Being Surprised + playing

Songs in our head Activate areas of the Brain In the Same way ACTUAL MUS DOES

Remembering in order to forget. forgetting in order to remember

No Feedback + MARILYN'S class the lesson is to Stop manufacturing Feedback

FORGETTING. WORST THING? BEST THING?
~~PHYSICAL ACTIVITY~~ TRYING

no narrative memories until language.
Prior to language memory takes the form of behavior
playing

WHAT IS IN FRONT OF YOU? LEFT? RIGHT? BEHIND? ABOVE? BELOW.
(expand circle)

WATCHING OTHERS — 13
○
ADULTS AND MENTAL HEALTH
○
CREATIVE CONCENTRATION
○
PLAY

LIFE ITS ALL MOVEMENT
What do you give up in the brain when you give up movement of the body

Activity always does more than embody purpose — it evolves purpose.
Follett

MEMORY
The new perishes before The old

Reading/writing ACTIVATING IMAGES we don't all day . to me A smell something that moves vs SUDDENLY Remember we forgot/

what is autobiographical? FEELING WE DON'T HAVE weirdo THE RIGHT TO DRAW, WRITE SING DANCE Thats FOR PROFESSIONALS imaginary friend MENTAL HEALTH TALK ABOUT PLAY → how we think we have to PUT SOMETHING IN INSTEAD OF FIND SOMETHING

PLAY TO KIDS CREATIVE CONCENTRATION AS ADULT IS THE ARTS

Playing ⋆ outside the individual But not in the external world LIVING BACON ⓣ

Freak out after

Planning play
• specific triggers in brain
• NAPOLEON — NOTHING SPECIFIC
• OBITUARY — has specific info but no images — imagination
• PLAYING/CREATIVE concentration SPECIFIC KID PLAYING w/ Truck
• CARS ⓣ
• X
• any word Fire, teeth doorways 100 DEMONS
• DOING IT RIGHT Read

specific exercise

Why are we able to remember something once we forget about trying to
Why we can't remember when we try

in order to remember something you have to forget it.
in order to forget you have to remember it

WHY WE DON'T READ IT OVER
The person reading it over is not the same person writing it.
The person reading + over only wants to know if it's any good

• NOT FOR OTHERS • ~~SATISFYING~~ • TAKES TIME NEEDS PLACE UNINTERRUPTED

THE GROOVE IS ABOUT A KIND OF FORGETTING

NO RIGHT TO DRAW SING DANCE ⋆
Karaoke ⓣ
play ✓
only professionals allowed

This solitary work that we do together

MARILYN'S instruction
Listen to the work
don't over load for info's sake
If it's there + coming up — teacher stand Back
No INTERFERE
Napoleon
monkey

the explanation of Realization children/writing about the uncultivated text the same implementations as for it

Images require some sort of representation in the world outside of us. that middle world

Who May be coming soon?

Printed in Singapore.

Drawn & Quarterly
Post Office Box 48056
Montreal, Quebec
Canada H2V 4S8
www.drawnandquarterly.com

First edition: May 2008. Second printing: June 2008. Third printing: July 2008. Fourth printing: March 2009. Fifth printing: October 2009. Sixth printing: March 2011.

10 9 8 7 6

"Two Questions" first appeared in "McSweeney's." "Dogs" first appeared in "The Bark." Some of the collage pages first appeared in "Tin House."

For Marilyn Frasca

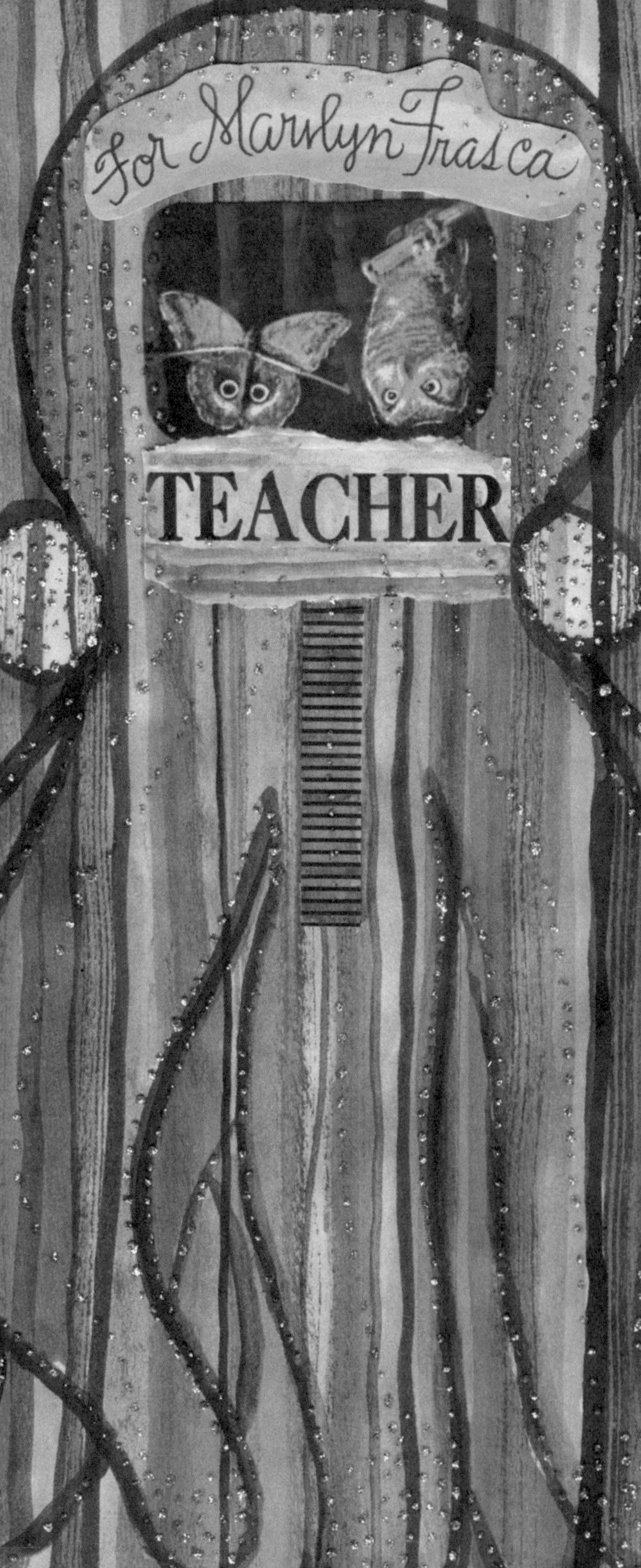
TEACHER

Library and Archives Canada Cataloguing in Publication
Barry, Lynda, 1956-
What it is / Lynda Barry.
ISBN 978-1-897299-35-7
1. Graphic novels. I. Title.
PN6727.B36W43 2008 741.5'973 C2007-904731-9

Distributed in the USA by:
Farrar, Straus and Giroux
18 West 18th Street
New York, NY 10011
Orders: 888.330.8477

Distributed in Canada by: Raincoast Books
9050 Shaughnessy Street
Vancouver, BC V6P 6E5
Orders: 800.663.5714

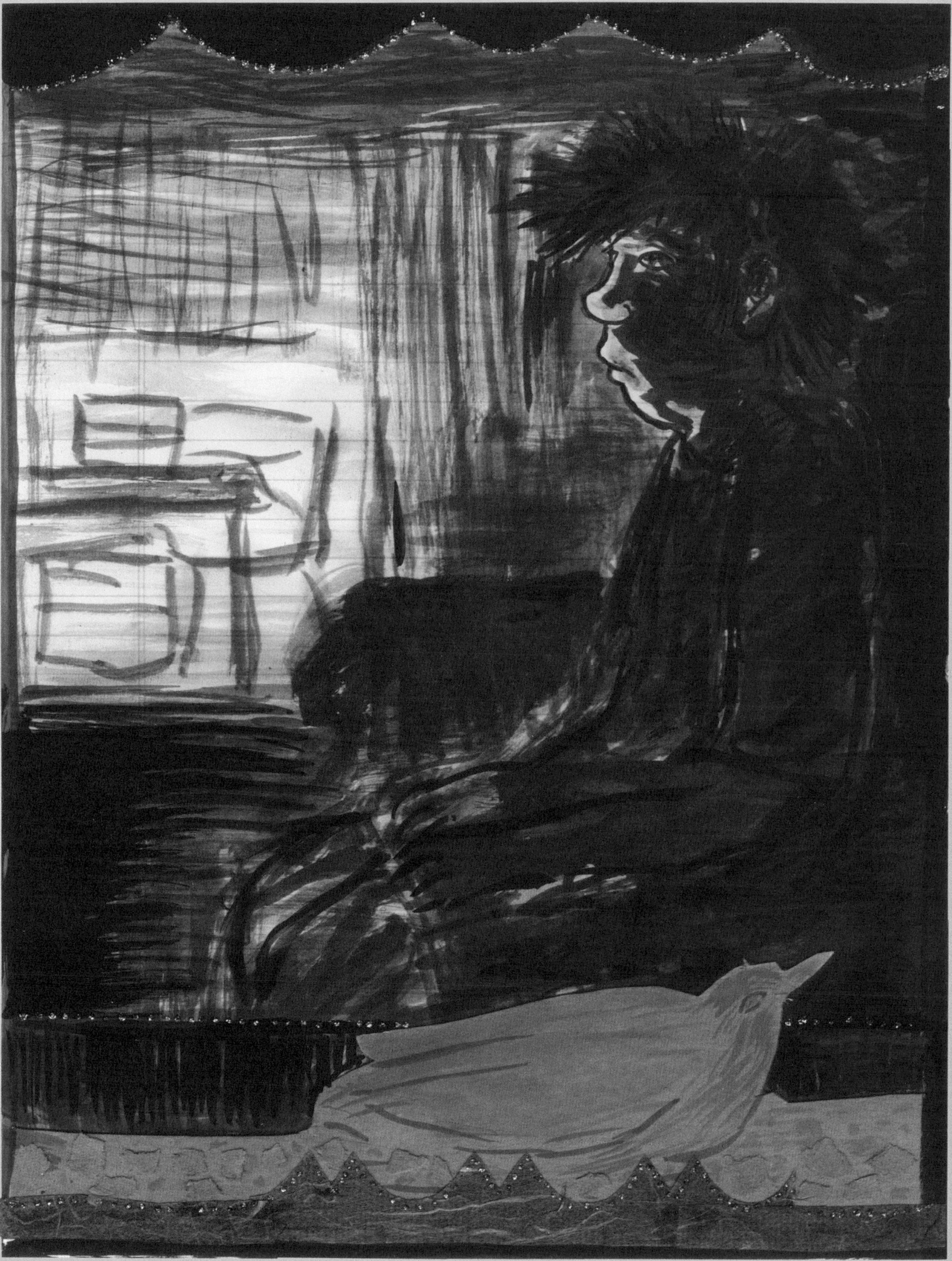

Chase me.
I will catch ye.
I will catlh ye

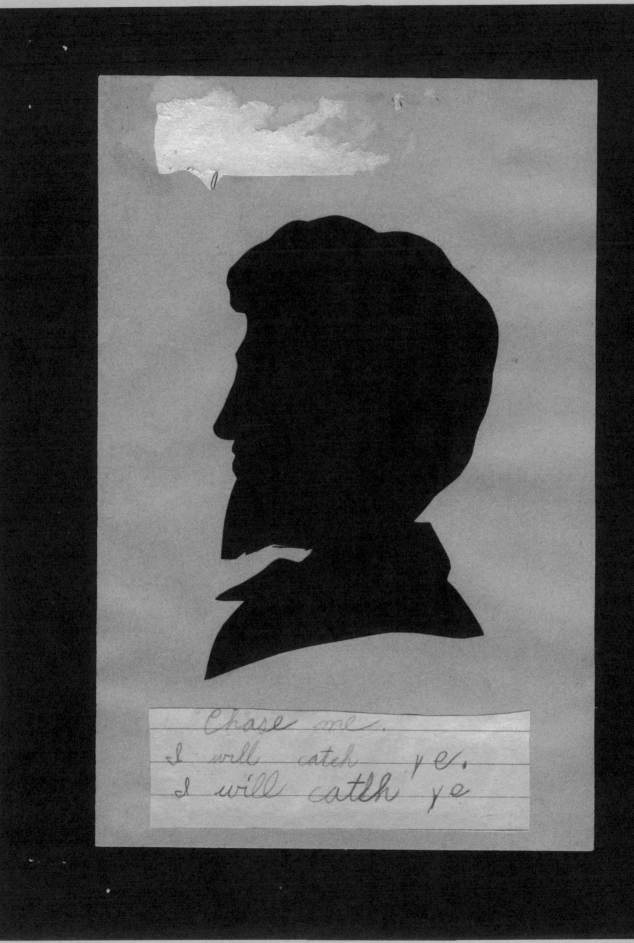

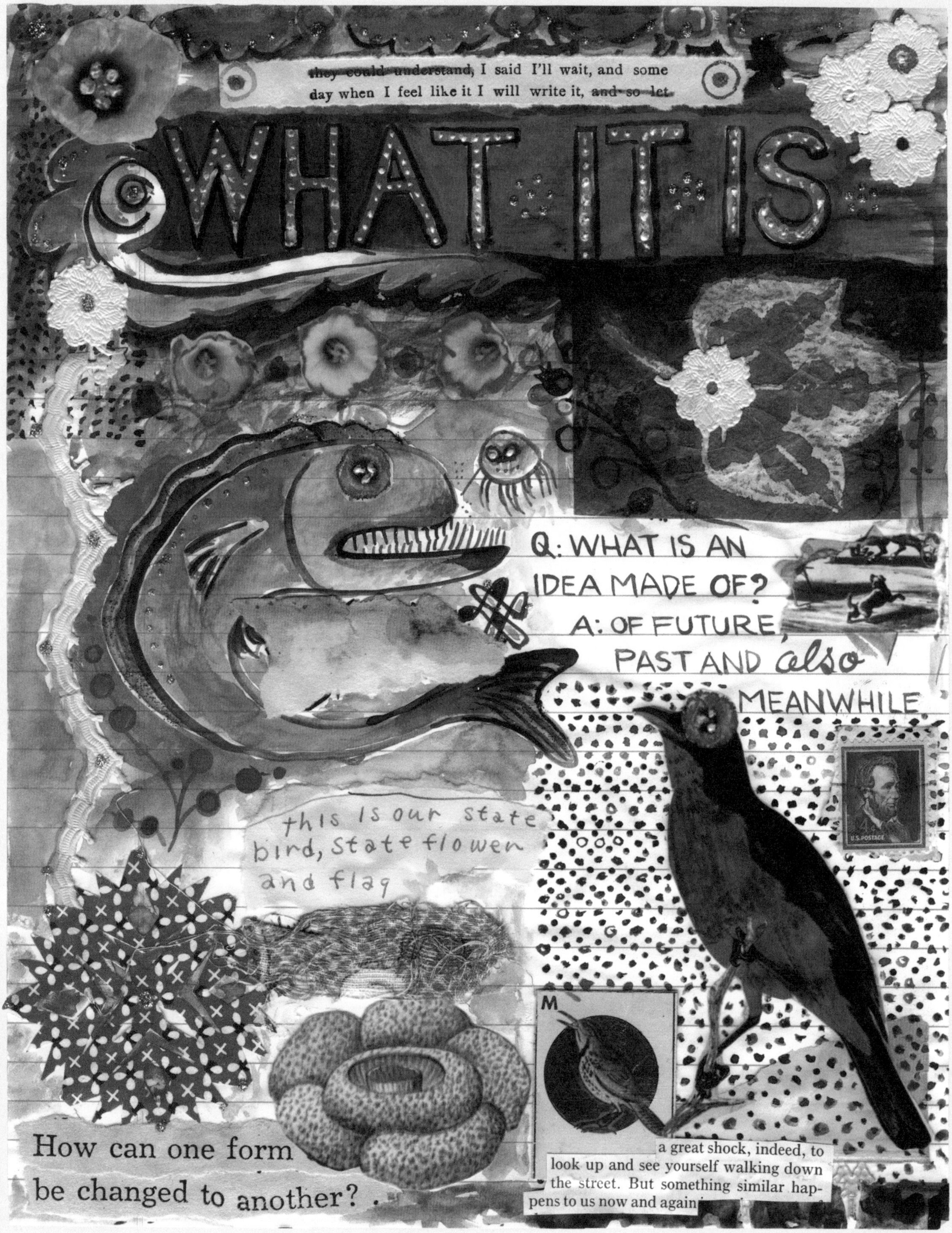
~~they could understand,~~ I said I'll wait, and some day when I feel like it I will write it, ~~and so let~~
WHAT IT IS
Q: WHAT IS AN IDEA MADE OF?
A: OF FUTURE, PAST AND also MEANWHILE
this is our state bird, state flower and flag
U.S. POSTAGE
M
How can one form be changed to another?
a great shock, indeed, to look up and see yourself walking down the street. But something similar happens to us now and again

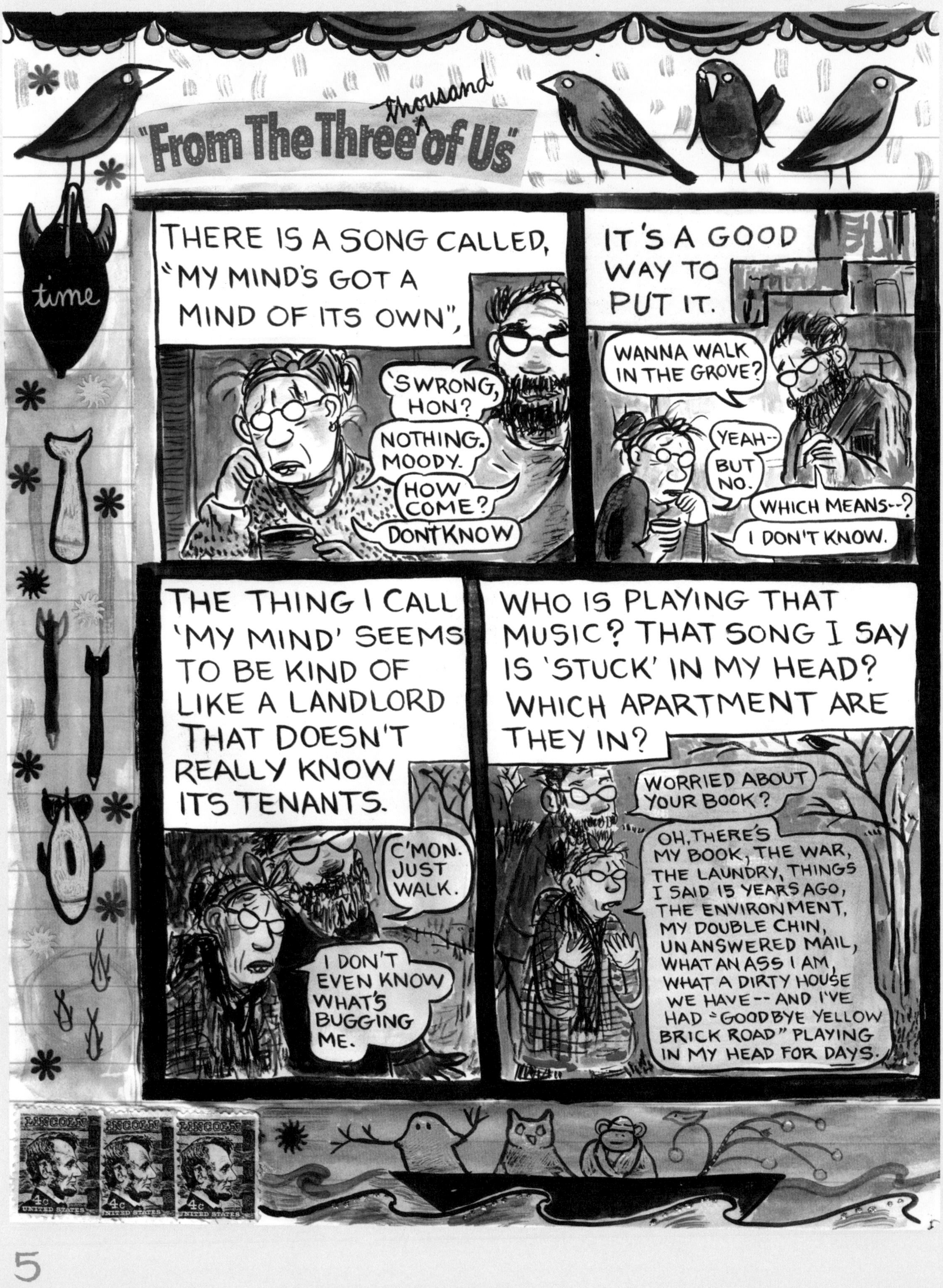
"From The Three thousand of Us"
time
THERE IS A SONG CALLED, "MY MIND'S GOT A MIND OF ITS OWN",
'SWRONG, HON?
NOTHING. MOODY.
HOW COME?
DONT KNOW
IT'S A GOOD WAY TO PUT IT.
WANNA WALK IN THE GROVE?
YEAH-- BUT NO.
WHICH MEANS--?
I DON'T KNOW.
THE THING I CALL 'MY MIND' SEEMS TO BE KIND OF LIKE A LANDLORD THAT DOESN'T REALLY KNOW ITS TENANTS.
C'MON. JUST WALK.
I DON'T EVEN KNOW WHAT'S BUGGING ME.
WHO IS PLAYING THAT MUSIC? THAT SONG I SAY IS 'STUCK' IN MY HEAD? WHICH APARTMENT ARE THEY IN?
WORRIED ABOUT YOUR BOOK?
OH, THERE'S MY BOOK, THE WAR, THE LAUNDRY, THINGS I SAID 15 YEARS AGO, THE ENVIRONMENT, MY DOUBLE CHIN, UNANSWERED MAIL, WHAT AN ASS I AM, WHAT A DIRTY HOUSE WE HAVE -- AND I'VE HAD "GOODBYE YELLOW BRICK ROAD" PLAYING IN MY HEAD FOR DAYS.
LINCOLN
4c
UNITED STATES
LINCOLN
4c
UNITED STATES
LINCOLN
4c
UNITED STATES

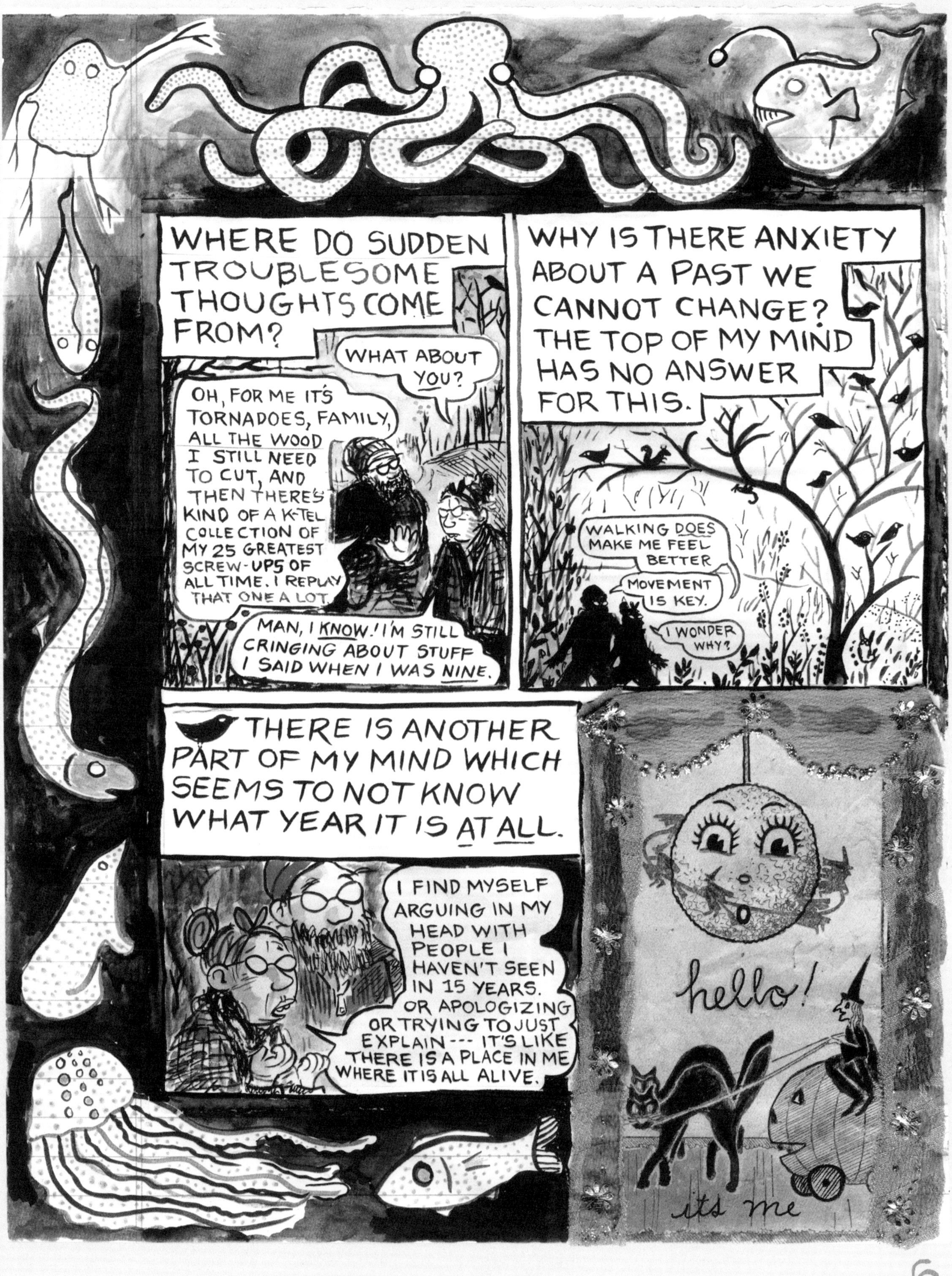

WHERE DO SUDDEN TROUBLESOME THOUGHTS COME FROM?
WHAT ABOUT YOU?
OH, FOR ME IT'S TORNADOES, FAMILY, ALL THE WOOD I STILL NEED TO CUT, AND THEN THERE'S KIND OF A K-TEL COLLECTION OF MY 25 GREATEST SCREW-UPS OF ALL TIME. I REPLAY THAT ONE A LOT.
MAN, I KNOW! I'M STILL CRINGING ABOUT STUFF I SAID WHEN I WAS NINE.
WHY IS THERE ANXIETY ABOUT A PAST WE CANNOT CHANGE? THE TOP OF MY MIND HAS NO ANSWER FOR THIS.
WALKING DOES MAKE ME FEEL BETTER
MOVEMENT IS KEY.
I WONDER WHY?
THERE IS ANOTHER PART OF MY MIND WHICH SEEMS TO NOT KNOW WHAT YEAR IT IS AT ALL.
I FIND MYSELF ARGUING IN MY HEAD WITH PEOPLE I HAVEN'T SEEN IN 15 YEARS. OR APOLOGIZING OR TRYING TO JUST EXPLAIN --- IT'S LIKE THERE IS A PLACE IN ME WHERE IT IS ALL ALIVE.
hello!
its me

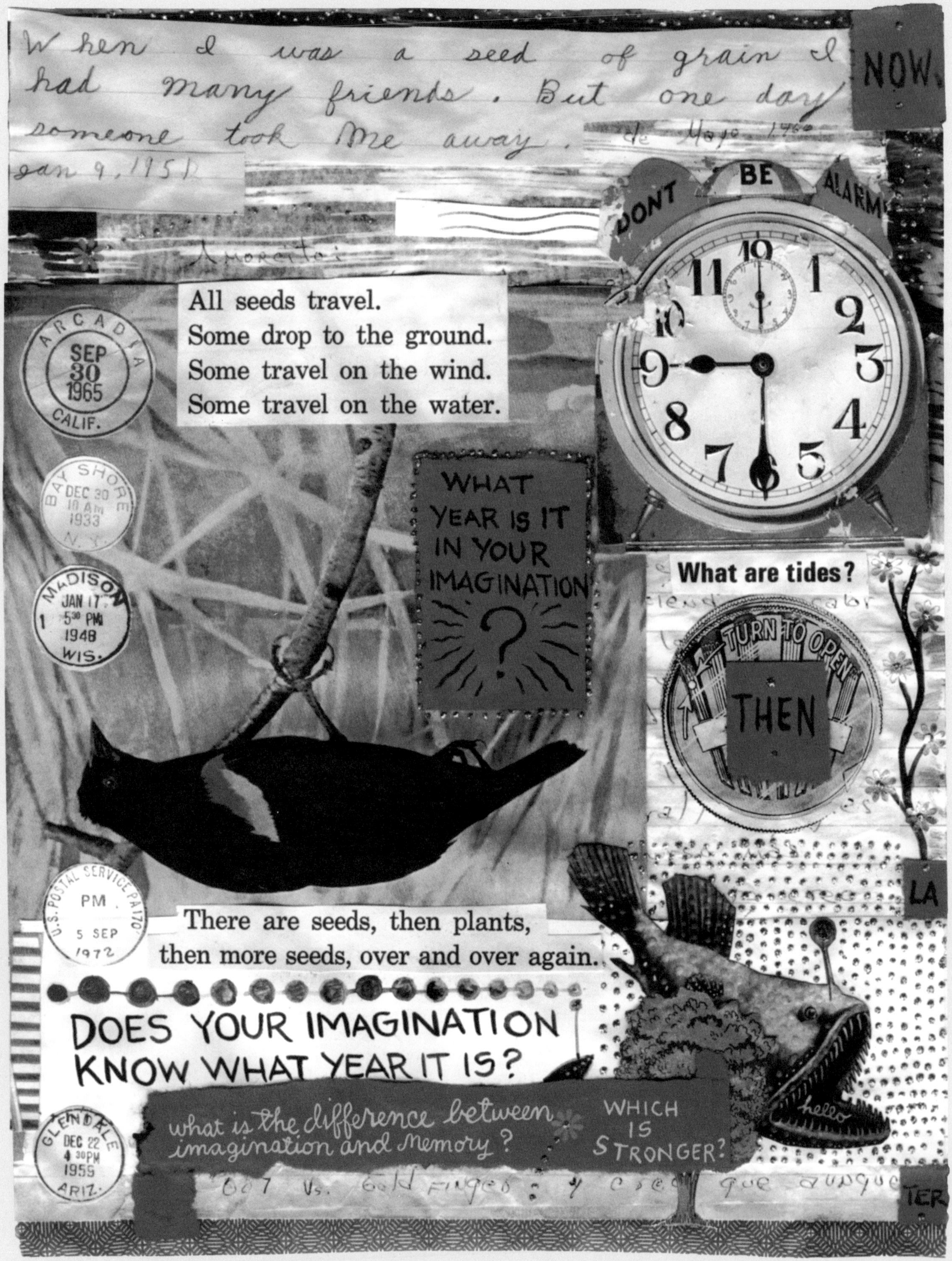
When I was a seed of grain I had many friends. But one day someone took me away.
NOW
DONT BE ALARMED
All seeds travel.
Some drop to the ground.
Some travel on the wind.
Some travel on the water.
ARCADIA SEP 30 1965 CALIF.
BAY SHORE DEC 30 10 AM 1933 N.Y.
MADISON JAN 17 5³⁰ PM 1948 WIS.
WHAT YEAR IS IT IN YOUR IMAGINATION ?
What are tides?
TURN TO OPEN
THEN
LA
U.S. POSTAL SERVICE PALTO PM 5 SEP 1972
There are seeds, then plants,
then more seeds, over and over again.
DOES YOUR IMAGINATION KNOW WHAT YEAR IT IS?
what is the difference between imagination and memory?
WHICH IS STRONGER?
hello
GLENDALE DEC 22 4 30PM 1955 ARIZ.
TER

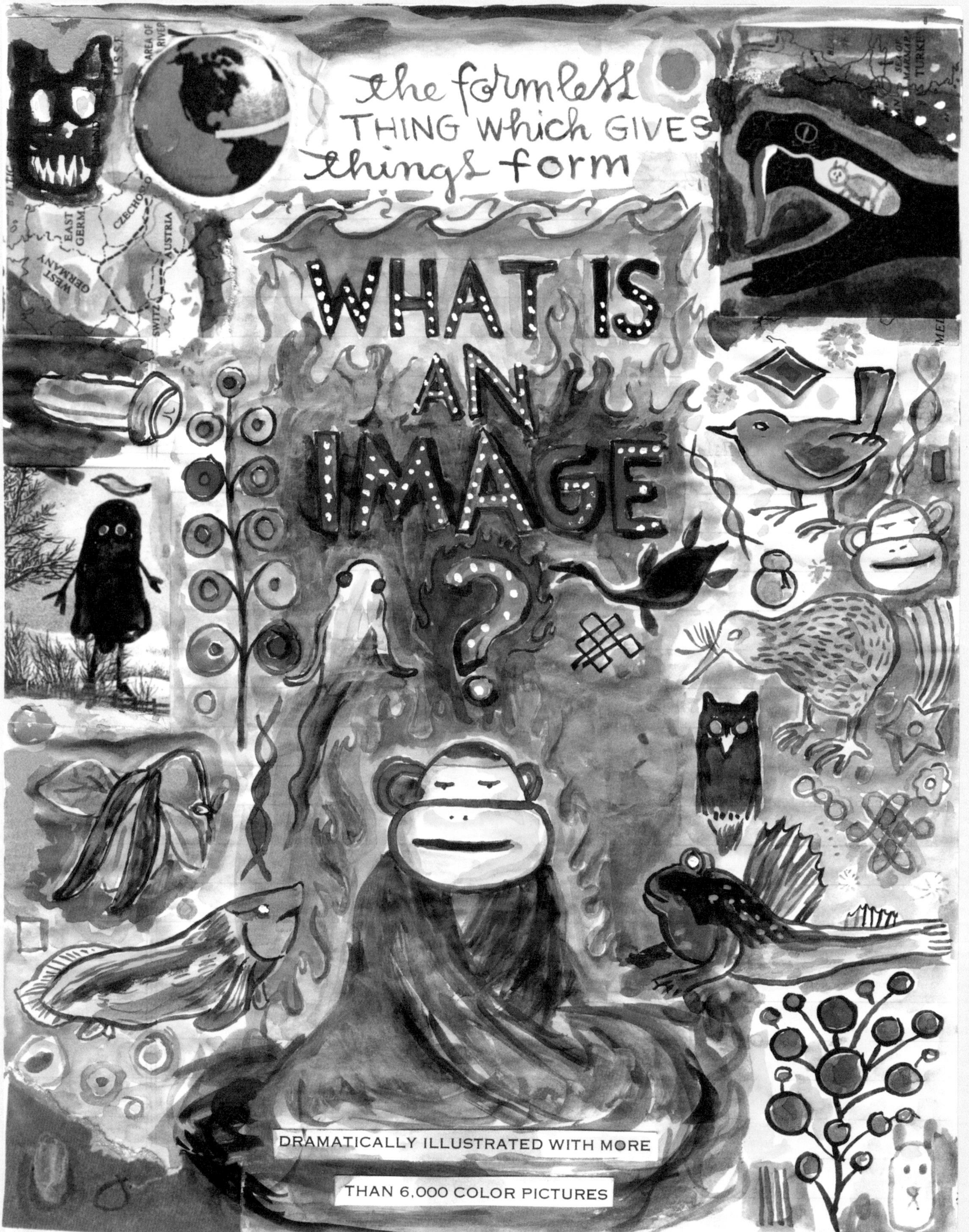
the formless
THING which GIVES
things form
WHAT IS AN IMAGE?
DRAMATICALLY ILLUSTRATED WITH MORE
THAN 6,000 COLOR PICTURES

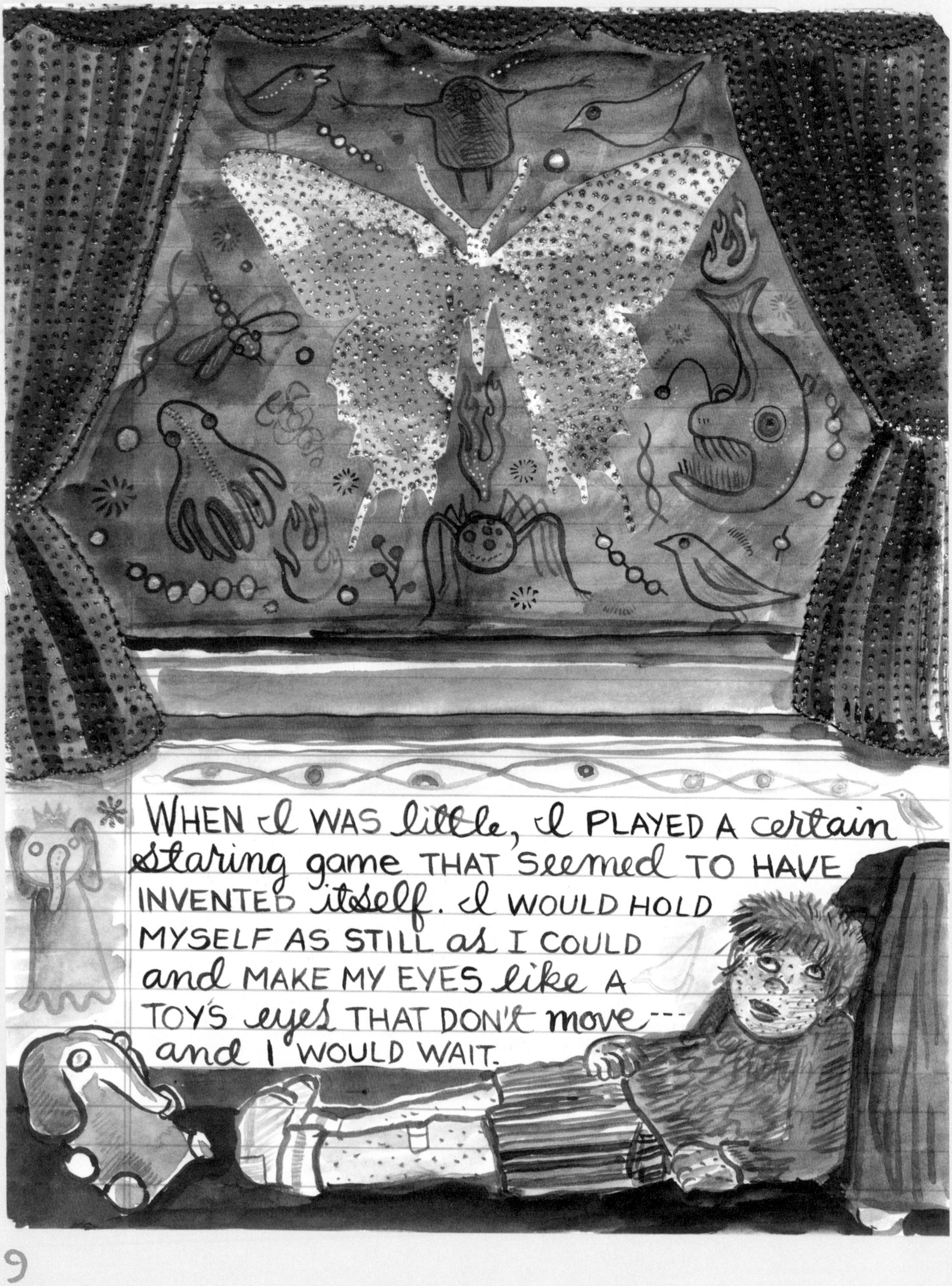
WHEN I WAS little, I PLAYED A certain staring game THAT seemed TO HAVE INVENTED itself. I WOULD HOLD MYSELF AS STILL as I COULD and MAKE MY EYES like A TOY'S eyes THAT DON'T move--- and I WOULD WAIT.

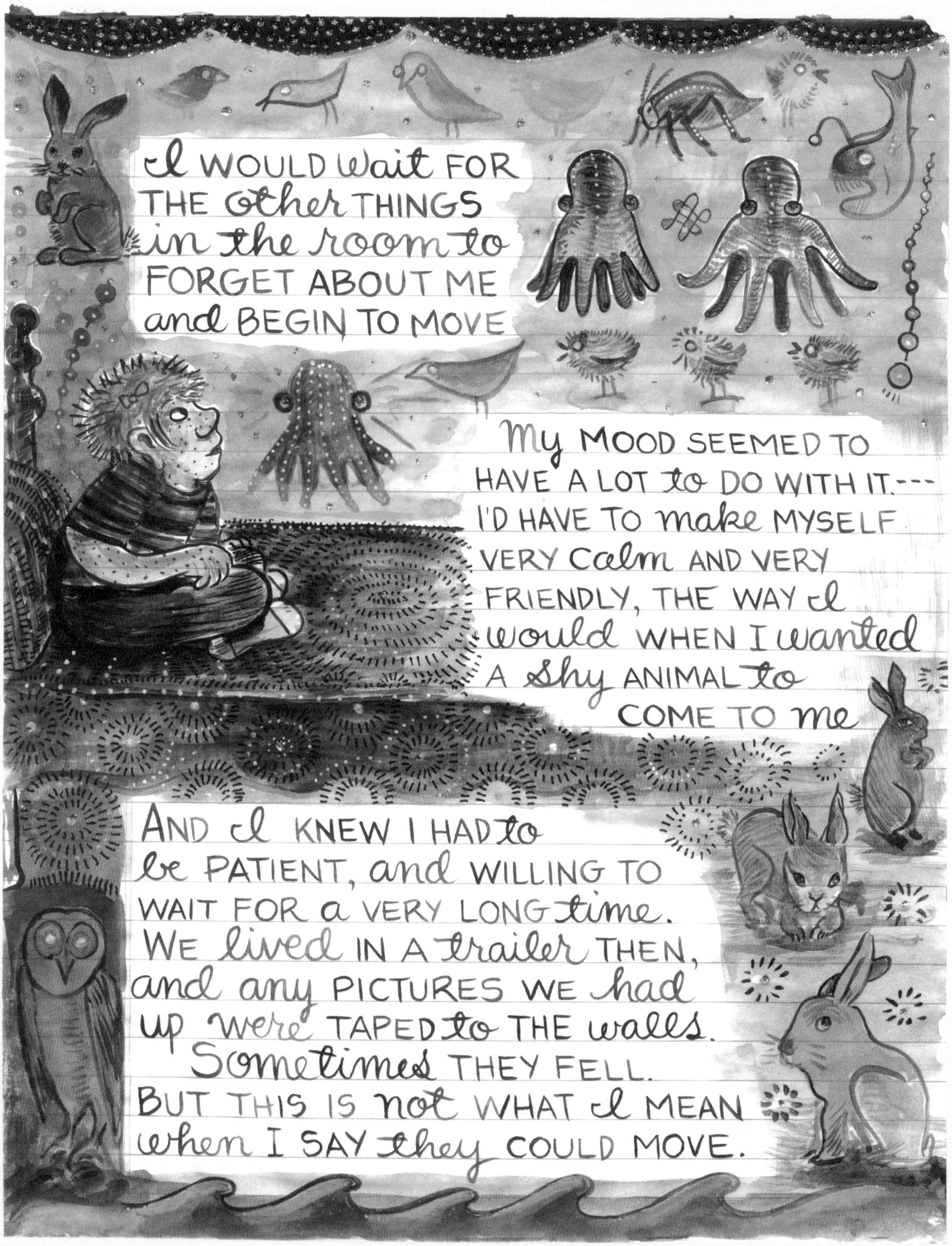
I WOULD wait FOR THE other THINGS in the room to FORGET ABOUT ME and BEGIN TO MOVE
My MOOD SEEMED TO HAVE A LOT to DO WITH IT--- I'D HAVE TO make MYSELF VERY calm AND VERY FRIENDLY, THE WAY I would WHEN I wanted A shy ANIMAL to COME TO me
AND I KNEW I HAD to be PATIENT, and WILLING TO WAIT FOR a VERY LONG time. WE lived IN A trailer THEN, and any PICTURES WE had up were TAPED to THE walls.
Sometimes THEY FELL.
BUT THIS IS not WHAT I MEAN when I SAY they COULD MOVE.

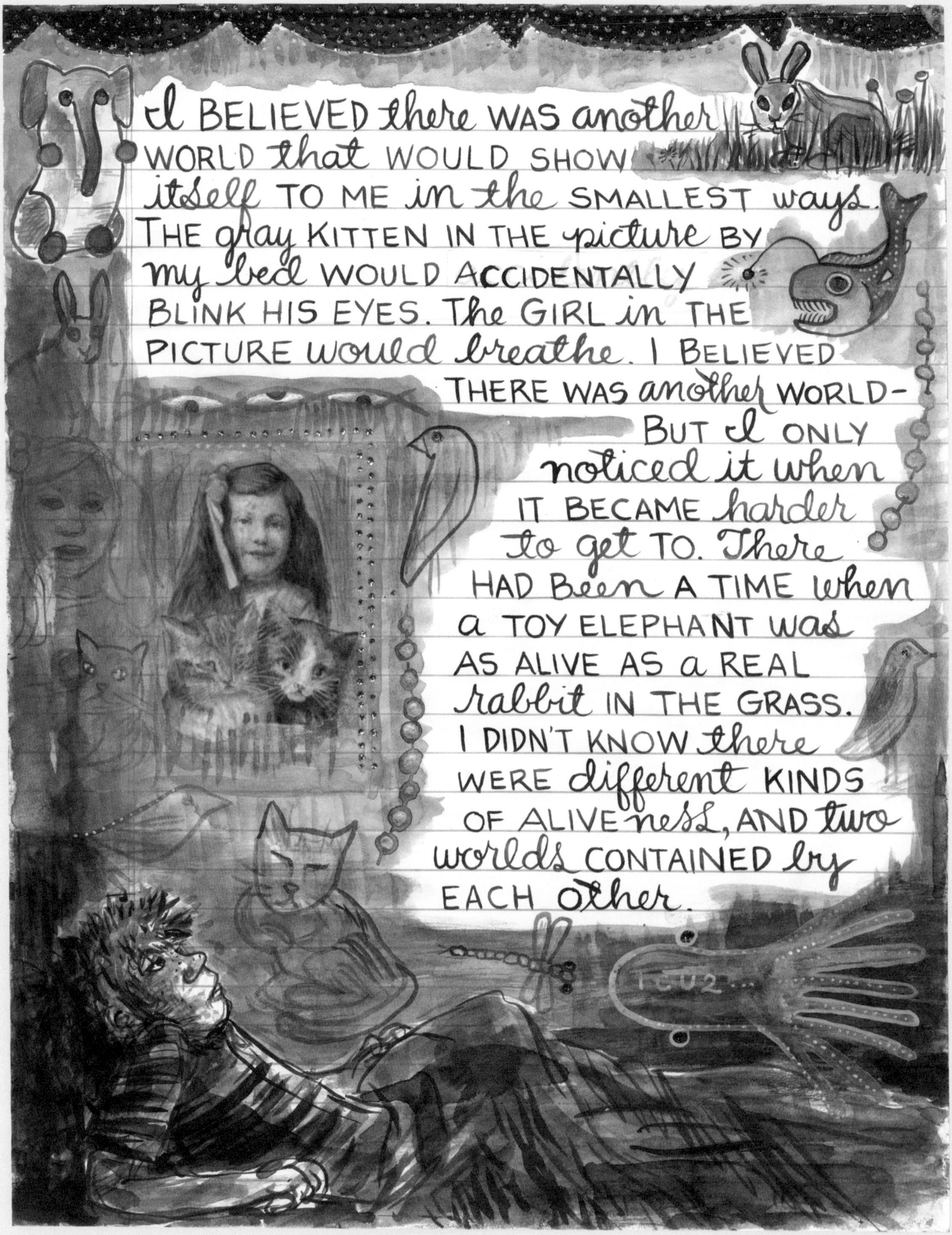
I BELIEVED there WAS another WORLD that WOULD SHOW itself TO ME in the SMALLEST ways. THE gray KITTEN IN THE picture BY my bed WOULD ACCIDENTALLY BLINK HIS EYES. The GIRL in THE PICTURE would breathe. I BELIEVED THERE WAS another WORLD- BUT I ONLY noticed it when IT BECAME harder to get TO. There HAD Been A TIME when a TOY ELEPHANT was AS ALIVE AS a REAL rabbit IN THE GRASS. I DIDN'T KNOW there WERE different KINDS OF ALIVEness, AND two worlds CONTAINED by EACH Other.
I C U 2

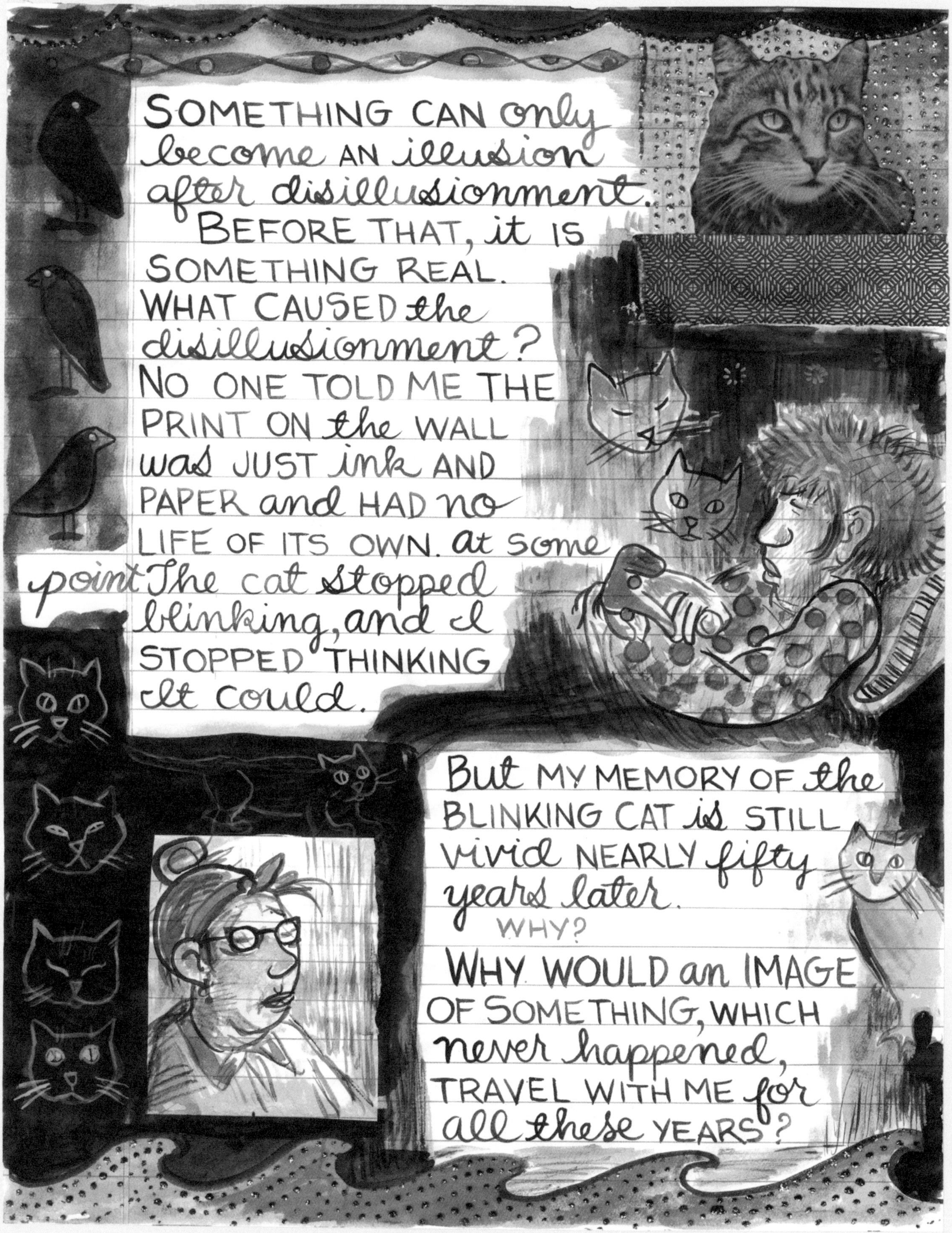
SOMETHING CAN only become AN illusion after disillusionment. BEFORE THAT, it IS SOMETHING REAL. WHAT CAUSED the disillusionment? NO ONE TOLD ME THE PRINT ON the WALL was JUST ink AND PAPER and HAD no LIFE OF ITS OWN. at some point The cat stopped blinking, and I STOPPED THINKING It could.
But MY MEMORY OF the BLINKING CAT is STILL vivid NEARLY fifty years later.
WHY?
WHY WOULD an IMAGE OF SOMETHING, WHICH never happened, TRAVEL WITH ME for all these YEARS?

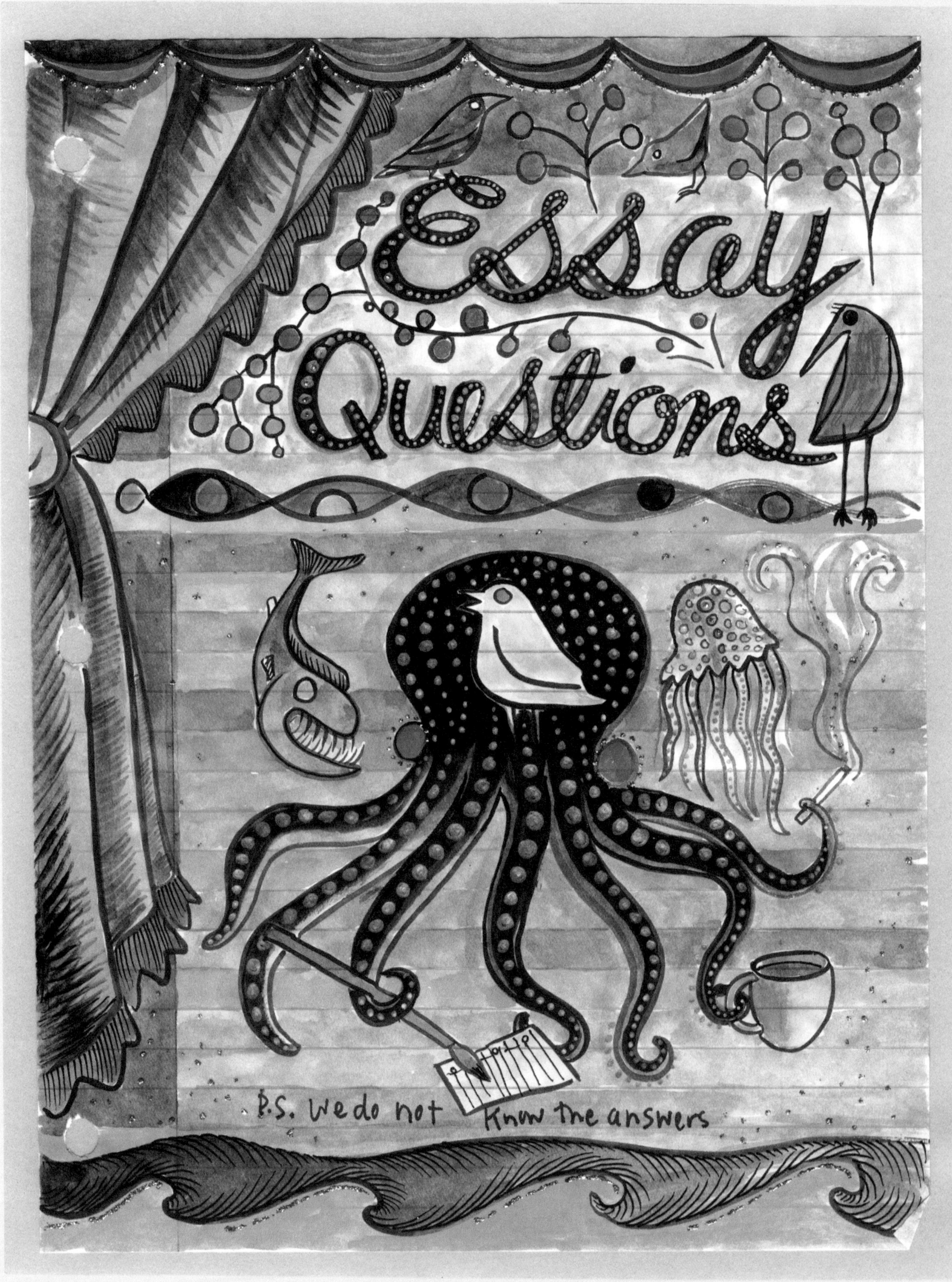
Essay Questions
P.S. We do not know the answers

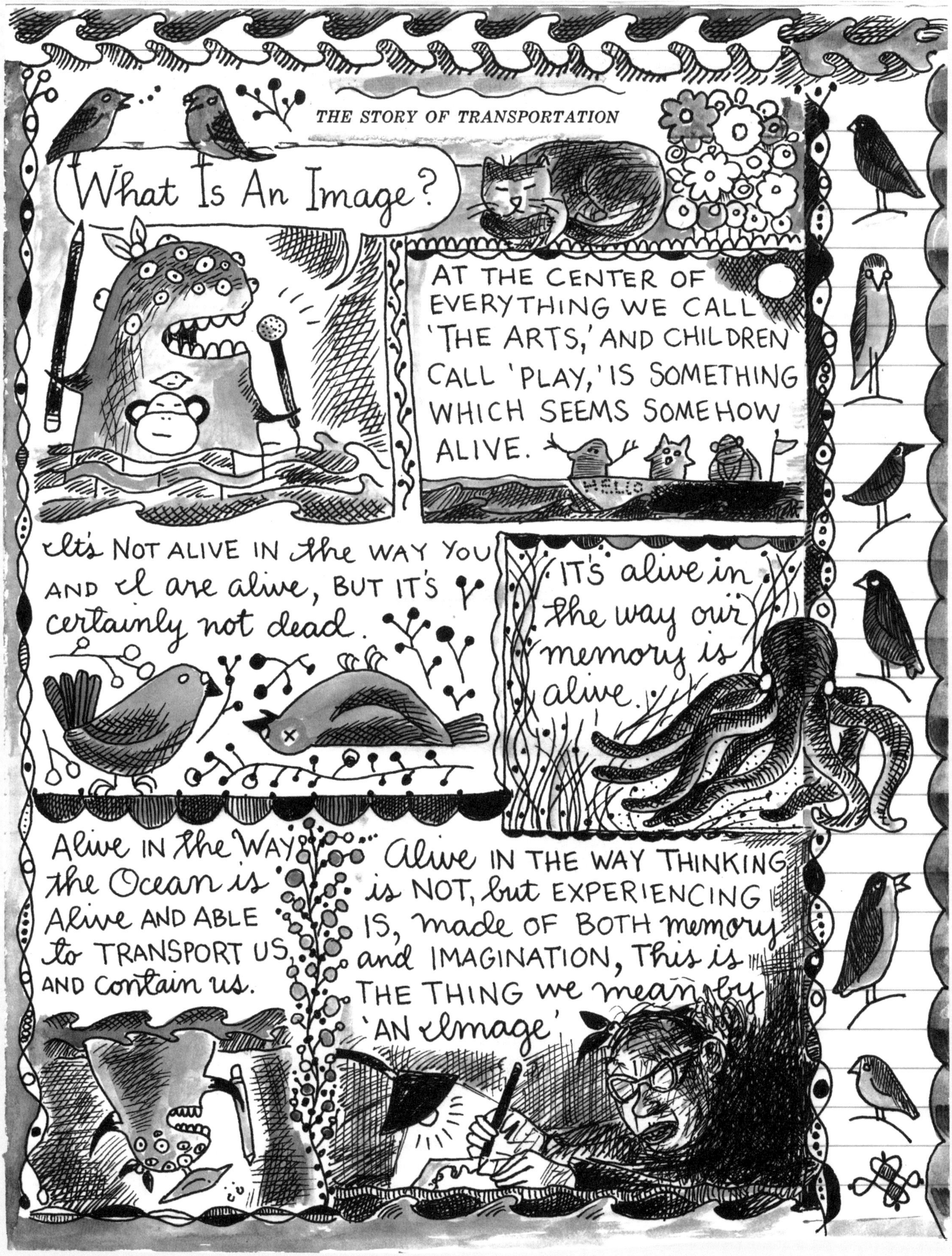
THE STORY OF TRANSPORTATION
What Is An Image?
AT THE CENTER OF EVERYTHING WE CALL 'THE ARTS,' AND CHILDREN CALL 'PLAY,' IS SOMETHING WHICH SEEMS SOMEHOW ALIVE.
It's NOT ALIVE IN the WAY YOU AND I are alive, BUT IT'S certainly not dead.
IT'S alive in the way our memory is alive.
Alive IN the WAY the Ocean is Alive AND ABLE to TRANSPORT US, AND contain us.
Alive IN THE WAY THINKING is NOT, but EXPERIENCING IS, made OF BOTH memory and IMAGINATION, This is THE THING we mean by 'AN Image'

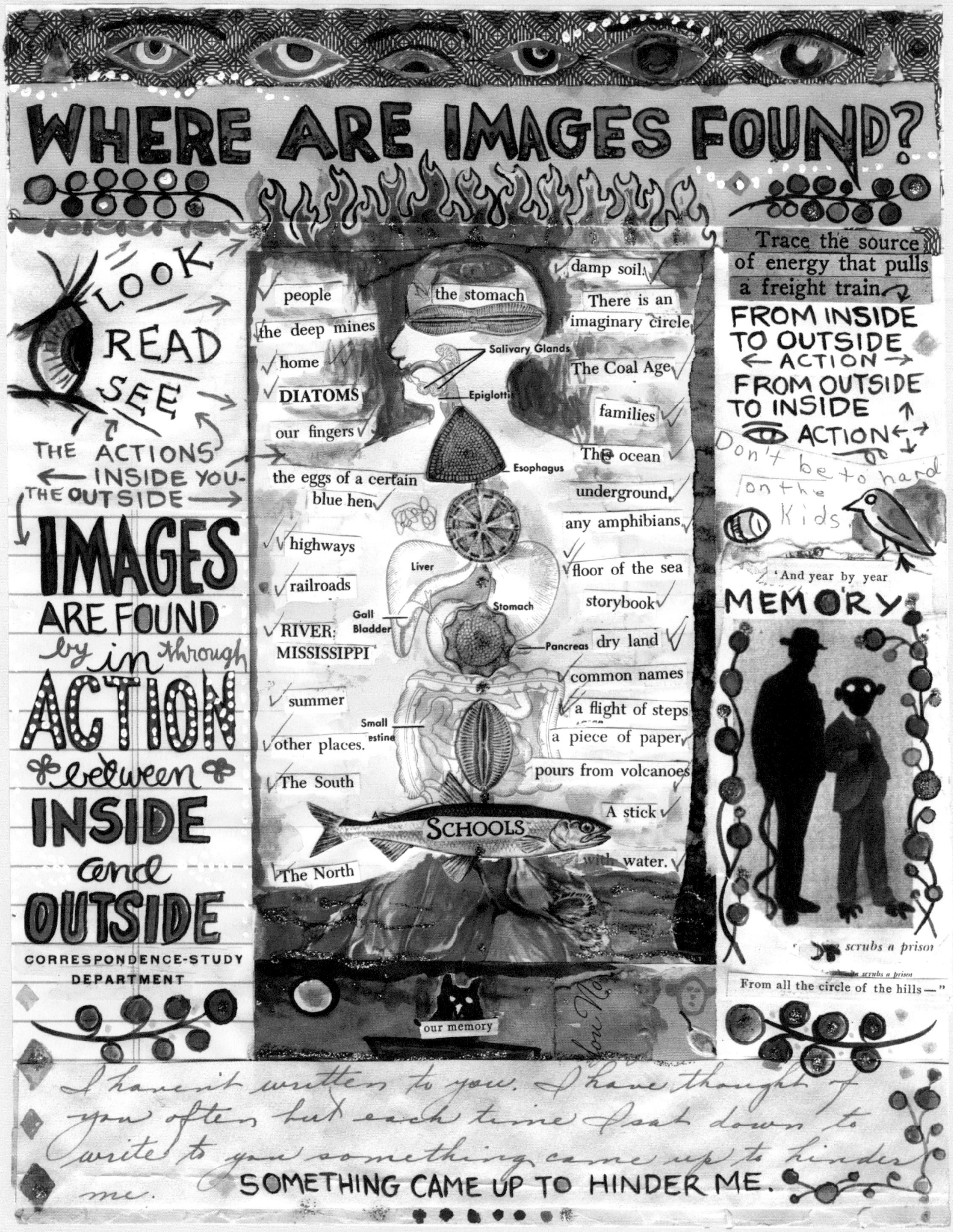
WHERE ARE IMAGES FOUND?
LOOK
READ
SEE
THE ACTIONS
INSIDE YOU-
THE OUTSIDE
IMAGES
ARE FOUND
by in through
ACTION
between
INSIDE
and
OUTSIDE
CORRESPONDENCE-STUDY
DEPARTMENT
people
the stomach
the deep mines
home
DIATOMS
our fingers
the eggs of a certain
blue hen
highways
railroads
RIVER:
MISSISSIPPI
summer
other places.
The South
The North
Salivary Glands
Epiglottis
Esophagus
Liver
Stomach
Gall
Bladder
Pancreas
Small
Intestine
SCHOOLS
damp soil.
There is an
imaginary circle
The Coal Age
families
The ocean
underground,
any amphibians,
floor of the sea
storybook
dry land
common names
a flight of steps
a piece of paper
pours from volcanoes
A stick
with water.
our memory
Trace the source
of energy that pulls
a freight train.
FROM INSIDE
TO OUTSIDE
← ACTION →
FROM OUTSIDE
TO INSIDE
ACTION
Don't be to hard
on the
Kids
'And year by year
MEMORY
scrubs a prison
From all the circle of the hills—"
I haven't written to you. I have thought of
you often but each time I sat down to
write to you something came up to hinder
me.
SOMETHING CAME UP TO HINDER ME.

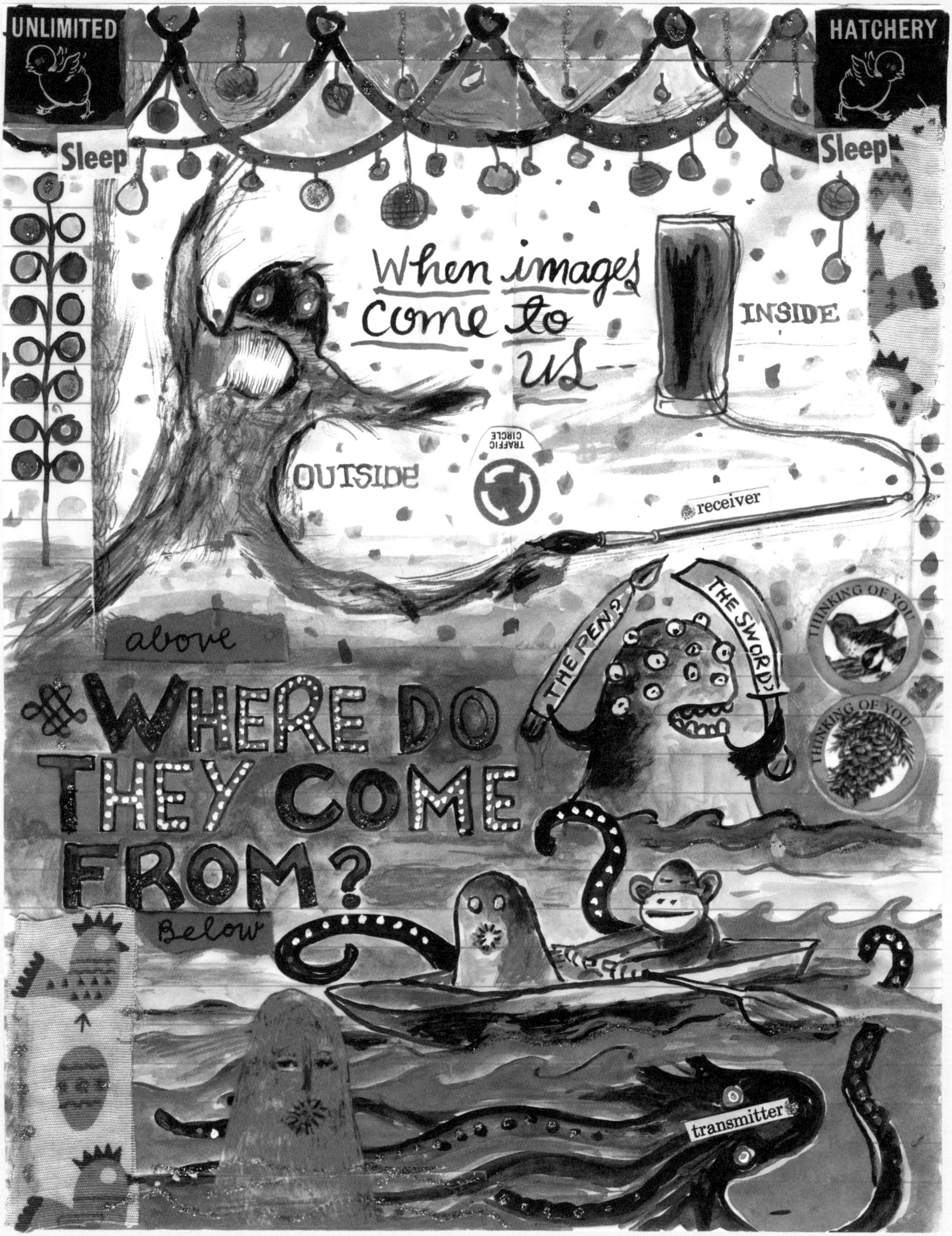
UNLIMITED
HATCHERY
Sleep
Sleep
When images come to us
INSIDE
TRAFFIC CIRCLE
OUTSIDE
receiver
above
THE PEN?
THE SWORD?
THINKING OF YOU
THINKING OF YOU
WHERE DO THEY COME FROM?
Below
transmitter

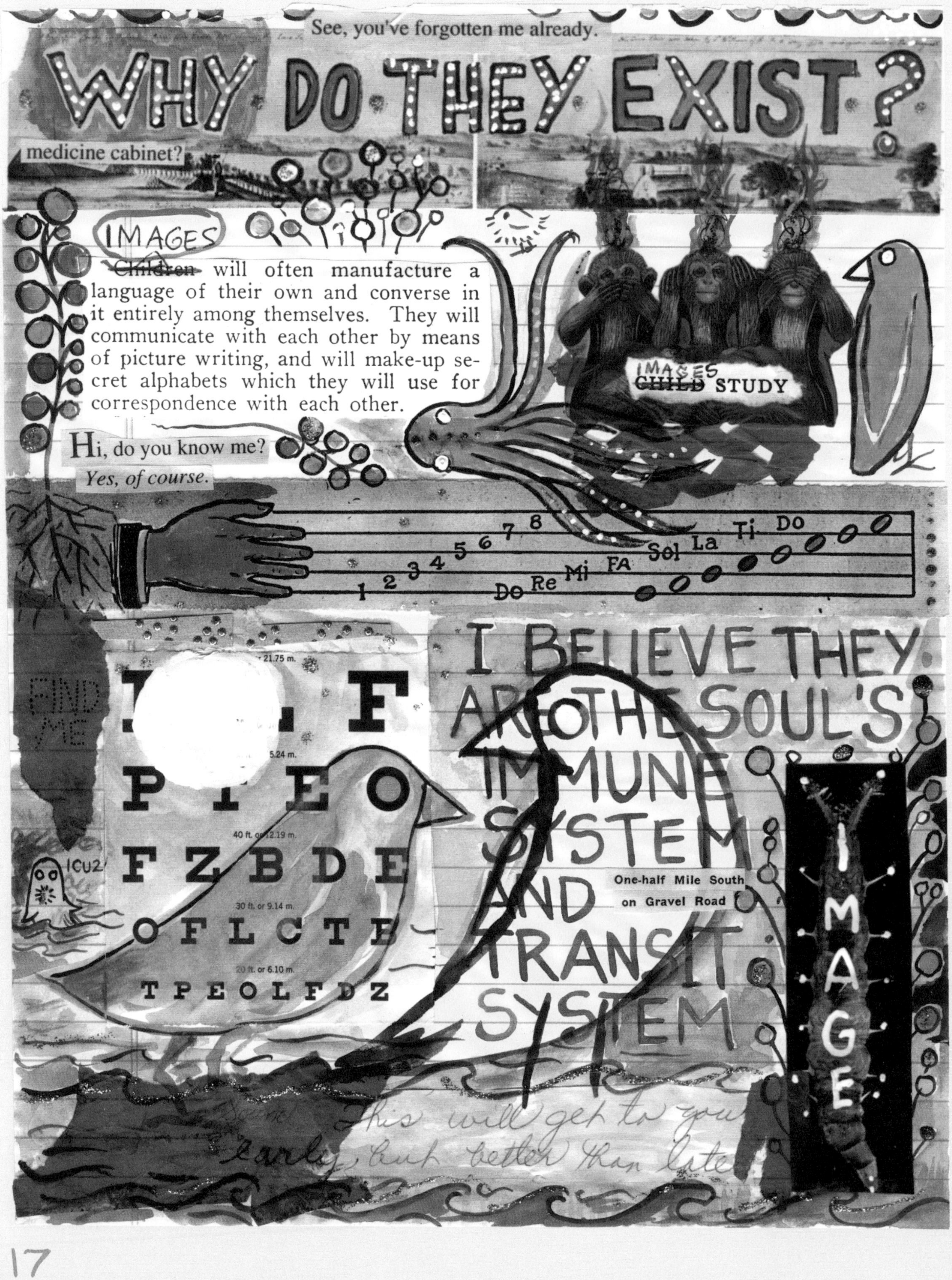
See, you've forgotten me already.
WHY DO THEY EXIST?
medicine cabinet?
IMAGES
~~Children~~ will often manufacture a language of their own and converse in it entirely among themselves. They will communicate with each other by means of picture writing, and will make-up secret alphabets which they will use for correspondence with each other.
Hi, do you know me?
Yes, of course.
IMAGES ~~CHILD~~ STUDY
1 2 3 4 5 6 7 8
Do Re Mi FA Sol La Ti DO
FIND ME
ICU2
21.75 m.
F
5.24 m.
P E O
40 ft. or 12.19 m.
F Z B D E
30 ft. or 9.14 m.
O F L C T E
20 ft. or 6.10 m.
T P E O L F D Z
I BELIEVE THEY ARE THE SOUL'S IMMUNE SYSTEM AND TRANSIT SYSTEM
One-half Mile South
on Gravel Road
IMAGE
This will get to you early, but better than late

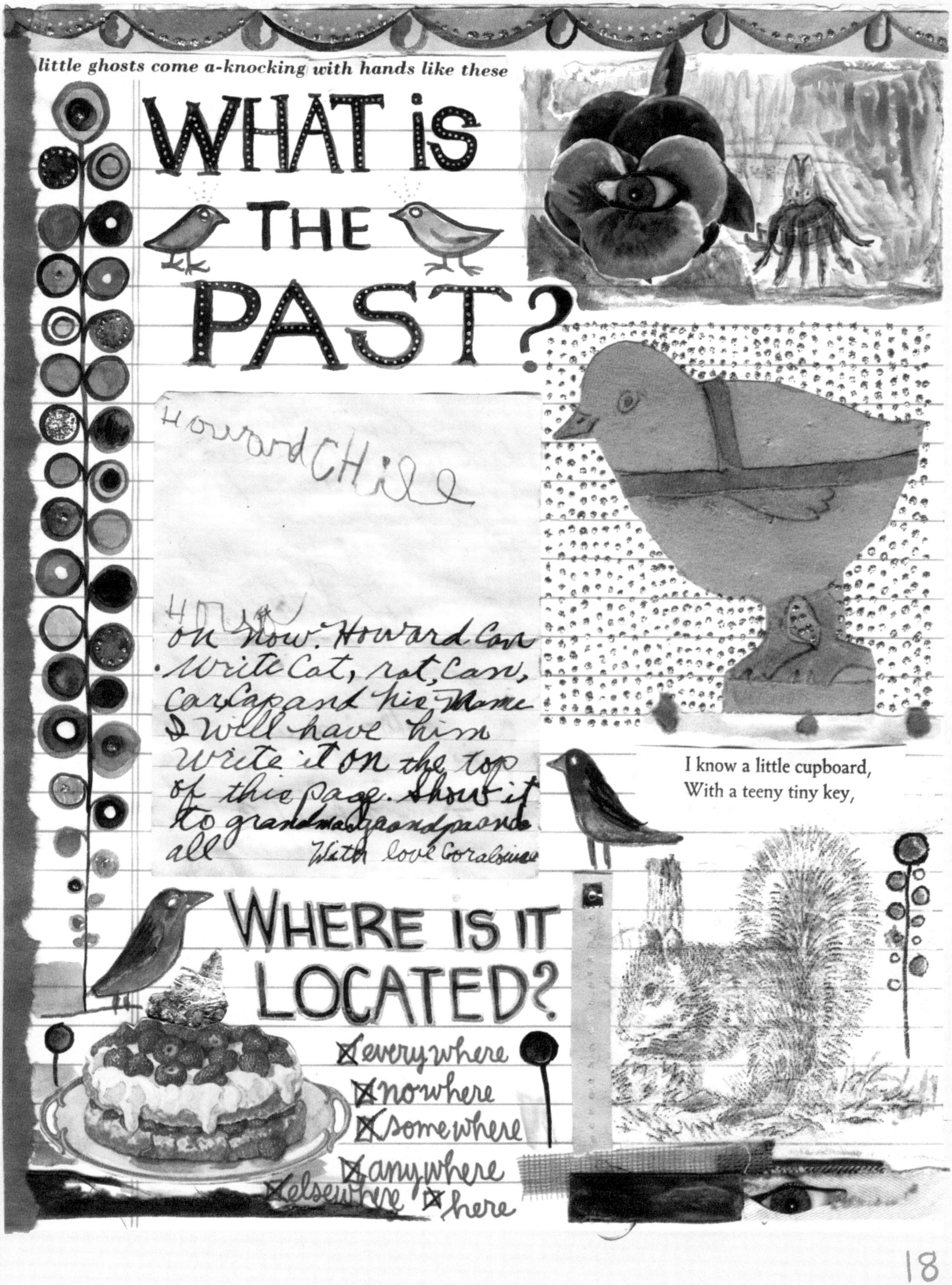

little ghosts come a-knocking with hands like these
WHAT is THE PAST?
Howard CHile
on now. Howard can
write cat, rat, can,
car, cap and his name
I will have him
write it on the top
of this page. Show it
to grandma grandpa
all With love
I know a little cupboard,
With a teeny tiny key,
WHERE IS IT LOCATED?
everywhere
nowhere
somewhere
anywhere
elsewhere
here

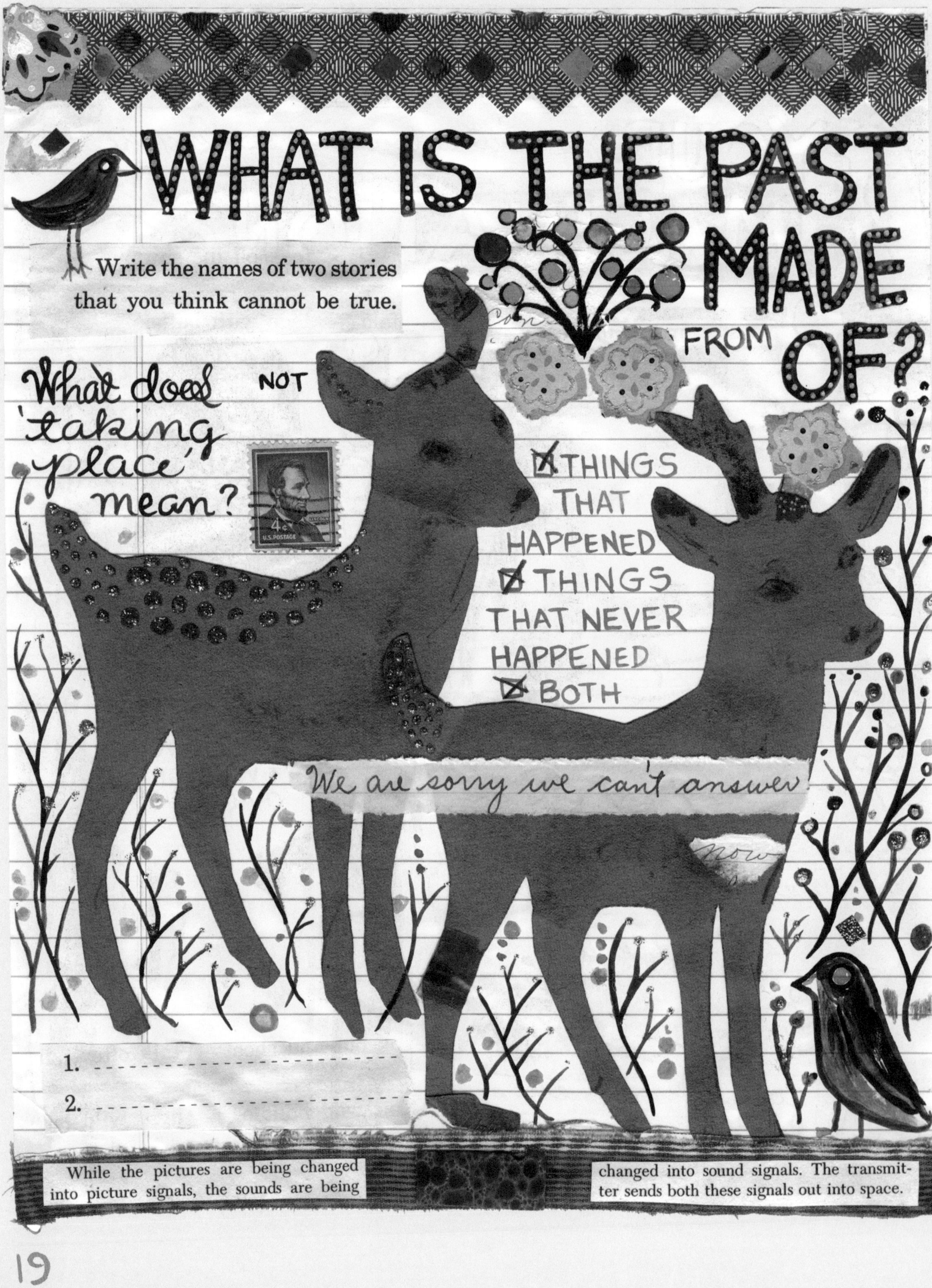

WHAT IS THE PAST MADE FROM OF?
Write the names of two stories that you think cannot be true.
What does NOT 'taking place' mean?
4¢ U.S. POSTAGE LINCOLN
☑ THINGS THAT HAPPENED
☑ THINGS THAT NEVER HAPPENED
☑ BOTH
We are sorry we can't answer
now
1. ----------------
2. ----------------
While the pictures are being changed into picture signals, the sounds are being
changed into sound signals. The transmitter sends both these signals out into space.

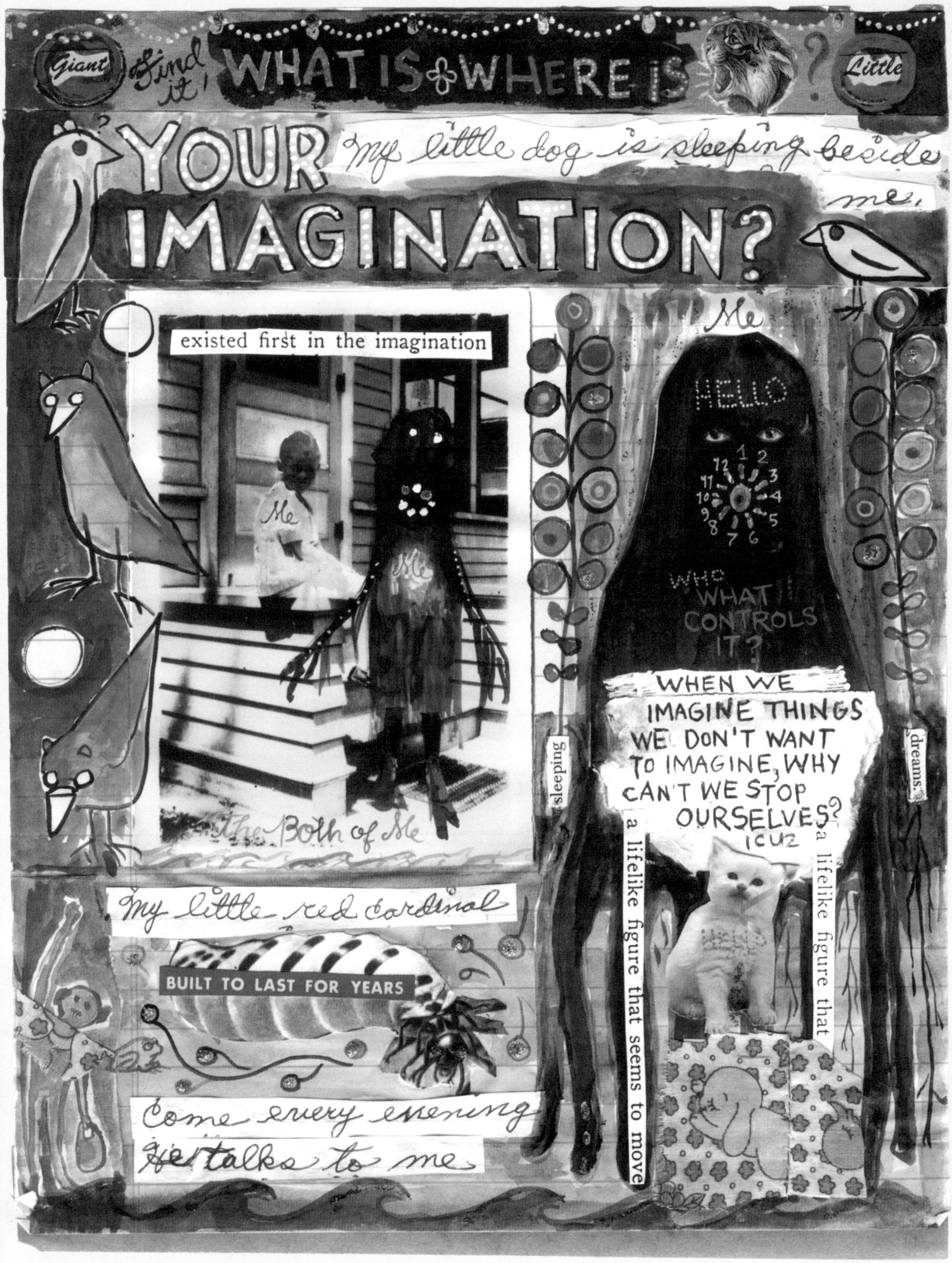
Giant
Find it,
WHAT IS WHERE IS
?
Little
YOUR
my little dog is sleeping beside
me.
IMAGINATION?
existed first in the imagination
Me
Me
The Both of Me
Me
HELLO
WHO
WHAT
CONTROLS
IT?
WHEN WE
IMAGINE THINGS
WE DON'T WANT
TO IMAGINE, WHY
CAN'T WE STOP
OURSELVES?
ICU2
sleeping
dreams.
a lifelike figure that seems to move
a lifelike figure that
my little red cardinal
BUILT TO LAST FOR YEARS
Come every evening
He talks to me

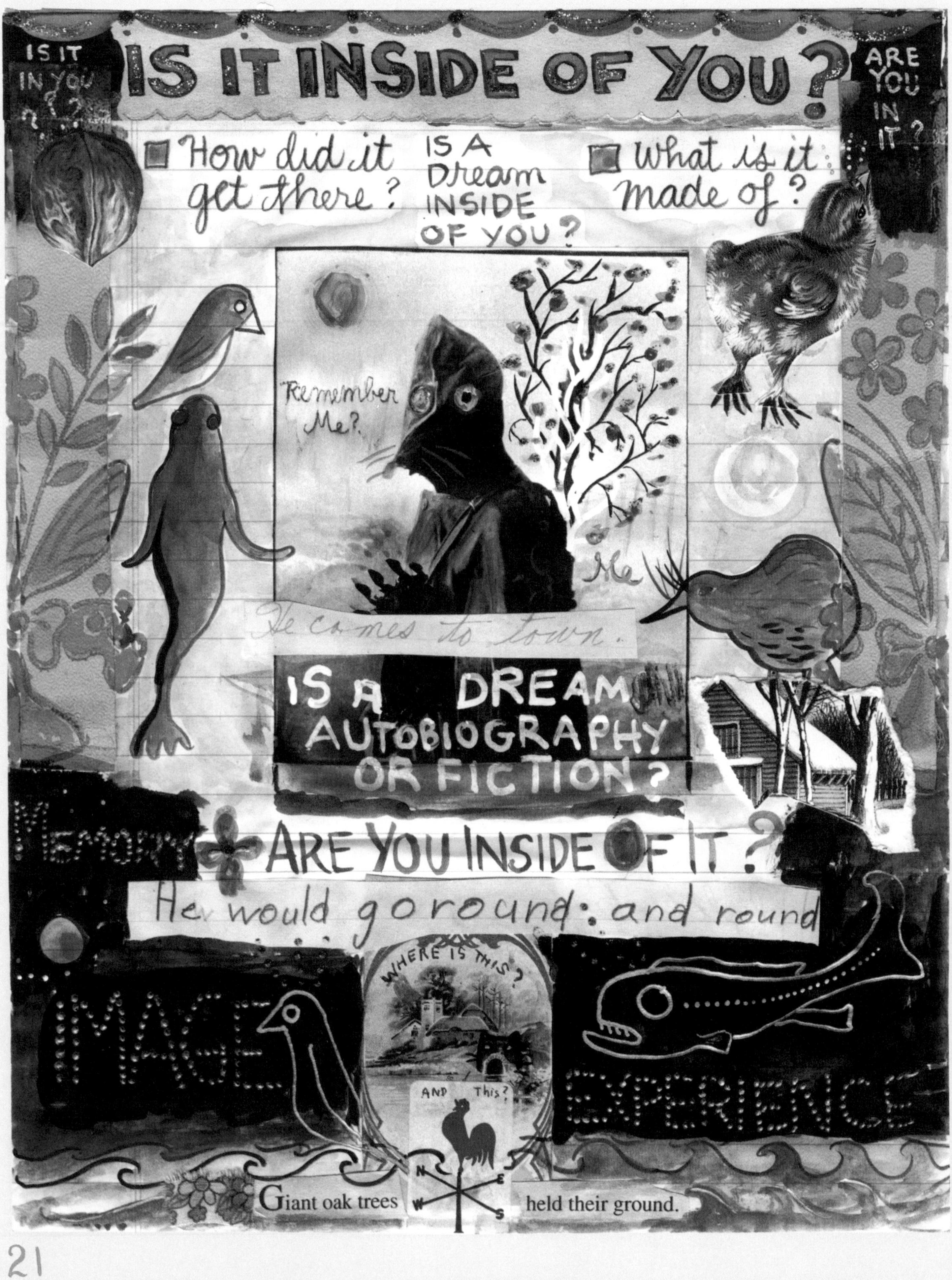
IS IT IN YOU ?
IS IT INSIDE OF YOU?
ARE YOU IN IT ?
How did it get there?
IS A DREAM INSIDE OF YOU?
What is it made of?
Remember Me?
Me
He comes to town.
IS A DREAM AUTOBIOGRAPHY OR FICTION?
Memory
ARE YOU INSIDE OF IT?
He would go round and round
WHERE IS THIS?
IMAGE
AND THIS?
EXPERIENCE
N E W S
Giant oak trees held their ground.

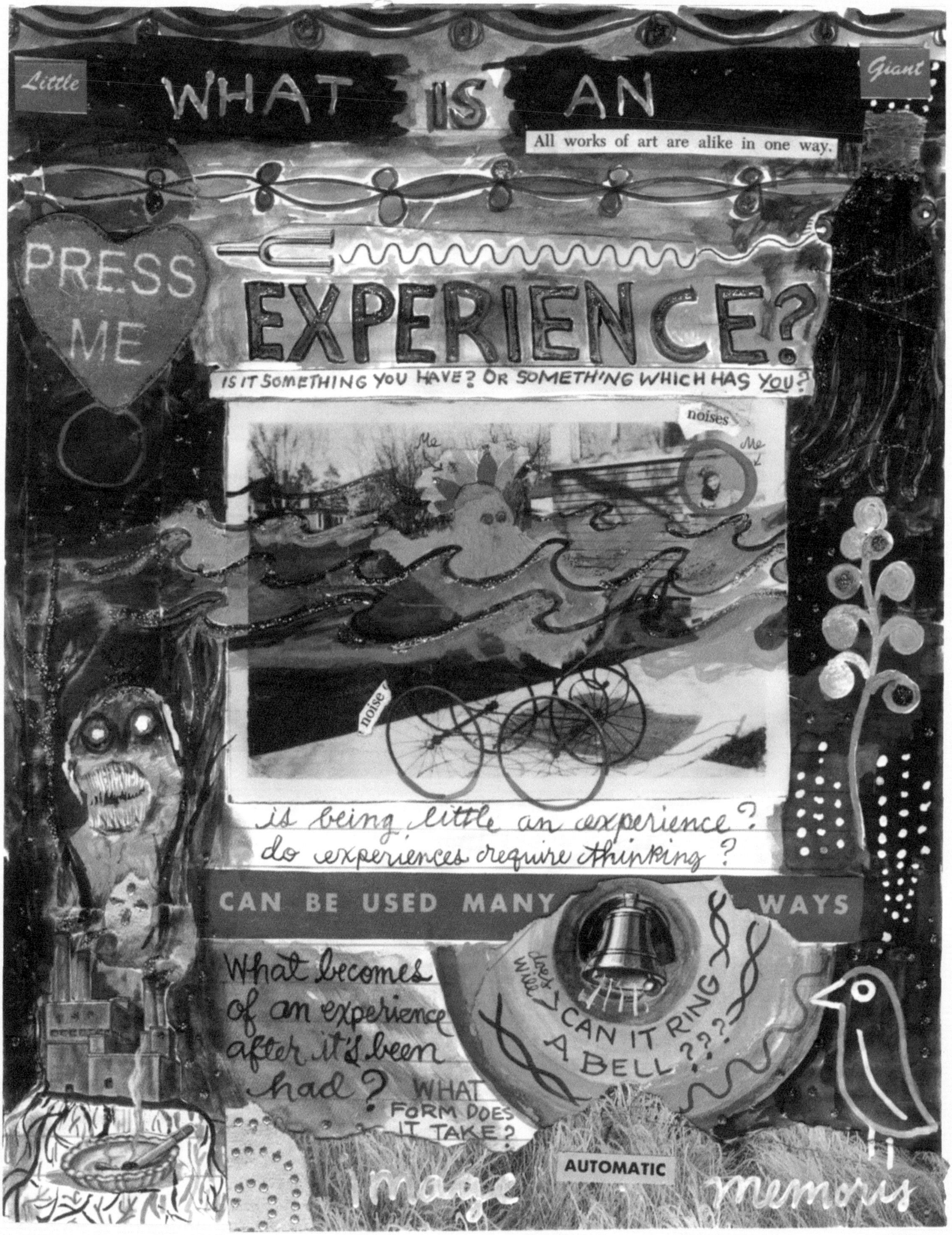
Little
WHAT IS AN
Giant
All works of art are alike in one way.
PRESS ME
EXPERIENCE?
IS IT SOMETHING YOU HAVE? OR SOMETHING WHICH HAS YOU?
noises
Me
Me
noise
is being little an experience?
do experiences require thinking?
CAN BE USED MANY
WAYS
What becomes of an experience after it's been had?
WHAT FORM DOES IT TAKE?
CAN IT RING A BELL???
AUTOMATIC
image
memories

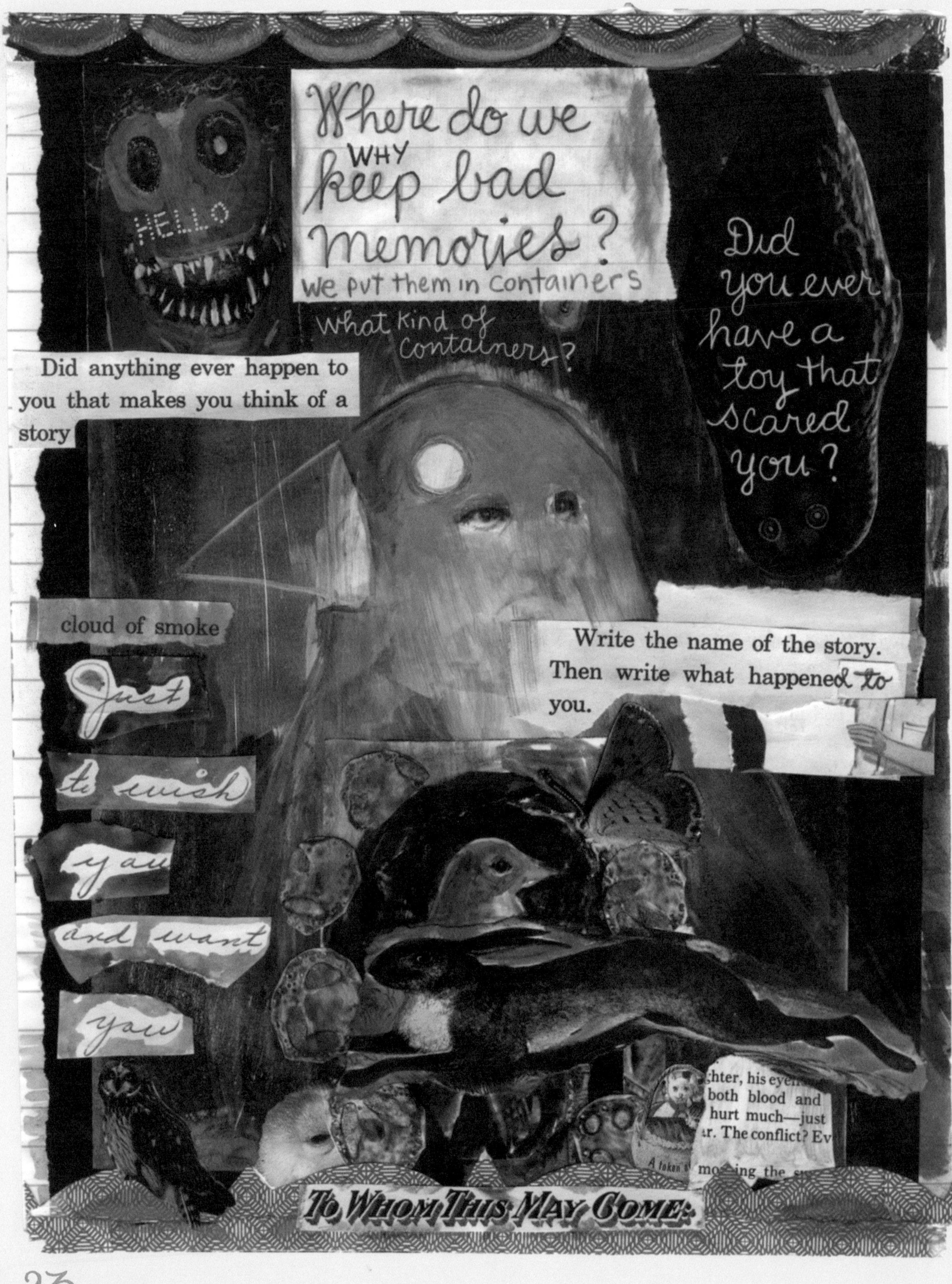
Where do we
WHY
keep bad
memories?
we put them in containers
what kind of
containers?
HELLO
Did you ever have a toy that scared you?
Did anything ever happen to you that makes you think of a story
cloud of smoke
Write the name of the story. Then write what happened ~~to~~ you.
just
to wish
you
and want
you
both blood and
hurt much—just
The conflict?
TO WHOM THIS MAY COME.

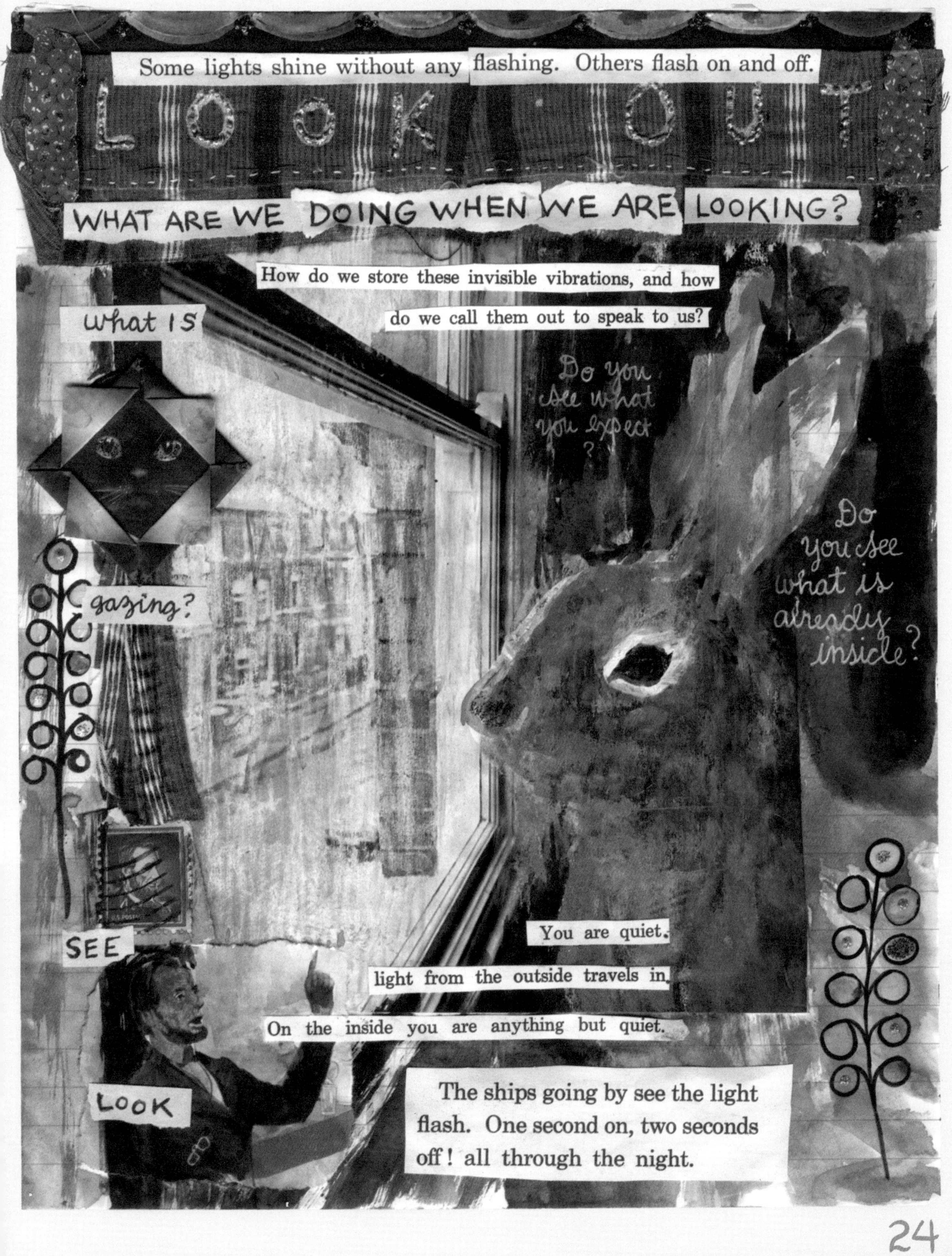
Some lights shine without any flashing. Others flash on and off.
LOOK OUT
WHAT ARE WE DOING WHEN WE ARE LOOKING?
How do we store these invisible vibrations, and how
do we call them out to speak to us?
What IS
Do you see what you expect ?
Do you see what is already inside?
gazing?
You are quiet.
light from the outside travels in.
SEE
On the inside you are anything but quiet.
LOOK
The ships going by see the light flash. One second on, two seconds off! all through the night.

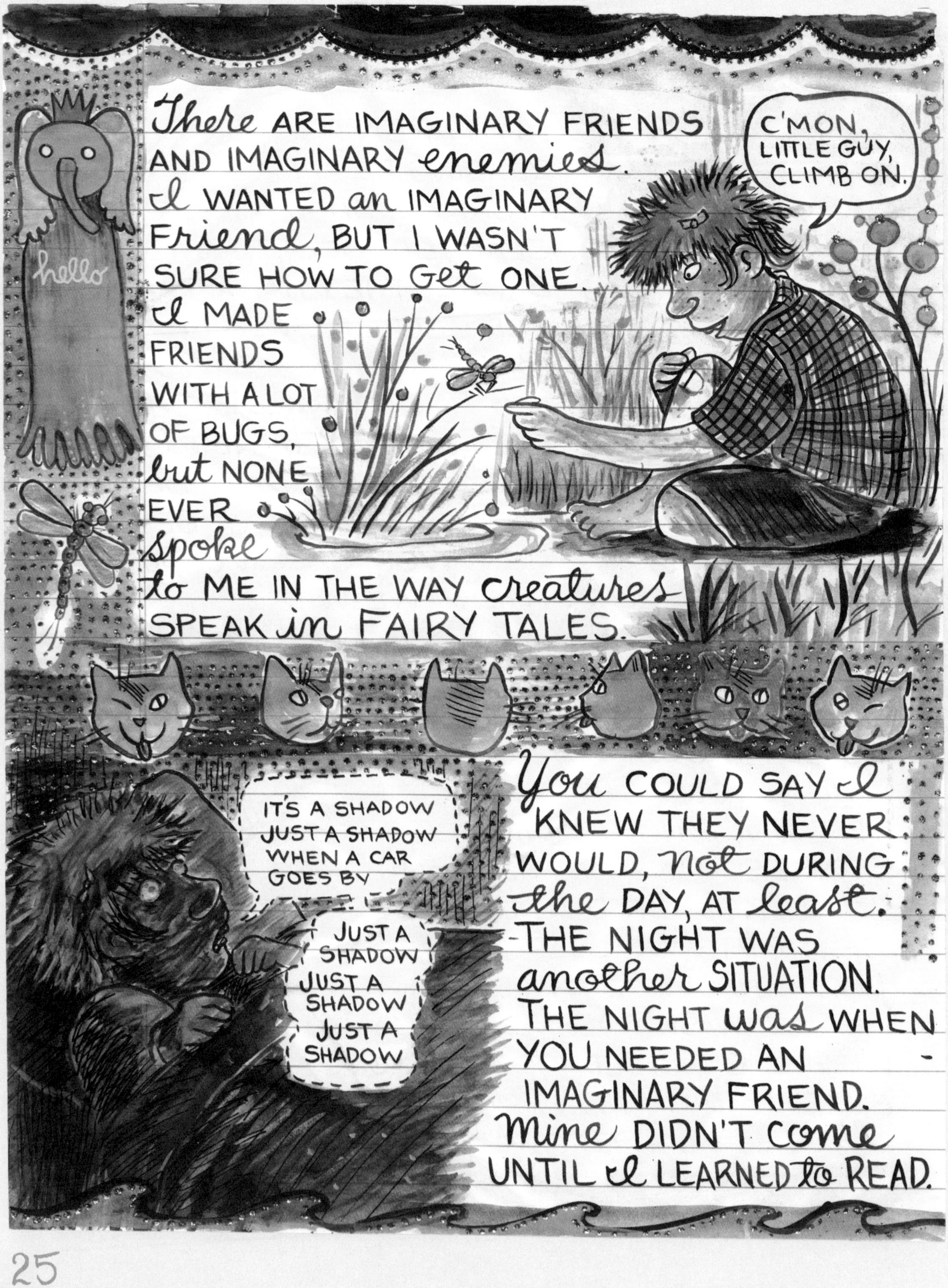
hello
There ARE IMAGINARY FRIENDS AND IMAGINARY enemies. I WANTED an IMAGINARY Friend, BUT I WASN'T SURE HOW TO Get ONE. I MADE FRIENDS WITH A LOT OF BUGS, but NONE EVER spoke to ME IN THE WAY creatures SPEAK in FAIRY TALES.
C'MON, LITTLE GUY, CLIMB ON.
IT'S A SHADOW JUST A SHADOW WHEN A CAR GOES BY
JUST A SHADOW JUST A SHADOW JUST A SHADOW
You COULD SAY I KNEW THEY NEVER WOULD, not DURING the DAY, AT least. THE NIGHT WAS another SITUATION. THE NIGHT was WHEN YOU NEEDED AN IMAGINARY FRIEND. Mine DIDN'T come UNTIL I LEARNED to READ.

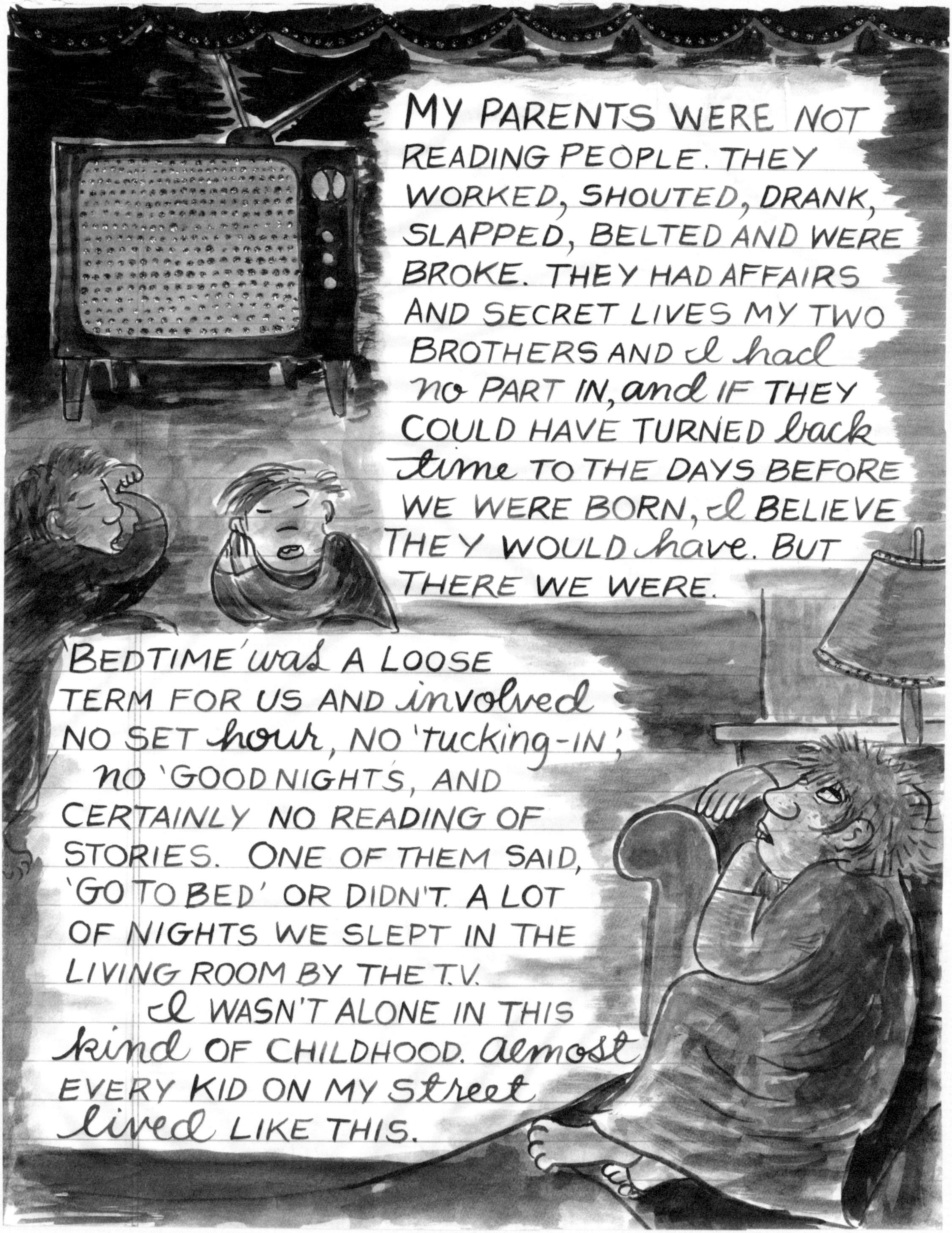
MY PARENTS WERE NOT READING PEOPLE. THEY WORKED, SHOUTED, DRANK, SLAPPED, BELTED AND WERE BROKE. THEY HAD AFFAIRS AND SECRET LIVES MY TWO BROTHERS AND I had no PART IN, and IF THEY COULD HAVE TURNED back time TO THE DAYS BEFORE WE WERE BORN, I BELIEVE THEY WOULD have. BUT THERE WE WERE.
'BEDTIME' was A LOOSE TERM FOR US AND involved NO SET hour, NO 'tucking-IN', no 'GOOD NIGHTS', AND CERTAINLY NO READING OF STORIES. ONE OF THEM SAID, 'GO TO BED' OR DIDN'T. A LOT OF NIGHTS WE SLEPT IN THE LIVING ROOM BY THE T.V.
I WASN'T ALONE IN THIS kind OF CHILDHOOD. almost EVERY KID ON MY street lived LIKE THIS.

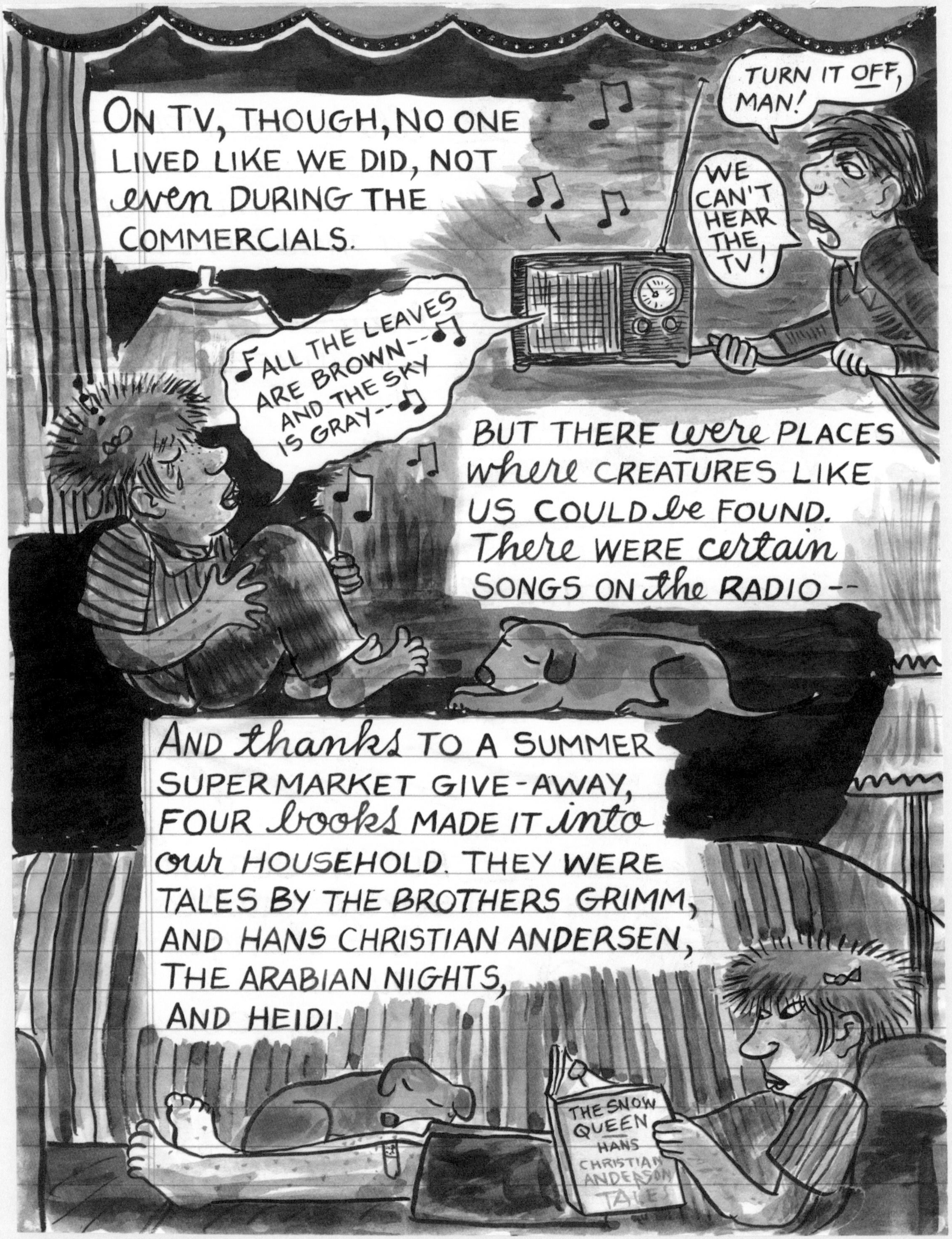

ON TV, THOUGH, NO ONE LIVED LIKE WE DID, NOT even DURING THE COMMERCIALS.
TURN IT OFF, MAN!
WE CAN'T HEAR THE TV!
ALL THE LEAVES ARE BROWN-- AND THE SKY IS GRAY--
BUT THERE were PLACES where CREATURES LIKE US COULD be FOUND. There WERE certain SONGS ON the RADIO--
AND thanks TO A SUMMER SUPERMARKET GIVE-AWAY, FOUR books MADE IT into our HOUSEHOLD. THEY WERE TALES BY THE BROTHERS GRIMM, AND HANS CHRISTIAN ANDERSEN, THE ARABIAN NIGHTS, AND HEIDI.
THE SNOW QUEEN
HANS CHRISTIAN ANDERSON TALES

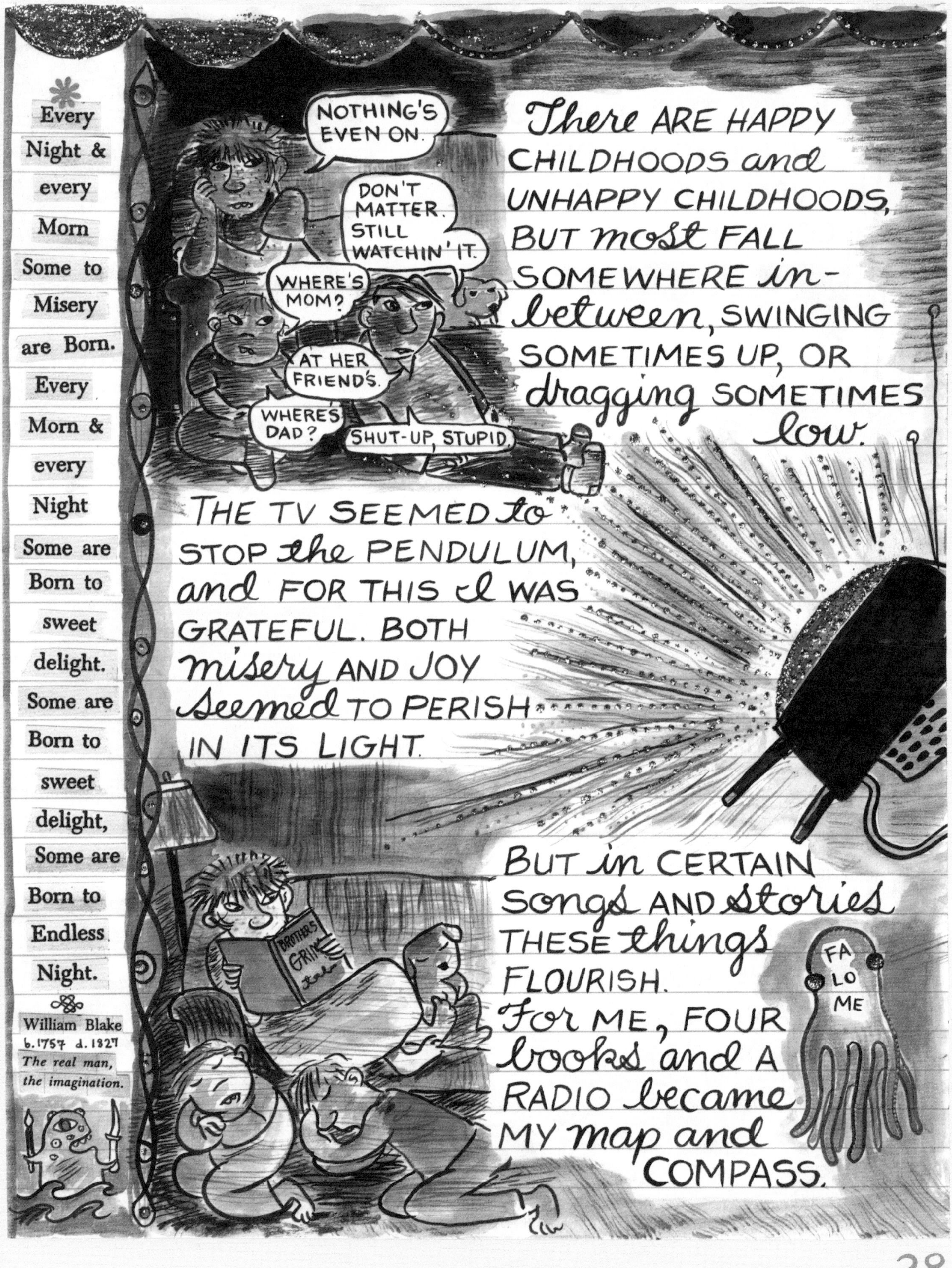

Every Night & every Morn Some to Misery are Born. Every Morn & every Night Some are Born to sweet delight. Some are Born to sweet delight, Some are Born to Endless Night.
William Blake b.1757 d.1827
The real man, the imagination.
NOTHING'S EVEN ON.
DON'T MATTER. STILL WATCHIN' IT.
WHERE'S MOM?
AT HER FRIEND'S.
WHERES DAD?
SHUT-UP, STUPID.
There ARE HAPPY CHILDHOODS and UNHAPPY CHILDHOODS, BUT most FALL SOMEWHERE in-between, SWINGING SOMETIMES UP, OR dragging SOMETIMES low.
THE TV SEEMED to STOP the PENDULUM, and FOR THIS I WAS GRATEFUL. BOTH misery AND JOY Seemed TO PERISH IN ITS LIGHT.
BROTHERS GRIM
BUT in CERTAIN Songs AND Stories THESE things FLOURISH.
FA LO ME
For ME, FOUR books and A RADIO became MY map and COMPASS.

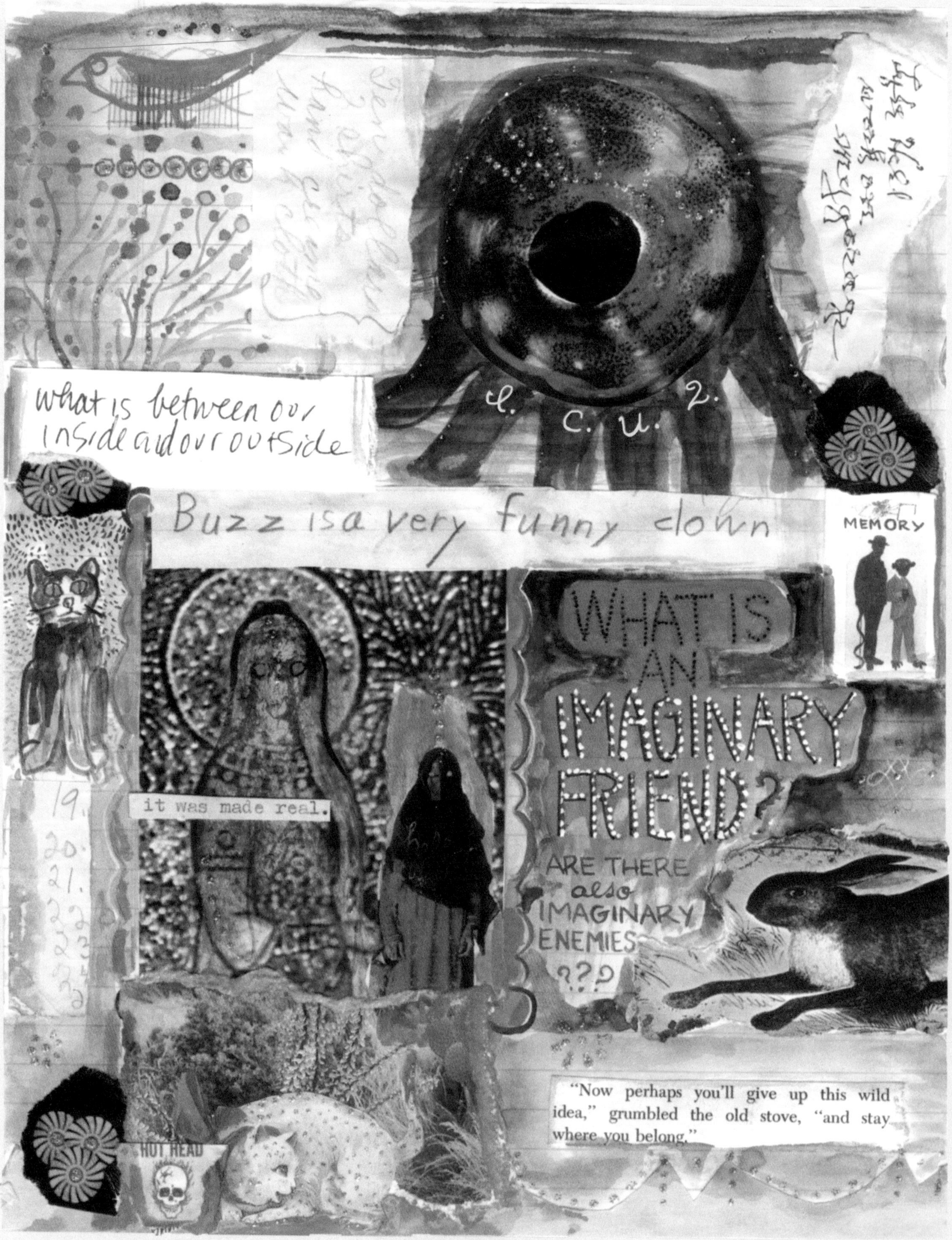
what is between our inside and our outside
Buzz is a very funny clown
MEMORY
WHAT IS AN IMAGINARY FRIEND?
ARE THERE also IMAGINARY ENEMIES ???
it was made real.
19.
20.
21.
"Now perhaps you'll give up this wild idea," grumbled the old stove, "and stay where you belong."
HOT HEAD

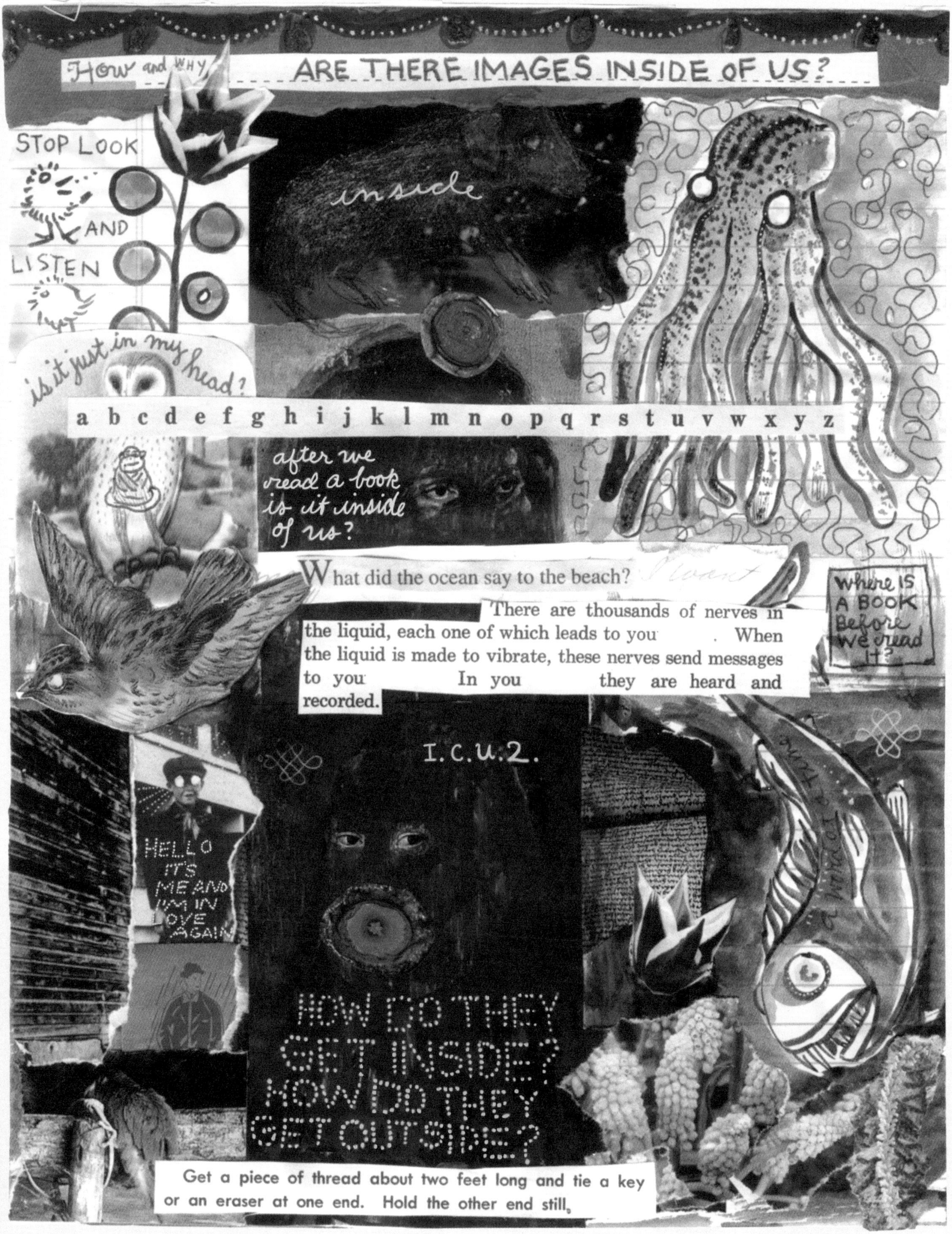
How and WHY ARE THERE IMAGES INSIDE OF US?
STOP LOOK AND LISTEN
inside
is it just in my head?
a b c d e f g h i j k l m n o p q r s t u v w x y z
after we read a book is it inside of us?
What did the ocean say to the beach?
There are thousands of nerves in the liquid, each one of which leads to you . When the liquid is made to vibrate, these nerves send messages to you In you they are heard and recorded.
Where IS A BOOK Before We read It?
I.C.U.2.
HELLO ITS ME AND I'M IN LOVE AGAIN
HOW DO THEY GET INSIDE? HOW DO THEY GET OUTSIDE?
Get a piece of thread about two feet long and tie a key or an eraser at one end. Hold the other end still.

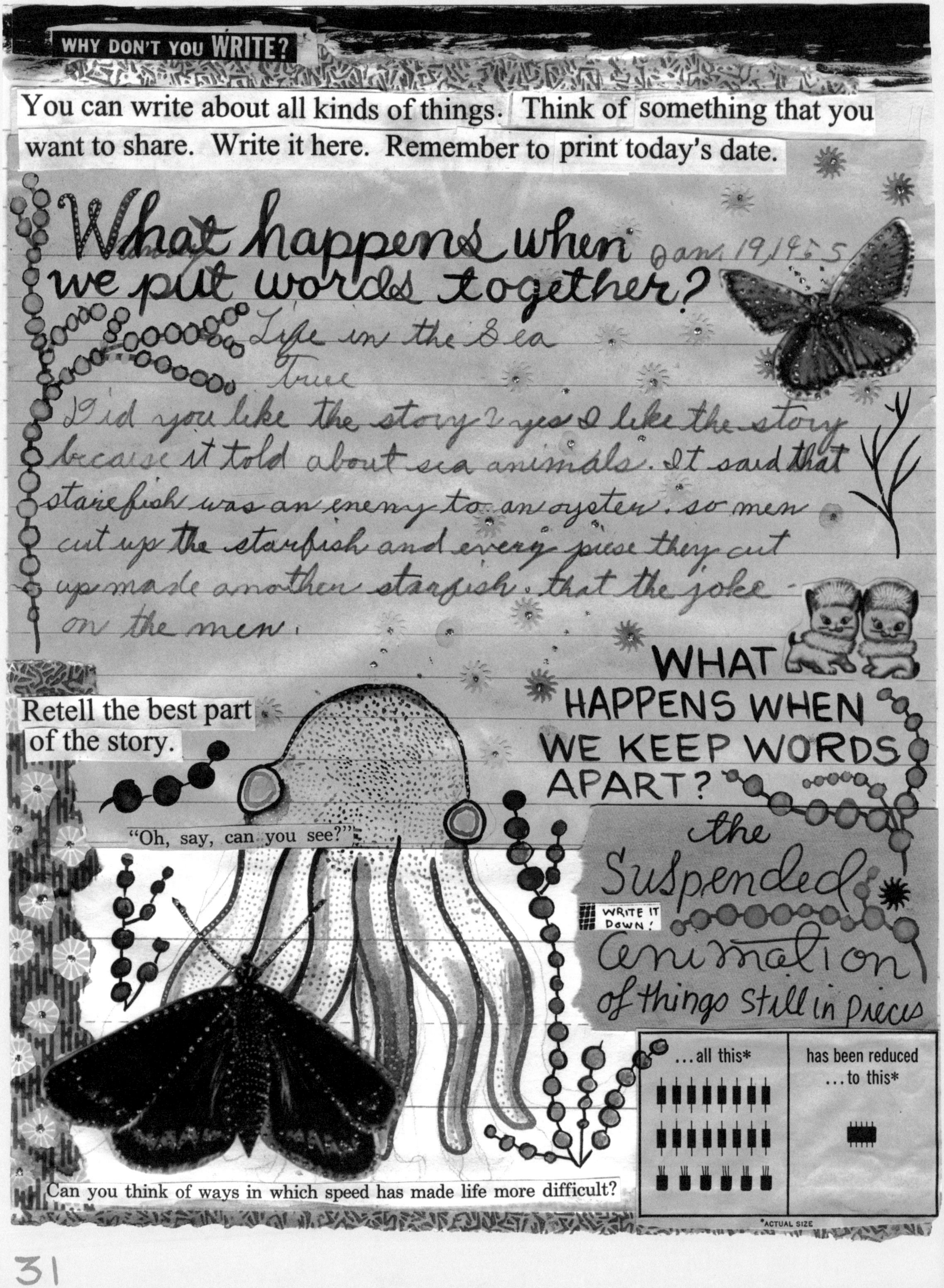
WHY DON'T YOU WRITE?
You can write about all kinds of things. Think of something that you want to share. Write it here. Remember to print today's date.
What happens when we put words together?
Jan. 19, 1955
Life in the Sea
True
Did you like the story? yes I like the story because it told about sea animals. It said that starefish was an enemy to an oyster. so men cut up the starfish and every piese they cut up made another starfish. that the joke on the men.
WHAT HAPPENS WHEN WE KEEP WORDS APART?
Retell the best part of the story.
"Oh, say, can you see?"
the Suspended Animation of things still in pieces
WRITE IT DOWN!
...all this*
has been reduced ...to this*
*ACTUAL SIZE
Can you think of ways in which speed has made life more difficult?

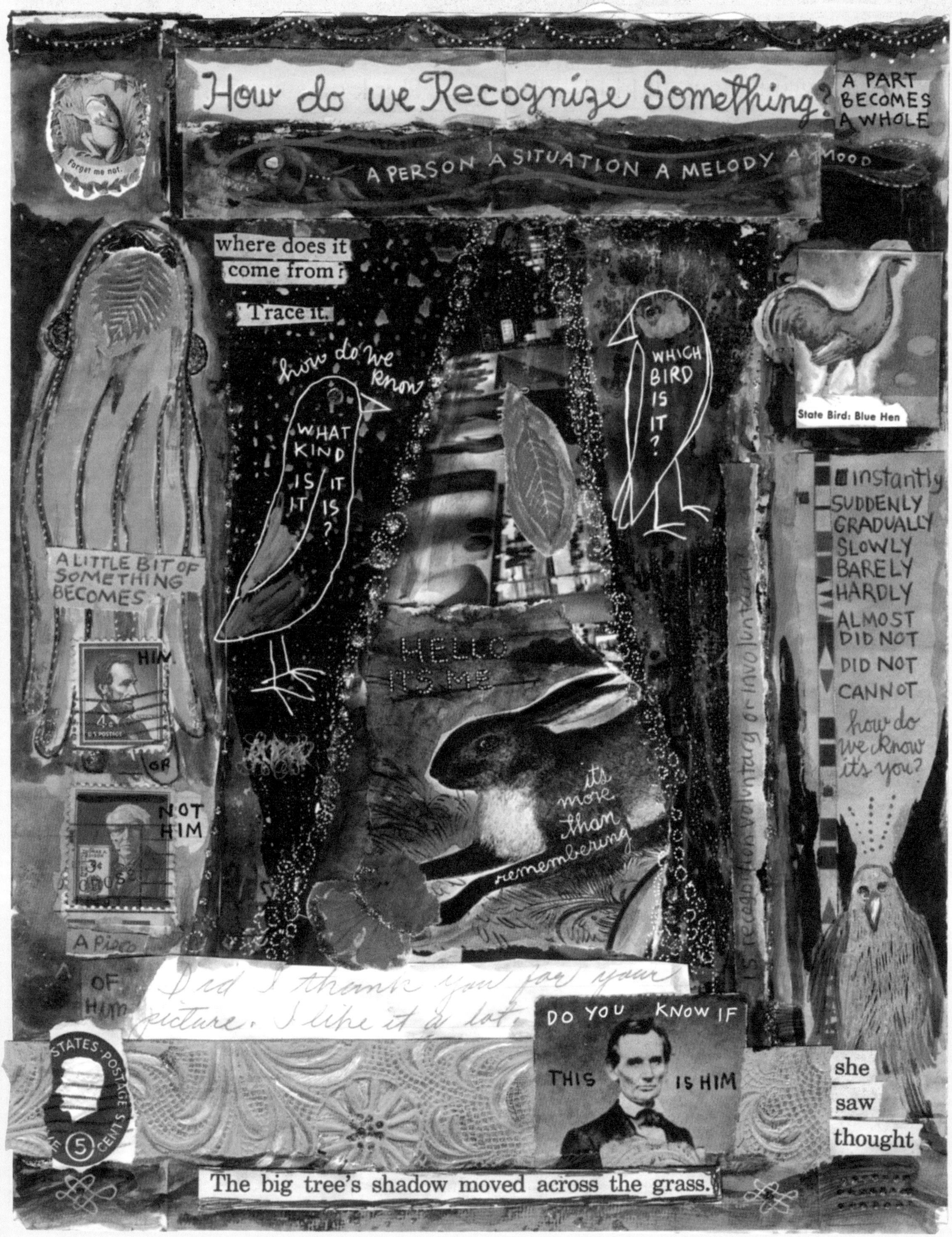
How do we Recognize Something?
A PART BECOMES A WHOLE
A PERSON A SITUATION A MELODY A MOOD
Forget me not.
where does it come from?
Trace it.
how do we know
WHAT KIND IS IT
IT IS?
WHICH BIRD IS IT?
State Bird: Blue Hen
instantly
SUDDENLY
GRADUALLY
SLOWLY
BARELY
HARDLY
ALMOST
DID NOT
DID NOT
CANNOT
how do we know its you?
A LITTLE BIT OF SOMETHING BECOMES
HIM
OR
NOT HIM
A Piece
OF
HIM
HELLO ITS ME
its more than remembering
IS recognition voluntary or involuntary
Did I thank you for your picture. I like it a lot.
DO YOU KNOW IF
THIS IS HIM
she
saw
thought
The big tree's shadow moved across the grass.

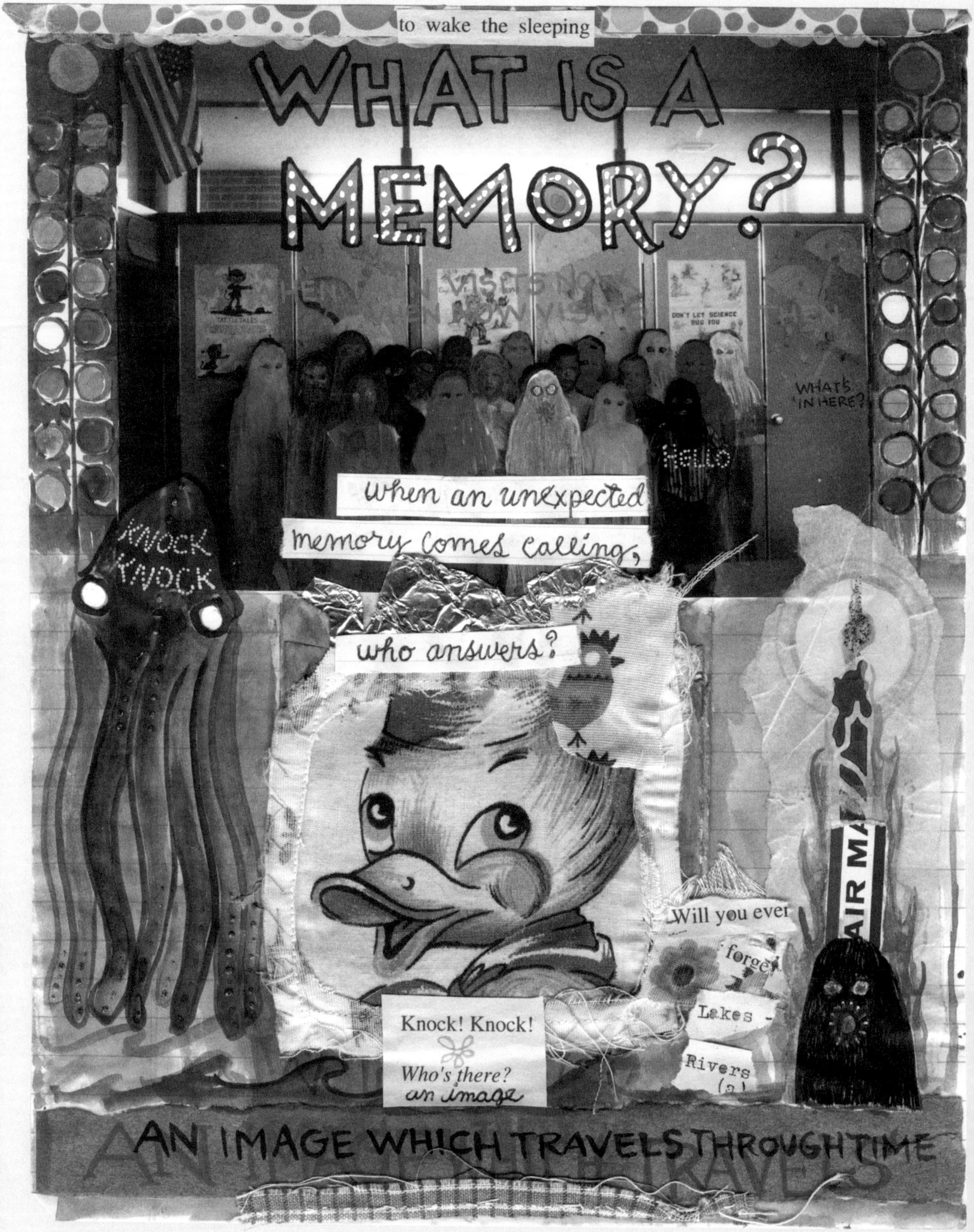

to wake the sleeping
WHAT IS A MEMORY?
WHAT'S IN HERE?
HELLO
KNOCK KNOCK
when an unexpected memory comes calling,
who answers?
Will you ever
forge
Lakes -
Rivers
(a)
AIR MA
Knock! Knock!
Who's there?
an image
AN IMAGE WHICH TRAVELS THROUGHTIME

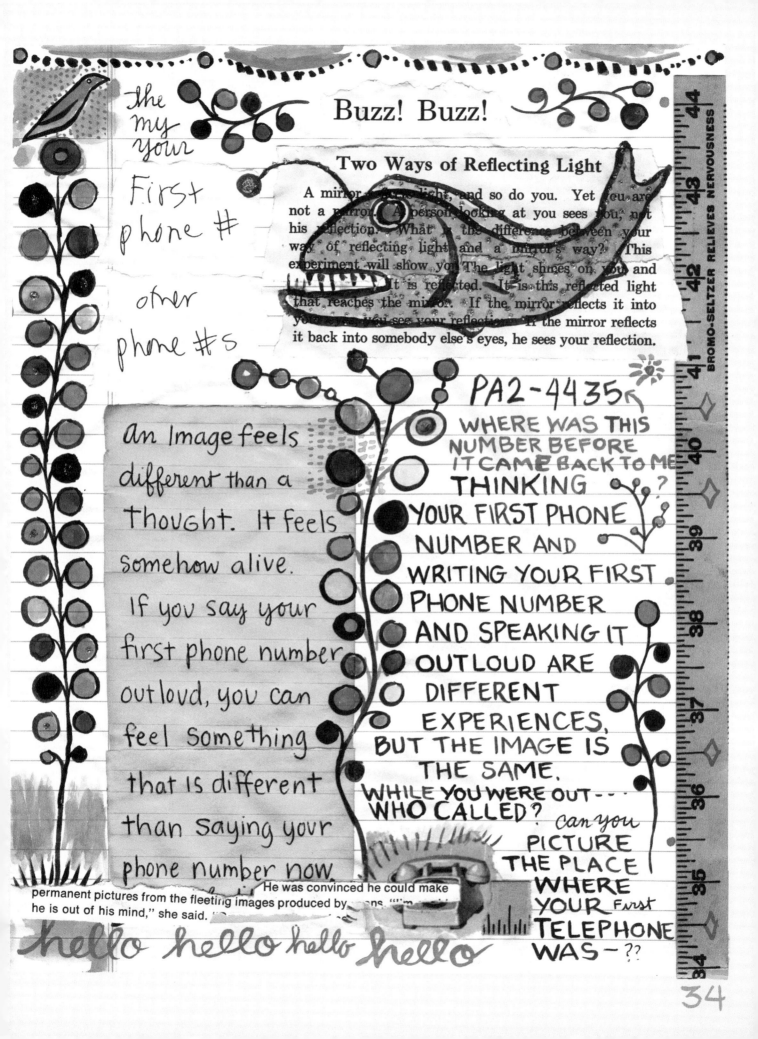

the
my
your

First
phone #

other
phone #s

Buzz! Buzz!

Two Ways of Reflecting Light

A mirror reflects light, and so do you. Yet you are not a mirror. A person looking at you sees you, not his reflection. What is the difference between your way of reflecting light and a mirror's way? This experiment will show you. The light shines on you and it is reflected. It is this reflected light that reaches the mirror. If the mirror reflects it into your eyes, you see your reflection. If the mirror reflects it back into somebody else's eyes, he sees your reflection.

PA2-4435

WHERE WAS THIS NUMBER BEFORE IT CAME BACK TO ME THINKING ?

An Image feels different than a thought. It feels somehow alive.

If you say your first phone number outloud, you can feel something that is different than saying your phone number now.

YOUR FIRST PHONE NUMBER AND WRITING YOUR FIRST PHONE NUMBER AND SPEAKING IT OUT LOUD ARE DIFFERENT EXPERIENCES, BUT THE IMAGE IS THE SAME.

WHILE YOU WERE OUT-- WHO CALLED? can you PICTURE THE PLACE WHERE YOUR First TELEPHONE WAS -- ??

permanent pictures from the fleeting images produced by lens. "I'm sure he is out of his mind," she said.

He was convinced he could make

hello hello hello hello

BROMO-SELTZER RELIEVES NERVOUSNESS

44 43 42 41 40 39 38 37 36 35 34

34

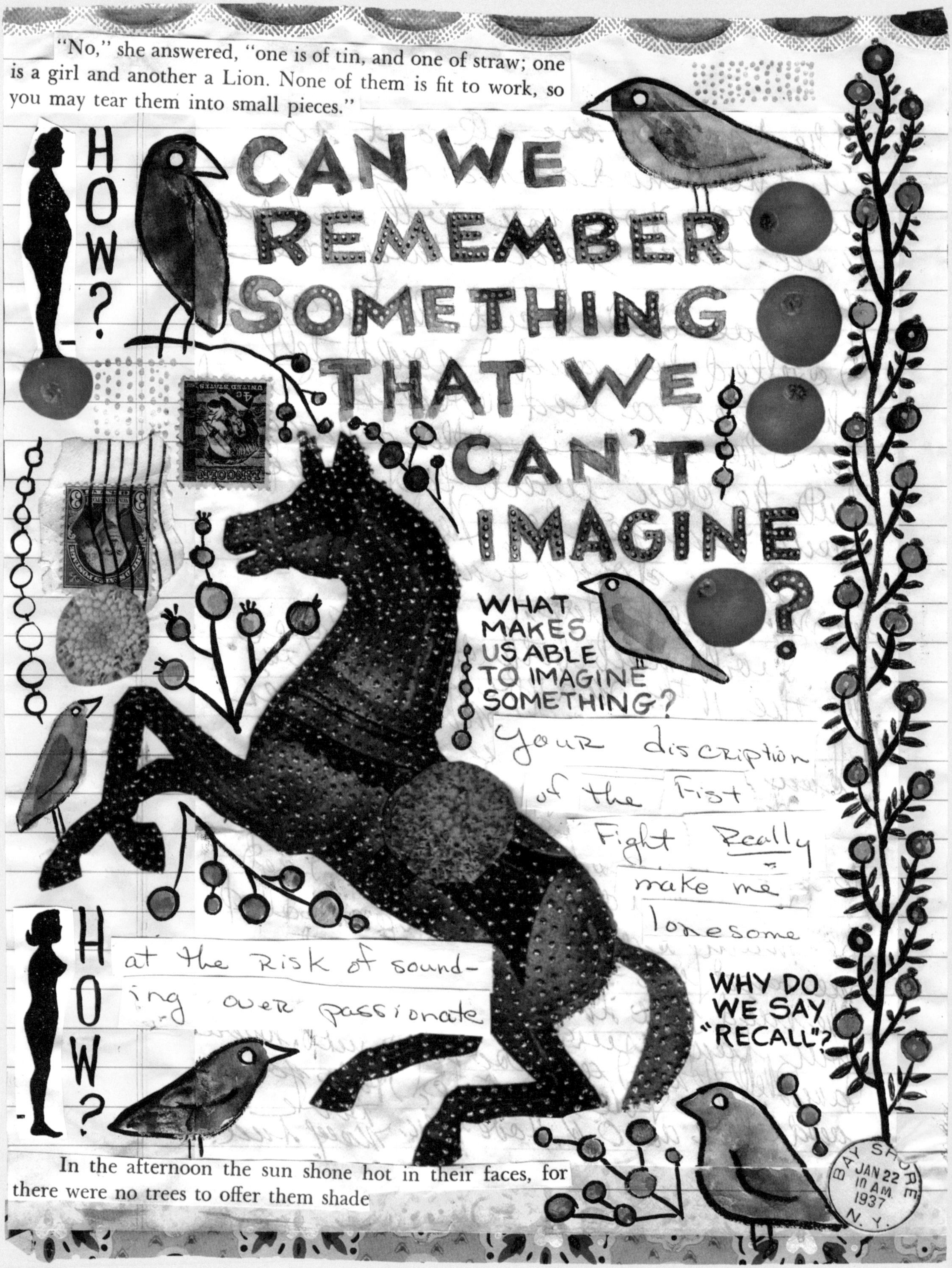
"No," she answered, "one is of tin, and one of straw; one is a girl and another a Lion. None of them is fit to work, so you may tear them into small pieces."
HOW?
CAN WE REMEMBER SOMETHING THAT WE CAN'T IMAGINE?
WHAT MAKES US ABLE TO IMAGINE SOMETHING?
your discription of the Fist Fight Really make me lonesome
at the Risk of sounding over passionate
HOW?
WHY DO WE SAY "RECALL"?
BAY SHORE JAN 22 10 AM 1937 N.Y.
In the afternoon the sun shone hot in their faces, for there were no trees to offer them shade

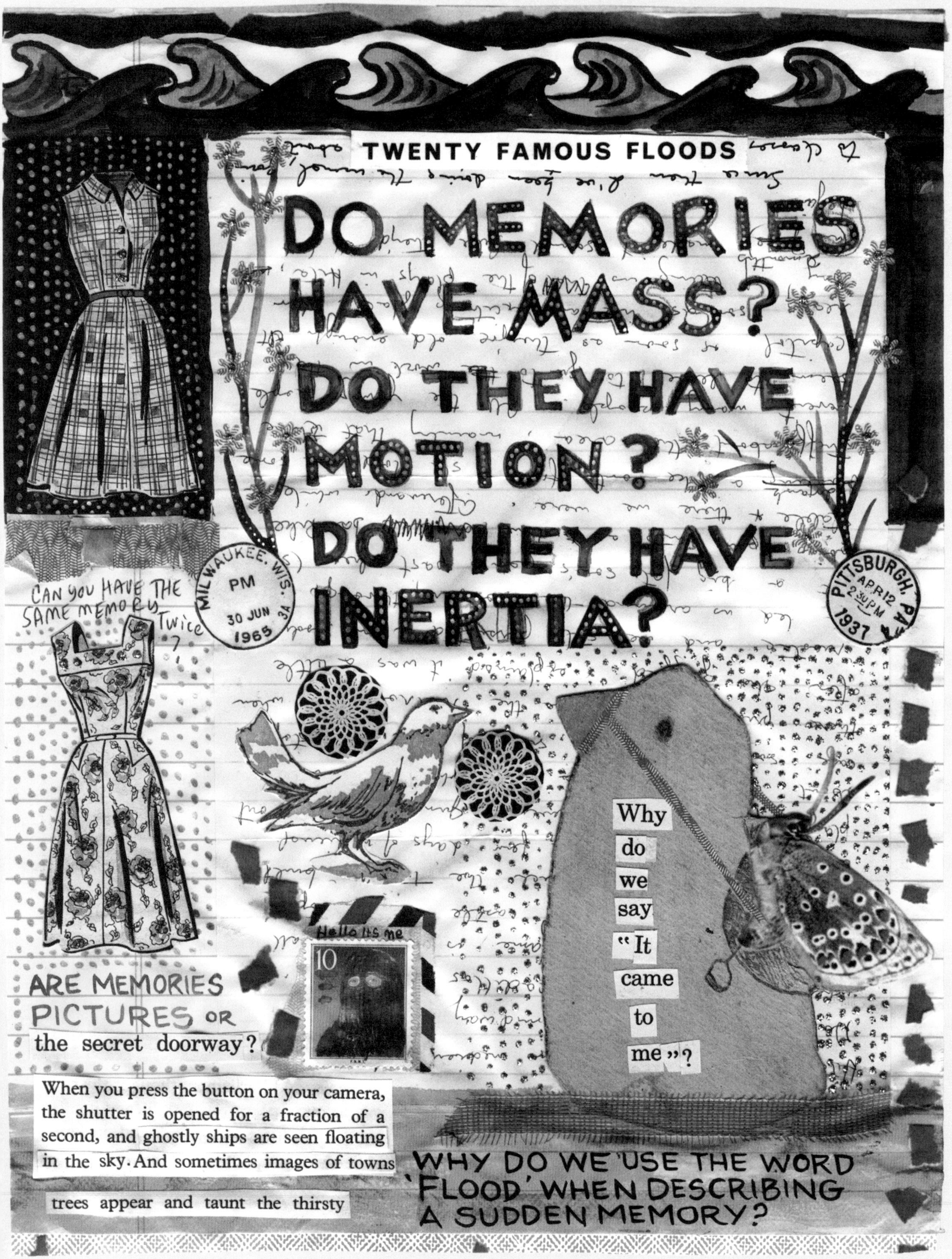
TWENTY FAMOUS FLOODS
DO MEMORIES HAVE MASS?
DO THEY HAVE MOTION?
DO THEY HAVE INERTIA?
CAN YOU HAVE THE SAME MEMORY TWICE?
MILWAUKEE, WIS. PM 30 JUN 1965 3A
PITTSBURGH, PA. APR 12 2:30 PM 1937
Hello it's me
10
Why do we say "It came to me"?
ARE MEMORIES PICTURES OR the secret doorway?
When you press the button on your camera, the shutter is opened for a fraction of a second, and ghostly ships are seen floating in the sky. And sometimes images of towns
trees appear and taunt the thirsty
WHY DO WE USE THE WORD 'FLOOD' WHEN DESCRIBING A SUDDEN MEMORY?

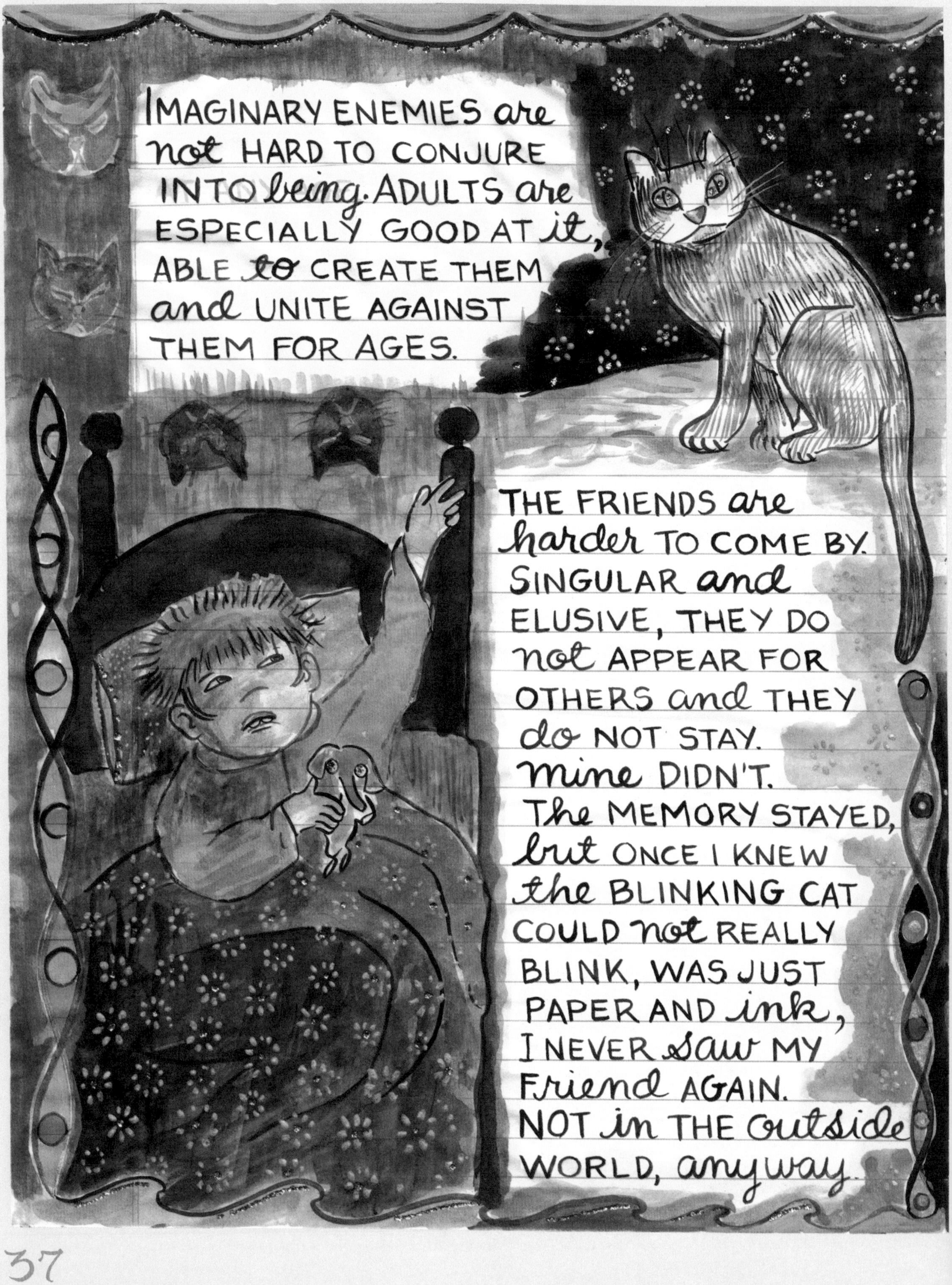
IMAGINARY ENEMIES are not HARD TO CONJURE INTO being. ADULTS are ESPECIALLY GOOD AT it, ABLE to CREATE THEM and UNITE AGAINST THEM FOR AGES.
THE FRIENDS are harder TO COME BY. SINGULAR and ELUSIVE, THEY DO not APPEAR FOR OTHERS and THEY do NOT STAY. mine DIDN'T. The MEMORY STAYED, but ONCE I KNEW the BLINKING CAT COULD not REALLY BLINK, WAS JUST PAPER AND ink, I NEVER saw MY Friend AGAIN. NOT in THE outside WORLD, anyway.

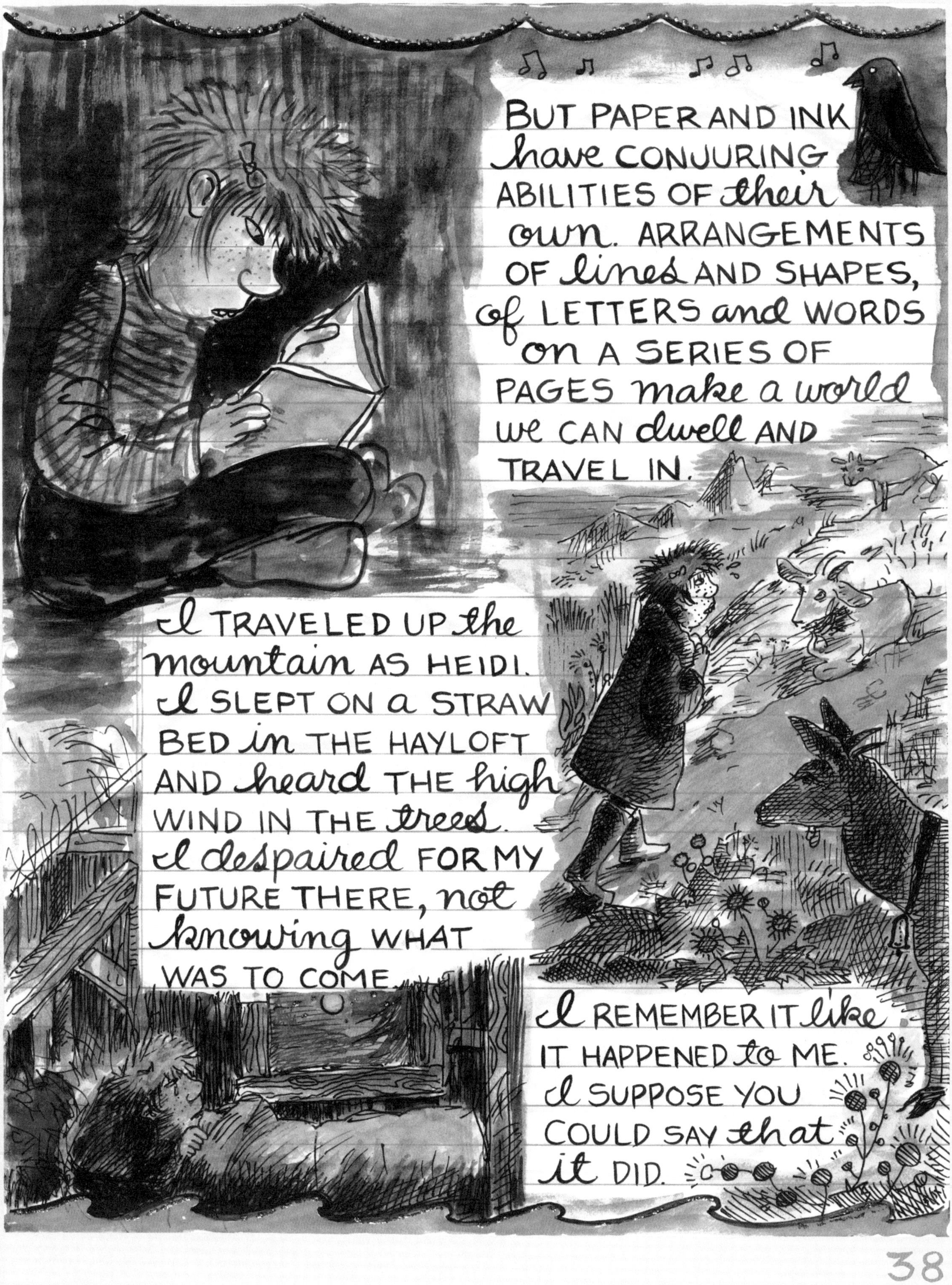
BUT PAPER AND INK have CONJURING ABILITIES OF their own. ARRANGEMENTS OF lines AND SHAPES, of LETTERS and WORDS on A SERIES OF PAGES make a world we CAN dwell AND TRAVEL IN.
I TRAVELED UP the mountain AS HEIDI. I SLEPT ON a STRAW BED in THE HAYLOFT AND heard THE high WIND IN THE trees. I despaired FOR MY FUTURE THERE, not knowing WHAT WAS TO COME.
I REMEMBER IT like IT HAPPENED to ME. I SUPPOSE YOU COULD SAY that it DID.

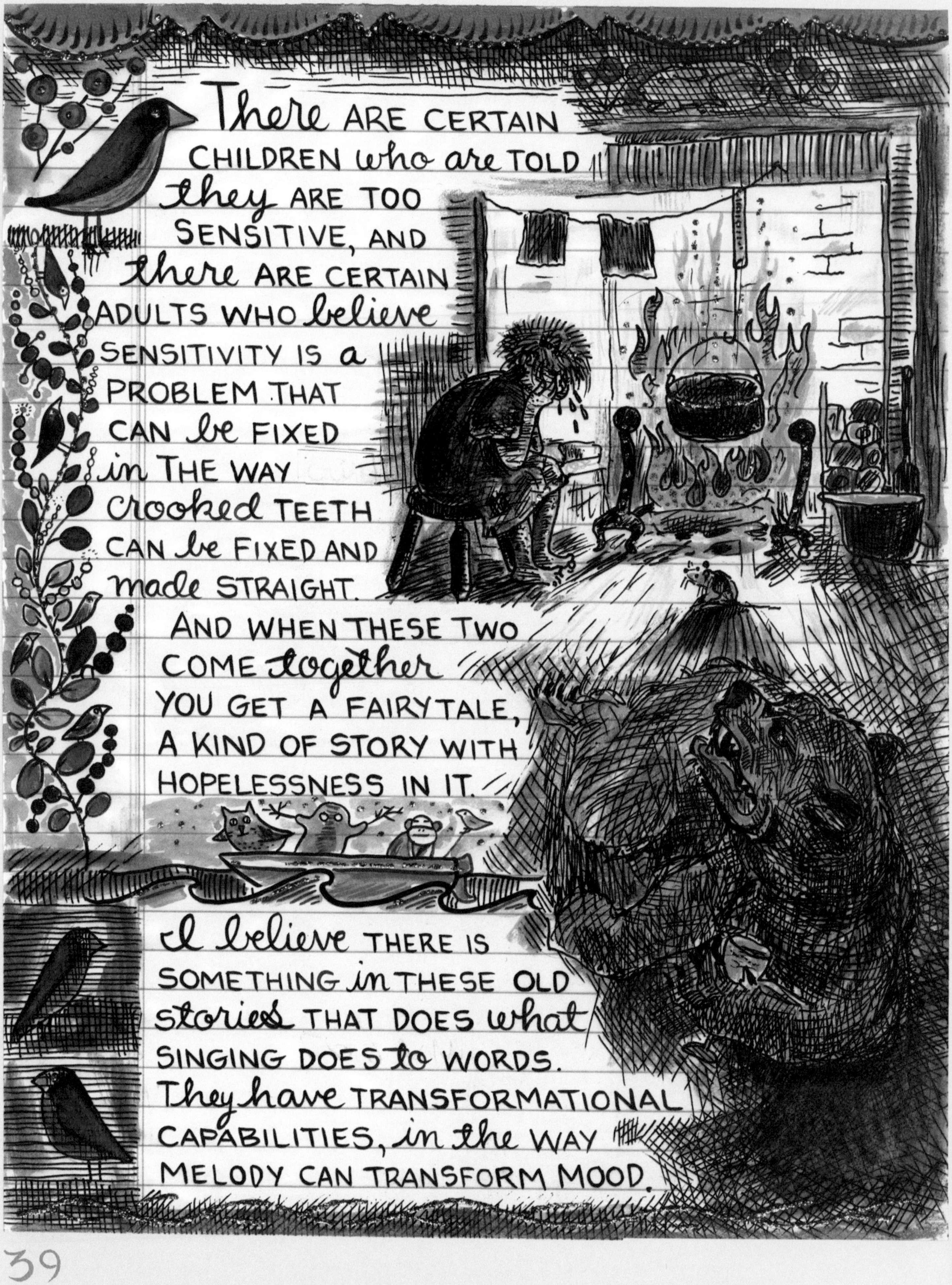
There are certain children who are told they are too sensitive, and there are certain adults who believe sensitivity is a problem that can be fixed in the way crooked teeth can be fixed and made straight.
And when these two come together you get a fairytale, a kind of story with hopelessness in it.
I believe there is something in these old stories that does what singing does to words. They have transformational capabilities, in the way melody can transform mood.

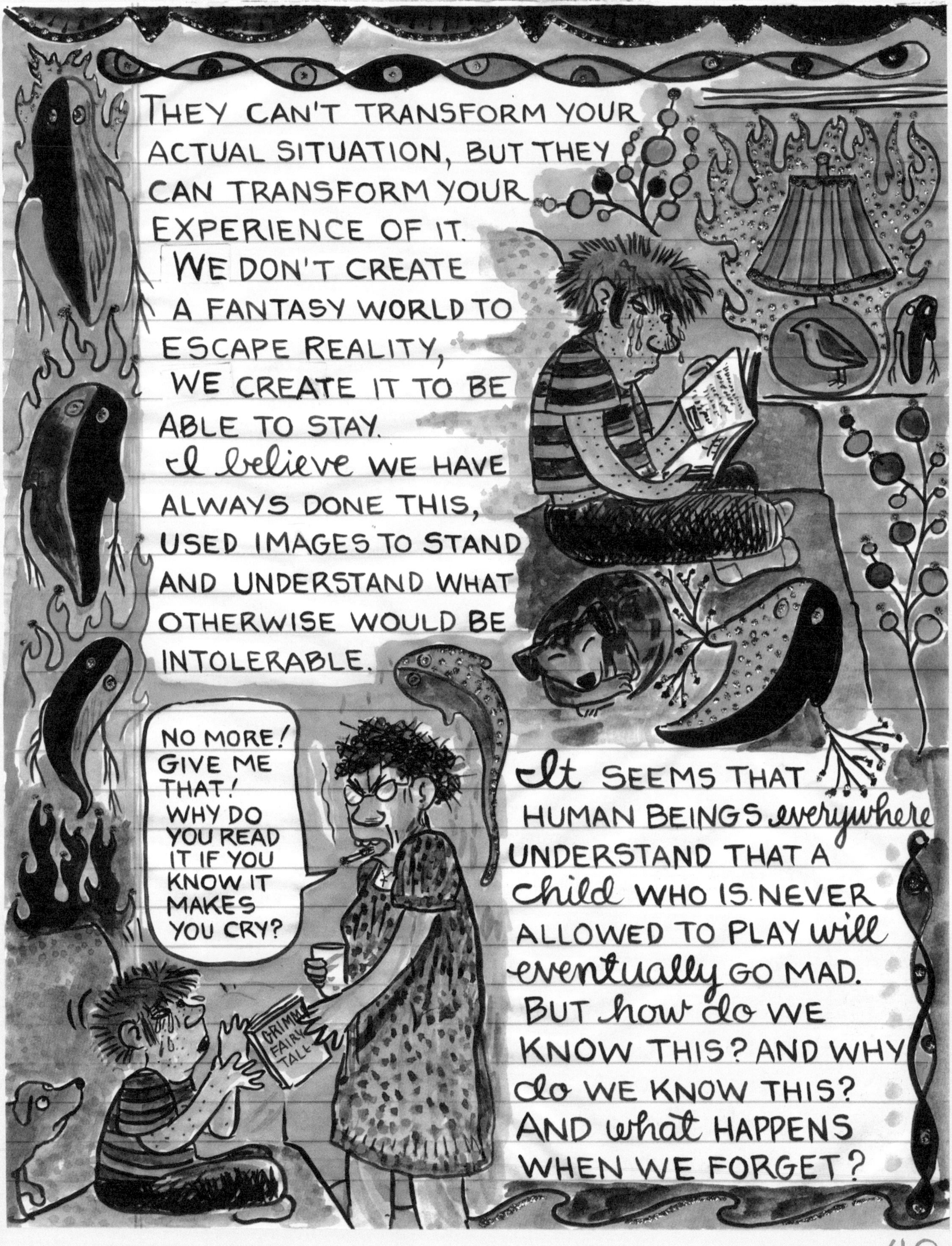
THEY CAN'T TRANSFORM YOUR ACTUAL SITUATION, BUT THEY CAN TRANSFORM YOUR EXPERIENCE OF IT.
WE DON'T CREATE A FANTASY WORLD TO ESCAPE REALITY, WE CREATE IT TO BE ABLE TO STAY.
I believe WE HAVE ALWAYS DONE THIS, USED IMAGES TO STAND AND UNDERSTAND WHAT OTHERWISE WOULD BE INTOLERABLE.
NO MORE! GIVE ME THAT! WHY DO YOU READ IT IF YOU KNOW IT MAKES YOU CRY?
GRIMM FAIRY TALE
It SEEMS THAT HUMAN BEINGS everywhere UNDERSTAND THAT A child WHO IS NEVER ALLOWED TO PLAY will eventually GO MAD.
BUT how do WE KNOW THIS? AND WHY do WE KNOW THIS? AND what HAPPENS WHEN WE FORGET?

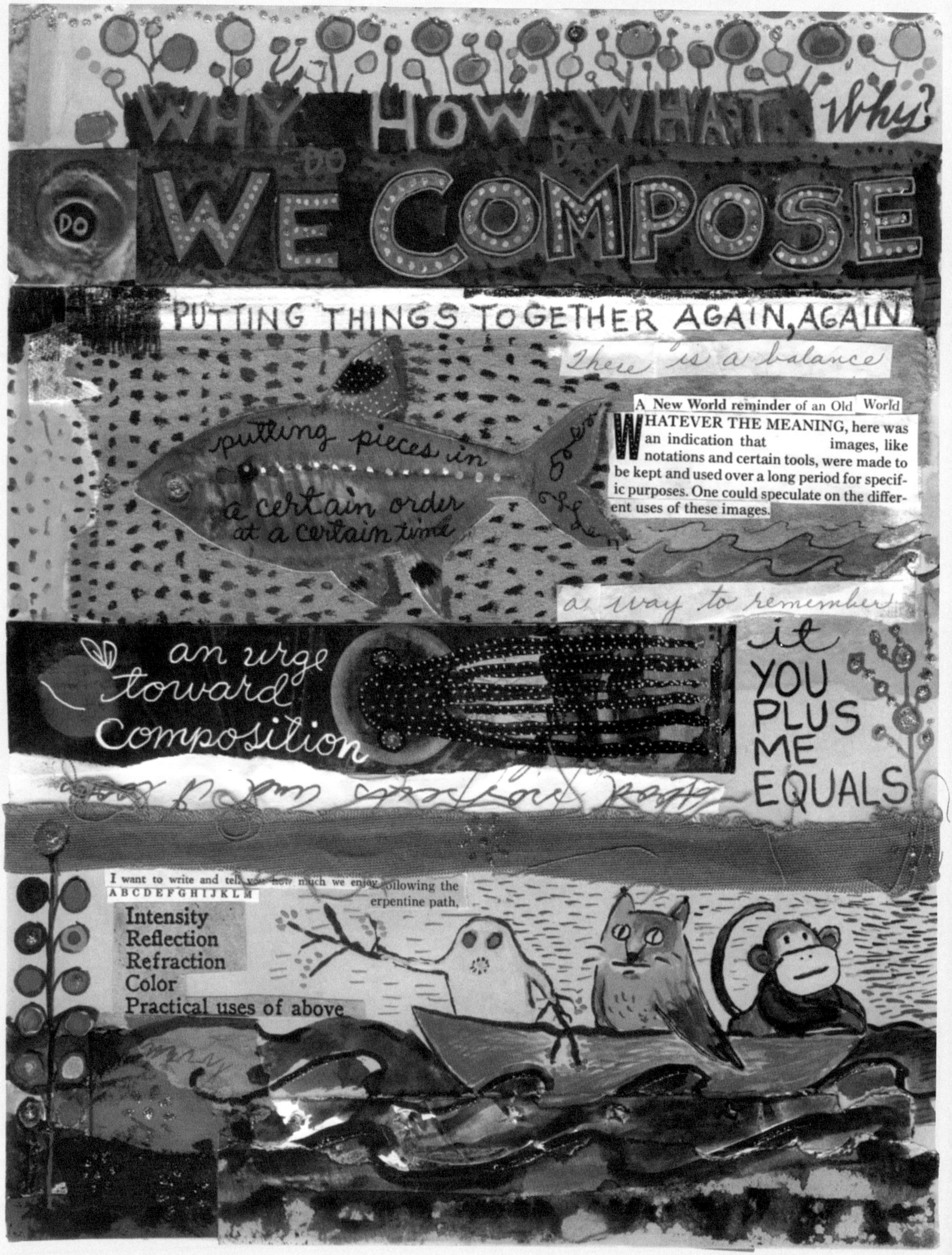
WHY HOW WHAT Why?
DO
WE COMPOSE
PUTTING THINGS TOGETHER AGAIN, AGAIN
There is a balance
putting pieces in
a certain order
at a certain time
A New World reminder of an Old World
WHATEVER THE MEANING, here was an indication that images, like notations and certain tools, were made to be kept and used over a long period for specific purposes. One could speculate on the different uses of these images.
a way to remember
an urge
toward
Composition
it
YOU
PLUS
ME
EQUALS
I want to write and tell
much we enjoy
ollowing the
erpentine path,
A B C D E F G H I J K L M
Intensity
Reflection
Refraction
Color
Practical uses of above

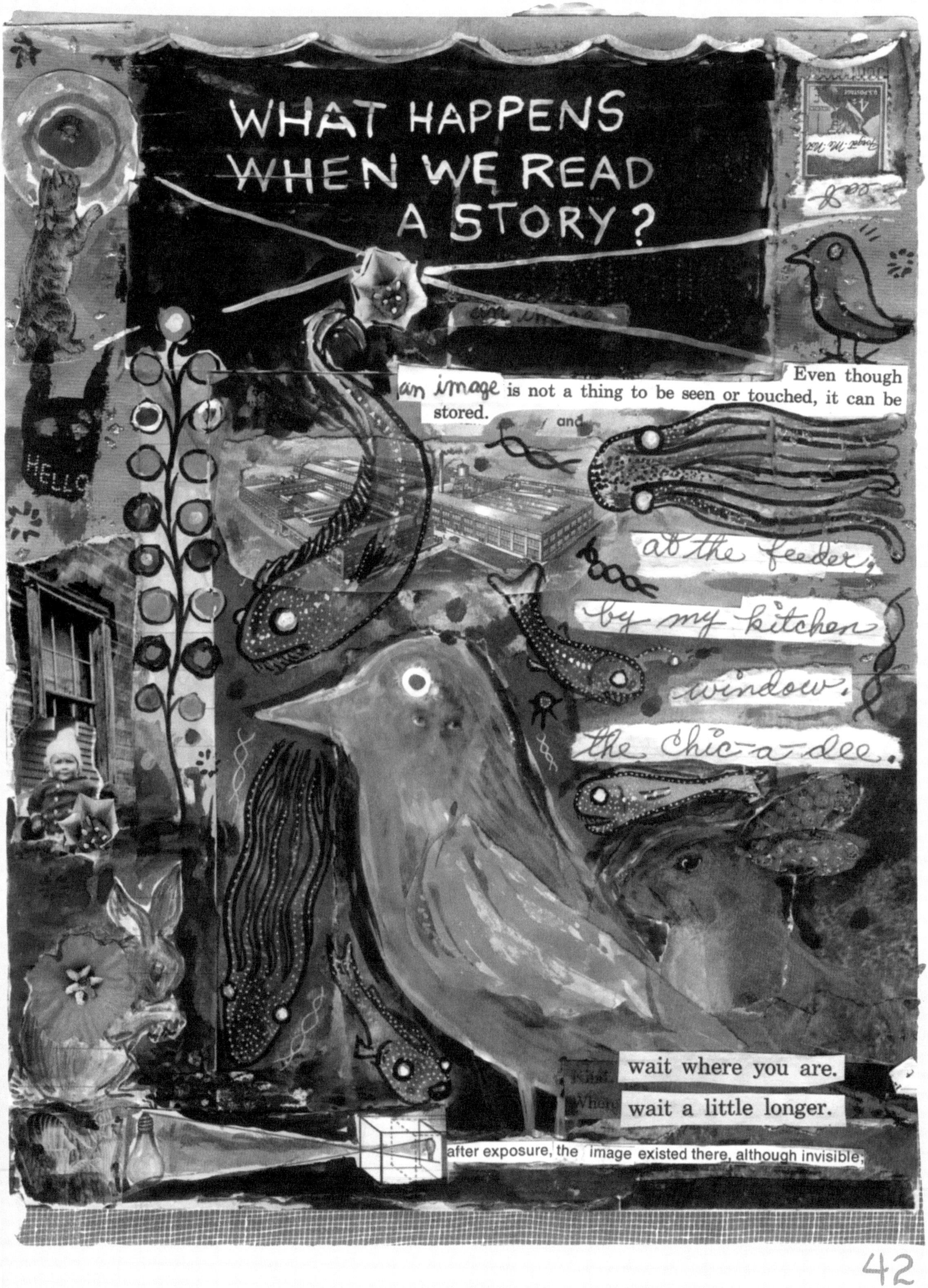
WHAT HAPPENS WHEN WE READ A STORY?
an image is not a thing to be seen or touched, it can be stored. Even though
and
HELLO
at the feeder,
by my kitchen
window,
the chic-a-dee.
wait where you are.
wait a little longer.
after exposure, the image existed there, although invisible,

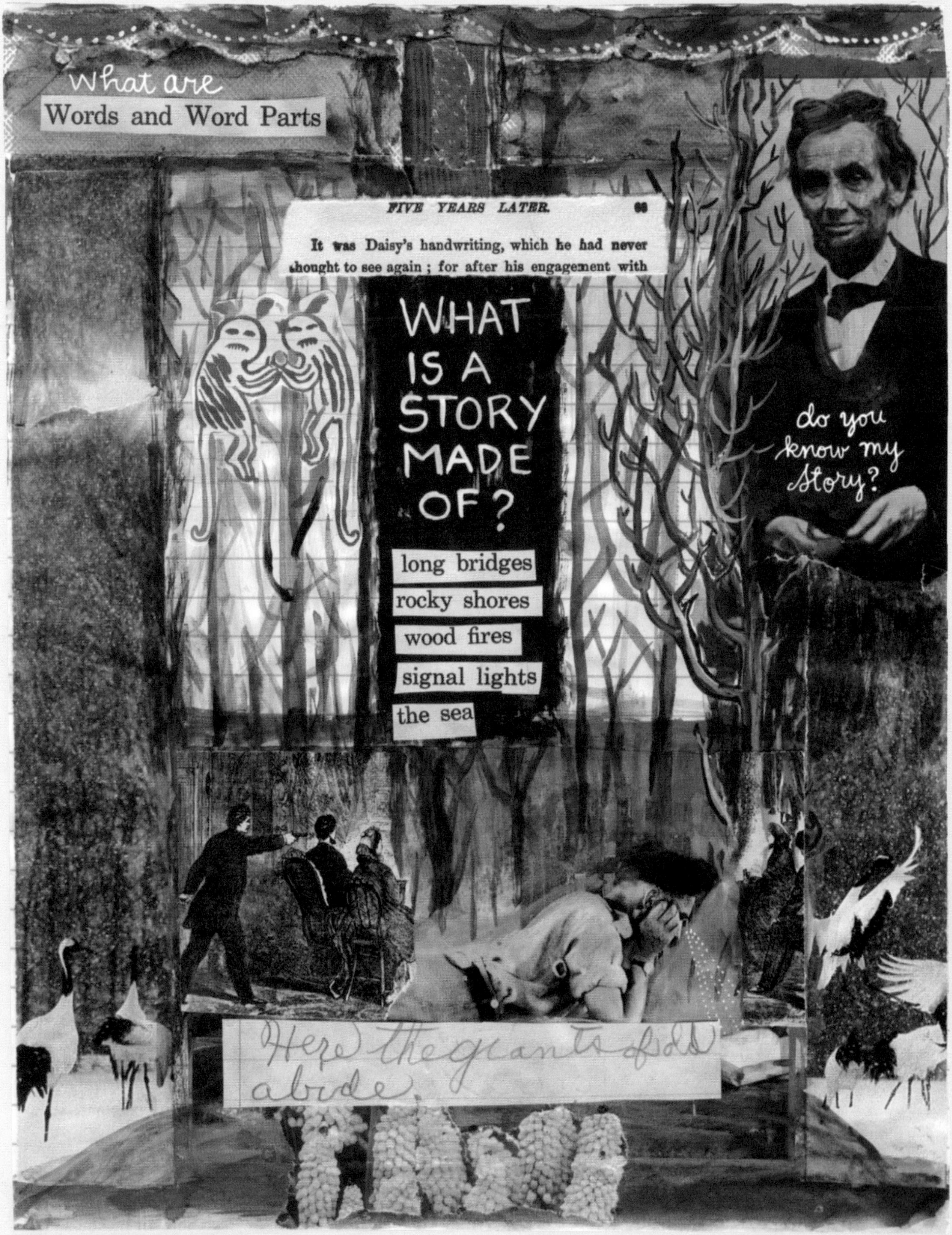
What are
Words and Word Parts
FIVE YEARS LATER.
It was Daisy's handwriting, which he had never thought to see again ; for after his engagement with
WHAT IS A STORY MADE OF?
long bridges
rocky shores
wood fires
signal lights
the sea
do you know my Story?
Here the giants of old abide

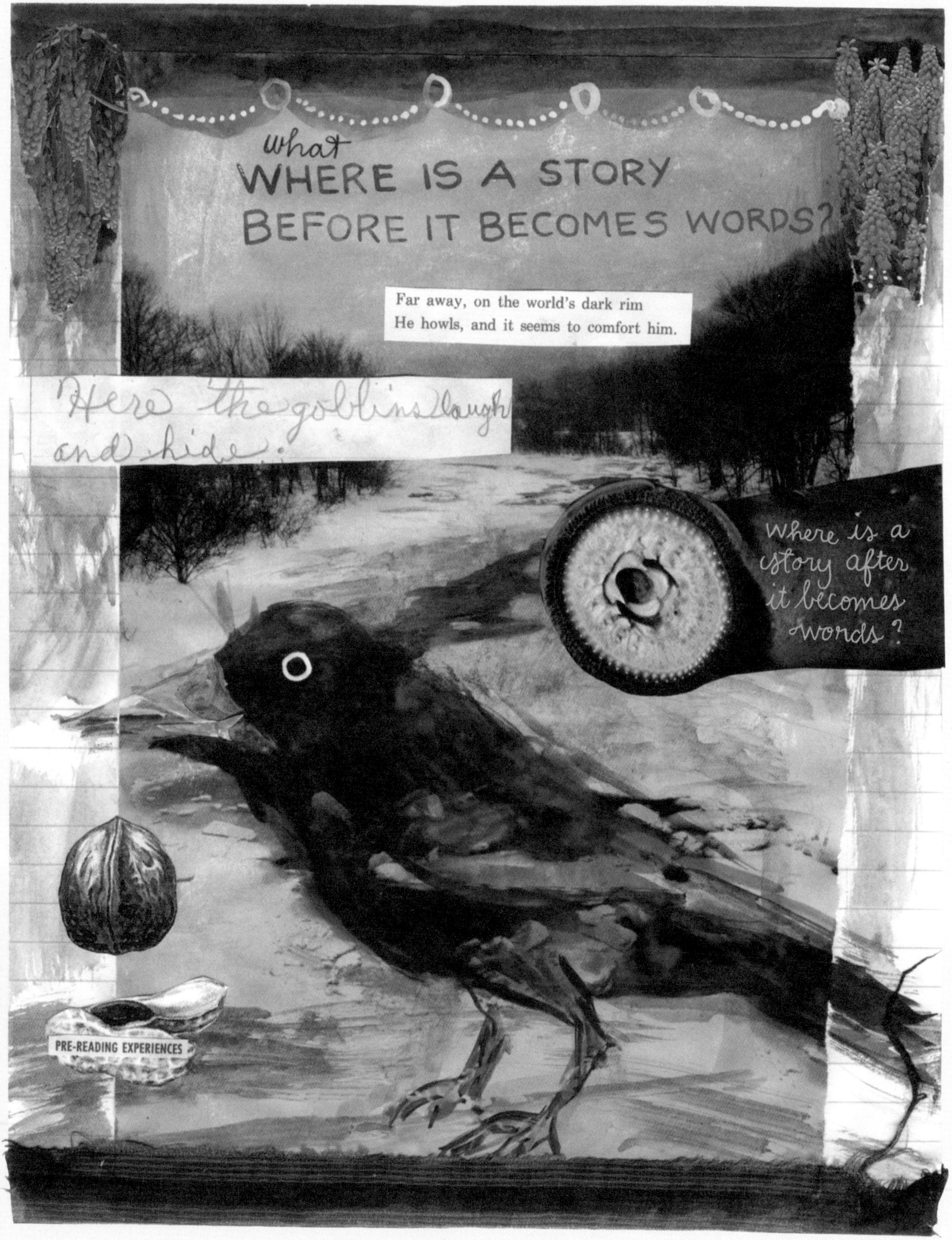
what
WHERE IS A STORY
BEFORE IT BECOMES WORDS?
Far away, on the world's dark rim
He howls, and it seems to comfort him.
Here the goblins laugh and hide.
Where is a story after it becomes words?
PRE-READING EXPERIENCES

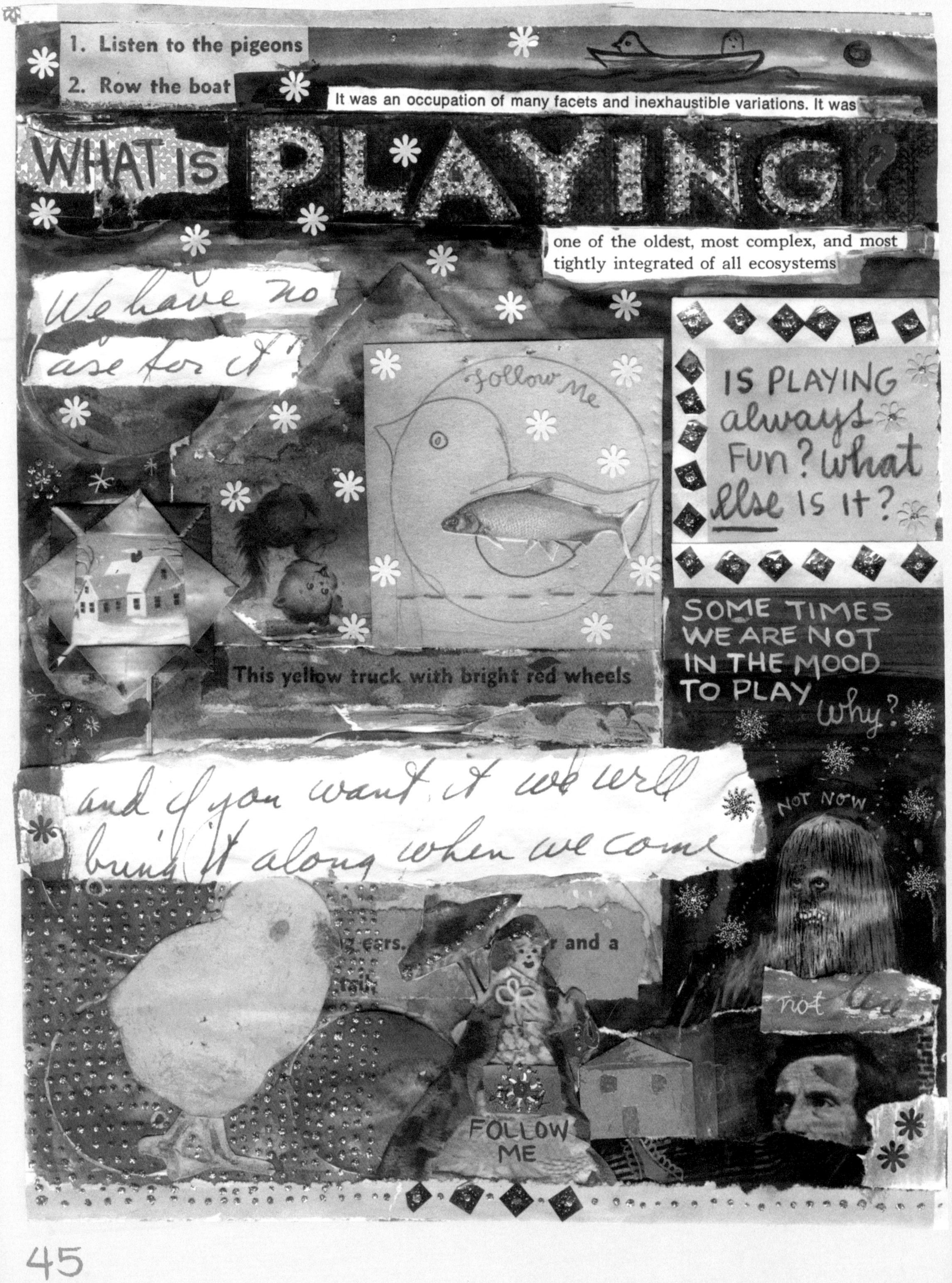
1. Listen to the pigeons
2. Row the boat
It was an occupation of many facets and inexhaustible variations. It was
WHAT IS PLAYING?
one of the oldest, most complex, and most tightly integrated of all ecosystems
We have no use for it!
Follow Me
IS PLAYING always Fun? what else is it?
This yellow truck with bright red wheels
SOME TIMES WE ARE NOT IN THE MOOD TO PLAY
Why?
and if you want it we will bring it along when we come
NOT NOW
FOLLOW ME

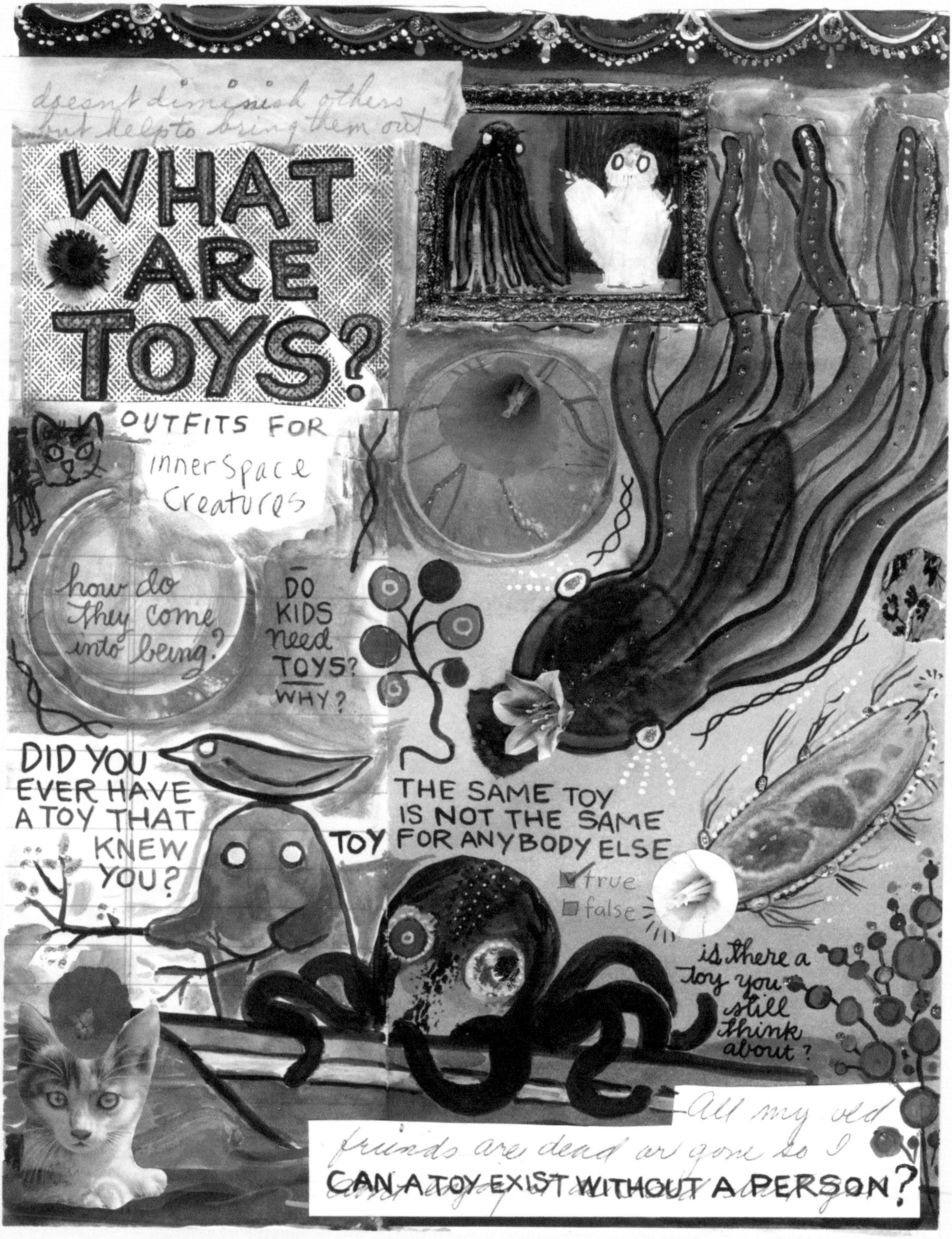
doesnt diminish others
but help to bring them out
WHAT ARE TOYS?
OUTFITS FOR
innerSpace
Creatures
how do
they come
into being?
DO
KIDS
need
TOYS?
WHY?
DID YOU
EVER HAVE
A TOY THAT
KNEW
YOU?
TOY
THE SAME TOY
IS NOT THE SAME
FOR ANYBODY ELSE
true
false
is there a
toy you
still
think
about?
All my old
friends are dead or gone so I
CAN A TOY EXIST WITHOUT A PERSON?

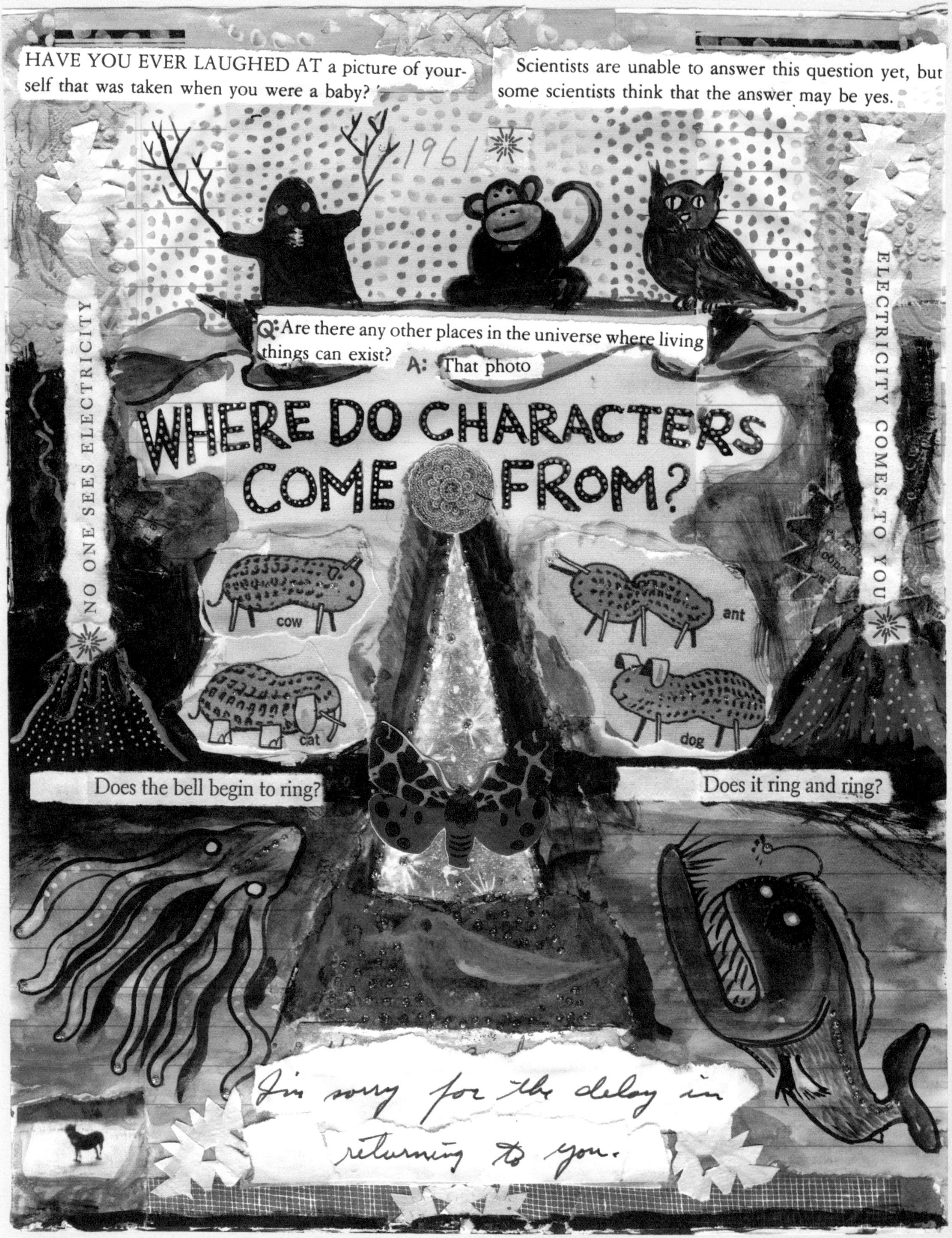
HAVE YOU EVER LAUGHED AT a picture of yourself that was taken when you were a baby?
Scientists are unable to answer this question yet, but some scientists think that the answer may be yes.
1961
NO ONE SEES ELECTRICITY
ELECTRICITY COMES TO YOU
Q: Are there any other places in the universe where living things can exist?
A: That photo
WHERE DO CHARACTERS COME FROM?
cow
ant
cat
dog
Does the bell begin to ring?
Does it ring and ring?
I'm sorry for the delay in returning to you.

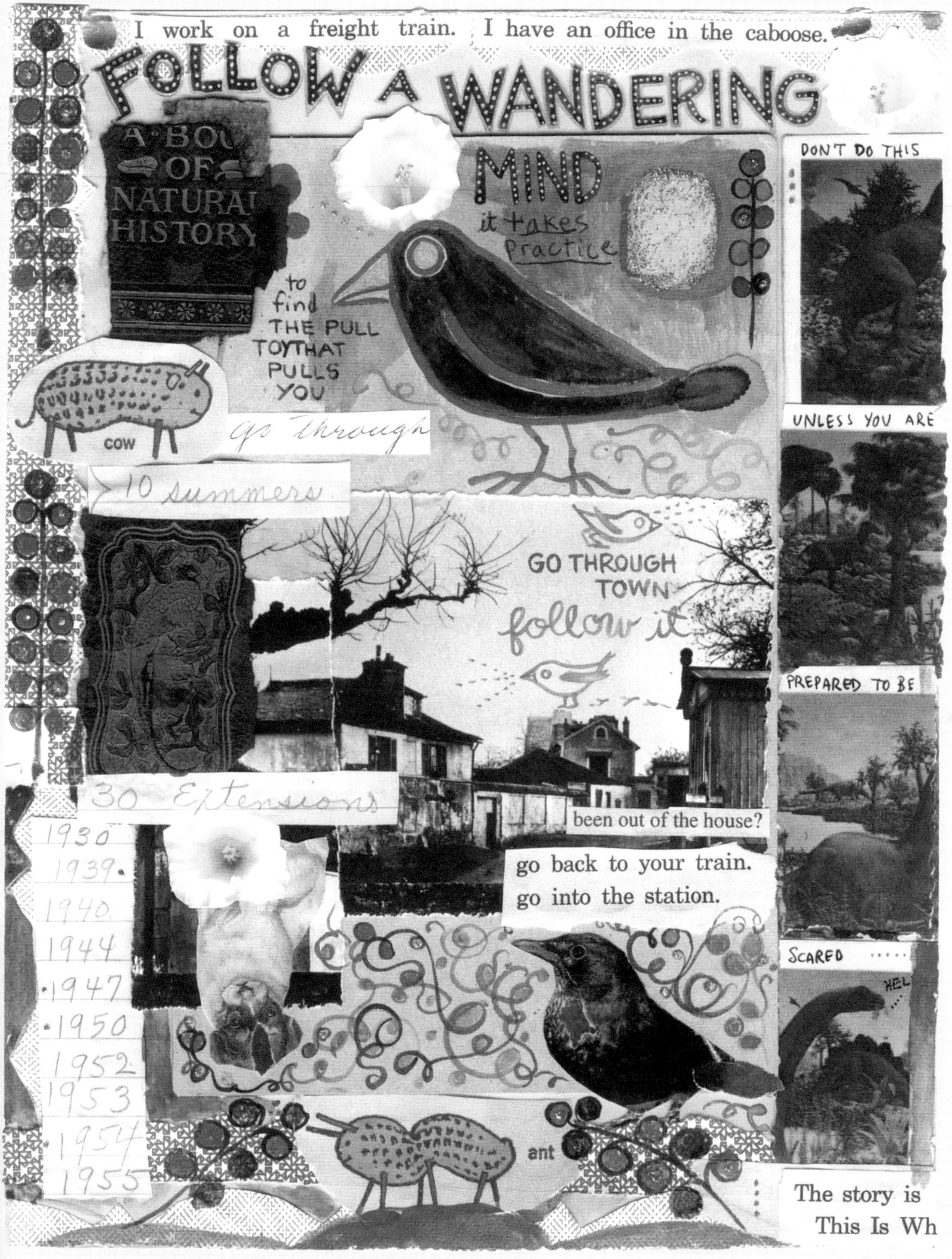
I work on a freight train. I have an office in the caboose.
FOLLOW A WANDERING
MIND
it takes practice
A BOOK OF NATURAL HISTORY
to find THE PULL TOY THAT PULLS YOU
COW
go through
10 summers
30 Extensions
DON'T DO THIS
UNLESS YOU ARE
PREPARED TO BE
SCARED
GO THROUGH TOWN
follow it
been out of the house?
go back to your train.
go into the station.
1930
1939
1940
1944
1947
1950
1952
1953
1954
1955
ant
The story is
This Is Wh

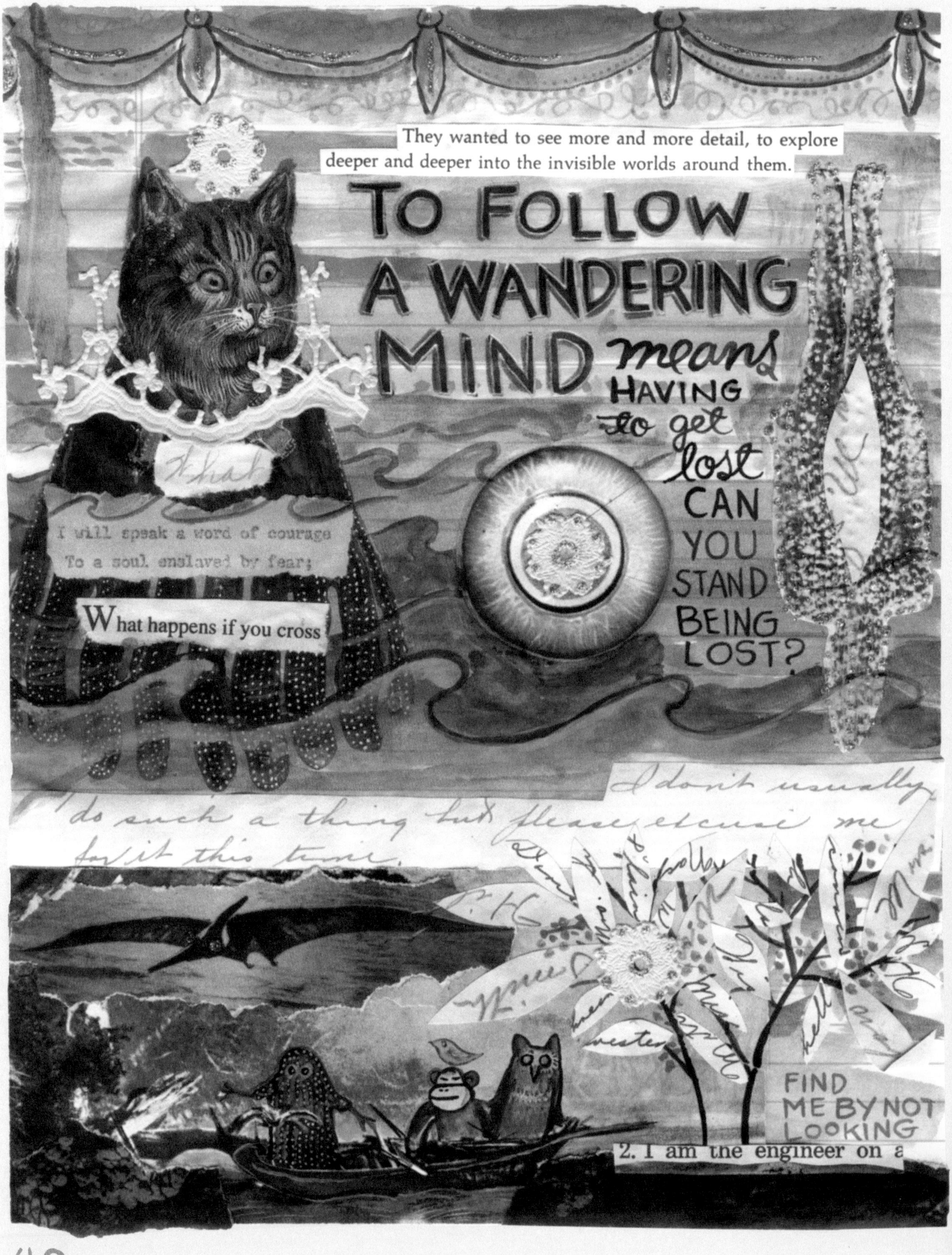

They wanted to see more and more detail, to explore deeper and deeper into the invisible worlds around them.
TO FOLLOW A WANDERING MIND means HAVING to get lost
CAN YOU STAND BEING LOST?
What
I will speak a word of courage
To a soul enslaved by fear;
What happens if you cross
I don't usually do such a thing but please excuse me for it this time.
FIND ME BY NOT LOOKING
2. I am the engineer on a

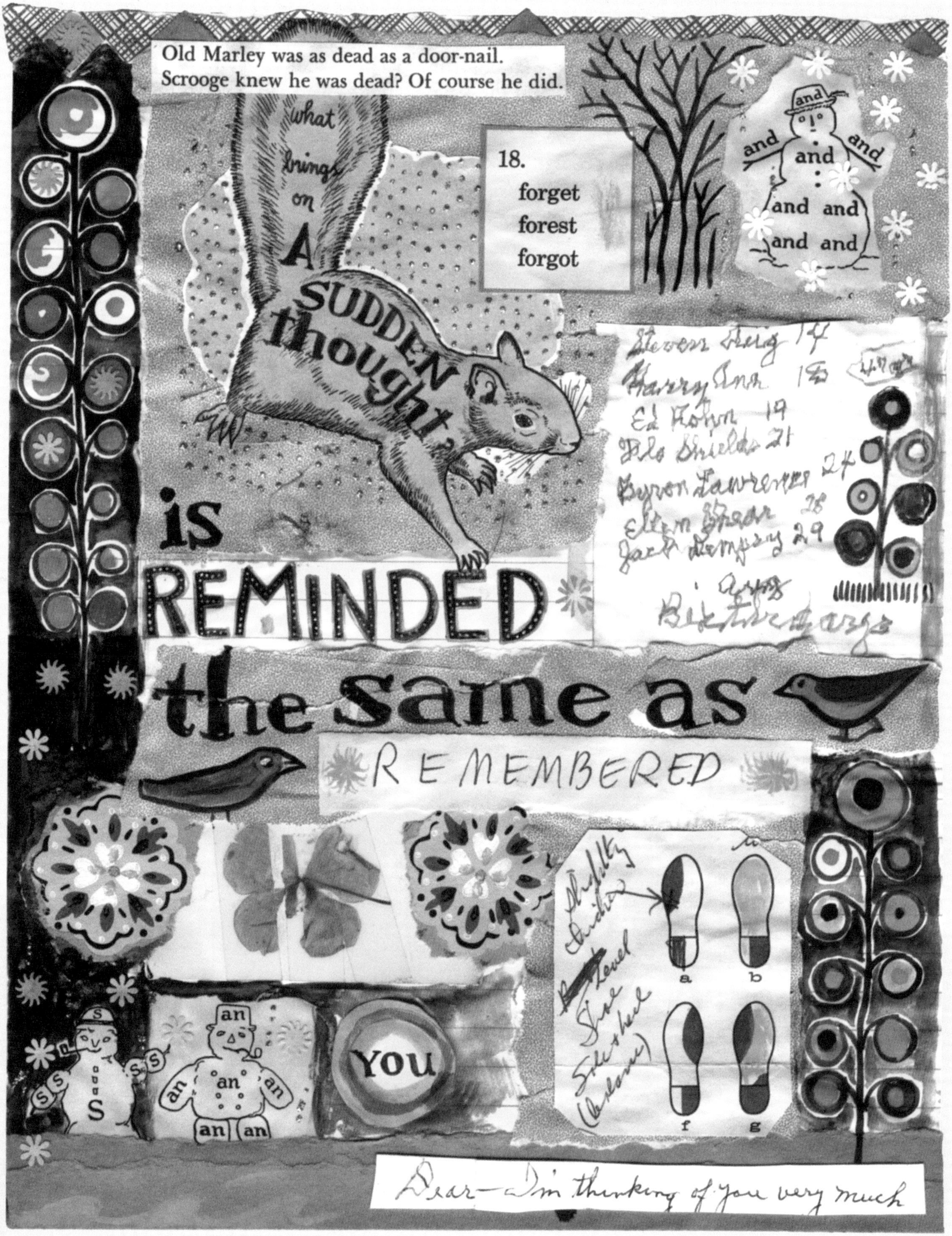

Old Marley was as dead as a door-nail.
Scrooge knew he was dead? Of course he did.
what brings on
A SUDDEN thought
18.
forget
forest
forgot
and and and and and and and and and
is
REMINDED
the same as
REMEMBERED
YOU
an an an an an an
S S S S S
a b f g
Dear — I'm thinking of you very much

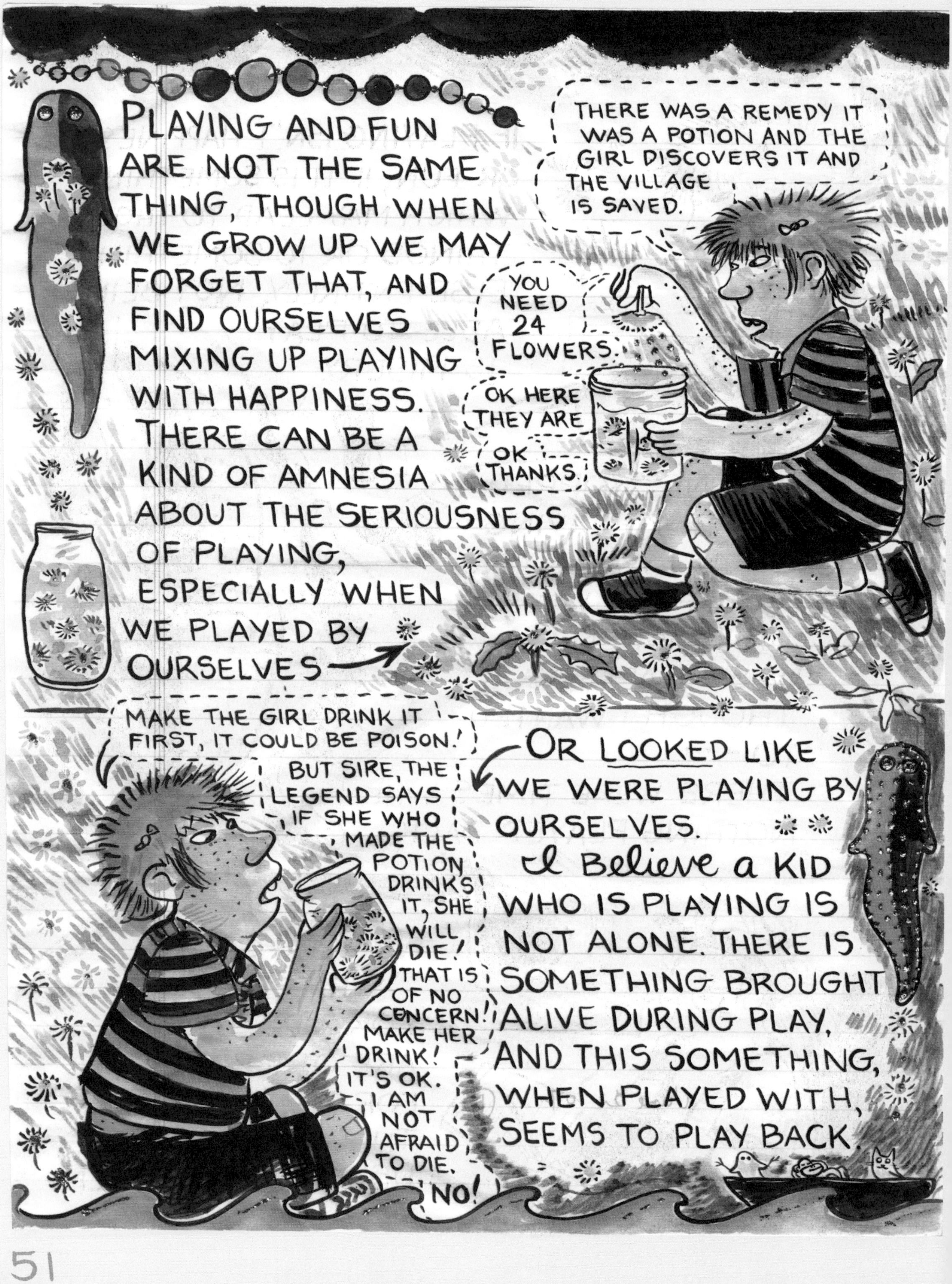
PLAYING AND FUN ARE NOT THE SAME THING, THOUGH WHEN WE GROW UP WE MAY FORGET THAT, AND FIND OURSELVES MIXING UP PLAYING WITH HAPPINESS. THERE CAN BE A KIND OF AMNESIA ABOUT THE SERIOUSNESS OF PLAYING, ESPECIALLY WHEN WE PLAYED BY OURSELVES
THERE WAS A REMEDY IT WAS A POTION AND THE GIRL DISCOVERS IT AND THE VILLAGE IS SAVED.
YOU NEED 24 FLOWERS.
OK HERE THEY ARE
OK THANKS.
MAKE THE GIRL DRINK IT FIRST, IT COULD BE POISON.
BUT SIRE, THE LEGEND SAYS IF SHE WHO MADE THE POTION DRINKS IT, SHE WILL DIE!
THAT IS OF NO CONCERN! MAKE HER DRINK!
IT'S OK. I AM NOT AFRAID TO DIE.
NO!
OR LOOKED LIKE WE WERE PLAYING BY OURSELVES.
I BELIEVE A KID WHO IS PLAYING IS NOT ALONE. THERE IS SOMETHING BROUGHT ALIVE DURING PLAY, AND THIS SOMETHING, WHEN PLAYED WITH, SEEMS TO PLAY BACK.

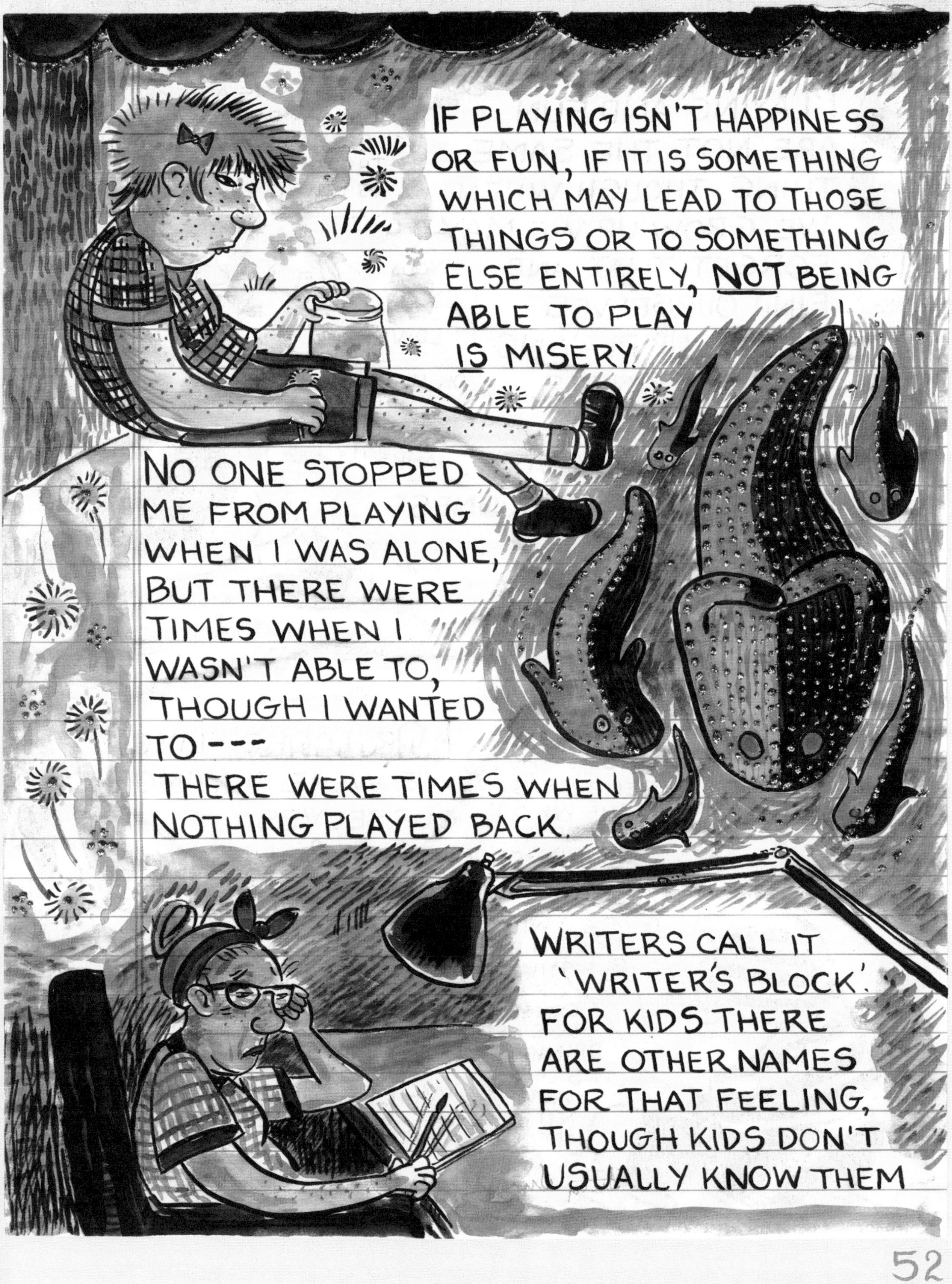
IF PLAYING ISN'T HAPPINESS OR FUN, IF IT IS SOMETHING WHICH MAY LEAD TO THOSE THINGS OR TO SOMETHING ELSE ENTIRELY, NOT BEING ABLE TO PLAY IS MISERY.
NO ONE STOPPED ME FROM PLAYING WHEN I WAS ALONE, BUT THERE WERE TIMES WHEN I WASN'T ABLE TO, THOUGH I WANTED TO ---
THERE WERE TIMES WHEN NOTHING PLAYED BACK.
WRITERS CALL IT 'WRITER'S BLOCK'. FOR KIDS THERE ARE OTHER NAMES FOR THAT FEELING, THOUGH KIDS DON'T USUALLY KNOW THEM

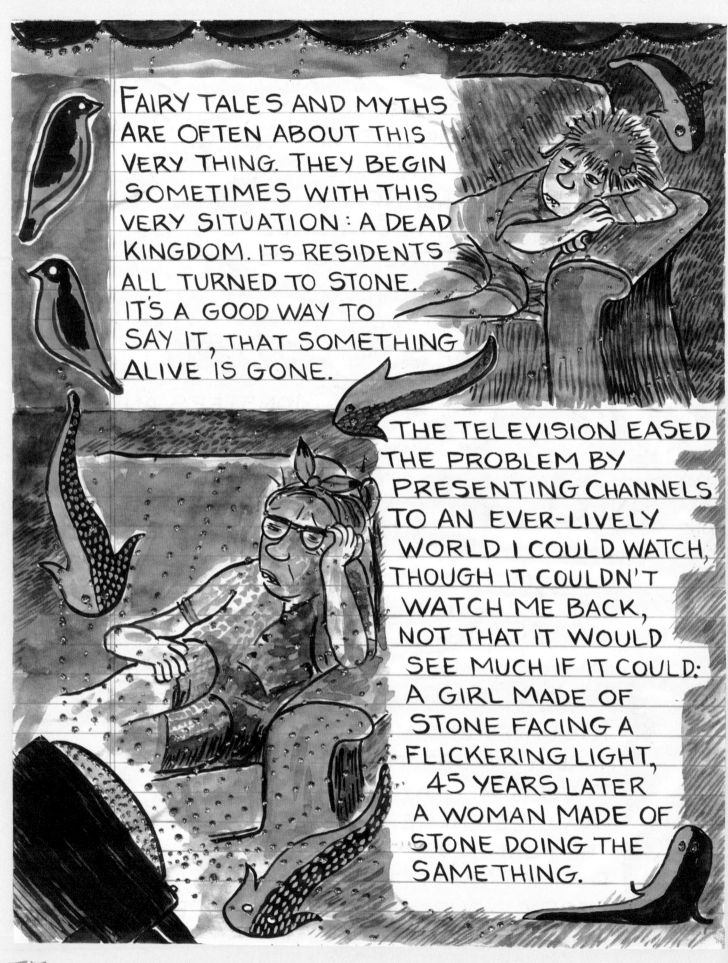

FAIRY TALES AND MYTHS ARE OFTEN ABOUT THIS VERY THING. THEY BEGIN SOMETIMES WITH THIS VERY SITUATION: A DEAD KINGDOM. ITS RESIDENTS ALL TURNED TO STONE. IT'S A GOOD WAY TO SAY IT, THAT SOMETHING ALIVE IS GONE.

THE TELEVISION EASED THE PROBLEM BY PRESENTING CHANNELS TO AN EVER-LIVELY WORLD I COULD WATCH, THOUGH IT COULDN'T WATCH ME BACK, NOT THAT IT WOULD SEE MUCH IF IT COULD: A GIRL MADE OF STONE FACING A FLICKERING LIGHT, 45 YEARS LATER A WOMAN MADE OF STONE DOING THE SAME THING.

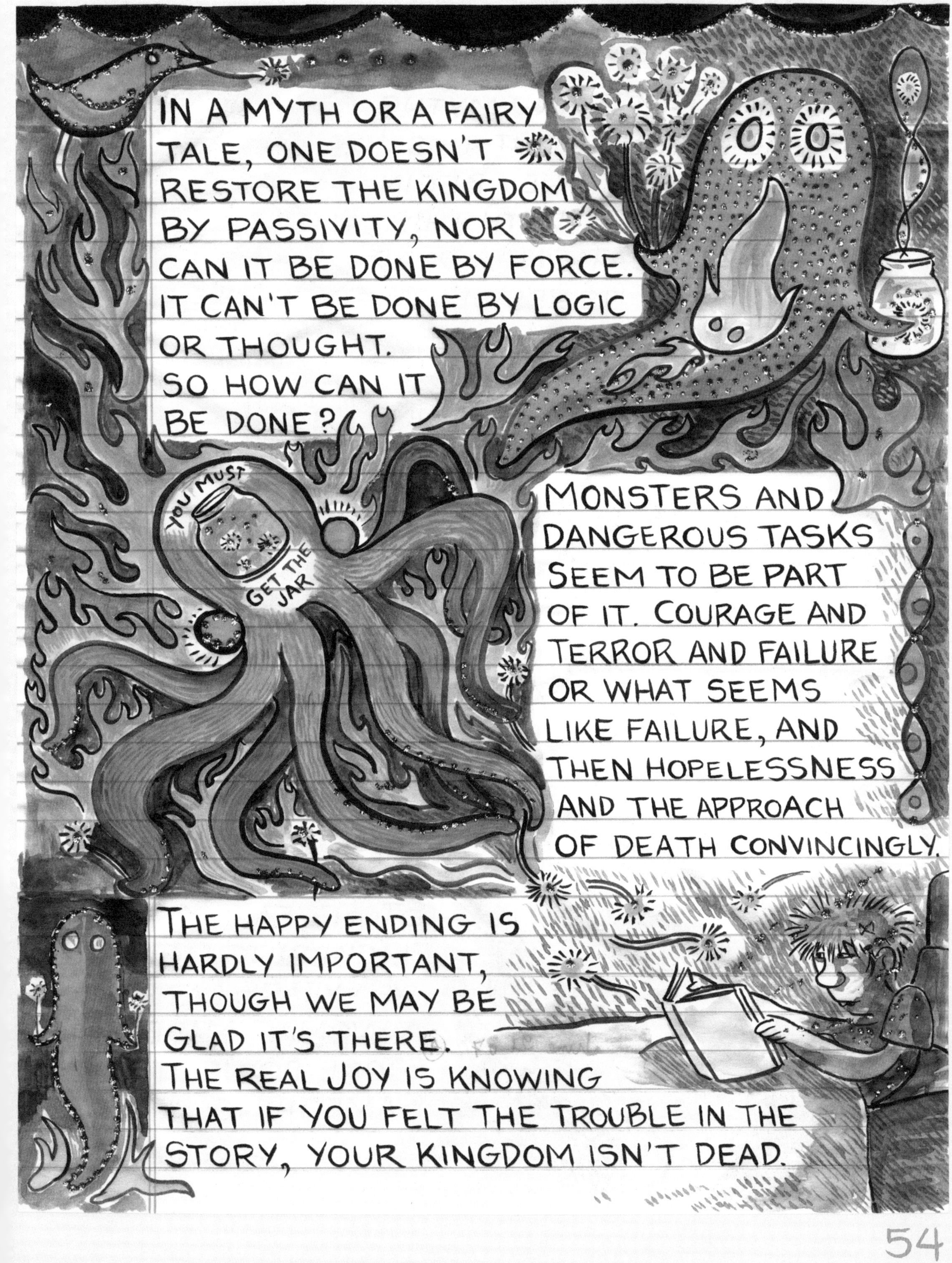
IN A MYTH OR A FAIRY TALE, ONE DOESN'T RESTORE THE KINGDOM BY PASSIVITY, NOR CAN IT BE DONE BY FORCE. IT CAN'T BE DONE BY LOGIC OR THOUGHT.
SO HOW CAN IT BE DONE?
YOU MUST GET THE JAR
MONSTERS AND DANGEROUS TASKS SEEM TO BE PART OF IT. COURAGE AND TERROR AND FAILURE OR WHAT SEEMS LIKE FAILURE, AND THEN HOPELESSNESS AND THE APPROACH OF DEATH CONVINCINGLY.
THE HAPPY ENDING IS HARDLY IMPORTANT, THOUGH WE MAY BE GLAD IT'S THERE.
THE REAL JOY IS KNOWING THAT IF YOU FELT THE TROUBLE IN THE STORY, YOUR KINGDOM ISN'T DEAD.

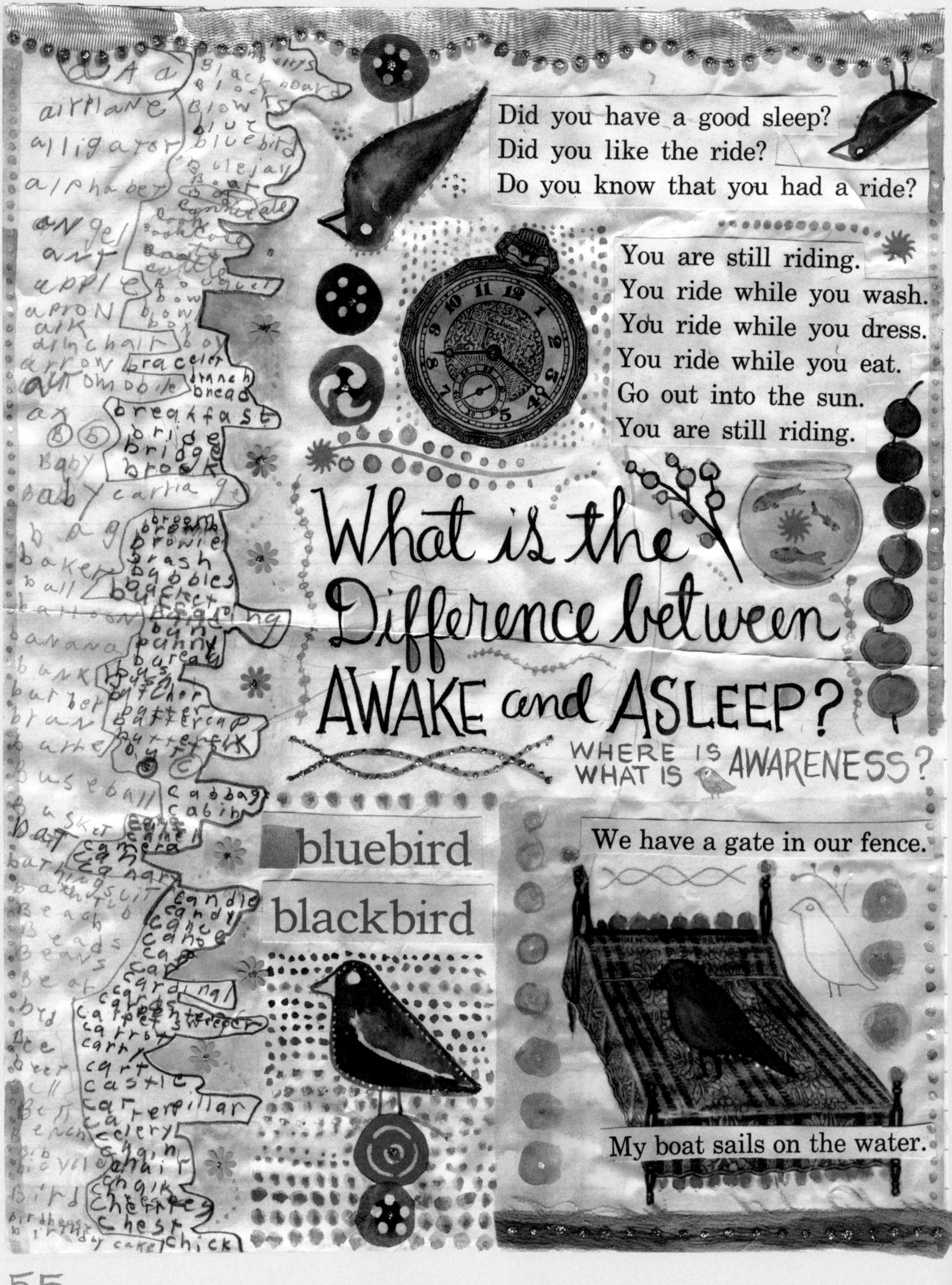
Did you have a good sleep?
Did you like the ride?
Do you know that you had a ride?
You are still riding.
You ride while you wash.
You ride while you dress.
You ride while you eat.
Go out into the sun.
You are still riding.
What is the Difference between AWAKE and ASLEEP?
WHERE IS AWARENESS?
WHAT IS AWARENESS?
bluebird
blackbird
We have a gate in our fence.
My boat sails on the water.

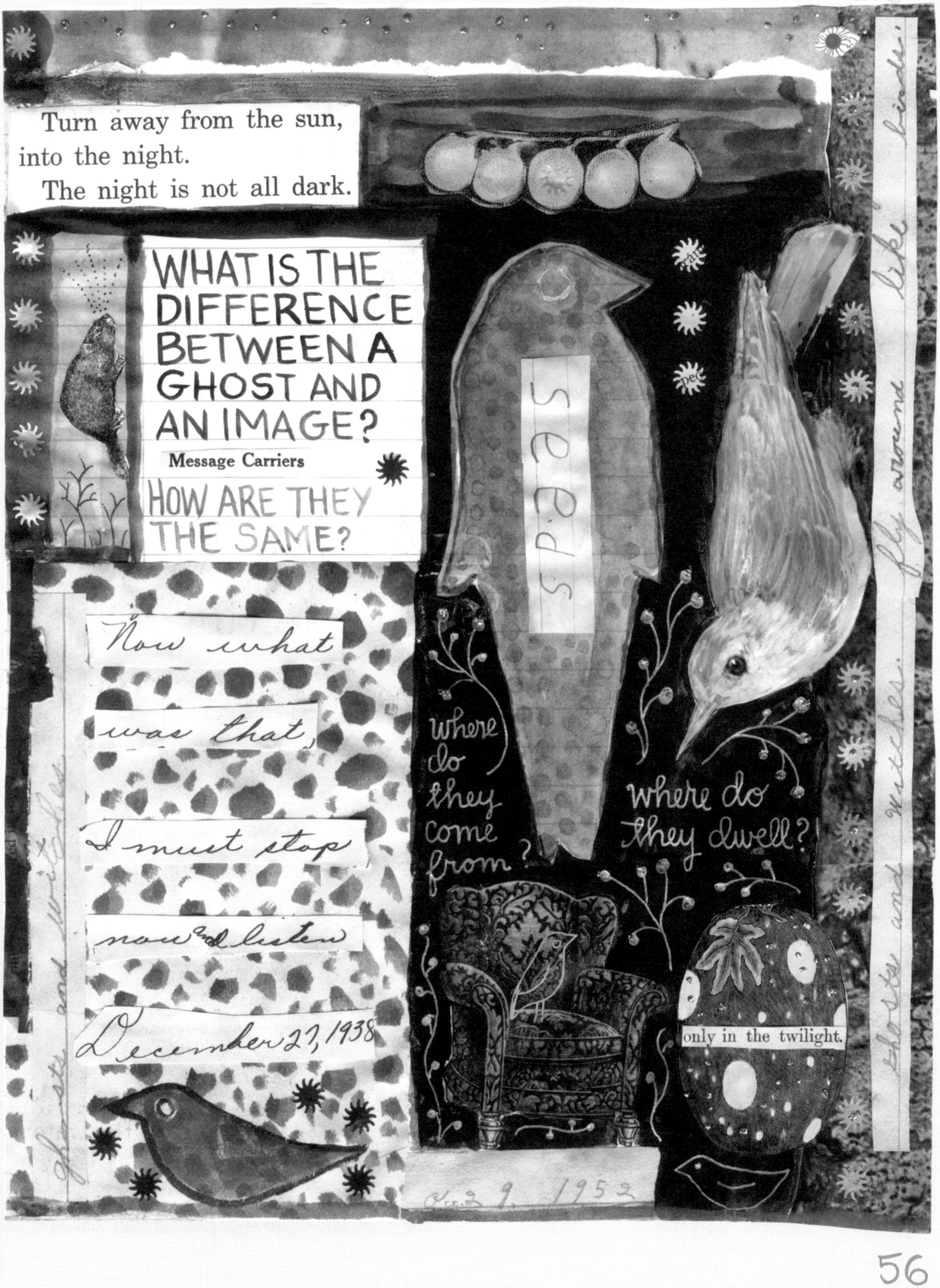
Turn away from the sun,
into the night.
The night is not all dark.
WHAT IS THE DIFFERENCE BETWEEN A GHOST AND AN IMAGE?
Message Carriers
HOW ARE THEY THE SAME?
seeds
Now what
was that,
I must stop
now & listen
December 27, 1938
where do they come from?
where do they dwell?
only in the twilight.
ghosts and witches fly around like birds.

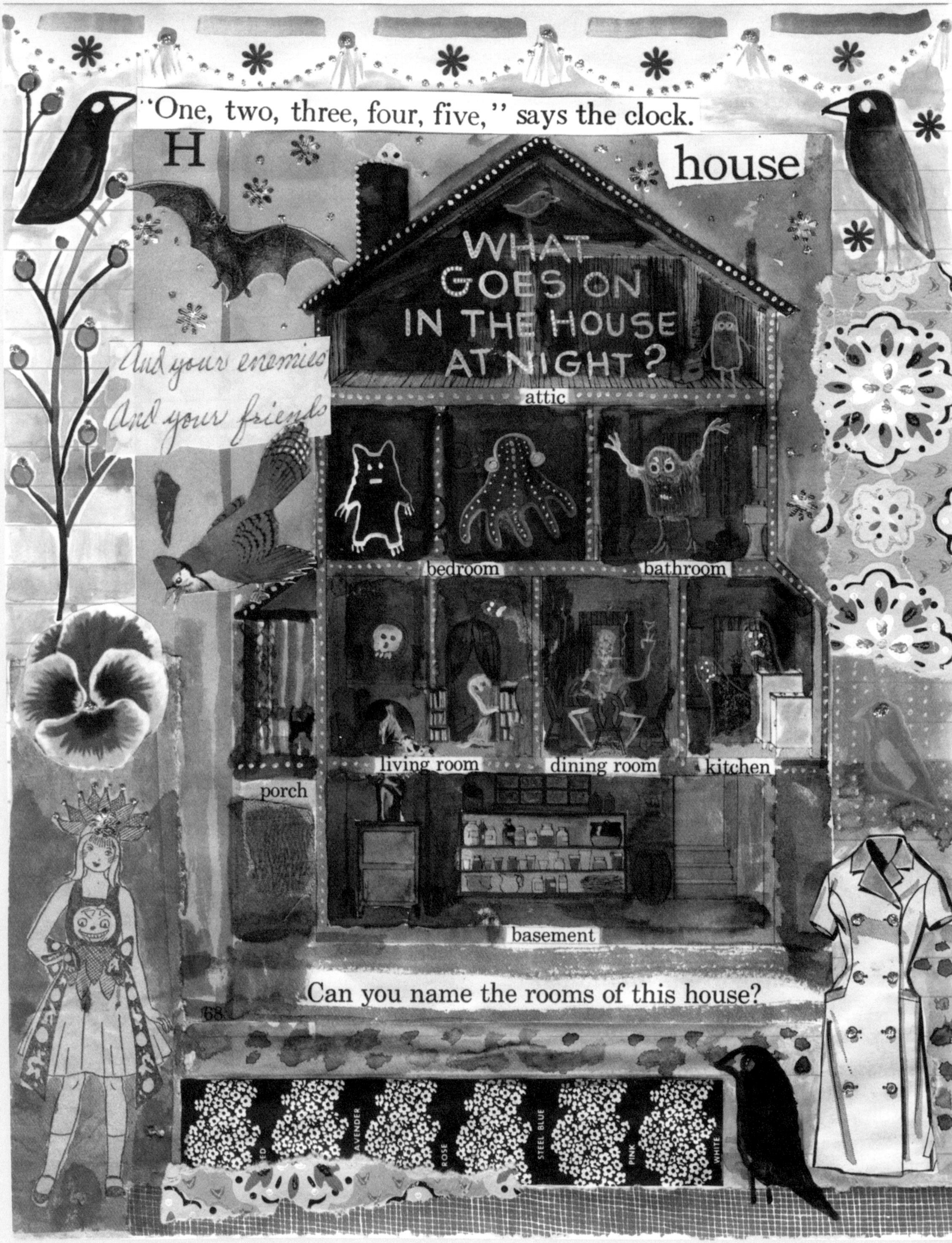
"One, two, three, four, five," says the clock.
H
house
WHAT GOES ON IN THE HOUSE AT NIGHT?
And your enemies
And your friends
attic
bedroom
bathroom
living room
dining room
kitchen
porch
basement
Can you name the rooms of this house?
68
LAVENDER
ROSE
STEEL BLUE
PINK
WHITE

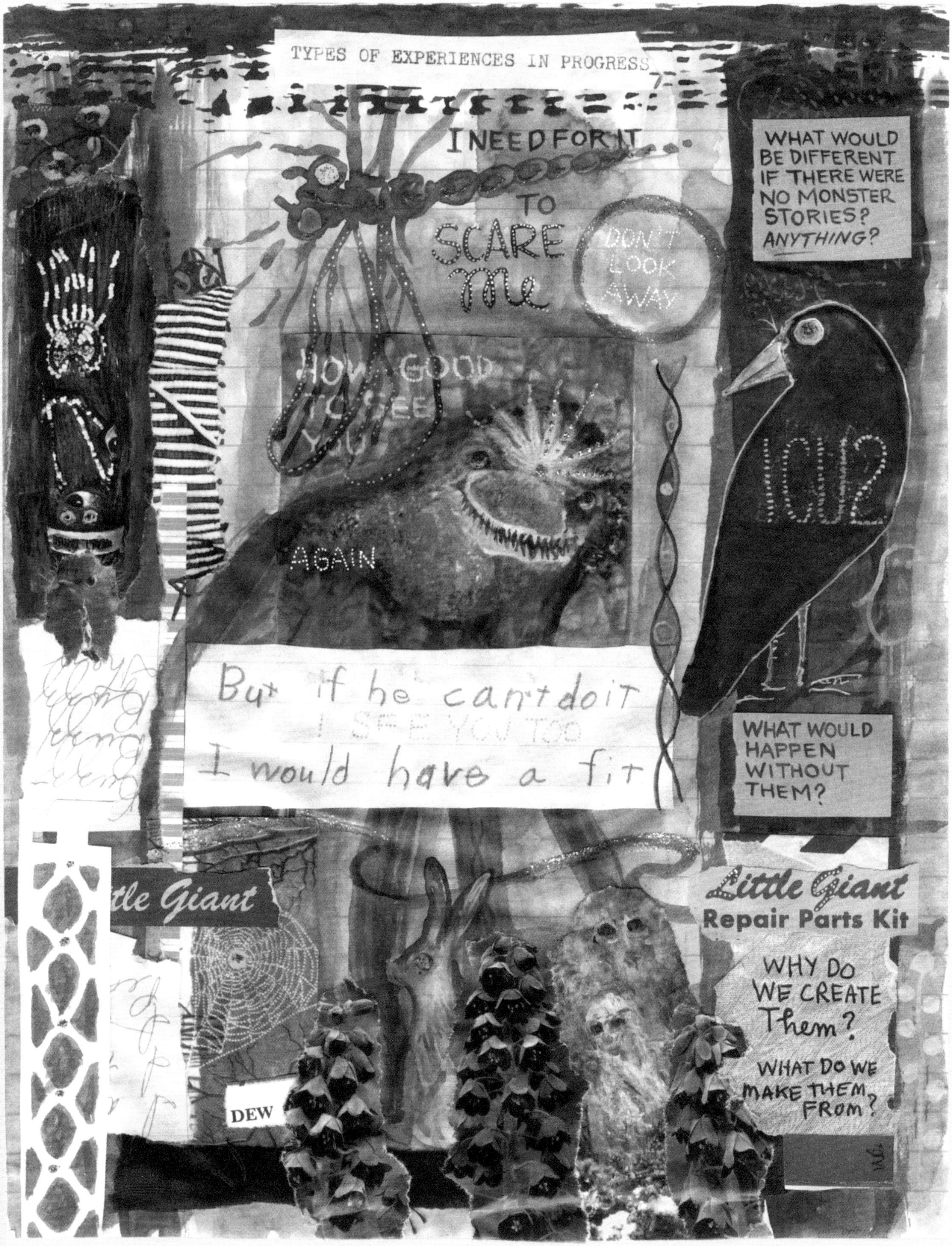
TYPES OF EXPERIENCES IN PROGRESS
I NEED FOR IT
TO
SCARE
me
DON'T
LOOK
AWAY
WHAT WOULD BE DIFFERENT IF THERE WERE NO MONSTER STORIES? ANYTHING?
HOW GOOD TO SEE YOU
AGAIN
ICU2
But if he can't do it
I SEE YOU TOO
I would have a fit
WHAT WOULD HAPPEN WITHOUT THEM?
ttle Giant
Little Giant
Repair Parts Kit
WHY DO WE CREATE Them?
WHAT DO WE MAKE THEM FROM?
DEW

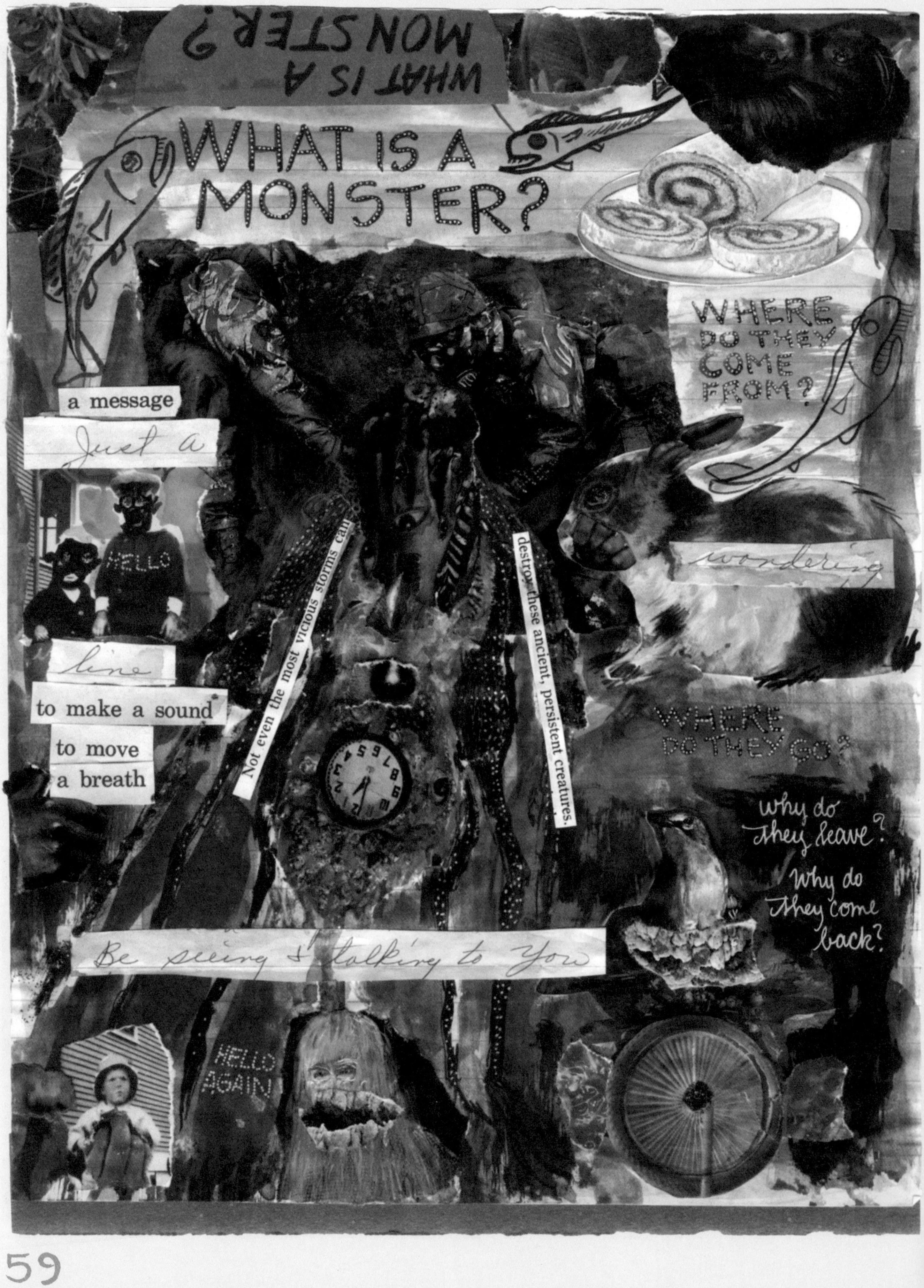
WHAT IS A MONSTER?
WHAT IS A MONSTER?
WHERE DO THEY COME FROM?
a message
Just a
HELLO
wondering
line
to make a sound
to move
a breath
Not even the most vicious storms can
destroy these ancient, persistent creatures.
WHERE DO THEY GO?
Why do they leave?
Why do they come back?
Be seeing & talking to You
HELLO AGAIN

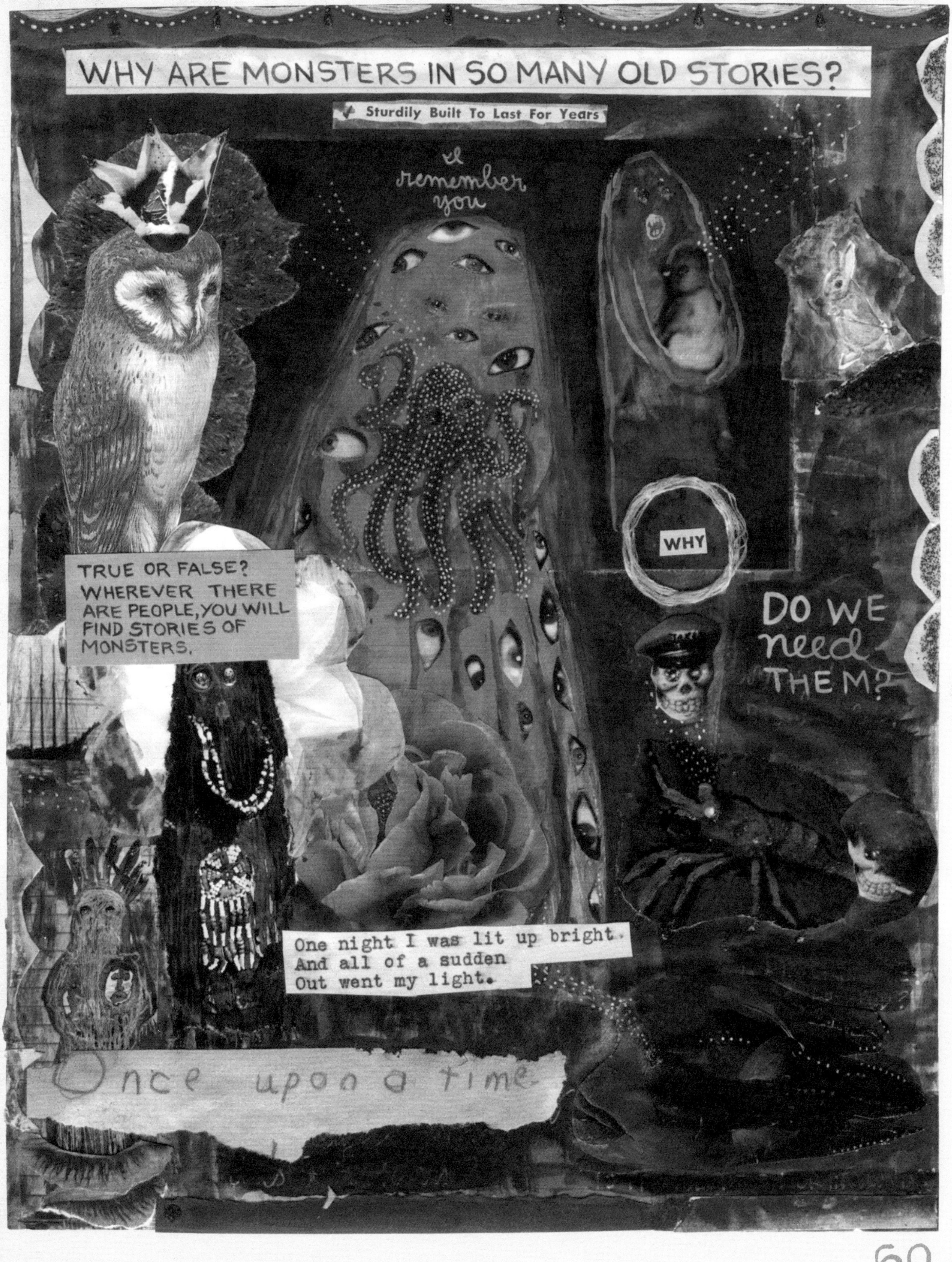
WHY ARE MONSTERS IN SO MANY OLD STORIES?
Sturdily Built To Last For Years
I remember you
TRUE OR FALSE? WHEREVER THERE ARE PEOPLE, YOU WILL FIND STORIES OF MONSTERS.
WHY
DO WE need THEM?
One night I was lit up bright.
And all of a sudden
Out went my light.
Once upon a time

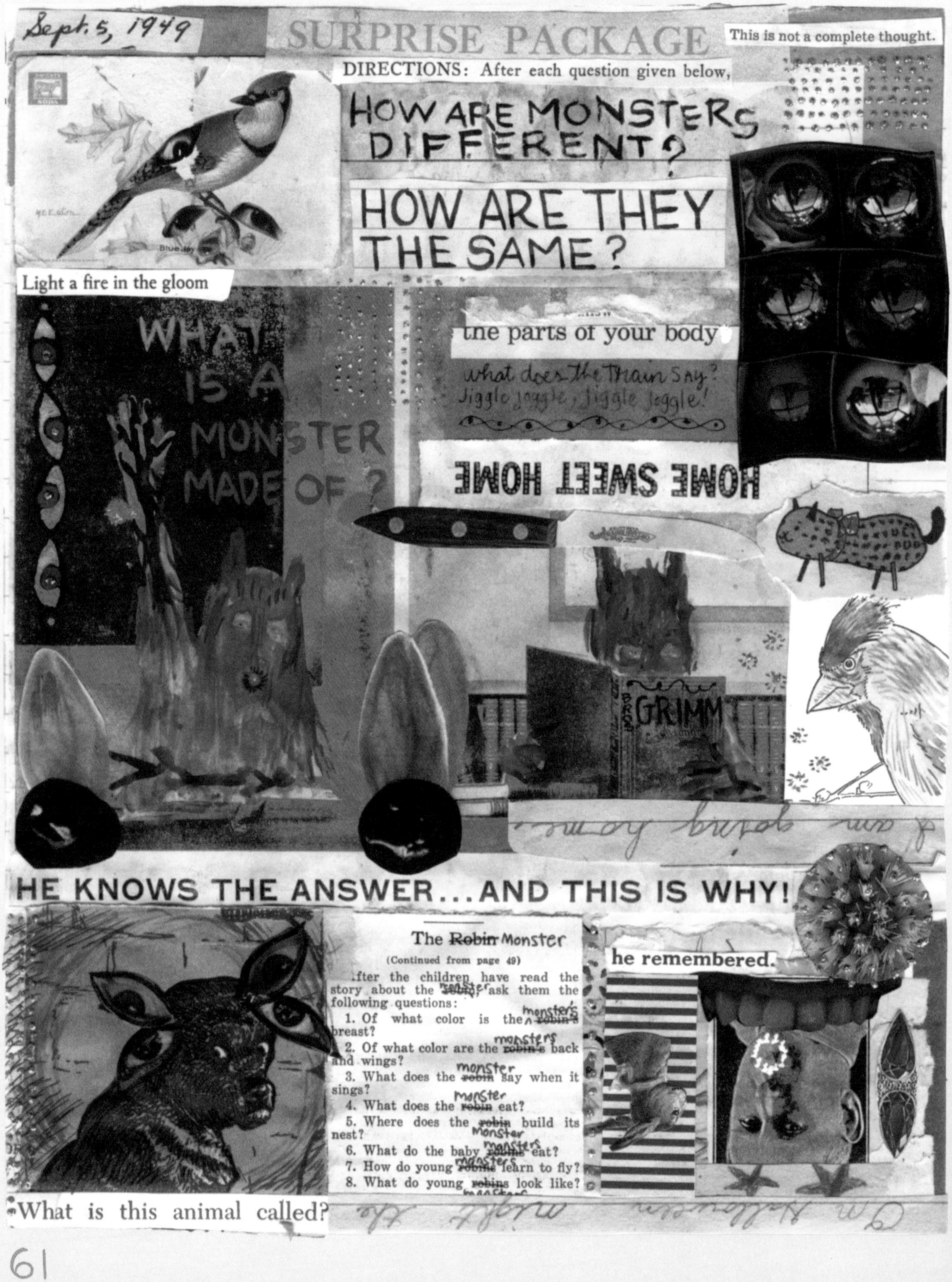

Sept. 5, 1949
SURPRISE PACKAGE
This is not a complete thought.
DIRECTIONS: After each question given below,
HOW ARE MONSTERS DIFFERENT?
HOW ARE THEY THE SAME?
Blue Jay
Light a fire in the gloom
WHAT IS A MONSTER MADE OF?
the parts of your body
what does the Train Say?
Jiggle Joggle, Jiggle Joggle!
HOME SWEET HOME
GRIMM
HE KNOWS THE ANSWER... AND THIS IS WHY!
The ~~Robin~~ Monster
(Continued from page 49)
After the children have read the story about the ~~robin~~ monster ask them the following questions:
1. Of what color is the ~~robin's~~ monster's breast?
2. Of what color are the ~~robin's~~ monsters back and wings?
3. What does the ~~robin~~ monster say when it sings?
4. What does the ~~robin~~ monster eat?
5. Where does the ~~robin~~ monster build its nest?
6. What do the baby ~~robins~~ monsters eat?
7. How do young ~~robins~~ monsters learn to fly?
8. What do young ~~robins~~ monsters look like?
he remembered.
What is this animal called?

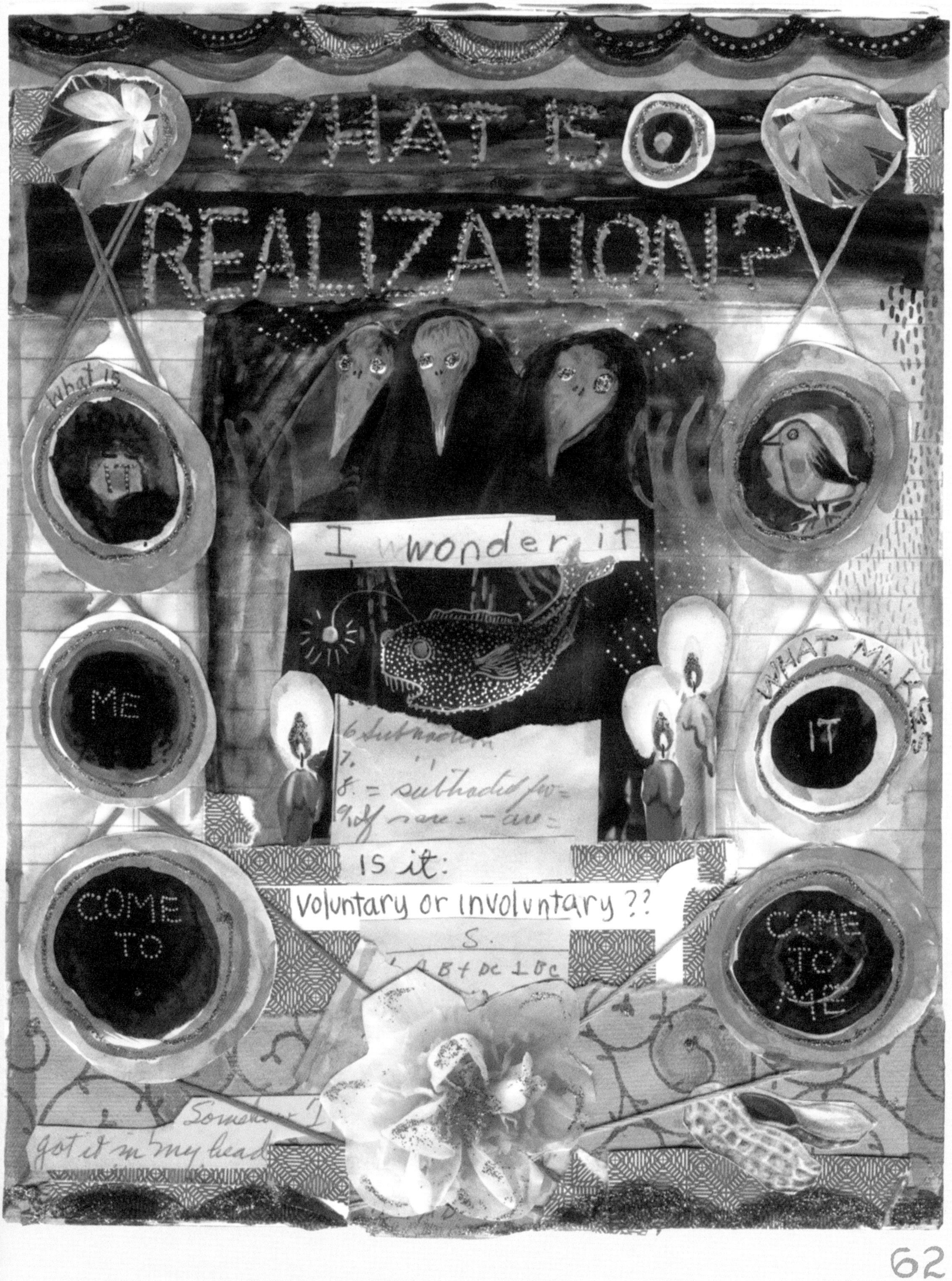
WHAT IS REALIZATION?
what is
ME
COME TO
WHAT MAKES
IT
COME TO ME
I wonder if
is it:
voluntary or involuntary ??
got it in my head

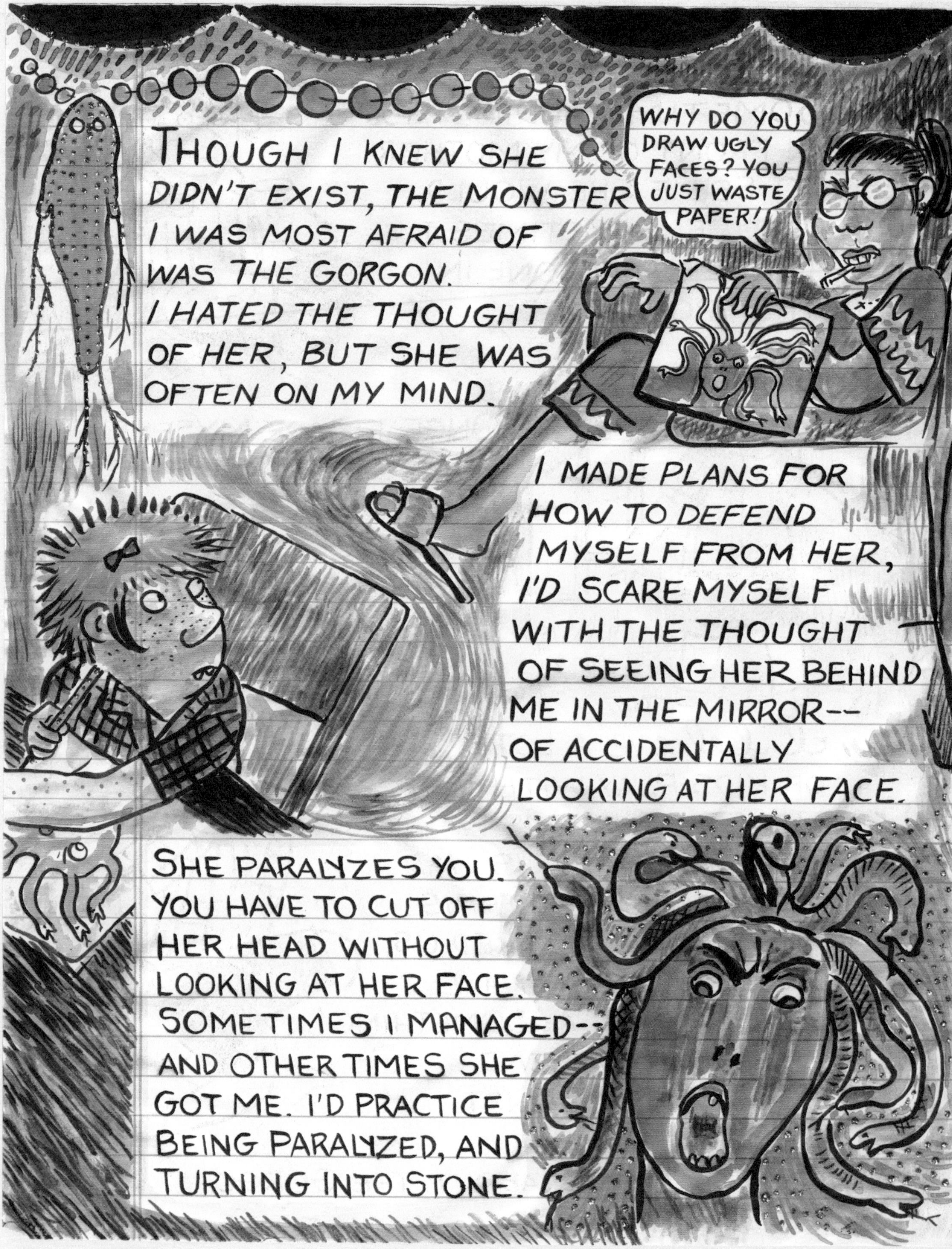
THOUGH I KNEW SHE DIDN'T EXIST, THE MONSTER I WAS MOST AFRAID OF WAS THE GORGON. I HATED THE THOUGHT OF HER, BUT SHE WAS OFTEN ON MY MIND.
WHY DO YOU DRAW UGLY FACES? YOU JUST WASTE PAPER!
I MADE PLANS FOR HOW TO DEFEND MYSELF FROM HER, I'D SCARE MYSELF WITH THE THOUGHT OF SEEING HER BEHIND ME IN THE MIRROR-- OF ACCIDENTALLY LOOKING AT HER FACE.
SHE PARALYZES YOU. YOU HAVE TO CUT OFF HER HEAD WITHOUT LOOKING AT HER FACE. SOMETIMES I MANAGED-- AND OTHER TIMES SHE GOT ME. I'D PRACTICE BEING PARALYZED, AND TURNING INTO STONE.

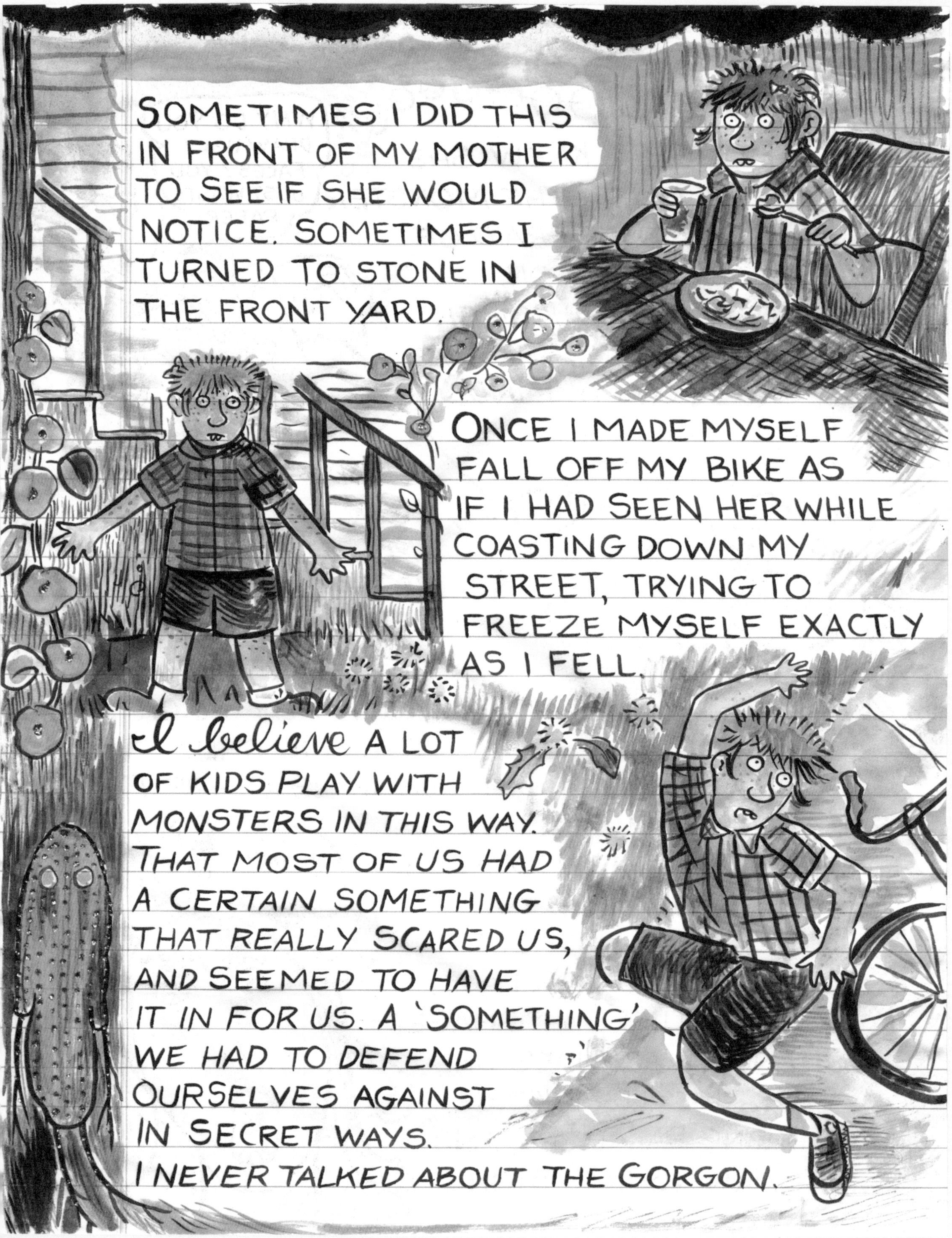

SOMETIMES I DID THIS IN FRONT OF MY MOTHER TO SEE IF SHE WOULD NOTICE. SOMETIMES I TURNED TO STONE IN THE FRONT YARD.
ONCE I MADE MYSELF FALL OFF MY BIKE AS IF I HAD SEEN HER WHILE COASTING DOWN MY STREET, TRYING TO FREEZE MYSELF EXACTLY AS I FELL.
I believe A LOT OF KIDS PLAY WITH MONSTERS IN THIS WAY. THAT MOST OF US HAD A CERTAIN SOMETHING THAT REALLY SCARED US, AND SEEMED TO HAVE IT IN FOR US. A 'SOMETHING' WE HAD TO DEFEND OURSELVES AGAINST IN SECRET WAYS.
I NEVER TALKED ABOUT THE GORGON.

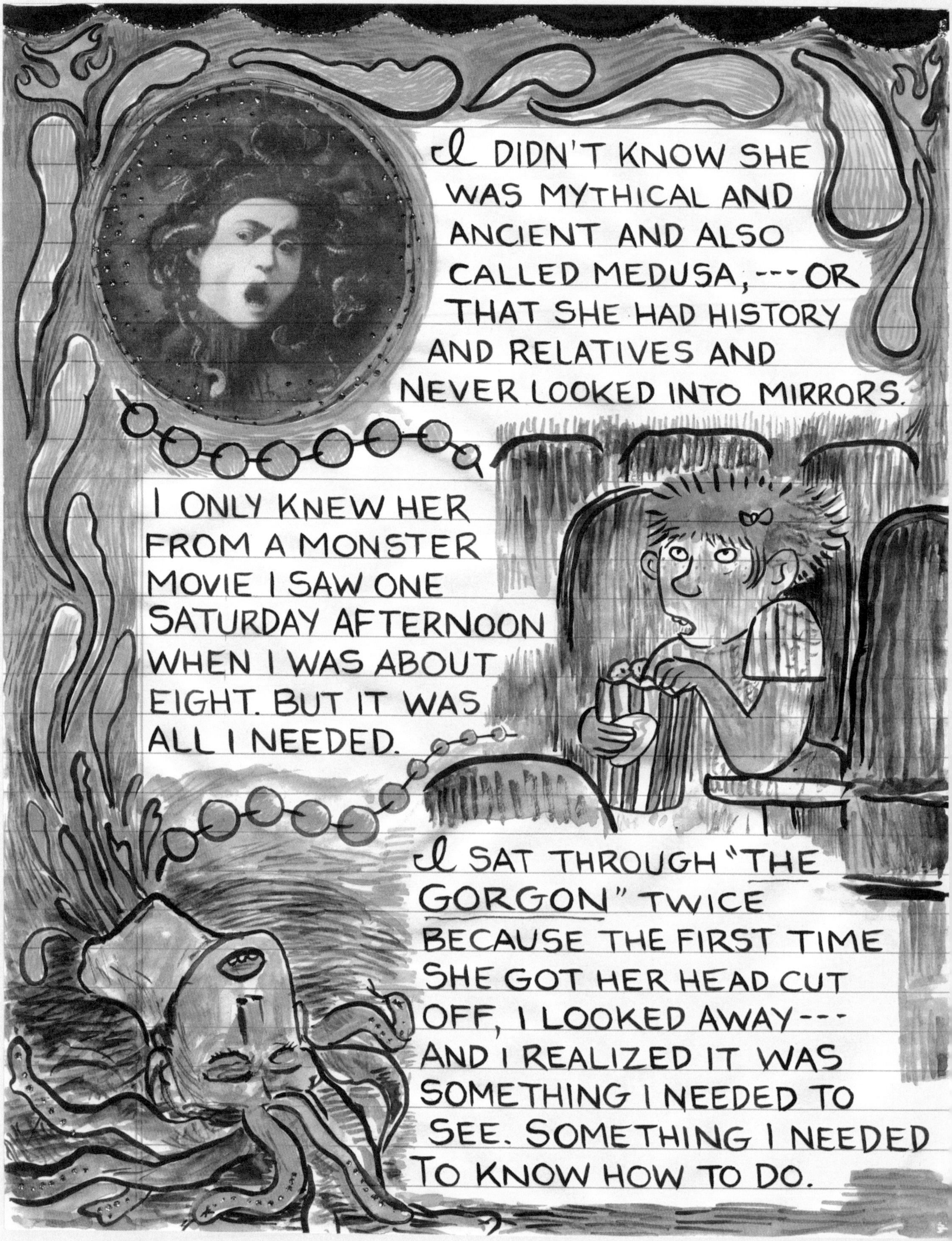
I DIDN'T KNOW SHE WAS MYTHICAL AND ANCIENT AND ALSO CALLED MEDUSA,---OR THAT SHE HAD HISTORY AND RELATIVES AND NEVER LOOKED INTO MIRRORS.
I ONLY KNEW HER FROM A MONSTER MOVIE I SAW ONE SATURDAY AFTERNOON WHEN I WAS ABOUT EIGHT. BUT IT WAS ALL I NEEDED.
I SAT THROUGH "THE GORGON" TWICE BECAUSE THE FIRST TIME SHE GOT HER HEAD CUT OFF, I LOOKED AWAY--- AND I REALIZED IT WAS SOMETHING I NEEDED TO SEE. SOMETHING I NEEDED TO KNOW HOW TO DO.

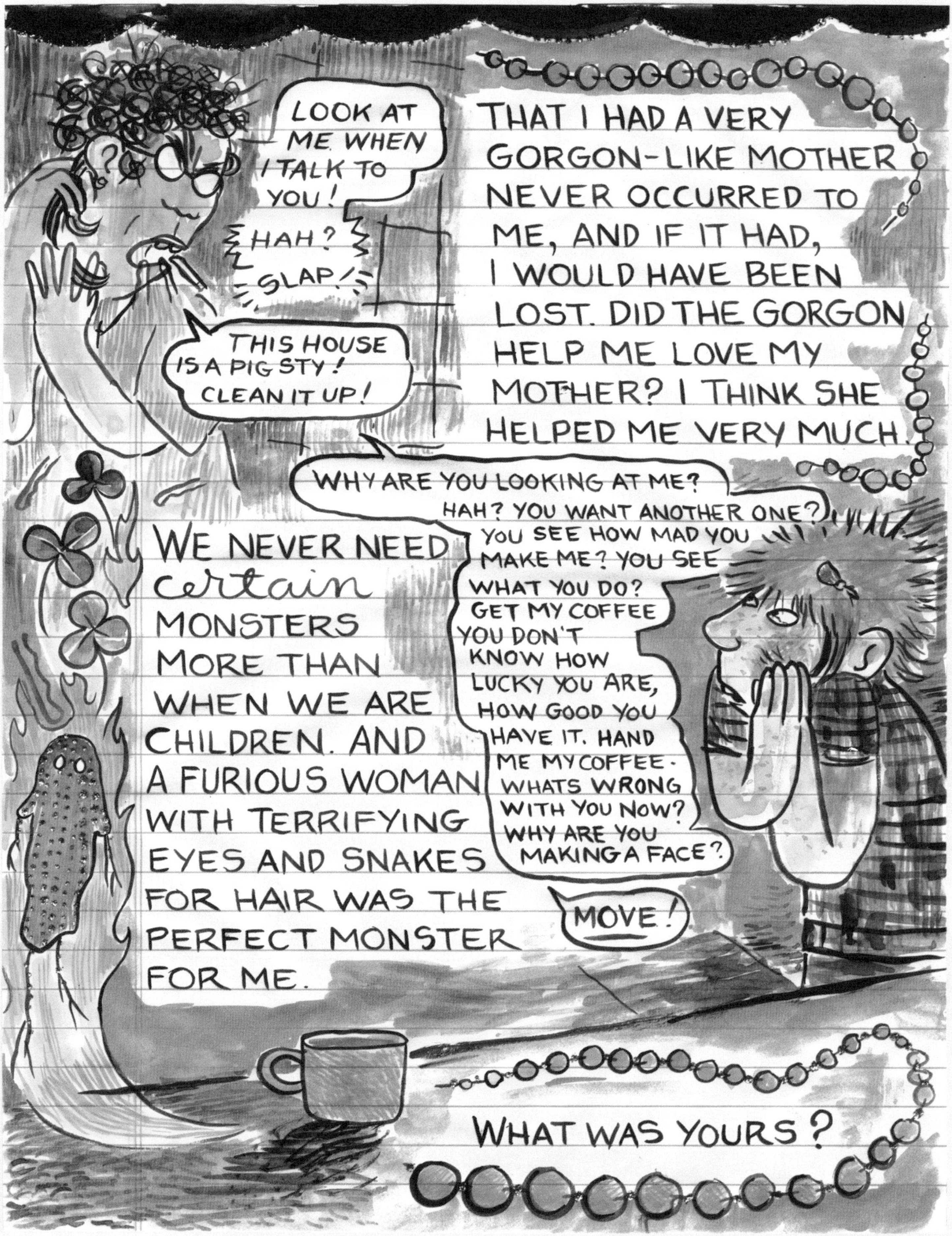
LOOK AT ME WHEN I TALK TO YOU!
HAH?
SLAP!
THIS HOUSE IS A PIG STY! CLEAN IT UP!
THAT I HAD A VERY GORGON-LIKE MOTHER NEVER OCCURRED TO ME, AND IF IT HAD, I WOULD HAVE BEEN LOST. DID THE GORGON HELP ME LOVE MY MOTHER? I THINK SHE HELPED ME VERY MUCH.
WHY ARE YOU LOOKING AT ME? HAH? YOU WANT ANOTHER ONE? YOU SEE HOW MAD YOU MAKE ME? YOU SEE WHAT YOU DO? GET MY COFFEE YOU DON'T KNOW HOW LUCKY YOU ARE, HOW GOOD YOU HAVE IT. HAND ME MY COFFEE. WHATS WRONG WITH YOU NOW? WHY ARE YOU MAKING A FACE?
WE NEVER NEED certain MONSTERS MORE THAN WHEN WE ARE CHILDREN. AND A FURIOUS WOMAN WITH TERRIFYING EYES AND SNAKES FOR HAIR WAS THE PERFECT MONSTER FOR ME.
MOVE!
WHAT WAS YOURS?

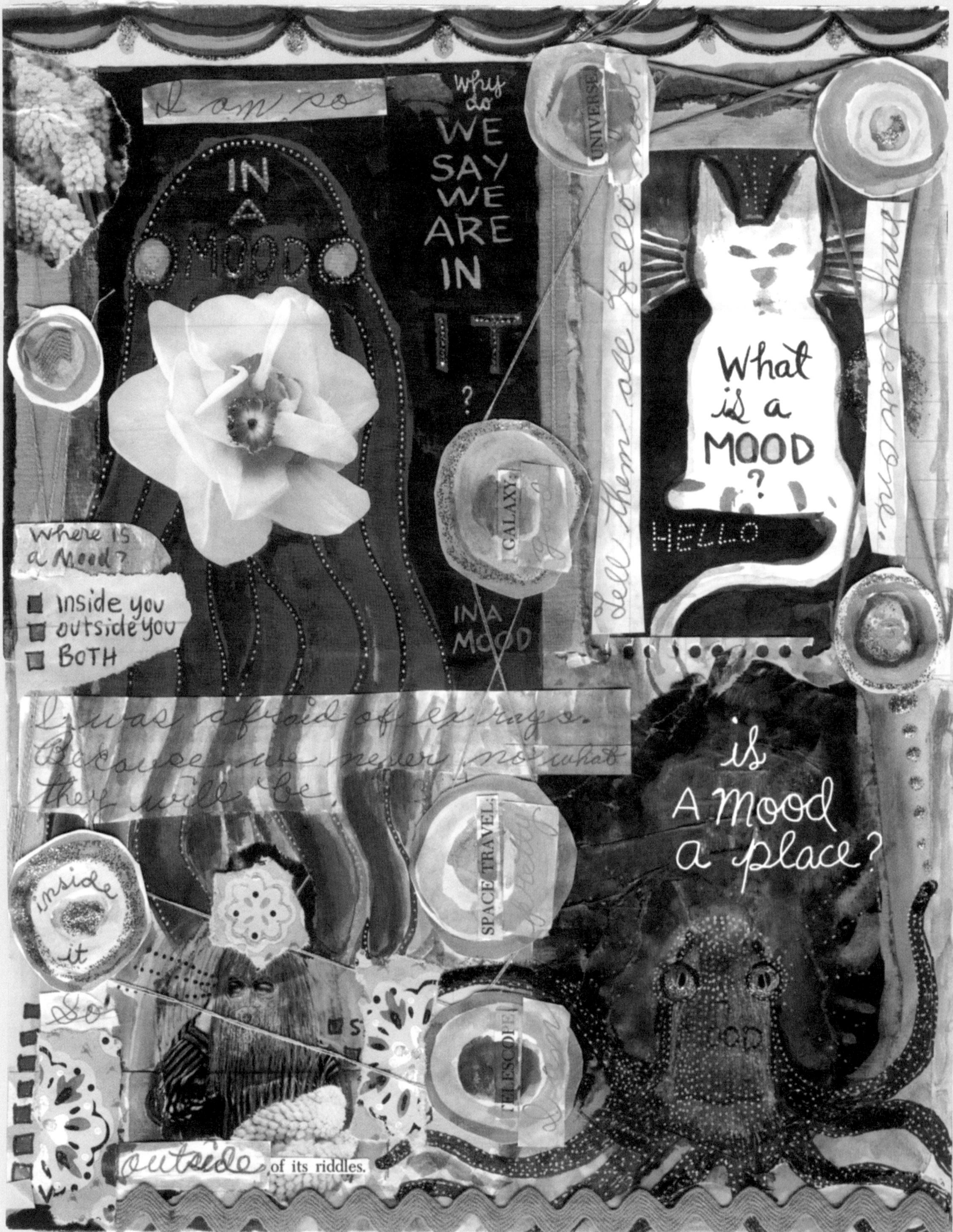

I am so
IN A MOOD
why do WE SAY WE ARE IN IT ?
UNIVERSE
Tell them all Hello
What is a MOOD ?
my dear one.
HELLO
GALAXY
Where is a Mood?
inside you
outside you
BOTH
IN A MOOD
I was afraid of ex rays. Because we never nos what they will be.
is A Mood a place?
SPACE TRAVEL
inside it
TELESCOPE
outside of its riddles.

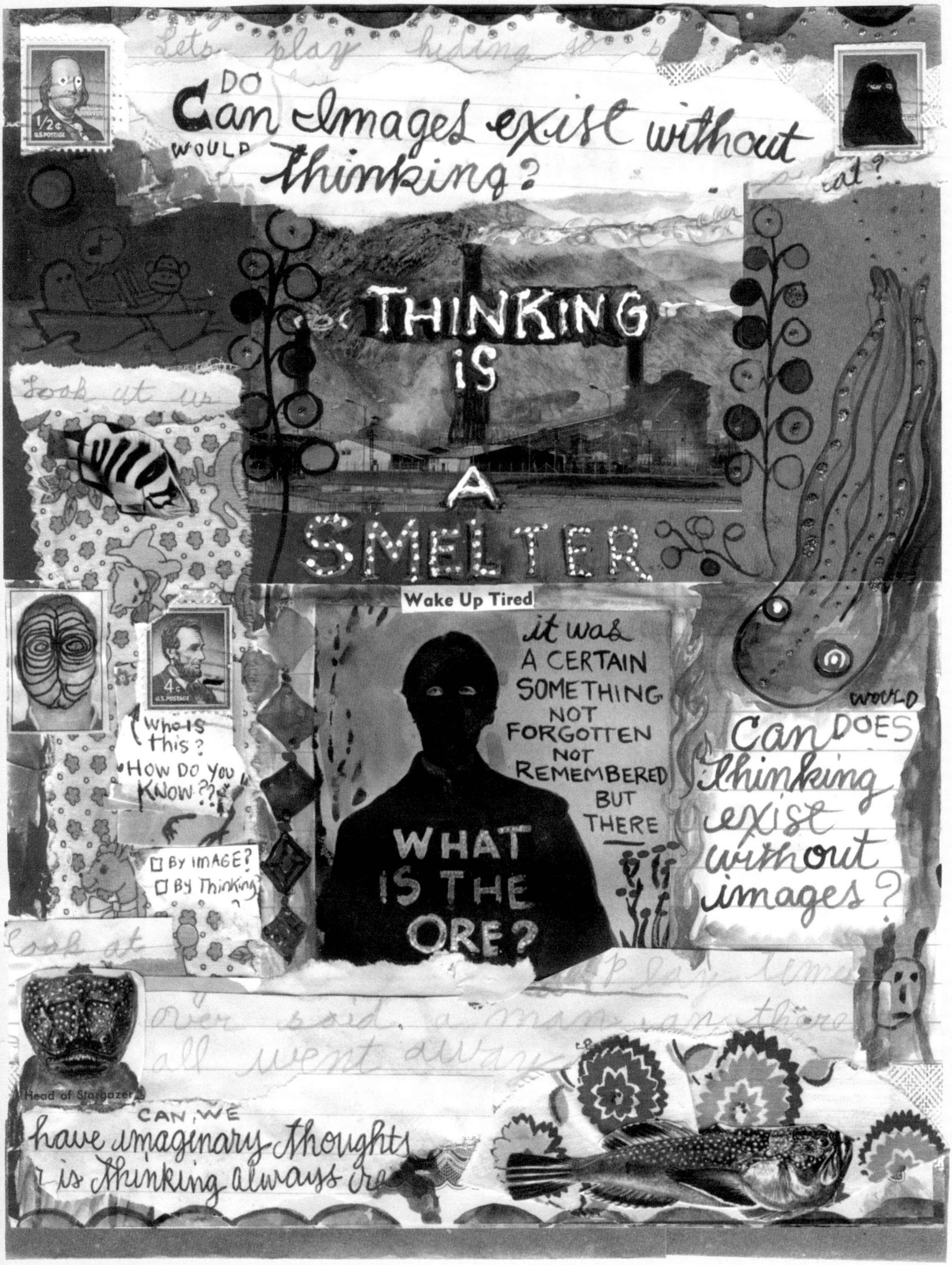
DO
Can Images exist without
WOULD
thinking?
THINKING
IS
A
SMELTER
Wake Up Tired
it was
A CERTAIN
SOMETHING
NOT
FORGOTTEN
NOT
REMEMBERED
BUT
THERE
WHAT
IS THE
ORE?
Who is this?
HOW DO YOU KNOW?
BY IMAGE?
BY Thinking
WOULD
Can DOES
Thinking
exist
without
images?
Head of Stargazer
CAN WE
have imaginary thoughts
is thinking always

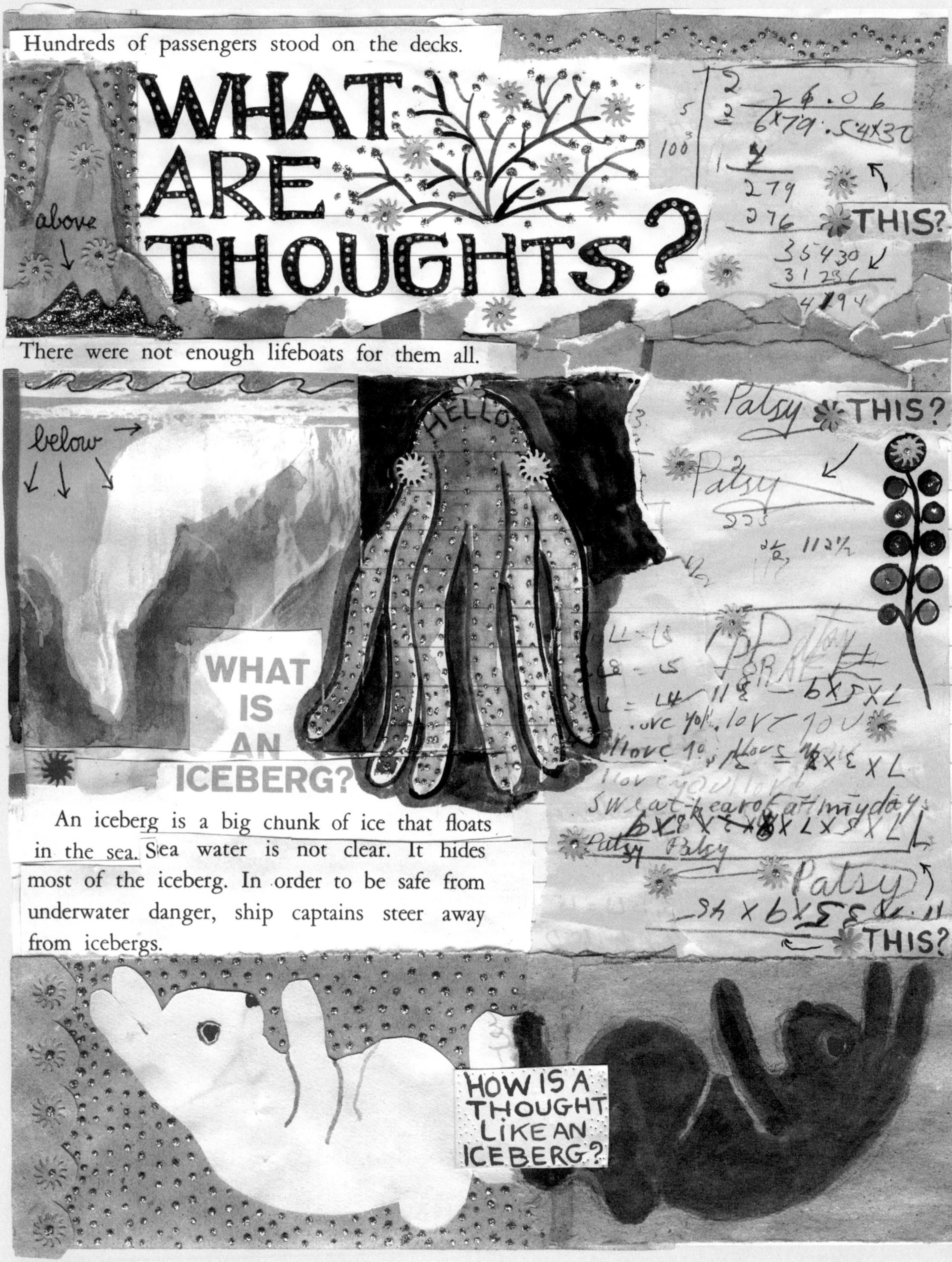
Hundreds of passengers stood on the decks.
WHAT ARE THOUGHTS?
above
THIS?
There were not enough lifeboats for them all.
below
HELLO
Patsy
THIS?
WHAT IS AN ICEBERG?
An iceberg is a big chunk of ice that floats in the sea. Sea water is not clear. It hides most of the iceberg. In order to be safe from underwater danger, ship captains steer away from icebergs.
Patsy
THIS?
HOW IS A THOUGHT LIKE AN ICEBERG?

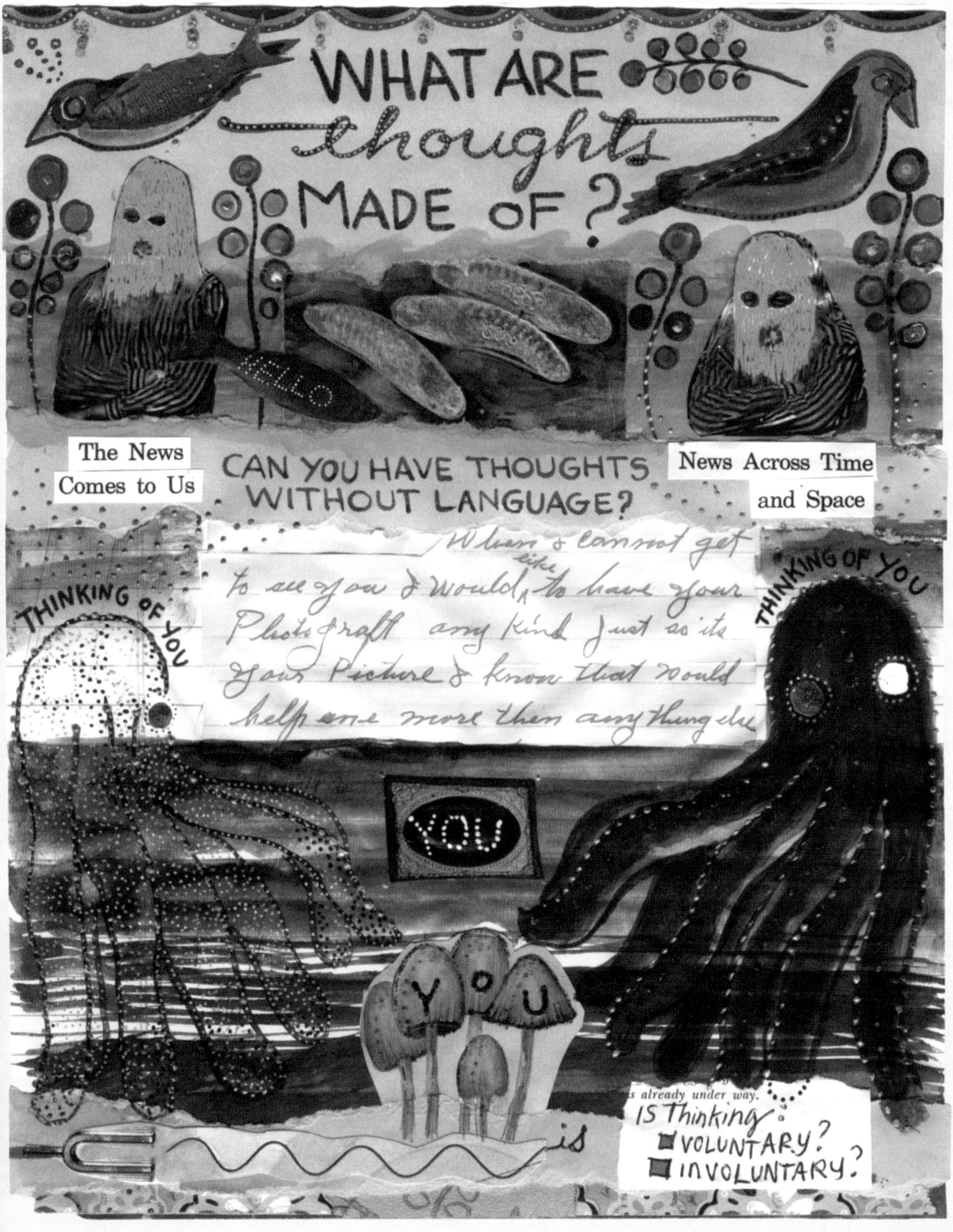
WHAT ARE thoughts MADE OF?
HELLO
The News Comes to Us
CAN YOU HAVE THOUGHTS WITHOUT LANGUAGE?
News Across Time and Space
When I cannot get to see you I would like to have your Photograft any kind just so its your Picture I know that would help me more then anything else
THINKING OF YOU
THINKING OF YOU
YOU
YOU
is
already under way.
IS Thinking:
VOLUNTARY?
INVOLUNTARY?

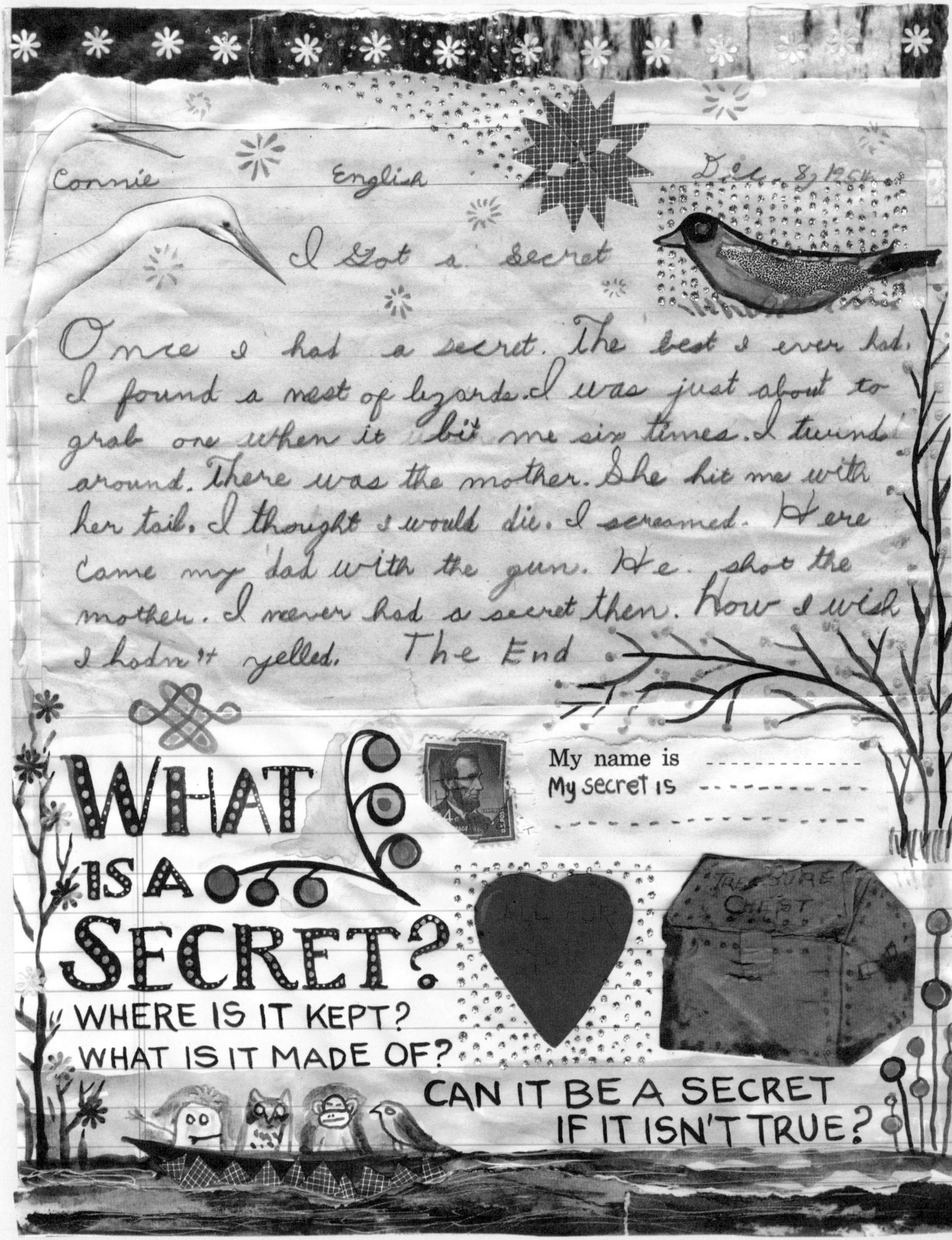
Connie English Dec. 8, 1964
I Got a Secret
Once i had a secret. The best i ever had. I found a nest of lizards. I was just about to grab one when it bit me six times. I turnd around. There was the mother. She hit me with her tail. I thought i would die. I screamed. Here came my dad with the gun. He shot the mother. I never had a secret then. How i wish I hadn't yelled. The End
My name is
My secret is
WHAT IS A SECRET?
WHERE IS IT KEPT?
WHAT IS IT MADE OF?
TREASURE CHEST
CAN IT BE A SECRET IF IT ISN'T TRUE?

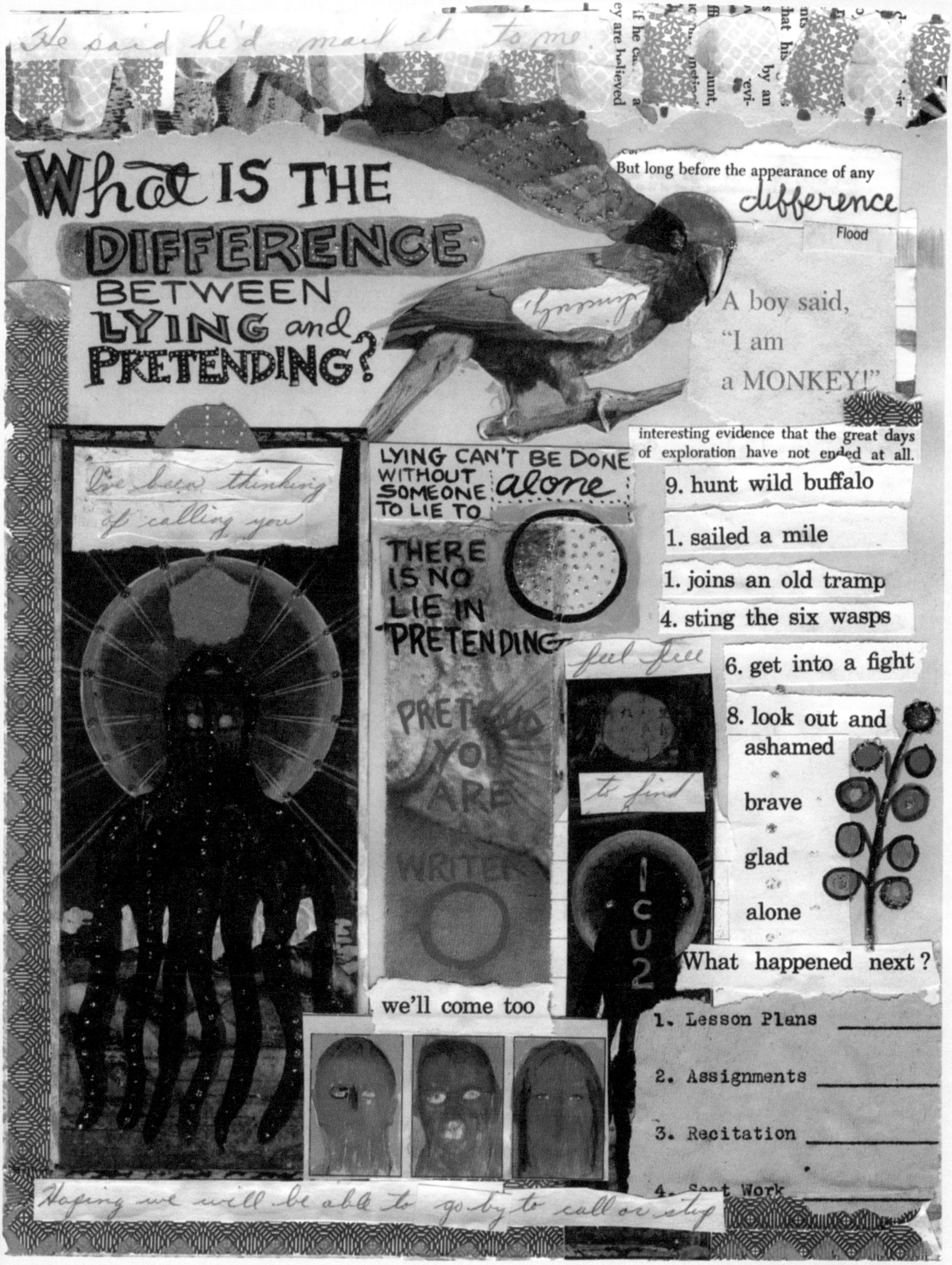
He said he'd mail it to me
What IS THE DIFFERENCE BETWEEN LYING and PRETENDING?
But long before the appearance of any
difference
Flood
A boy said, "I am a MONKEY!"
interesting evidence that the great days of exploration have not ended at all.
I've been thinking of calling you
LYING CAN'T BE DONE WITHOUT SOMEONE TO LIE TO
alone
THERE IS NO LIE IN PRETENDING
feel free
9. hunt wild buffalo
1. sailed a mile
1. joins an old tramp
4. sting the six wasps
6. get into a fight
8. look out and
ashamed
brave
glad
alone
to find
ICU2
What happened next?
we'll come too
1. Lesson Plans
2. Assignments
3. Recitation
4. Seat Work
Hoping we will be able to go by to call or stop

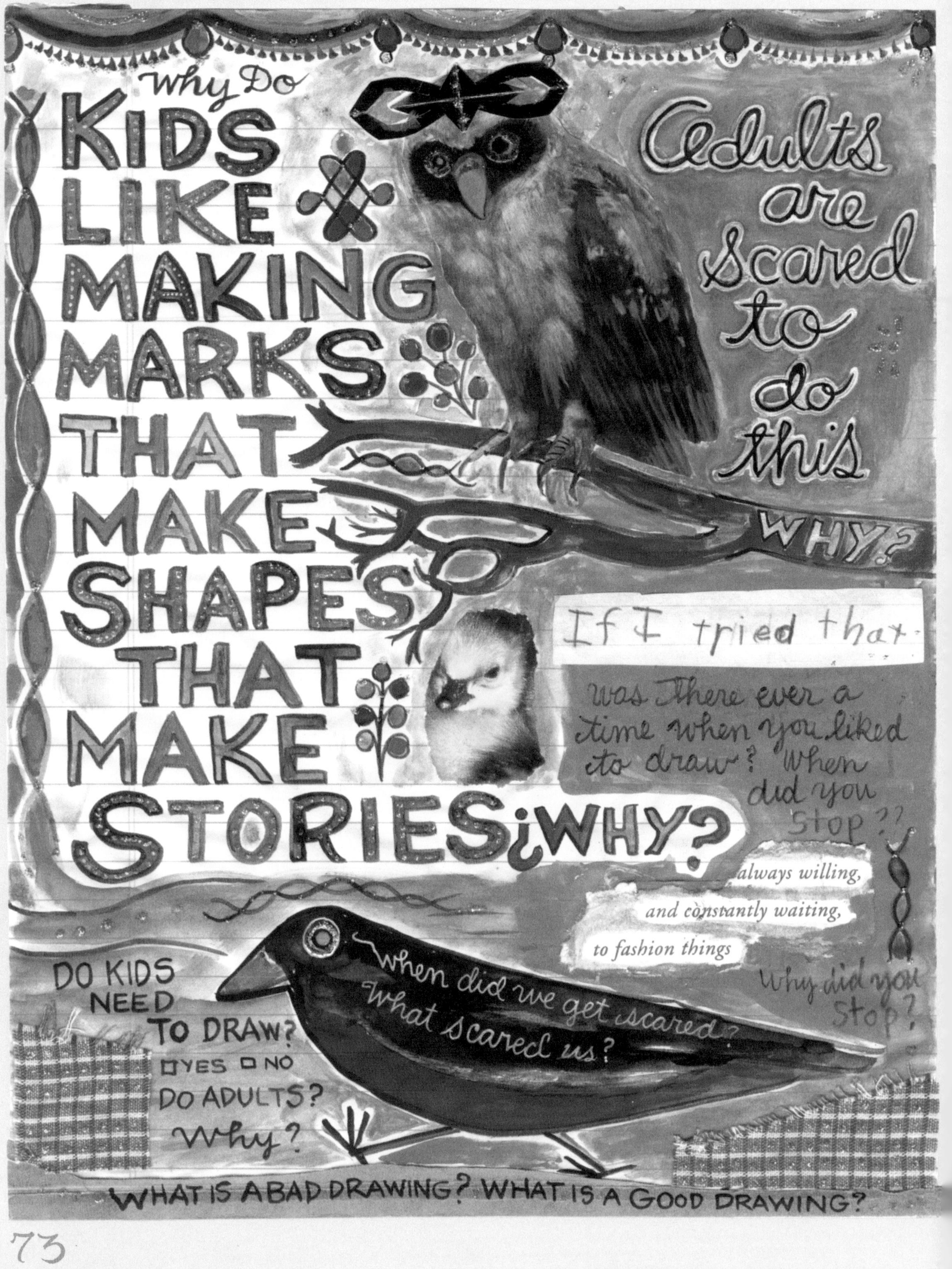
Why Do
KIDS LIKE MAKING MARKS THAT MAKE SHAPES THAT MAKE STORIES ¿WHY?
Adults are Scared to do this
WHY?
If I tried that
was There ever a time when you liked to draw? When did you Stop??
always willing,
and constantly waiting,
to fashion things
Why did you Stop?
DO KIDS NEED TO DRAW?
☐YES ☐NO
DO ADULTS?
Why?
when did we get scared? What scared us?
WHAT IS A BAD DRAWING? WHAT IS A GOOD DRAWING?

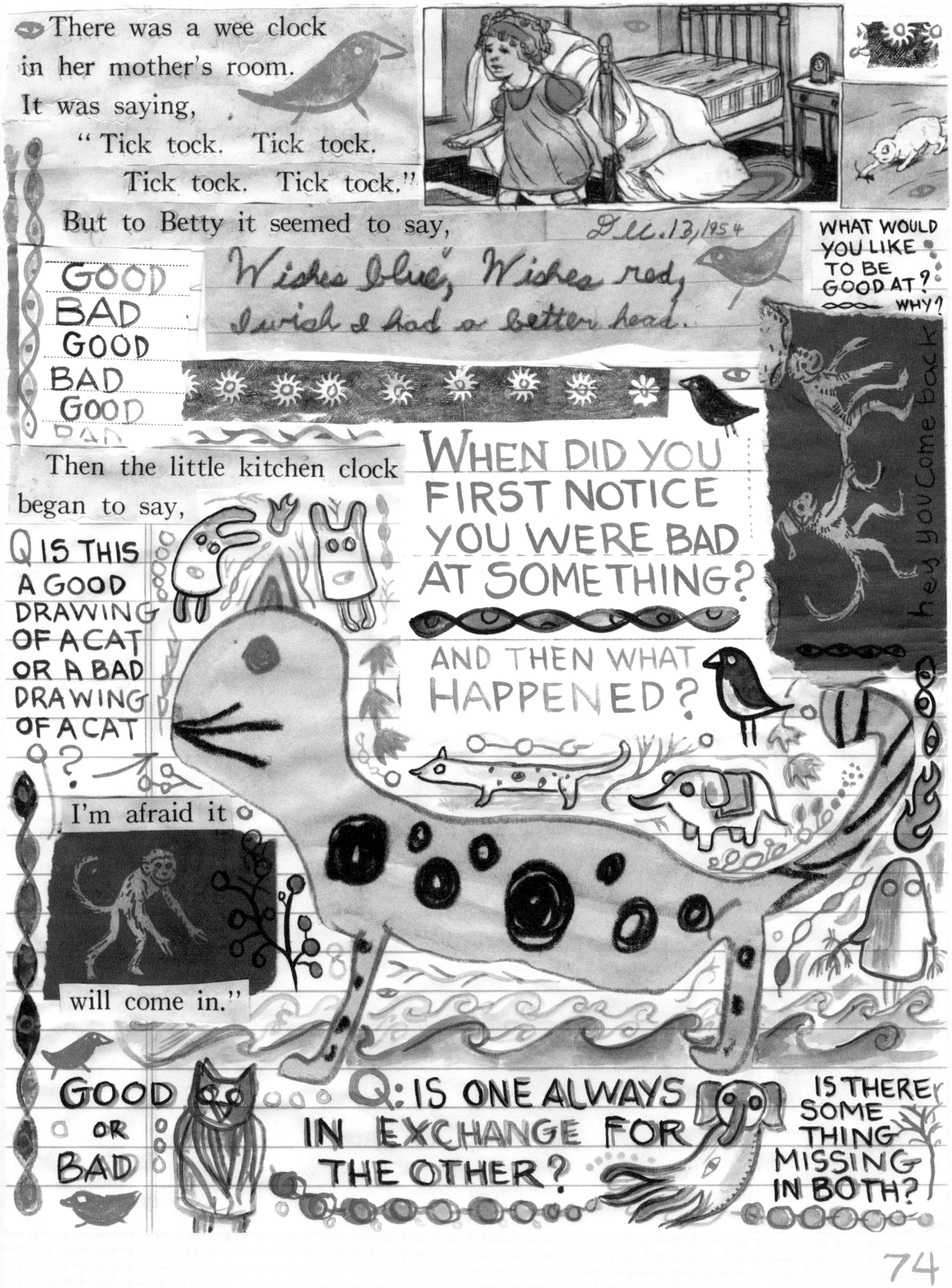
There was a wee clock
in her mother's room.
It was saying,
"Tick tock. Tick tock.
Tick tock. Tick tock."
But to Betty it seemed to say,
Dec. 13, 1954
Wishes blue, Wishes red,
I wish I had a better head.
WHAT WOULD YOU LIKE TO BE GOOD AT? WHY?
GOOD
BAD
GOOD
BAD
GOOD
hey you come back
Then the little kitchen clock
began to say,
WHEN DID YOU FIRST NOTICE YOU WERE BAD AT SOMETHING?
AND THEN WHAT HAPPENED?
Q IS THIS A GOOD DRAWING OF A CAT OR A BAD DRAWING OF A CAT ?
I'm afraid it
will come in."
GOOD OR BAD
Q: IS ONE ALWAYS IN EXCHANGE FOR THE OTHER?
IS THERE SOME THING MISSING IN BOTH?

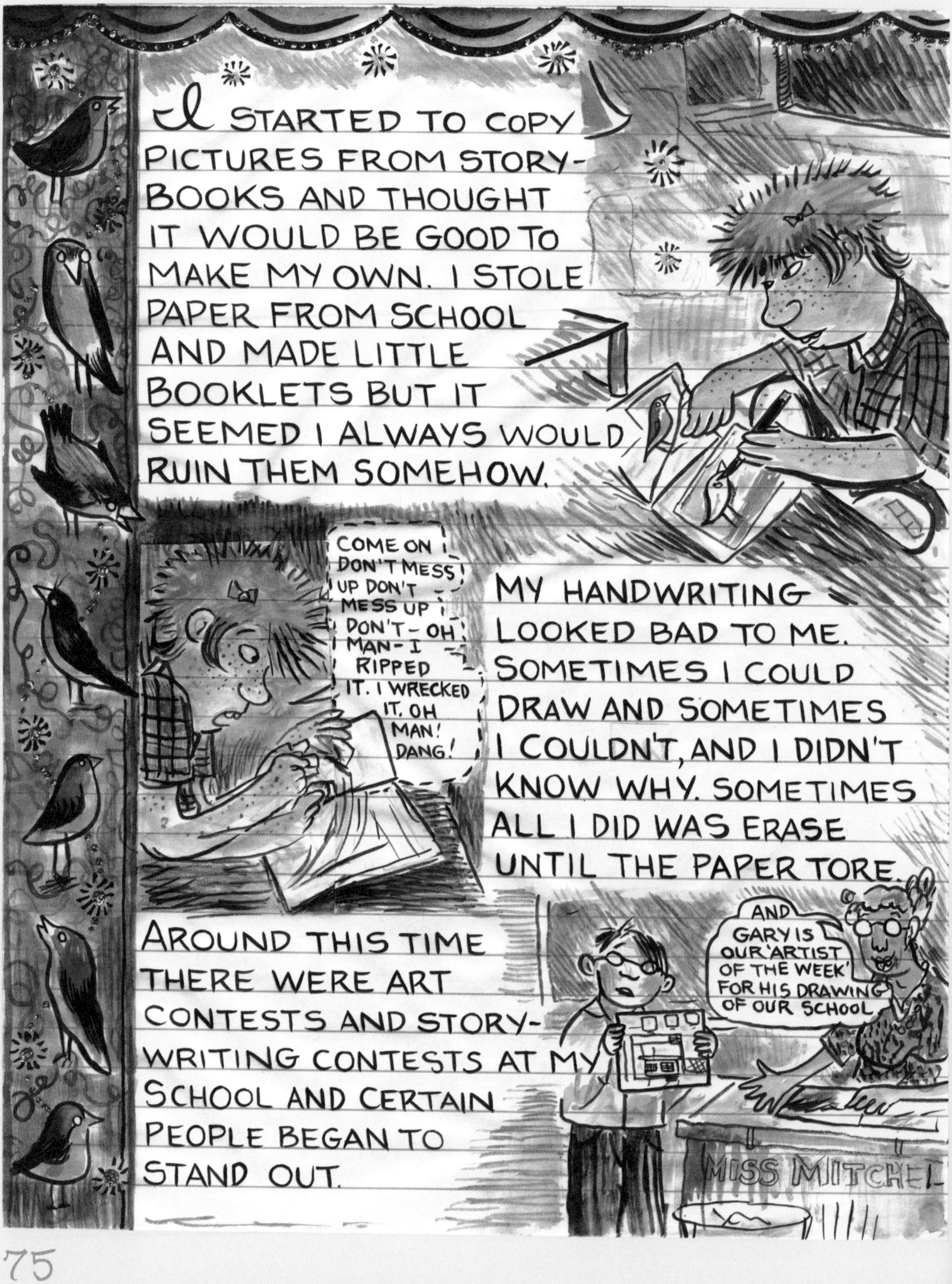
I STARTED TO COPY PICTURES FROM STORY-BOOKS AND THOUGHT IT WOULD BE GOOD TO MAKE MY OWN. I STOLE PAPER FROM SCHOOL AND MADE LITTLE BOOKLETS BUT IT SEEMED I ALWAYS WOULD RUIN THEM SOMEHOW.
COME ON DON'T MESS UP DON'T MESS UP DON'T- OH MAN- I RIPPED IT. I WRECKED IT. OH MAN! DANG!
MY HANDWRITING LOOKED BAD TO ME. SOMETIMES I COULD DRAW AND SOMETIMES I COULDN'T, AND I DIDN'T KNOW WHY. SOMETIMES ALL I DID WAS ERASE UNTIL THE PAPER TORE.
AROUND THIS TIME THERE WERE ART CONTESTS AND STORY-WRITING CONTESTS AT MY SCHOOL AND CERTAIN PEOPLE BEGAN TO STAND OUT.
AND GARY IS OUR 'ARTIST OF THE WEEK' FOR HIS DRAWING OF OUR SCHOOL
MISS MITCHEL

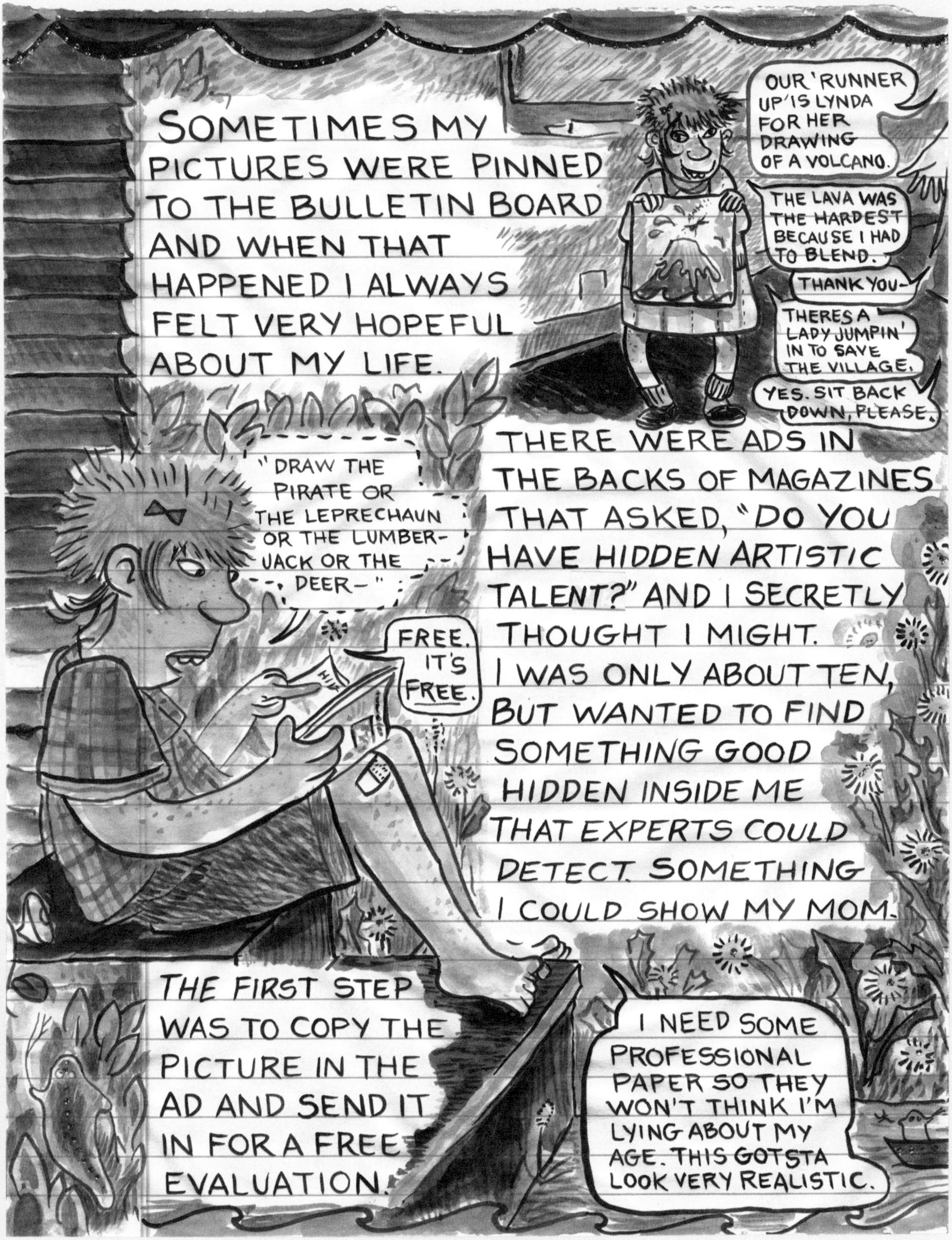
SOMETIMES MY PICTURES WERE PINNED TO THE BULLETIN BOARD AND WHEN THAT HAPPENED I ALWAYS FELT VERY HOPEFUL ABOUT MY LIFE.
OUR 'RUNNER UP' IS LYNDA FOR HER DRAWING OF A VOLCANO.
THE LAVA WAS THE HARDEST BECAUSE I HAD TO BLEND.
THANK YOU-
THERES A LADY JUMPIN' IN TO SAVE THE VILLAGE.
YES. SIT BACK DOWN, PLEASE.
THERE WERE ADS IN THE BACKS OF MAGAZINES THAT ASKED, "DO YOU HAVE HIDDEN ARTISTIC TALENT?" AND I SECRETLY THOUGHT I MIGHT. I WAS ONLY ABOUT TEN, BUT WANTED TO FIND SOMETHING GOOD HIDDEN INSIDE ME THAT EXPERTS COULD DETECT. SOMETHING I COULD SHOW MY MOM.
"DRAW THE PIRATE OR THE LEPRECHAUN OR THE LUMBER-JACK OR THE DEER-"
FREE. IT'S FREE.
THE FIRST STEP WAS TO COPY THE PICTURE IN THE AD AND SEND IT IN FOR A FREE EVALUATION.
I NEED SOME PROFESSIONAL PAPER SO THEY WON'T THINK I'M LYING ABOUT MY AGE. THIS GOTSTA LOOK VERY REALISTIC.

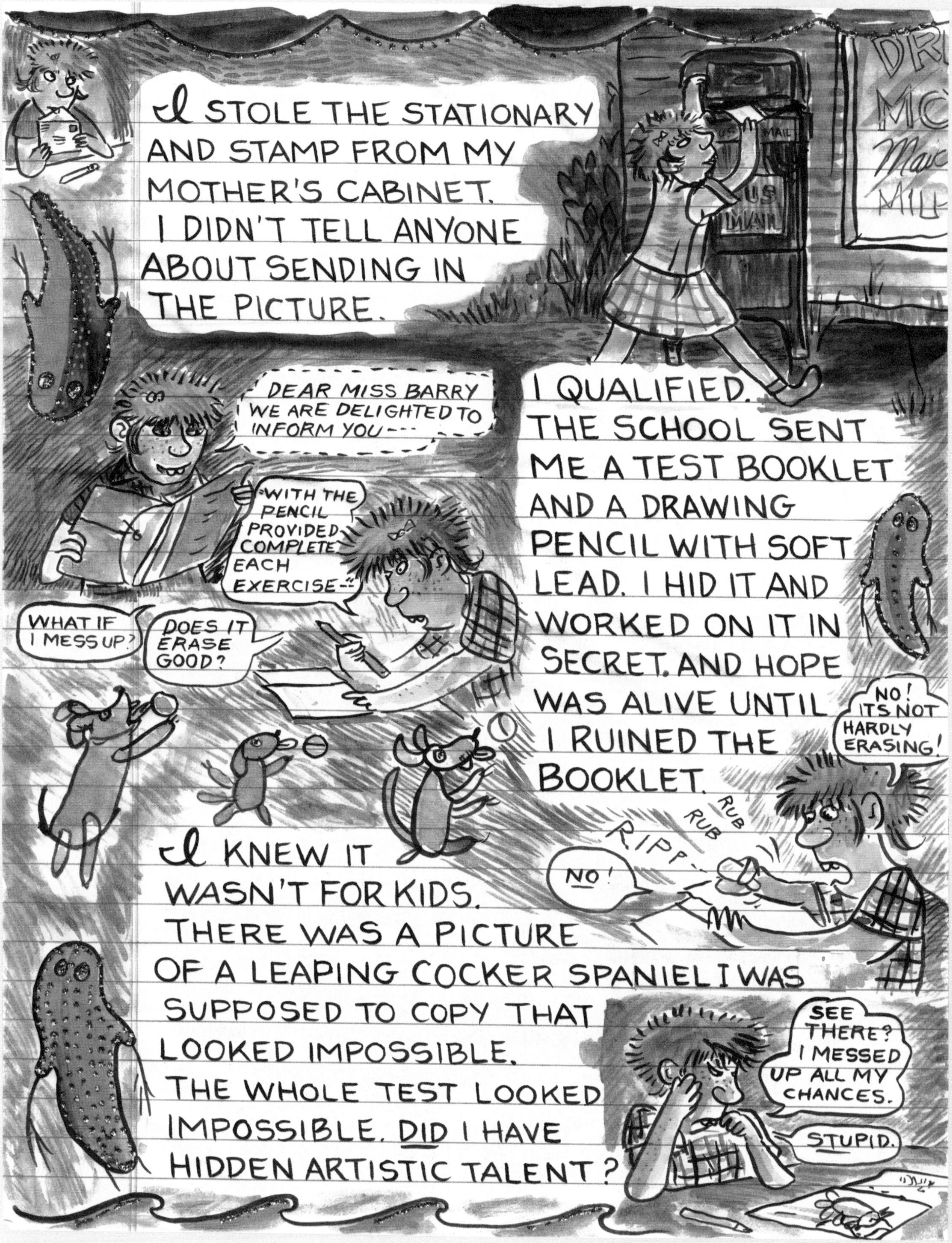
I STOLE THE STATIONARY AND STAMP FROM MY MOTHER'S CABINET. I DIDN'T TELL ANYONE ABOUT SENDING IN THE PICTURE.
US MAIL
DEAR MISS BARRY WE ARE DELIGHTED TO INFORM YOU---
"WITH THE PENCIL PROVIDED COMPLETE EACH EXERCISE--"
WHAT IF I MESS UP?
DOES IT ERASE GOOD?
I QUALIFIED. THE SCHOOL SENT ME A TEST BOOKLET AND A DRAWING PENCIL WITH SOFT LEAD. I HID IT AND WORKED ON IT IN SECRET. AND HOPE WAS ALIVE UNTIL I RUINED THE BOOKLET.
NO! ITS NOT HARDLY ERASING!
RUB
RUB
RIPP
NO!
I KNEW IT WASN'T FOR KIDS. THERE WAS A PICTURE OF A LEAPING COCKER SPANIEL I WAS SUPPOSED TO COPY THAT LOOKED IMPOSSIBLE. THE WHOLE TEST LOOKED IMPOSSIBLE. DID I HAVE HIDDEN ARTISTIC TALENT?
SEE THERE? I MESSED UP ALL MY CHANCES.
STUPID.

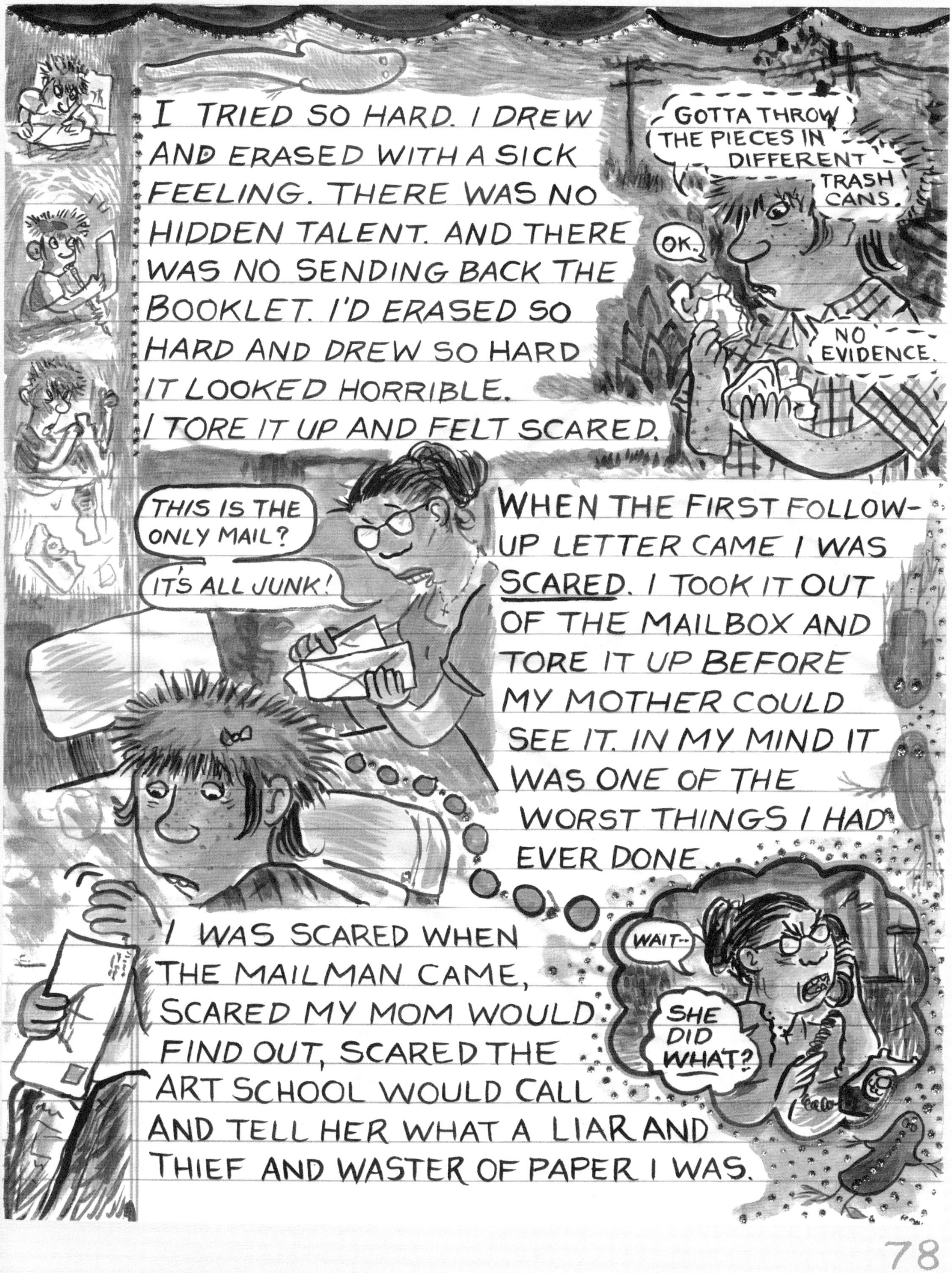
I TRIED SO HARD. I DREW AND ERASED WITH A SICK FEELING. THERE WAS NO HIDDEN TALENT. AND THERE WAS NO SENDING BACK THE BOOKLET. I'D ERASED SO HARD AND DREW SO HARD IT LOOKED HORRIBLE.
I TORE IT UP AND FELT SCARED.
GOTTA THROW THE PIECES IN DIFFERENT TRASH CANS.
OK.
NO EVIDENCE.
THIS IS THE ONLY MAIL?
IT'S ALL JUNK!
WHEN THE FIRST FOLLOW-UP LETTER CAME I WAS SCARED. I TOOK IT OUT OF THE MAILBOX AND TORE IT UP BEFORE MY MOTHER COULD SEE IT. IN MY MIND IT WAS ONE OF THE WORST THINGS I HAD EVER DONE.
I WAS SCARED WHEN THE MAILMAN CAME, SCARED MY MOM WOULD FIND OUT, SCARED THE ART SCHOOL WOULD CALL AND TELL HER WHAT A LIAR AND THIEF AND WASTER OF PAPER I WAS.
WAIT--
SHE DID WHAT?

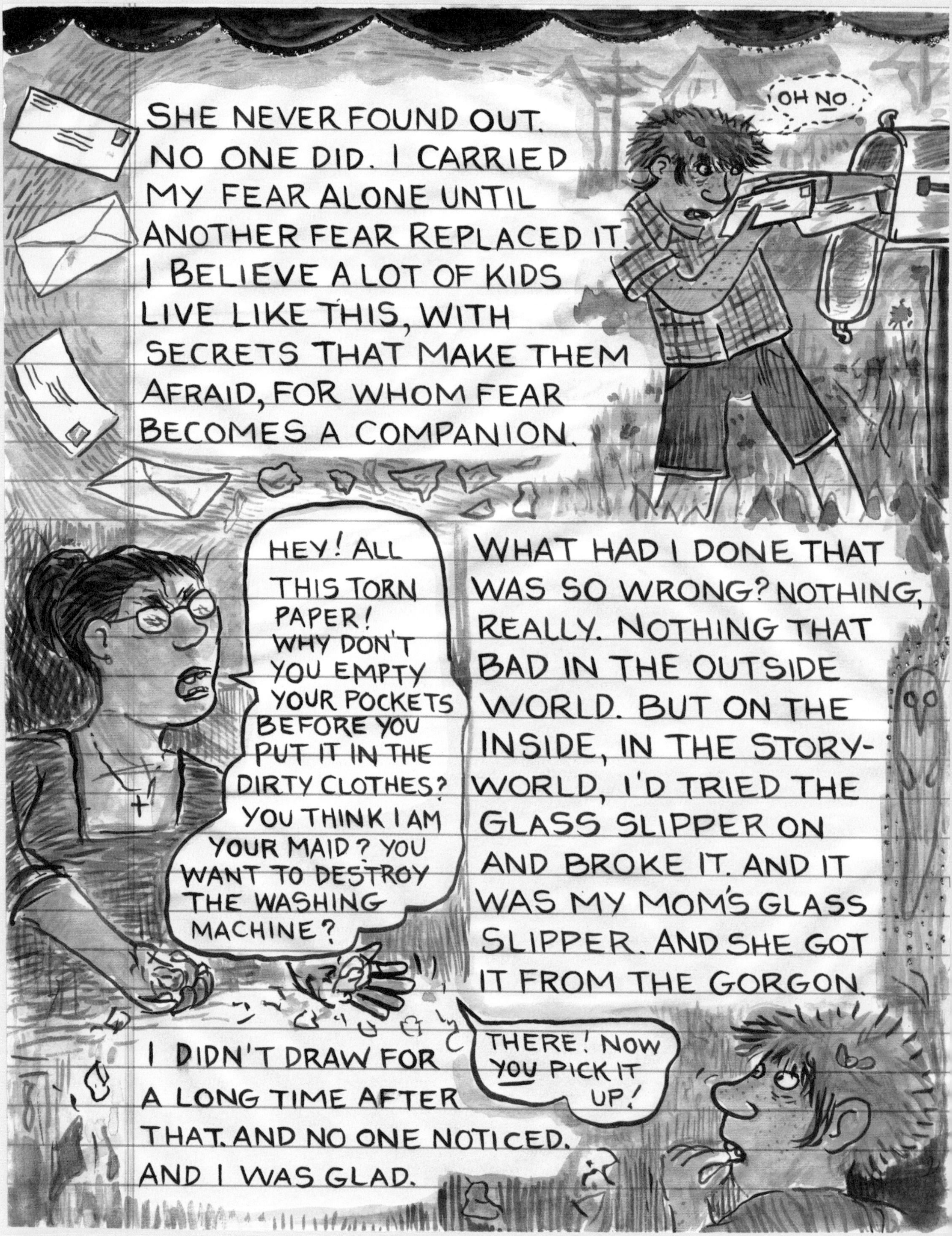
SHE NEVER FOUND OUT. NO ONE DID. I CARRIED MY FEAR ALONE UNTIL ANOTHER FEAR REPLACED IT. I BELIEVE A LOT OF KIDS LIVE LIKE THIS, WITH SECRETS THAT MAKE THEM AFRAID, FOR WHOM FEAR BECOMES A COMPANION.
OH NO.
HEY! ALL THIS TORN PAPER! WHY DON'T YOU EMPTY YOUR POCKETS BEFORE YOU PUT IT IN THE DIRTY CLOTHES? YOU THINK I AM YOUR MAID? YOU WANT TO DESTROY THE WASHING MACHINE?
WHAT HAD I DONE THAT WAS SO WRONG? NOTHING, REALLY. NOTHING THAT BAD IN THE OUTSIDE WORLD. BUT ON THE INSIDE, IN THE STORY-WORLD, I'D TRIED THE GLASS SLIPPER ON AND BROKE IT. AND IT WAS MY MOM'S GLASS SLIPPER. AND SHE GOT IT FROM THE GORGON.
I DIDN'T DRAW FOR A LONG TIME AFTER THAT. AND NO ONE NOTICED. AND I WAS GLAD.
THERE! NOW YOU PICK IT UP!

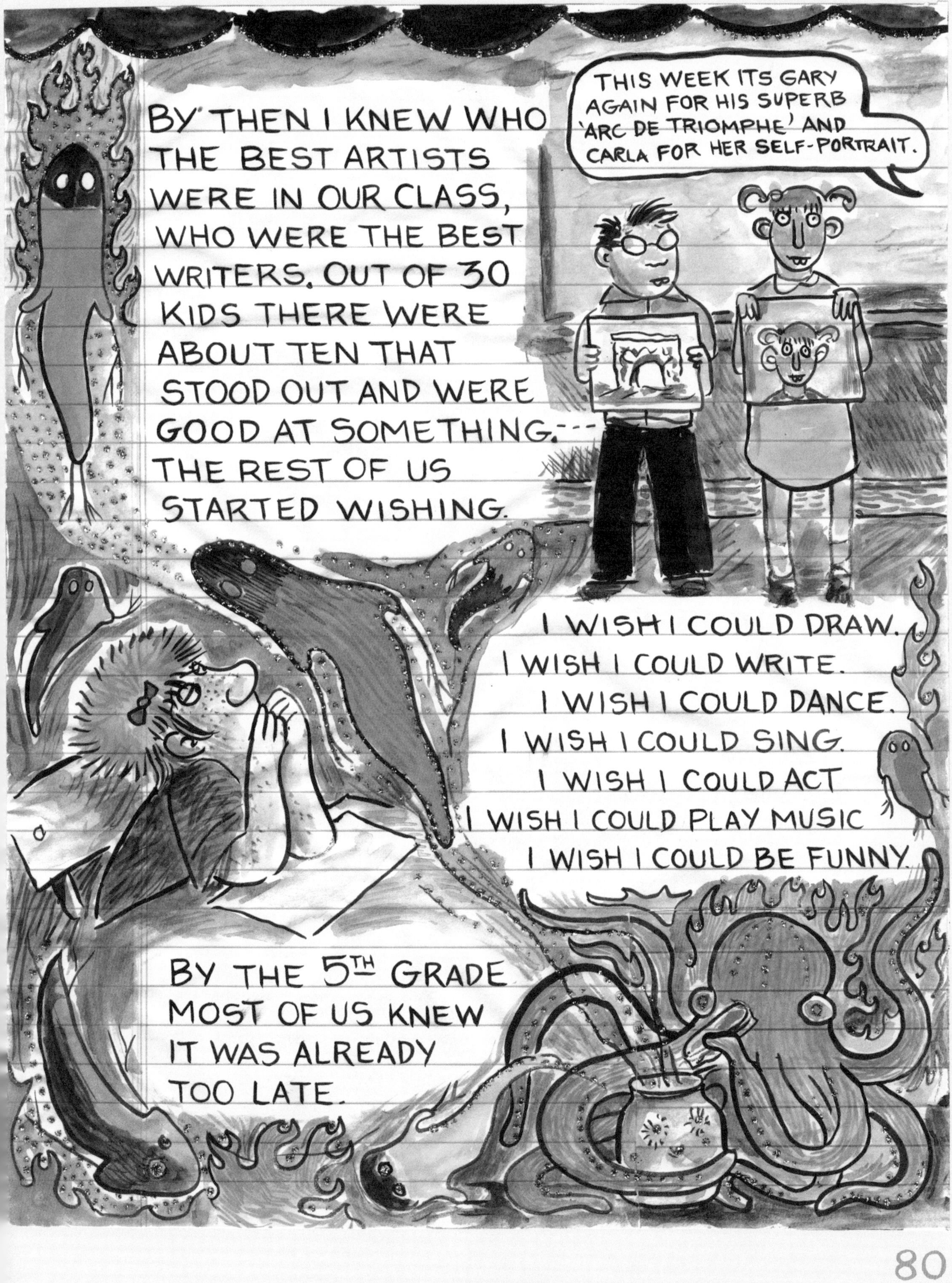
BY THEN I KNEW WHO THE BEST ARTISTS WERE IN OUR CLASS, WHO WERE THE BEST WRITERS. OUT OF 30 KIDS THERE WERE ABOUT TEN THAT STOOD OUT AND WERE GOOD AT SOMETHING.--- THE REST OF US STARTED WISHING.
THIS WEEK ITS GARY AGAIN FOR HIS SUPERB 'ARC DE TRIOMPHE' AND CARLA FOR HER SELF-PORTRAIT.
I WISH I COULD DRAW.
I WISH I COULD WRITE.
I WISH I COULD DANCE.
I WISH I COULD SING.
I WISH I COULD ACT
I WISH I COULD PLAY MUSIC
I WISH I COULD BE FUNNY.
BY THE 5TH GRADE MOST OF US KNEW IT WAS ALREADY TOO LATE.

Although every hour is 60 minutes long
We notice some hours are shorter than others

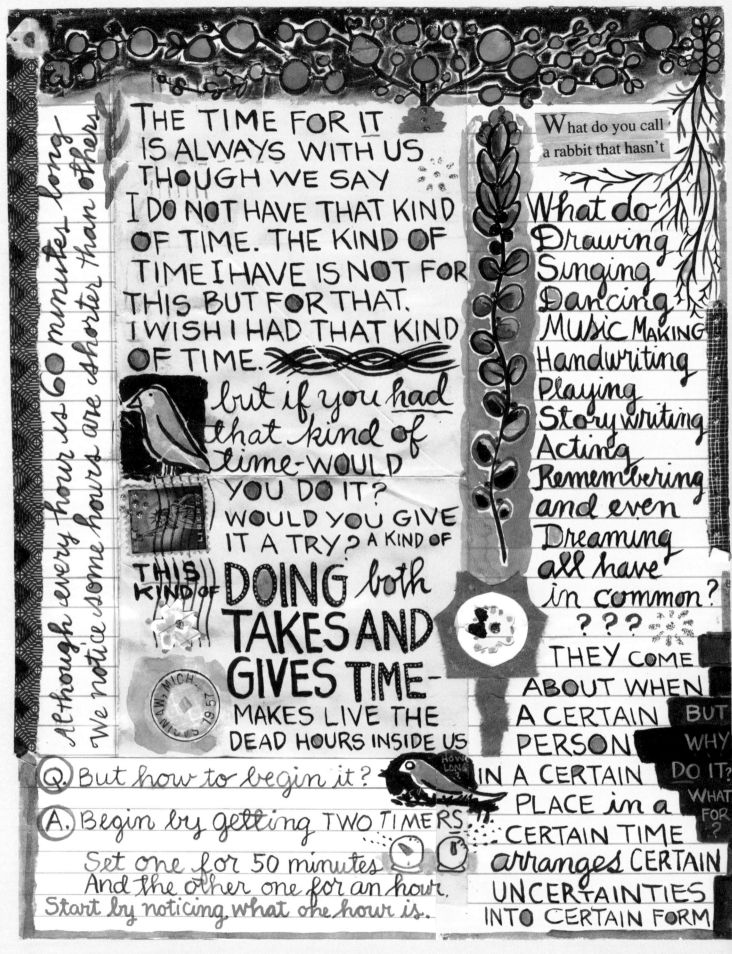

THE TIME FOR IT
IS ALWAYS WITH US
THOUGH WE SAY
I DO NOT HAVE THAT KIND
OF TIME. THE KIND OF
TIME I HAVE IS NOT FOR
THIS BUT FOR THAT.
I WISH I HAD THAT KIND
OF TIME.

but if you *had*
that kind of
time-WOULD
YOU DO IT?
WOULD YOU GIVE
IT A TRY? A KIND OF
THIS KIND OF DOING both
TAKES AND
GIVES TIME-
MAKES LIVE THE
DEAD HOURS INSIDE US

What do you call
a rabbit that hasn't

What do
Drawing
Singing
Dancing
MUSIC MAKING
Handwriting
Playing
Storywriting
Acting
Remembering
and even
Dreaming
all have
in common?
???

THEY COME
ABOUT WHEN
A CERTAIN
PERSON
IN A CERTAIN
PLACE in a
CERTAIN TIME
arranges CERTAIN
UNCERTAINTIES
INTO CERTAIN FORM

BUT
WHY
DO IT?
WHAT
FOR?

HOW LONG?

Q. But how to begin it?

A. Begin by getting TWO TIMERS
Set one for 50 minutes
And the other one for an hour.
Start by noticing what one hour is.

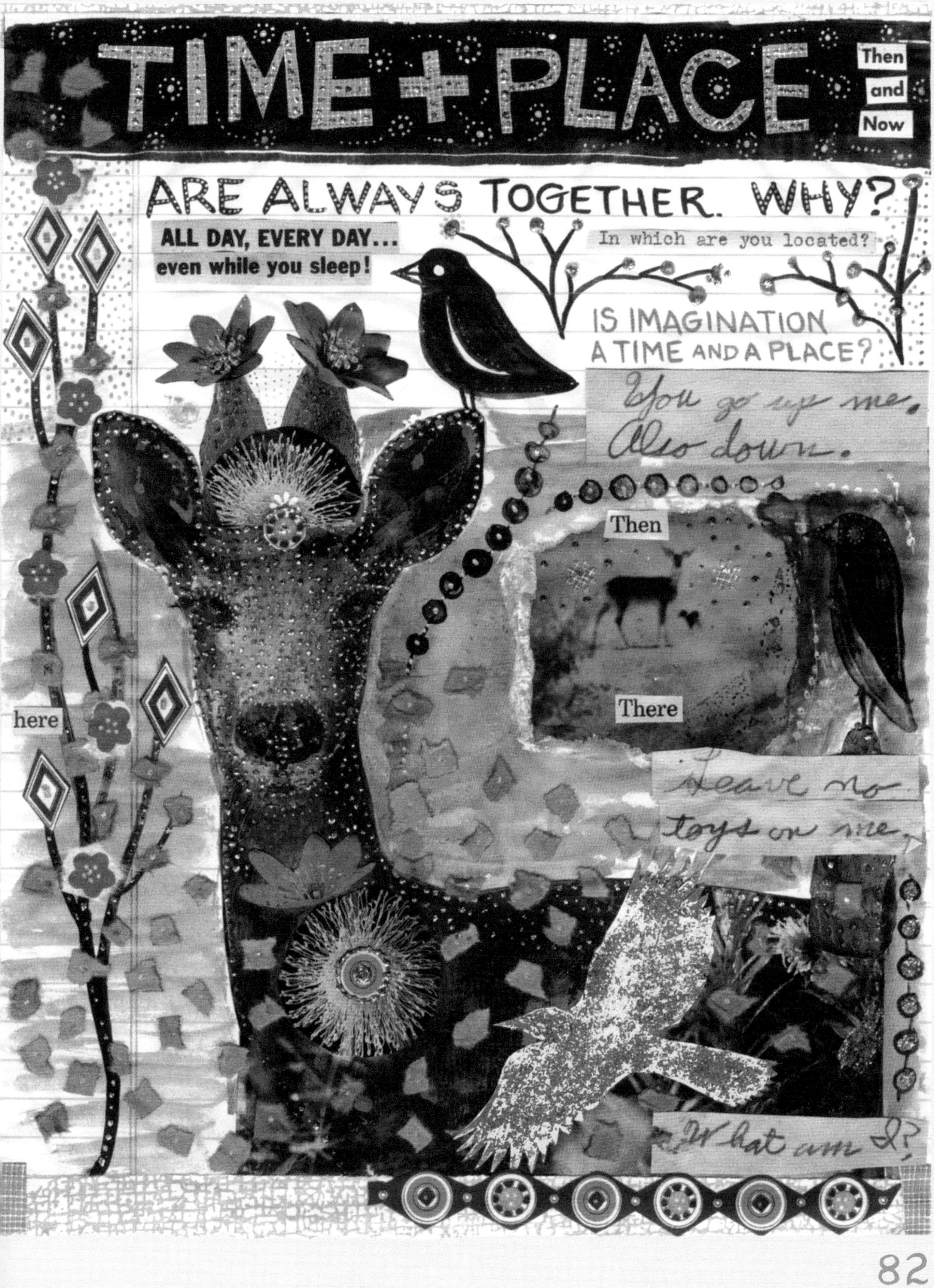
TIME + PLACE
Then and Now
ARE ALWAYS TOGETHER. WHY?
ALL DAY, EVERY DAY...
even while you sleep!
In which are you located?
IS IMAGINATION A TIME AND A PLACE?
You go up me. Also down.
Then
There
here
Leave no toys on me.
What am I?

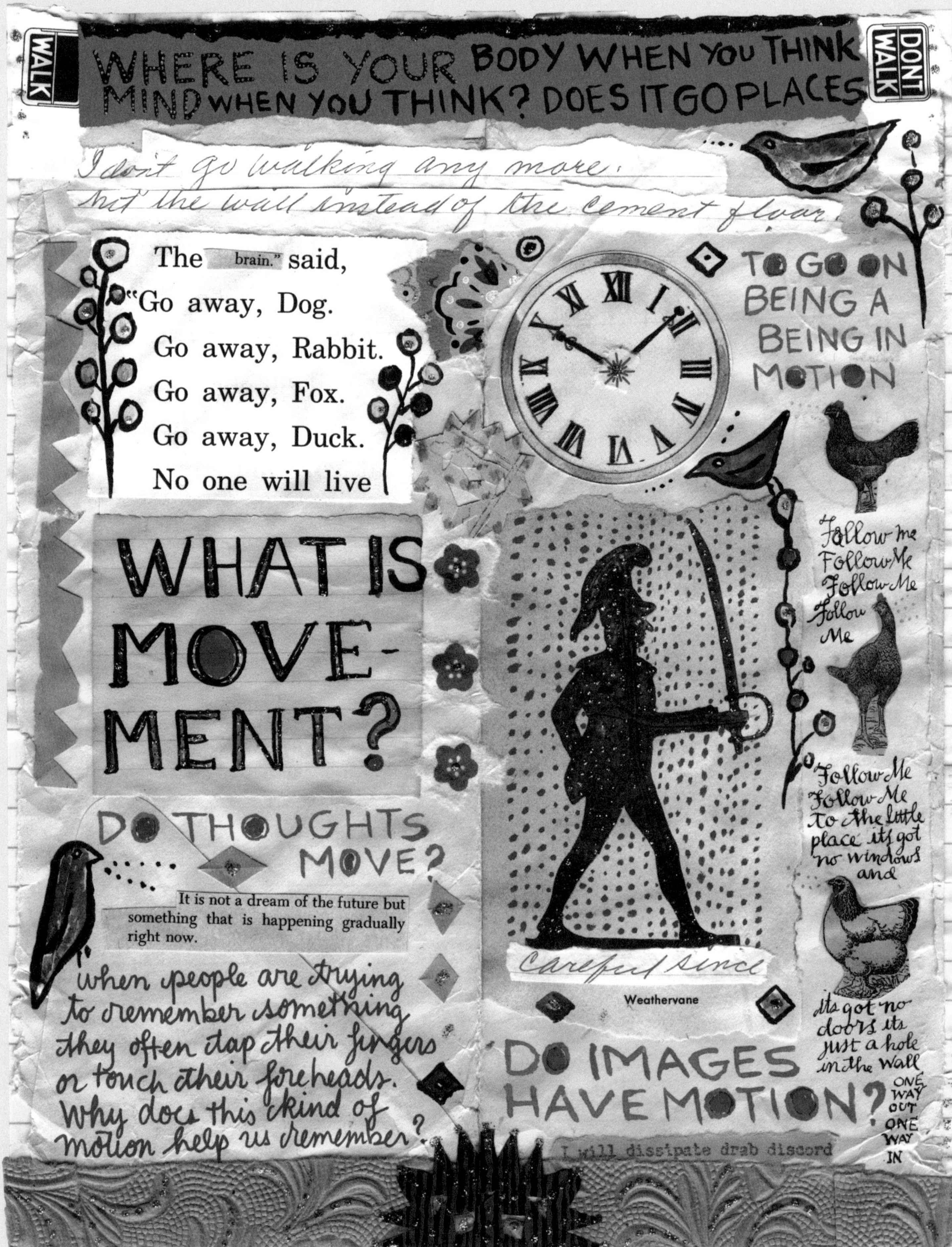
WALK
WHERE IS YOUR BODY WHEN YOU THINK
MIND WHEN YOU THINK? DOES IT GO PLACES
DONT WALK
I don't go walking any more.
hit the wall instead of the cement floor.
The brain." said,
"Go away, Dog.
Go away, Rabbit.
Go away, Fox.
Go away, Duck.
No one will live
TO GO ON BEING A BEING IN MOTION
WHAT IS MOVE-MENT?
Follow me Follow Me Follow Me Follow Me
Follow Me Follow Me To the little place its got no windows and
DO THOUGHTS MOVE?
It is not a dream of the future but something that is happening gradually right now.
when people are trying to remember something they often tap their fingers or touch their foreheads. Why does this kind of motion help us remember?
Careful Since
Weathervane
its got no doors its just a hole in the wall
DO IMAGES HAVE MOTION?
ONE WAY OUT ONE WAY IN
I will dissipate drab discord

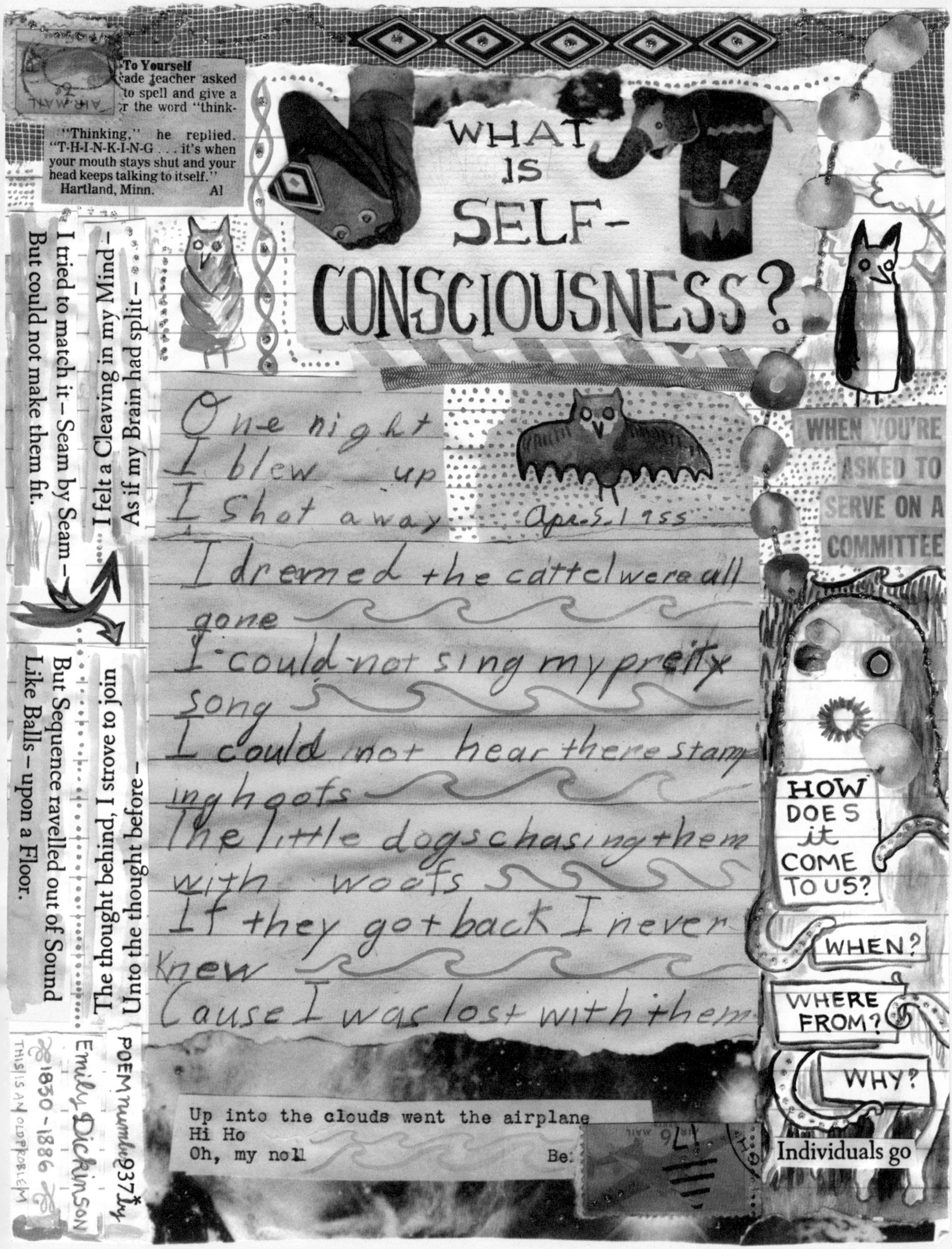
WHAT IS SELF-CONSCIOUSNESS?
To Yourself
ade teacher asked
to spell and give a
r the word "think-
"Thinking," he replied. "T-H-I-N-K-I-N-G . . . it's when your mouth stays shut and your head keeps talking to itself."
Hartland, Minn. Al
I felt a Cleaving in my Mind –
As if my Brain had split –
I tried to match it – Seam by Seam –
But could not make them fit.
The thought behind, I strove to join
Unto the thought before –
But Sequence ravelled out of Sound
Like Balls – upon a Floor.
POEM number 937
Emily Dickinson
1830-1886
THIS IS AN OLD PROBLEM
One night
I blew up
I Shot away Apr. 5. 1955
I dremed the cattel were all gone
I could not sing my pretty song
I could not hear there stamping hoofs
The little dogs chasing them with woofs
If they got back I never knew
Cause I was lost with them
WHEN YOU'RE ASKED TO SERVE ON A COMMITTEE
HOW DOES it COME TO US?
WHEN?
WHERE FROM?
WHY?
Individuals go
Up into the clouds went the airplane
Hi Ho
Oh, my noll
Be:

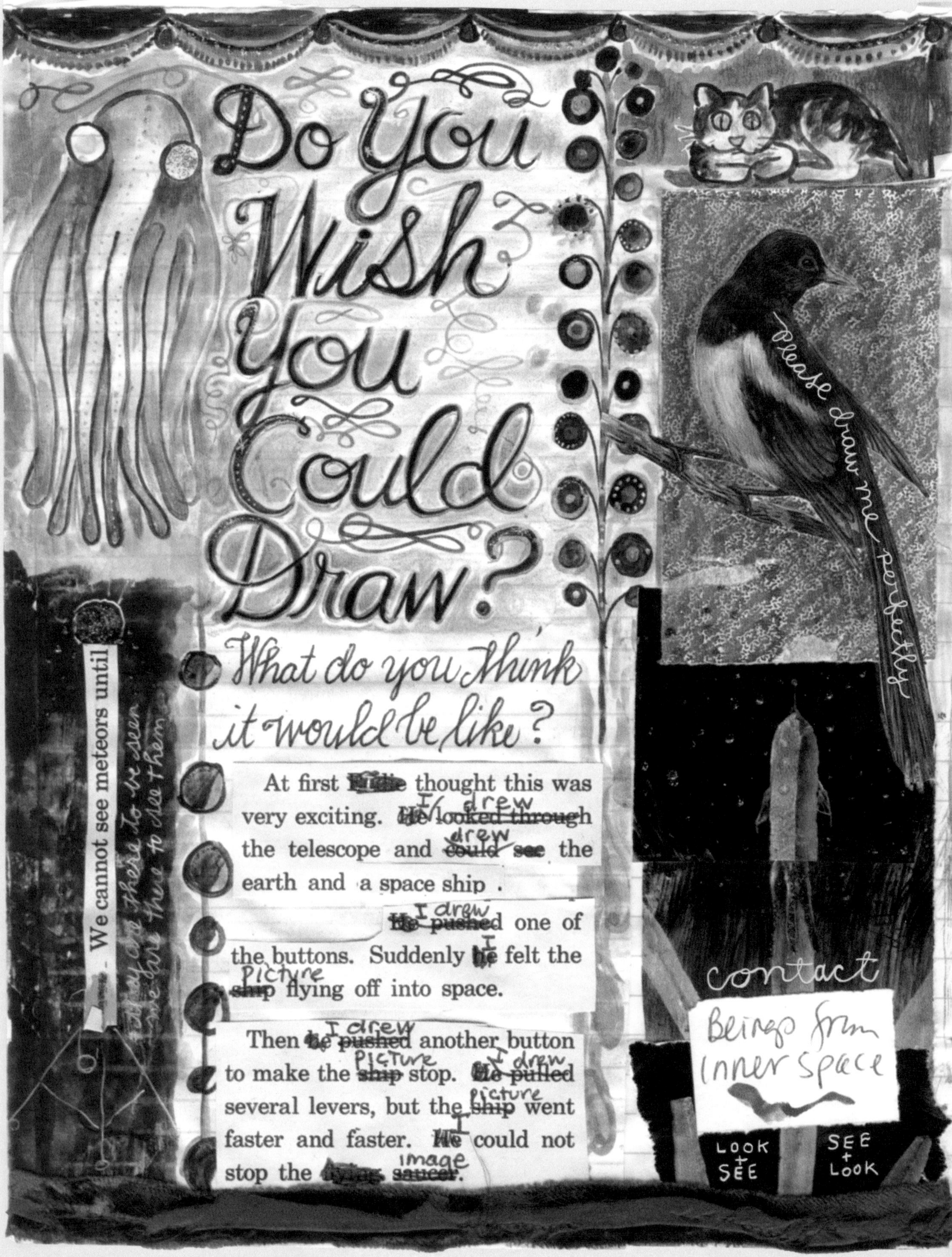
Do You Wish You Could Draw?
What do you think it would be like?
At first ~~Eddie~~ thought this was very exciting. I/ drew ~~He looked through~~ the telescope and drew ~~could see~~ the earth and a space ship .
I drew ~~He pushed~~ one of the buttons. Suddenly I ~~he~~ felt the picture ~~ship~~ flying off into space.
Then I drew ~~he pushed~~ another button to make the picture ~~ship~~ stop. I drew ~~He pulled~~ several levers, but the picture ~~ship~~ went faster and faster. I ~~He~~ could not stop the image ~~flying saucer~~.
We cannot see meteors until
they are there to be seen
we are there to see them
please draw me perfectly
contact
Beings from Inner Space
LOOK + SEE
SEE + LOOK

---- to move along on the water into the open sea.

ILLUSTRATED MUSIC

WHAT IS SINGING?

feel something inside you that is shaking back and forth, vibrating.

why is there SINGING ??? IS IT JUST ENTER-TAIN-MENT ???

Do you

Do You Wish you Could Sing?

Human beings everywhere sing to babies but they hardly ever notice that babies are also singing right back

Singing comes before Speaking

Things We Could Sing About

- high hollow tree
- slow-ringing bells
- hide with buffalo
- saddle the horse
- keep on dancing
- swing with Henry
- high swallows fly
- big campers road

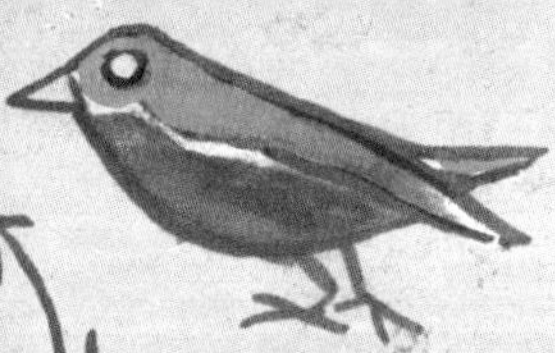

IF WE SPOKE OF THESE THINGS INSTEAD OF SINGING ABOUT THEM, WHAT WOULD BE DIFFERENT ABOUT THE experience?

WHAT DO YOU imagine BEING ABLE to SING would Feel LIKE?

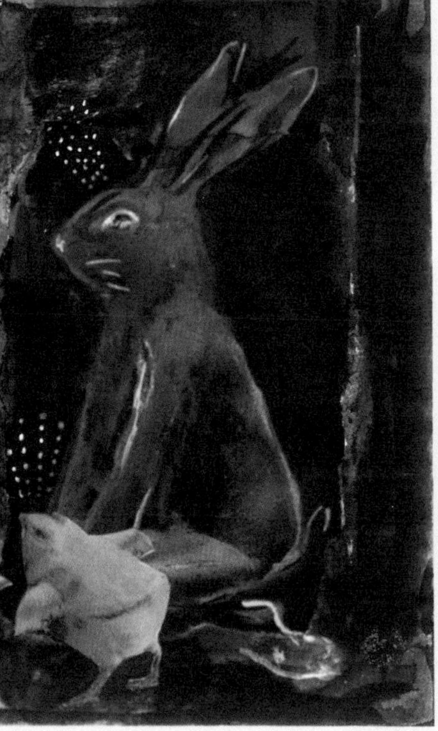

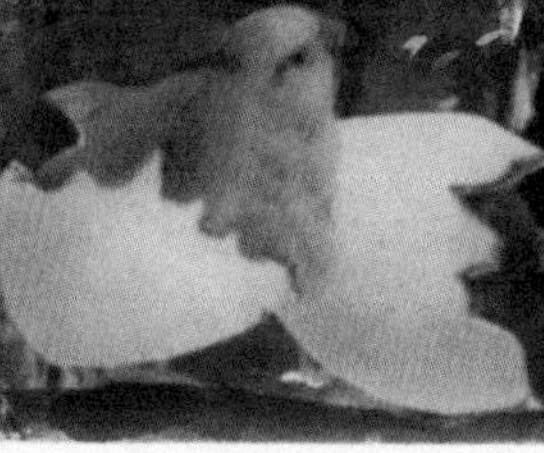

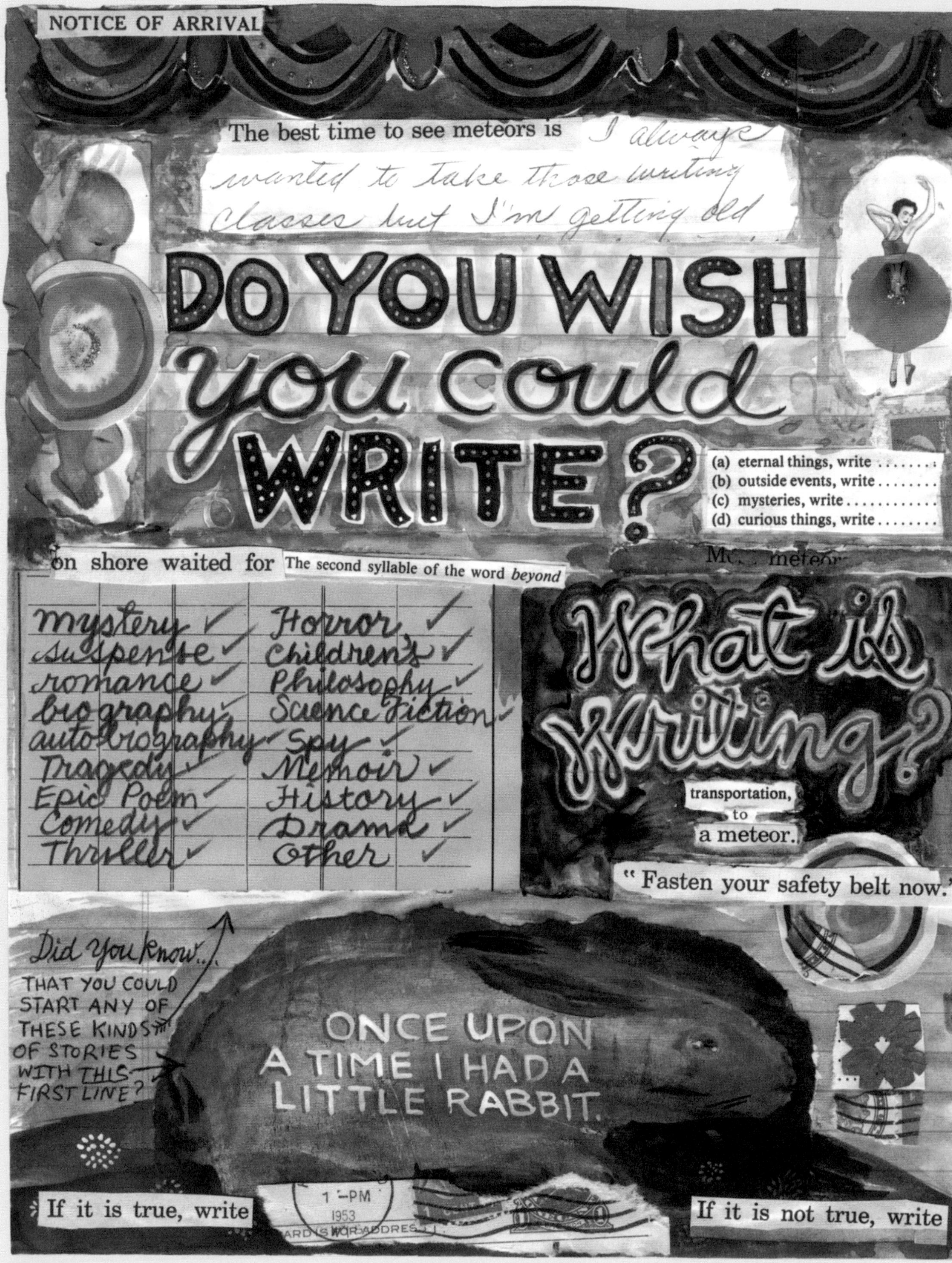
NOTICE OF ARRIVAL
The best time to see meteors is I always wanted to take those writing classes but I'm getting old
DO YOU WISH you could WRITE?
(a) eternal things, write . . . .
(b) outside events, write . . . .
(c) mysteries, write . . . .
(d) curious things, write . . . .
on shore waited for The second syllable of the word beyond
mystery ✓ suspense ✓ romance ✓ biography ✓ autobiography ✓ Tragedy ✓ Epic Poem ✓ Comedy ✓ Thriller ✓
Horror ✓ Children's ✓ Philosophy ✓ Science Fiction ✓ Spy ✓ Memoir ✓ History ✓ Drama ✓ Other ✓
What is Writing?
transportation, to a meteor.
" Fasten your safety belt now."
Did You Know... THAT YOU COULD START ANY OF THESE KINDS OF STORIES WITH THIS FIRST LINE?
ONCE UPON A TIME I HAD A LITTLE RABBIT.
If it is true, write
1953
If it is not true, write

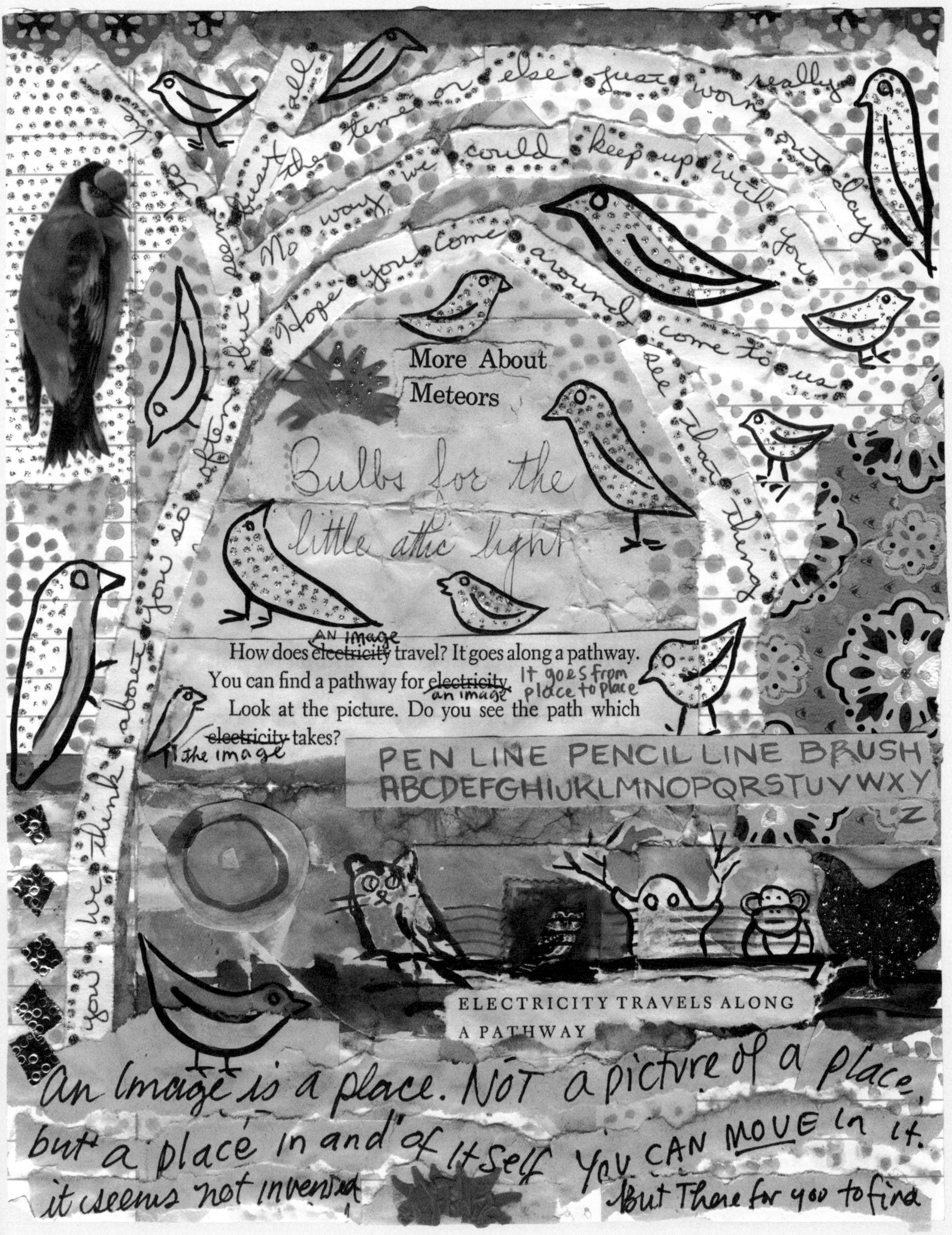
Hope you come around come to us
No way we could keep up with you
More About
Meteors
Bulbs for the
little attic light
How does ~~electricity~~ an image travel? It goes along a pathway.
You can find a pathway for ~~electricity~~ an image. It goes from place to place
Look at the picture. Do you see the path which
~~electricity~~ the image takes?
PEN LINE PENCIL LINE BRUSH
ABCDEFGHIUKLMNOPQRSTUVWXY
Z
ELECTRICITY TRAVELS ALONG
A PATHWAY
An Image is a place. NOT a picture of a place,
but a place in and of itself. YOU CAN MOVE in it.
it seems not invented
But There for you to find

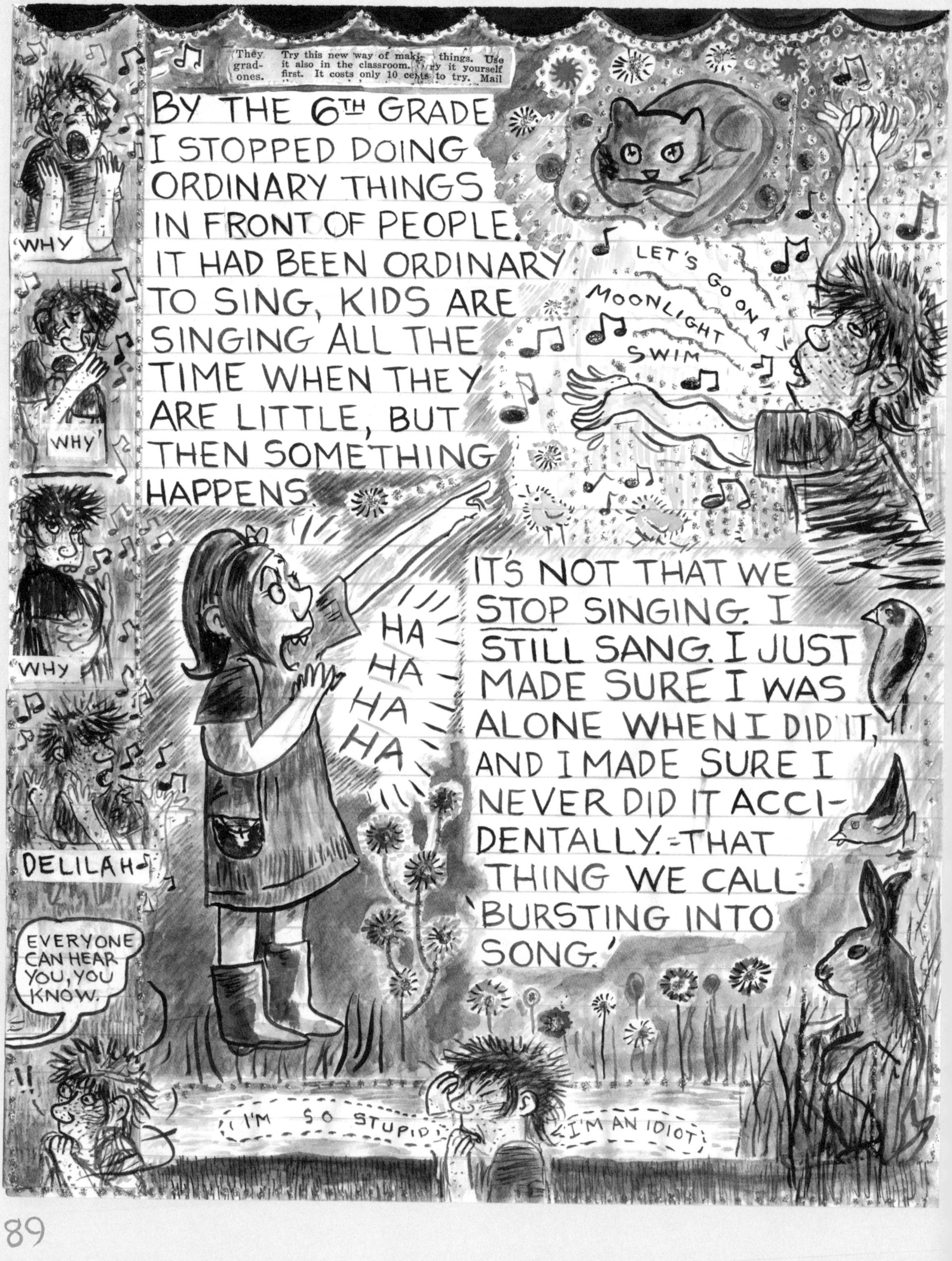
They grad- ones. Try this new way of making things. Use it also in the classroom. Try it yourself first. It costs only 10 cents to try. Mail
BY THE 6TH GRADE I STOPPED DOING ORDINARY THINGS IN FRONT OF PEOPLE. IT HAD BEEN ORDINARY TO SING, KIDS ARE SINGING ALL THE TIME WHEN THEY ARE LITTLE, BUT THEN SOMETHING HAPPENS.
WHY
WHY
WHY
DELILAH
LET'S GO ON A MOONLIGHT SWIM
HA HA HA HA
IT'S NOT THAT WE STOP SINGING. I STILL SANG. I JUST MADE SURE I WAS ALONE WHEN I DID IT, AND I MADE SURE I NEVER DID IT ACCIDENTALLY. THAT THING WE CALL 'BURSTING INTO SONG.'
EVERYONE CAN HEAR YOU, YOU KNOW.
!!
I'M SO STUPID
I'M AN IDIOT

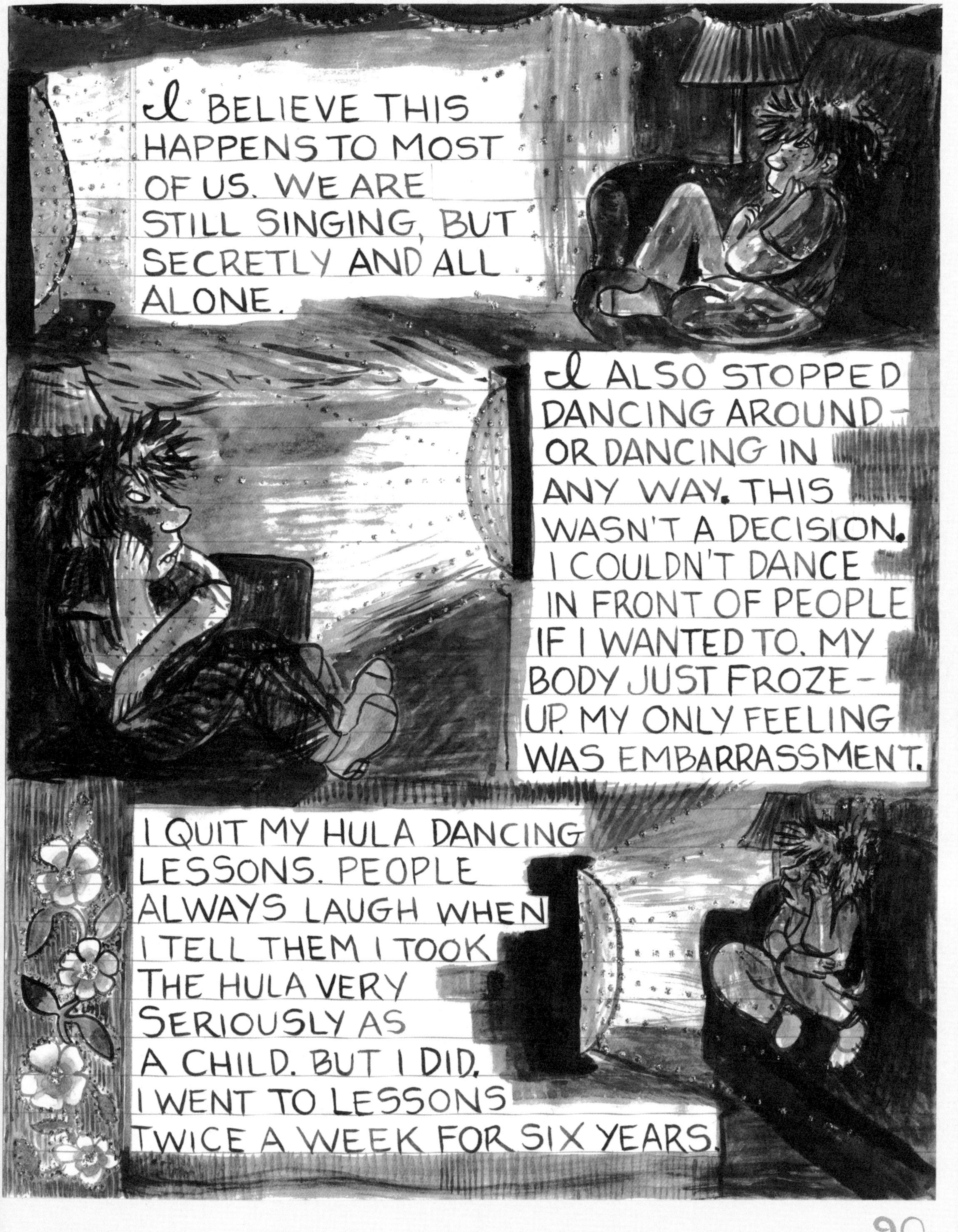
I BELIEVE THIS HAPPENS TO MOST OF US. WE ARE STILL SINGING, BUT SECRETLY AND ALL ALONE.
I ALSO STOPPED DANCING AROUND - OR DANCING IN ANY WAY. THIS WASN'T A DECISION. I COULDN'T DANCE IN FRONT OF PEOPLE IF I WANTED TO. MY BODY JUST FROZE - UP. MY ONLY FEELING WAS EMBARRASSMENT.
I QUIT MY HULA DANCING LESSONS. PEOPLE ALWAYS LAUGH WHEN I TELL THEM I TOOK THE HULA VERY SERIOUSLY AS A CHILD. BUT I DID. I WENT TO LESSONS TWICE A WEEK FOR SIX YEARS.

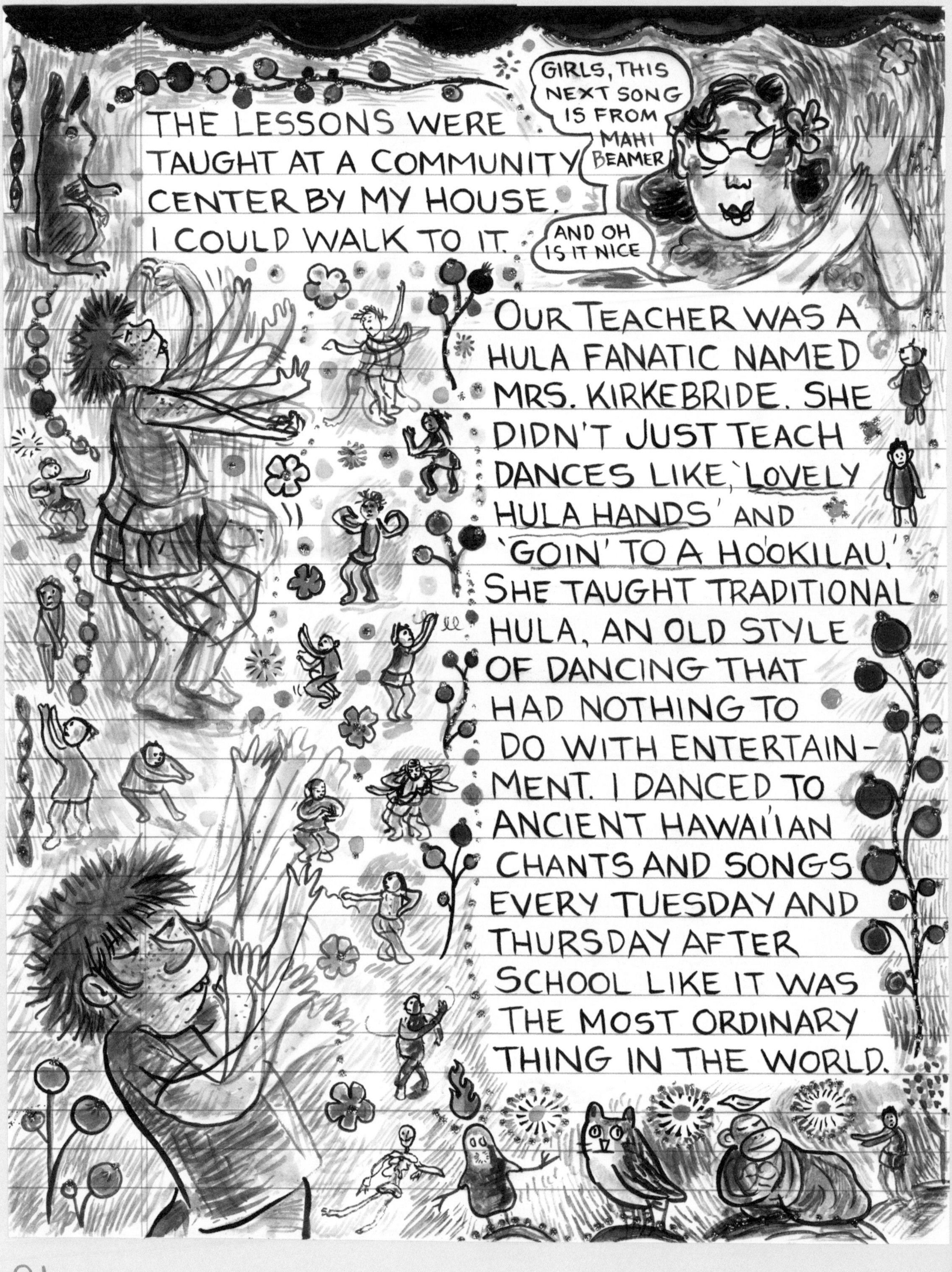
THE LESSONS WERE TAUGHT AT A COMMUNITY CENTER BY MY HOUSE. I COULD WALK TO IT.
GIRLS, THIS NEXT SONG IS FROM MAHI BEAMER
AND OH IS IT NICE
OUR TEACHER WAS A HULA FANATIC NAMED MRS. KIRKEBRIDE. SHE DIDN'T JUST TEACH DANCES LIKE 'LOVELY HULA HANDS' AND 'GOIN' TO A HO'OKILAU.' SHE TAUGHT TRADITIONAL HULA, AN OLD STYLE OF DANCING THAT HAD NOTHING TO DO WITH ENTERTAINMENT. I DANCED TO ANCIENT HAWAI'IAN CHANTS AND SONGS EVERY TUESDAY AND THURSDAY AFTER SCHOOL LIKE IT WAS THE MOST ORDINARY THING IN THE WORLD.

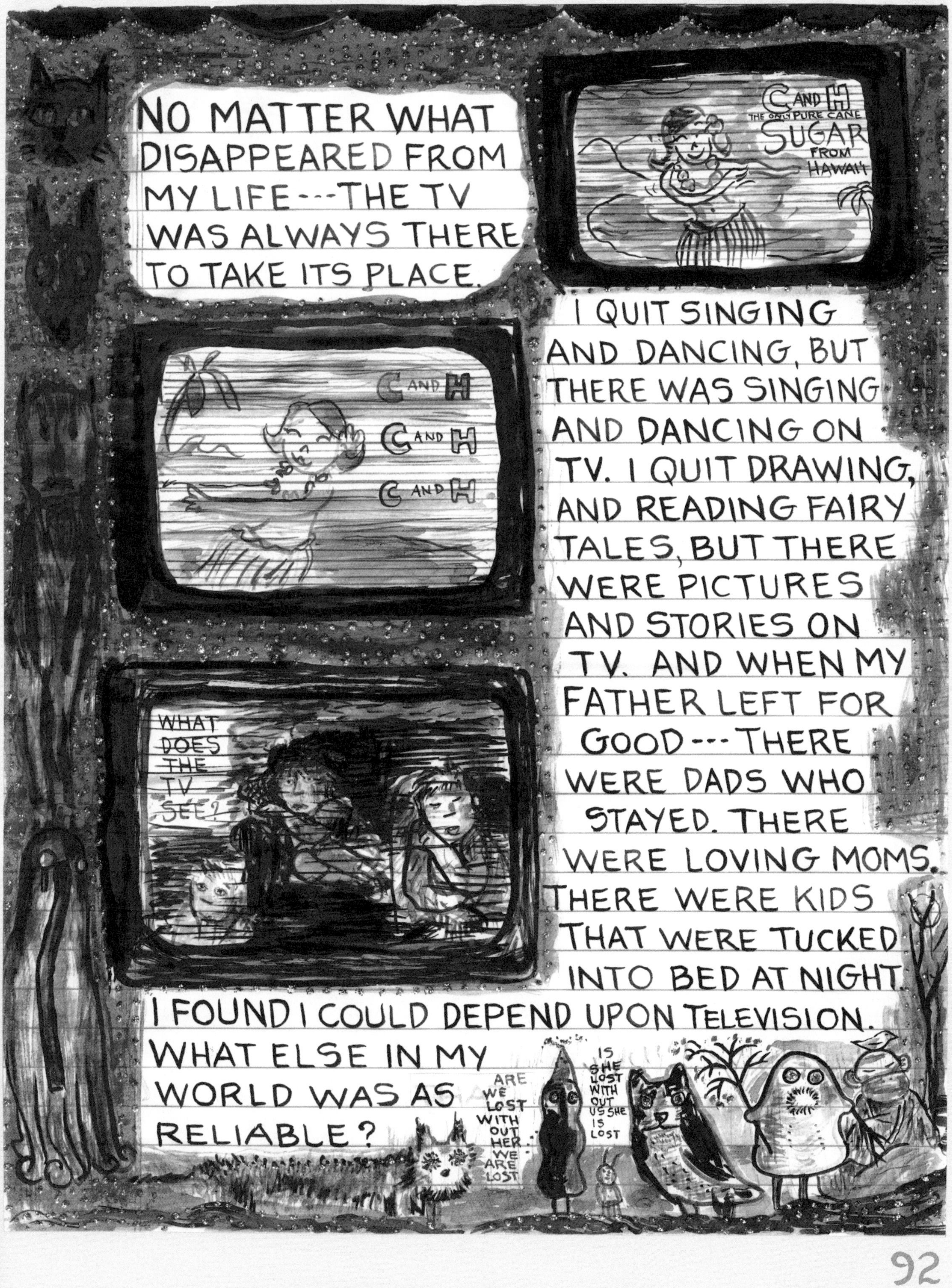
NO MATTER WHAT DISAPPEARED FROM MY LIFE---THE TV WAS ALWAYS THERE TO TAKE ITS PLACE.
C AND H
THE ONLY PURE CANE
SUGAR
FROM HAWAI'I
C AND H
C AND H
C AND H
I QUIT SINGING AND DANCING, BUT THERE WAS SINGING AND DANCING ON TV. I QUIT DRAWING, AND READING FAIRY TALES, BUT THERE WERE PICTURES AND STORIES ON TV. AND WHEN MY FATHER LEFT FOR GOOD---THERE WERE DADS WHO STAYED. THERE WERE LOVING MOMS. THERE WERE KIDS THAT WERE TUCKED INTO BED AT NIGHT.
WHAT DOES THE TV SEE?
I FOUND I COULD DEPEND UPON TELEVISION. WHAT ELSE IN MY WORLD WAS AS RELIABLE?
ARE WE LOST WITH OUT HER. WE ARE LOST
IS SHE LOST WITH OUT US SHE IS LOST

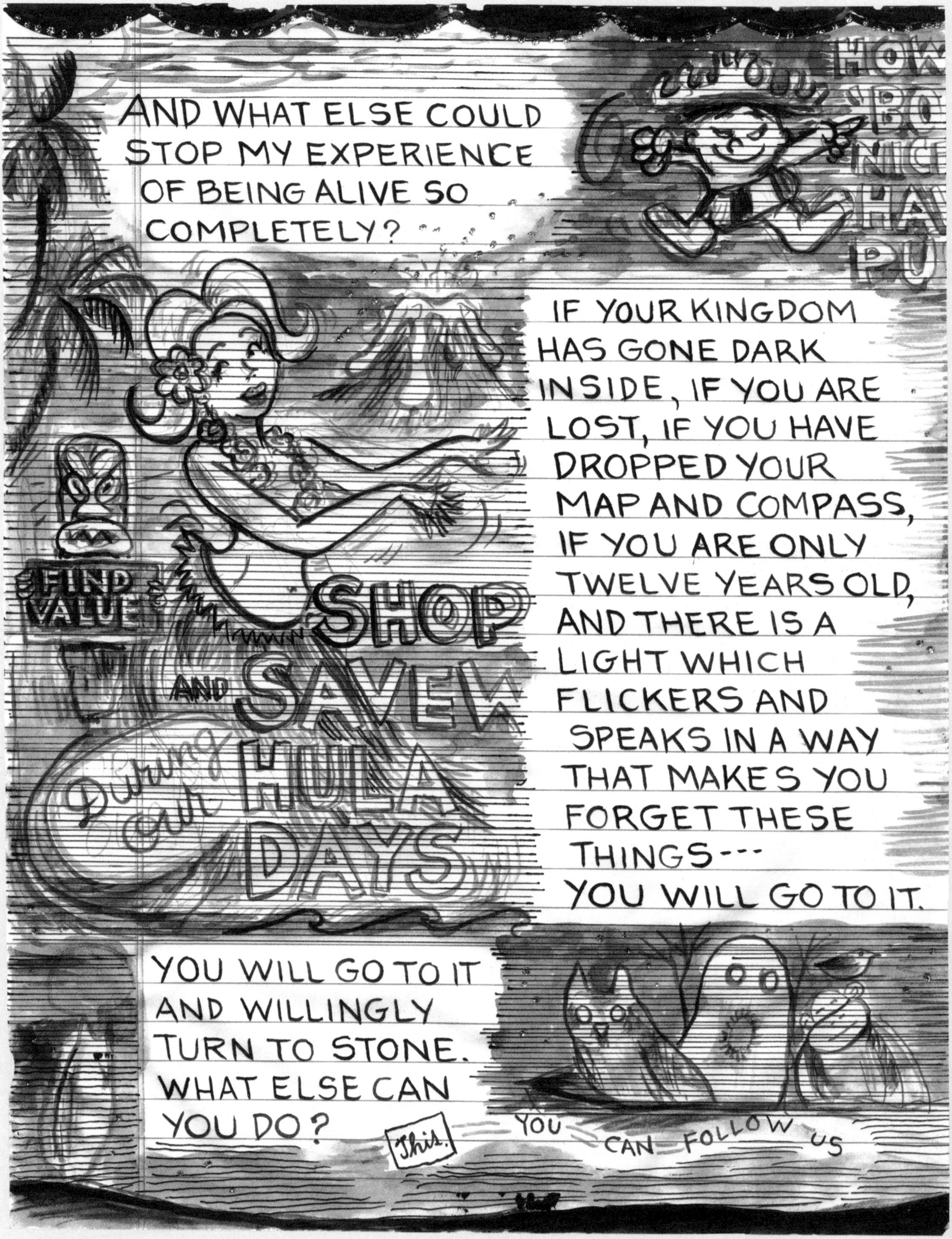
AND WHAT ELSE COULD STOP MY EXPERIENCE OF BEING ALIVE SO COMPLETELY?
IF YOUR KINGDOM HAS GONE DARK INSIDE, IF YOU ARE LOST, IF YOU HAVE DROPPED YOUR MAP AND COMPASS, IF YOU ARE ONLY TWELVE YEARS OLD, AND THERE IS A LIGHT WHICH FLICKERS AND SPEAKS IN A WAY THAT MAKES YOU FORGET THESE THINGS--- YOU WILL GO TO IT.
FIND VALUE
SHOP AND SAVE
During our HULA DAYS
YOU WILL GO TO IT AND WILLINGLY TURN TO STONE. WHAT ELSE CAN YOU DO?
This.
YOU CAN FOLLOW US

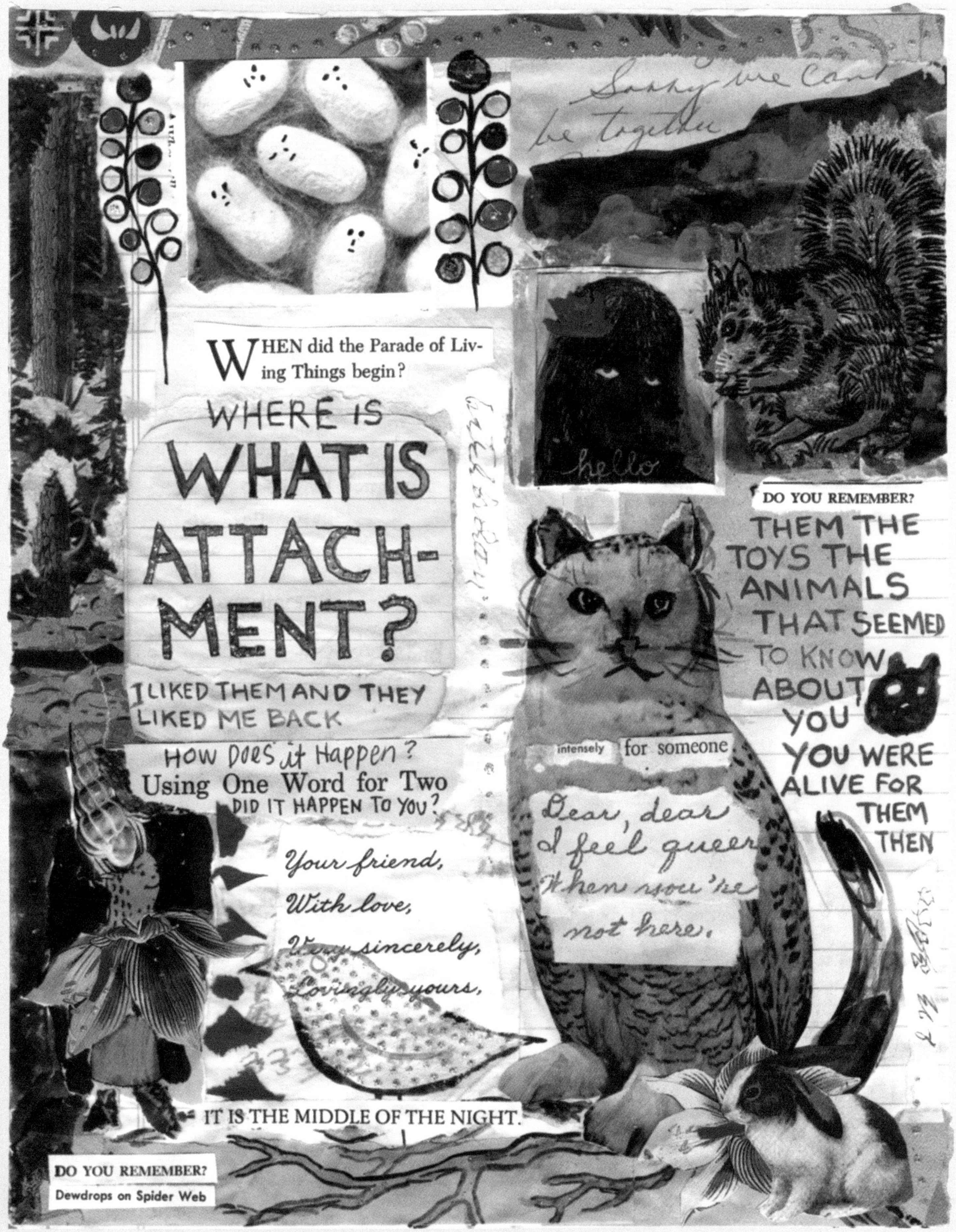
Sorry we Cant be together
WHEN did the Parade of Living Things begin?
WHERE IS
WHAT IS ATTACH-MENT?
I LIKED THEM AND THEY LIKED ME BACK
HOW DOES it Happen?
Using One Word for Two
DID IT HAPPEN TO YOU?
Your friend,
With love,
Very sincerely,
Lovingly yours,
IT IS THE MIDDLE OF THE NIGHT.
DO YOU REMEMBER?
Dewdrops on Spider Web
hello
DO YOU REMEMBER?
THEM THE TOYS THE ANIMALS THAT SEEMED TO KNOW ABOUT YOU YOU WERE ALIVE FOR THEM THEN
intensely
for someone
Dear, dear I feel queer When you're not here.

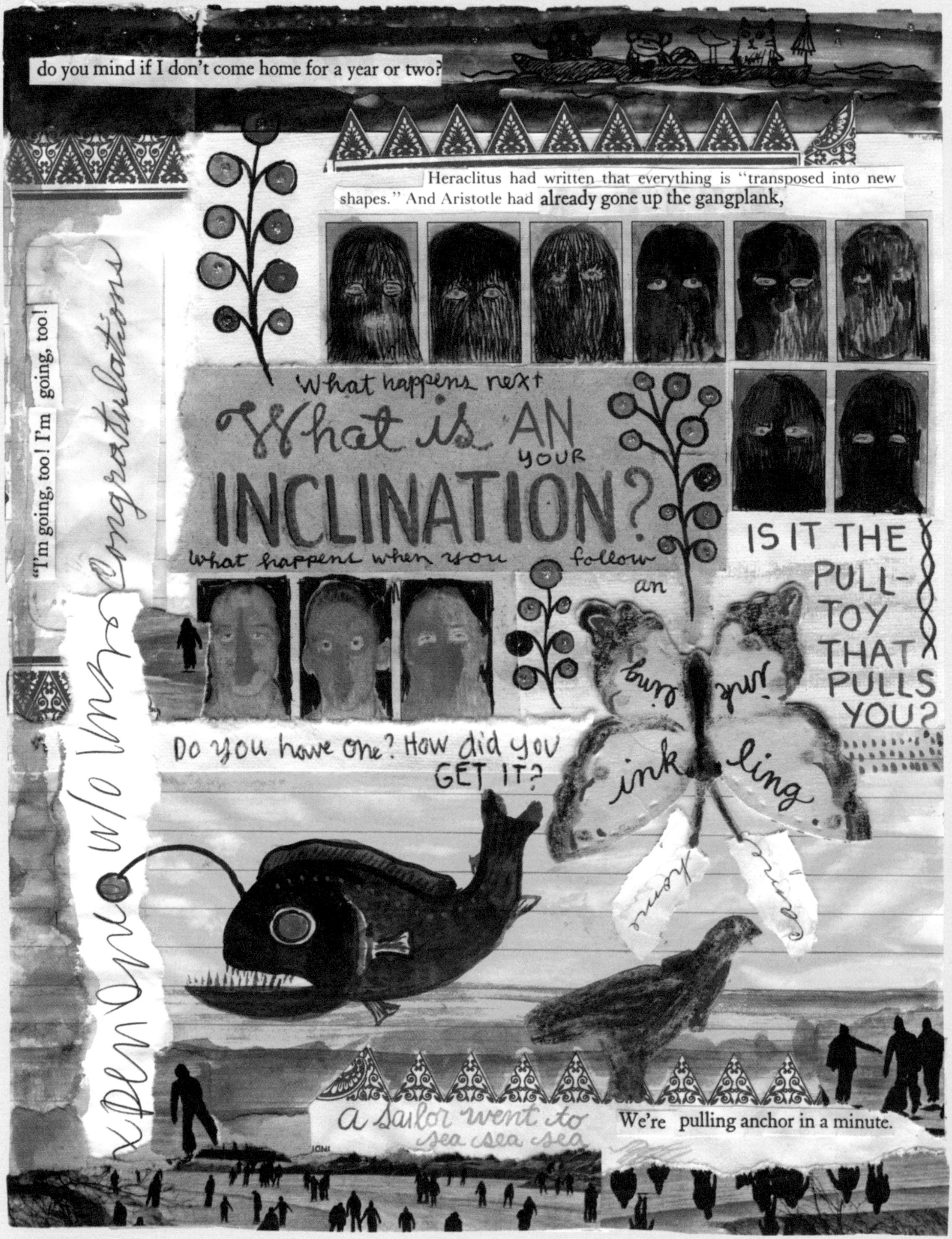
do you mind if I don't come home for a year or two?
Heraclitus had written that everything is "transposed into new shapes." And Aristotle had already gone up the gangplank,
"I'm going, too! I'm going, too!
congratulations
What happens next
What is AN
YOUR
INCLINATION?
What happens when you follow
an
IS IT THE PULL-TOY THAT PULLS YOU?
ink ling
ink ling
Do you have one? How did you GET IT?
a sailor went to sea sea sea
We're pulling anchor in a minute.

Can something be meaningful even if we can't say what the meaning is?

☐ yes
☐ no

News from faraway places

WHY DO SOME IMAGES COME BACK AGAIN AND AGAIN? WHAT MAKES SOMething MEANINGFUL?

Hello There!

Choose the books you want. Then give this coupon and your money to the teacher.

Your name __Happened to Me__

☐ Little Fish That Got Away, 25¢	☒ Caroline & Her Kettle, Maud, 35¢	☐ Curious George Gets a Medal, 35
☐ My Box and String, 25¢	☒ Magnets and How to Use Them, 35¢	How Big Is Big?, 35¢
☐ Adventures Three Blind Mice, 25¢	☐ Clifford, the Big Red Dog, 25¢	☐ Days of the Dinosaurs, 35¢
☒ Five Chinese Brothers, 35¢	☐ Secret Place & Other Poems, 25¢	☐ Johnny Appleseed, 35
☒ Adventures George Washington, 35¢	☐ Look Out, Mrs. Doodlepunk, 25¢	☐ Pony for the Winter, 35¢
☐ Benny and the Bear, 25¢	DO NOT MAIL THIS COUPON	

Club must order 15 or more books.
PAYMENT____1.40____ (This offer not valid in Canada)

Did you ever wonder how people would get along if they had no words?

Which came first? Language or Meaning?

96

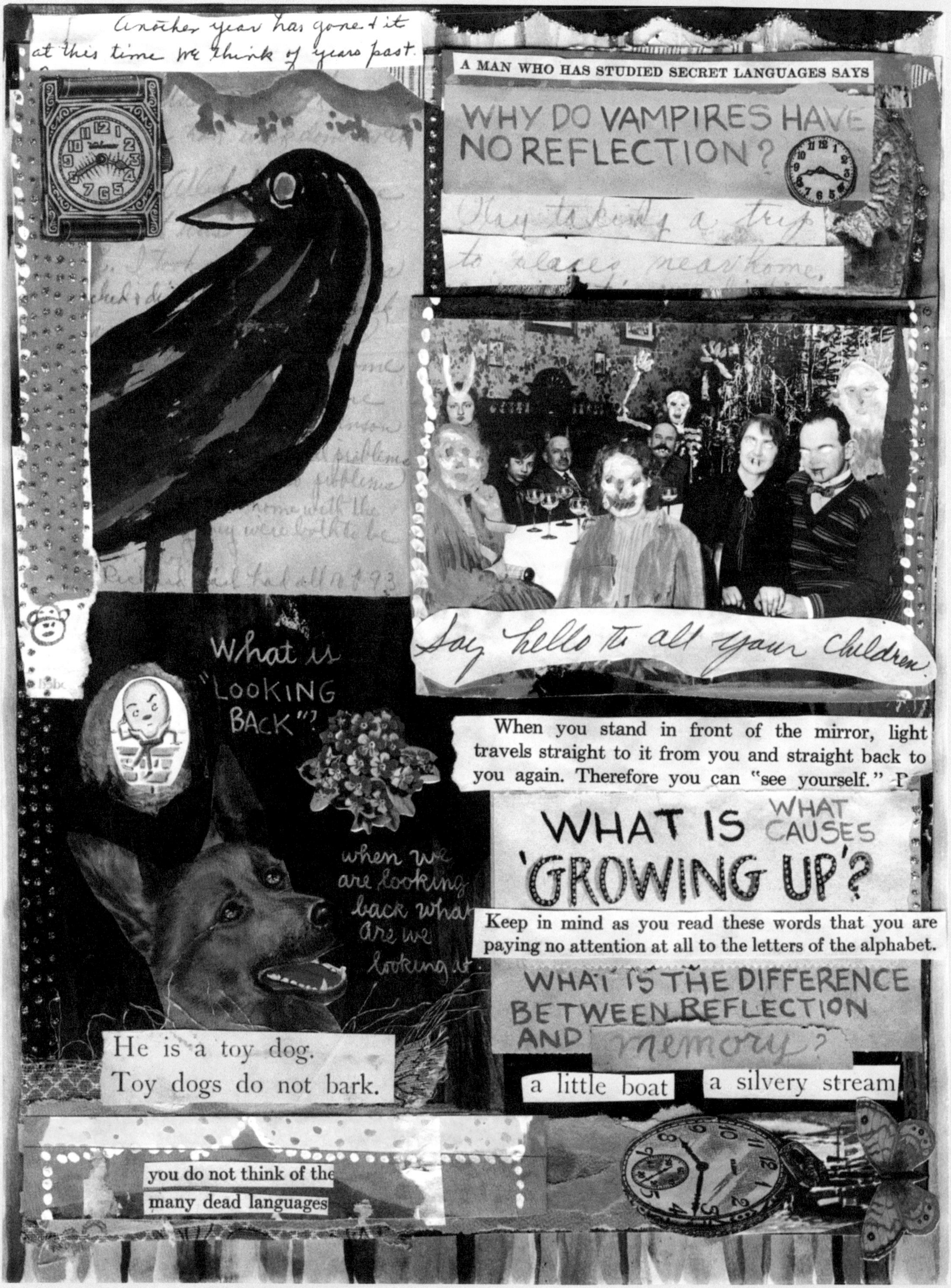
Another year has gone & it at this time we think of years past.
A MAN WHO HAS STUDIED SECRET LANGUAGES SAYS
WHY DO VAMPIRES HAVE NO REFLECTION?
Okay taking a trip
to places near home,
Say hello to all your children
What is "LOOKING BACK"?
When you stand in front of the mirror, light travels straight to it from you and straight back to you again. Therefore you can "see yourself."
WHAT IS WHAT CAUSES 'GROWING UP'?
when we are looking back what are we looking at.
Keep in mind as you read these words that you are paying no attention at all to the letters of the alphabet.
WHAT IS THE DIFFERENCE BETWEEN REFLECTION AND memory?
He is a toy dog.
Toy dogs do not bark.
a little boat
a silvery stream
you do not think of the
many dead languages

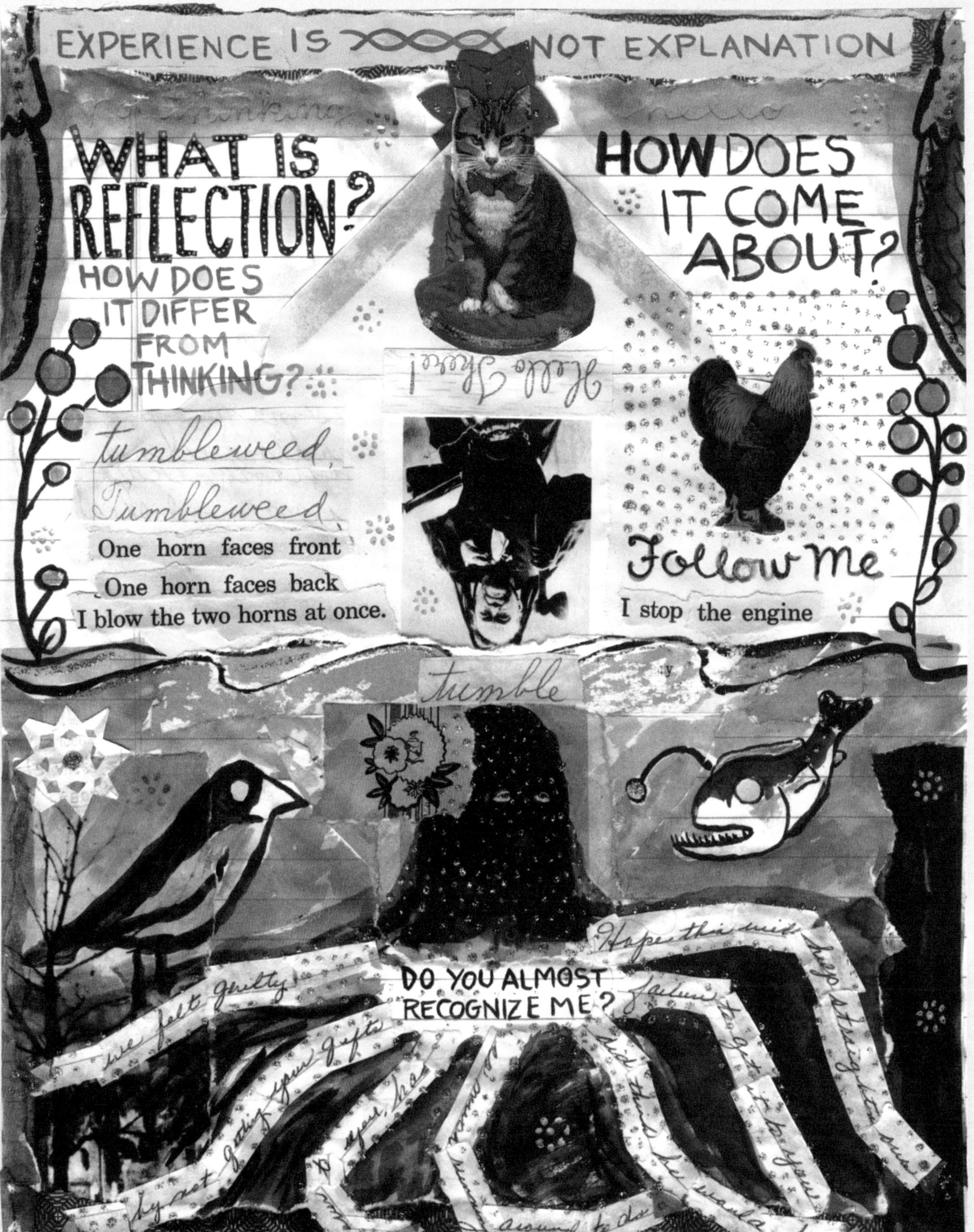
EXPERIENCE IS NOT EXPLANATION
WHAT IS REFLECTION?
HOW DOES IT DIFFER FROM THINKING?
HOW DOES IT COME ABOUT?
tumbleweed,
Tumbleweed,
One horn faces front
One horn faces back
I blow the two horns at once.
Follow me
I stop the engine
tumble
DO YOU ALMOST RECOGNIZE ME?
we felt guilty

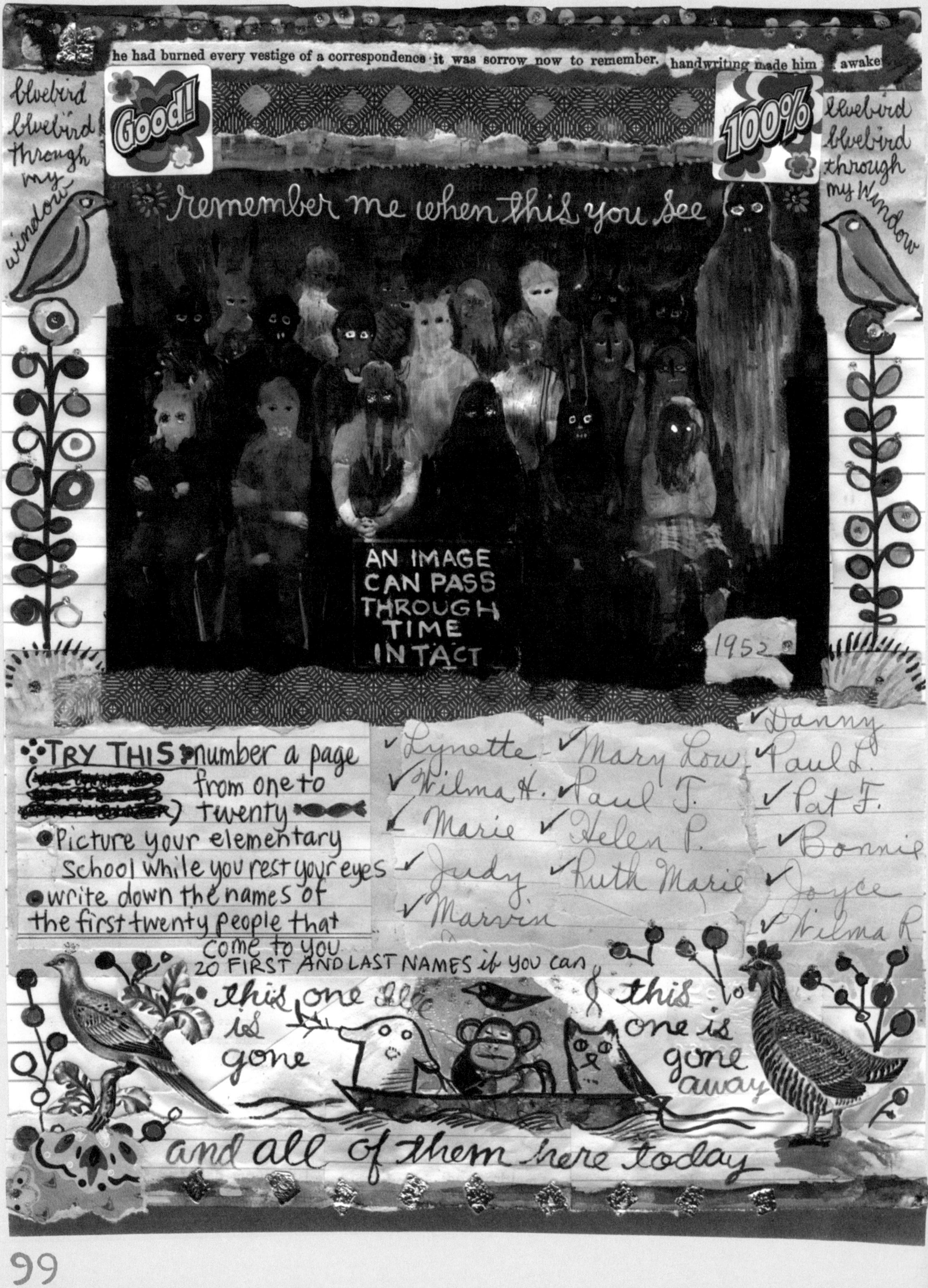
he had burned every vestige of a correspondence it was sorrow now to remember.
handwriting made him
awake
Good!
100%
bluebird bluebird through my window
bluebird bluebird through my window
remember me when this you see
AN IMAGE CAN PASS THROUGH TIME INTACT
1952
TRY THIS: number a page ([redacted]) from one to twenty
Picture your elementary school while you rest your eyes
write down the names of the first twenty people that come to you
20 FIRST AND LAST NAMES if you can
Lynette
Wilma H.
Marie
Judy
Marvin
Mary Lou
Paul T.
Helen P.
Ruth Marie
Danny
Paul L.
Pat F.
Bonnie
Joyce
Wilma R
this one is gone
& this one is gone away
and all of them here today

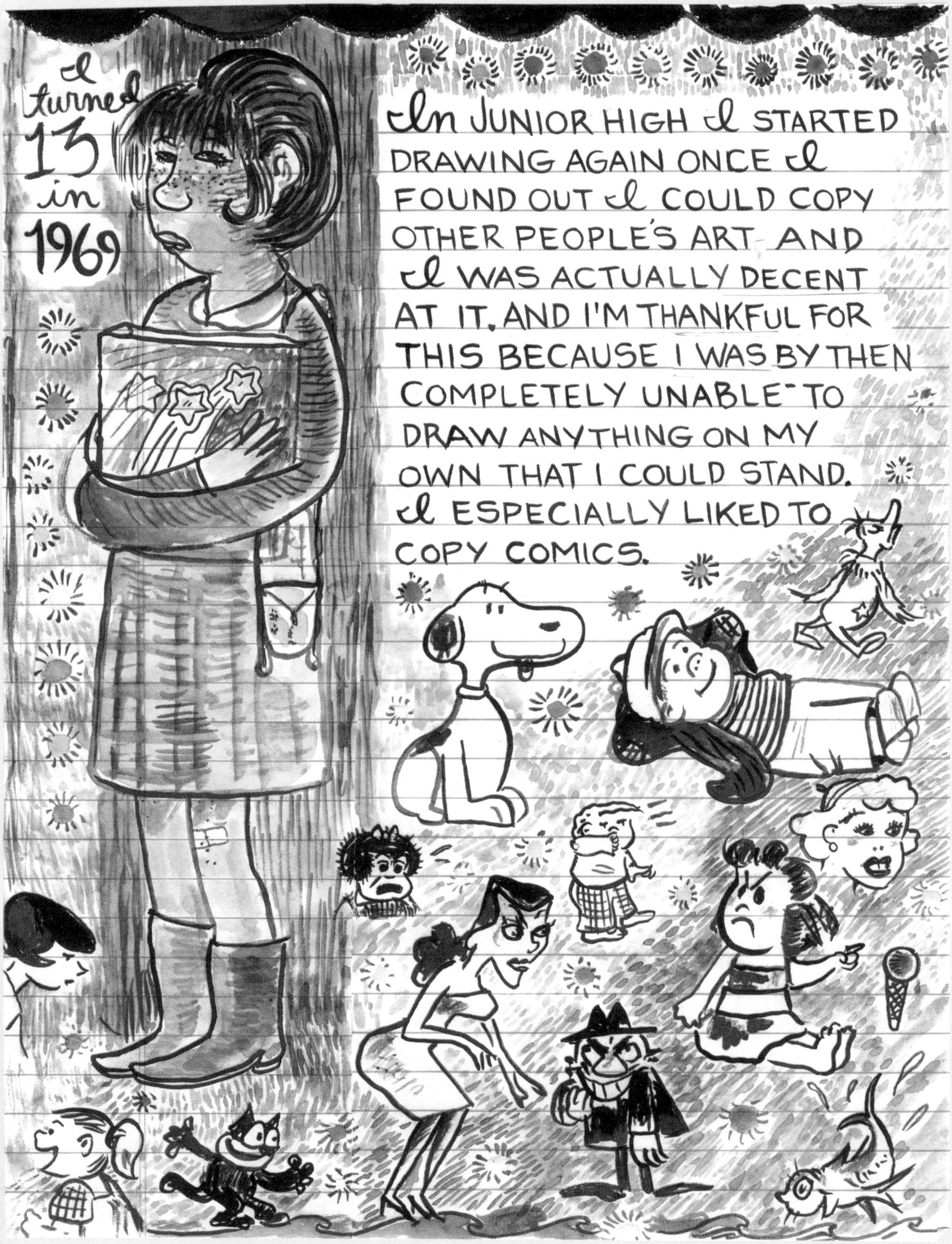
I turned 13 in 1969
In JUNIOR HIGH I STARTED DRAWING AGAIN ONCE I FOUND OUT I COULD COPY OTHER PEOPLE'S ART AND I WAS ACTUALLY DECENT AT IT. AND I'M THANKFUL FOR THIS BECAUSE I WAS BY THEN COMPLETELY UNABLE TO DRAW ANYTHING ON MY OWN THAT I COULD STAND. I ESPECIALLY LIKED TO COPY COMICS.

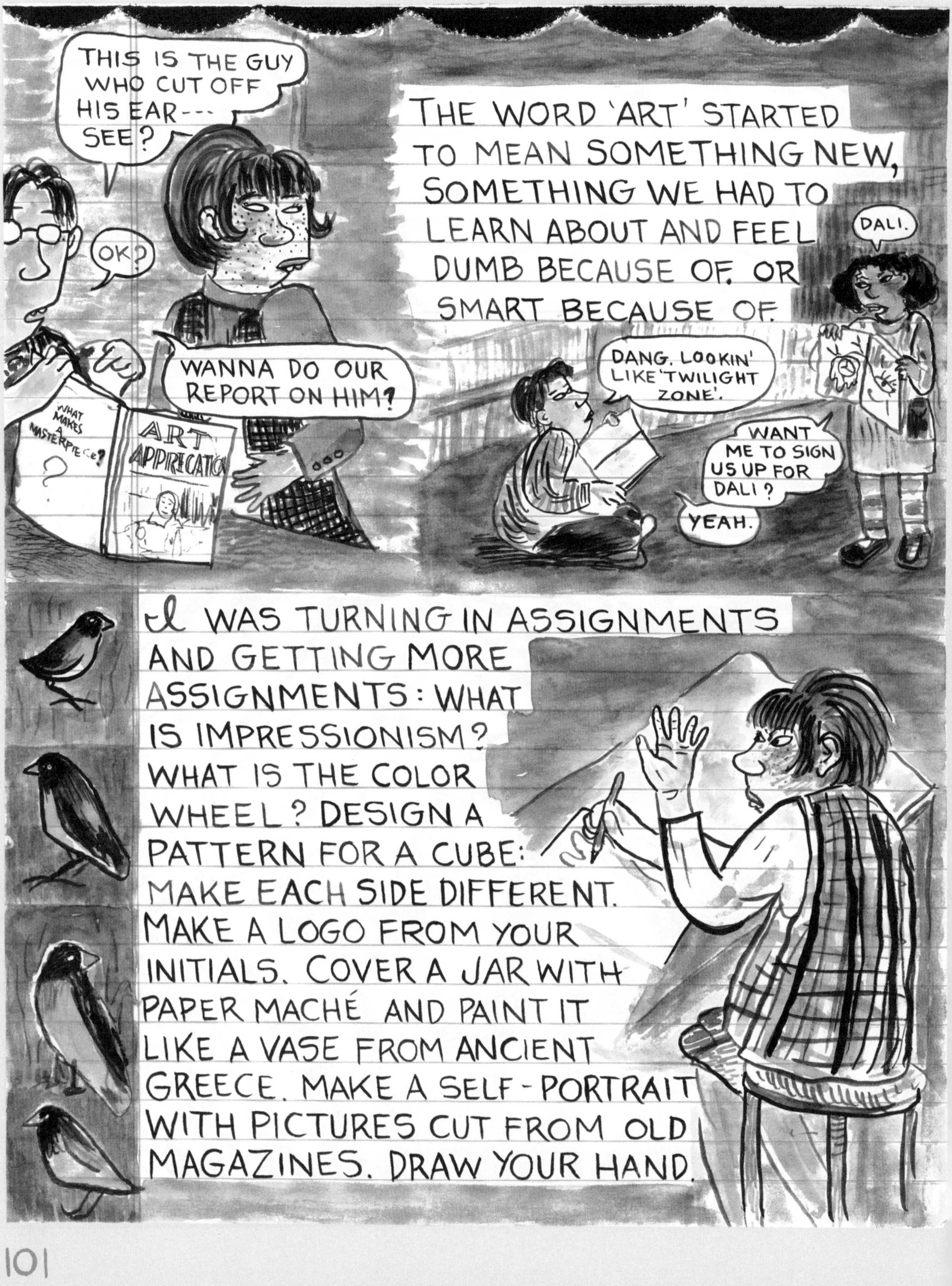
THIS IS THE GUY WHO CUT OFF HIS EAR--- SEE?
OK?
WANNA DO OUR REPORT ON HIM?
WHAT MAKES A MASTERPIECE?
ART
THE WORD 'ART' STARTED TO MEAN SOMETHING NEW, SOMETHING WE HAD TO LEARN ABOUT AND FEEL DUMB BECAUSE OF. OR SMART BECAUSE OF.
DALI.
DANG. LOOKIN' LIKE 'TWILIGHT ZONE'.
WANT ME TO SIGN US UP FOR DALI?
YEAH.
I WAS TURNING IN ASSIGNMENTS AND GETTING MORE ASSIGNMENTS: WHAT IS IMPRESSIONISM? WHAT IS THE COLOR WHEEL? DESIGN A PATTERN FOR A CUBE: MAKE EACH SIDE DIFFERENT. MAKE A LOGO FROM YOUR INITIALS. COVER A JAR WITH PAPER MACHÉ AND PAINT IT LIKE A VASE FROM ANCIENT GREECE. MAKE A SELF-PORTRAIT WITH PICTURES CUT FROM OLD MAGAZINES. DRAW YOUR HAND.

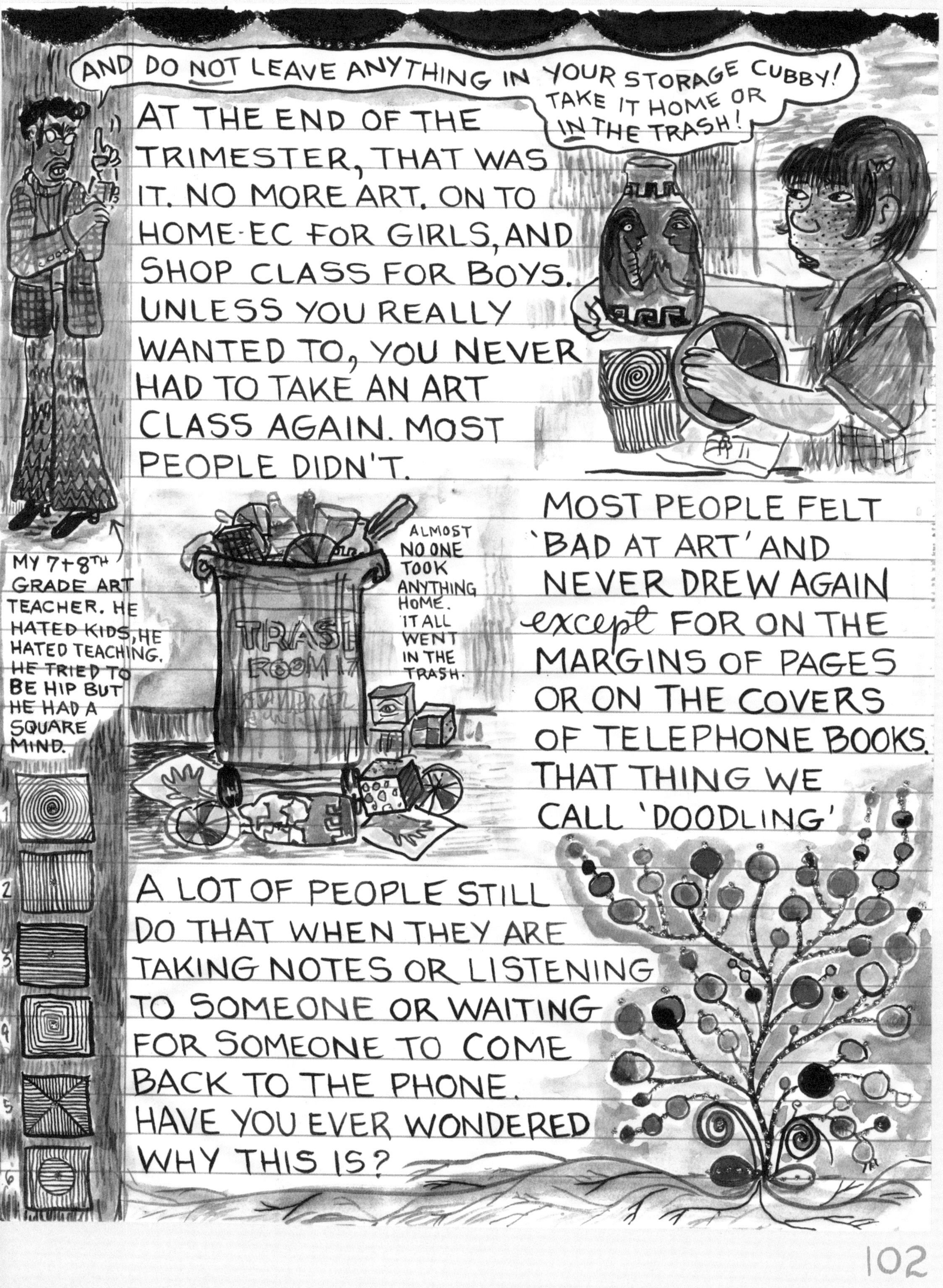
AND DO NOT LEAVE ANYTHING IN YOUR STORAGE CUBBY! TAKE IT HOME OR IN THE TRASH!
AT THE END OF THE TRIMESTER, THAT WAS IT. NO MORE ART. ON TO HOME-EC FOR GIRLS, AND SHOP CLASS FOR BOYS. UNLESS YOU REALLY WANTED TO, YOU NEVER HAD TO TAKE AN ART CLASS AGAIN. MOST PEOPLE DIDN'T.
MY 7+8TH GRADE ART TEACHER. HE HATED KIDS, HE HATED TEACHING. HE TRIED TO BE HIP BUT HE HAD A SQUARE MIND.
TRASH
ROOM 17
ALMOST NO ONE TOOK ANYTHING HOME. IT ALL WENT IN THE TRASH.
MOST PEOPLE FELT 'BAD AT ART' AND NEVER DREW AGAIN except FOR ON THE MARGINS OF PAGES OR ON THE COVERS OF TELEPHONE BOOKS. THAT THING WE CALL 'DOODLING'
1
2
3
4
5
6
A LOT OF PEOPLE STILL DO THAT WHEN THEY ARE TAKING NOTES OR LISTENING TO SOMEONE OR WAITING FOR SOMEONE TO COME BACK TO THE PHONE. HAVE YOU EVER WONDERED WHY THIS IS?

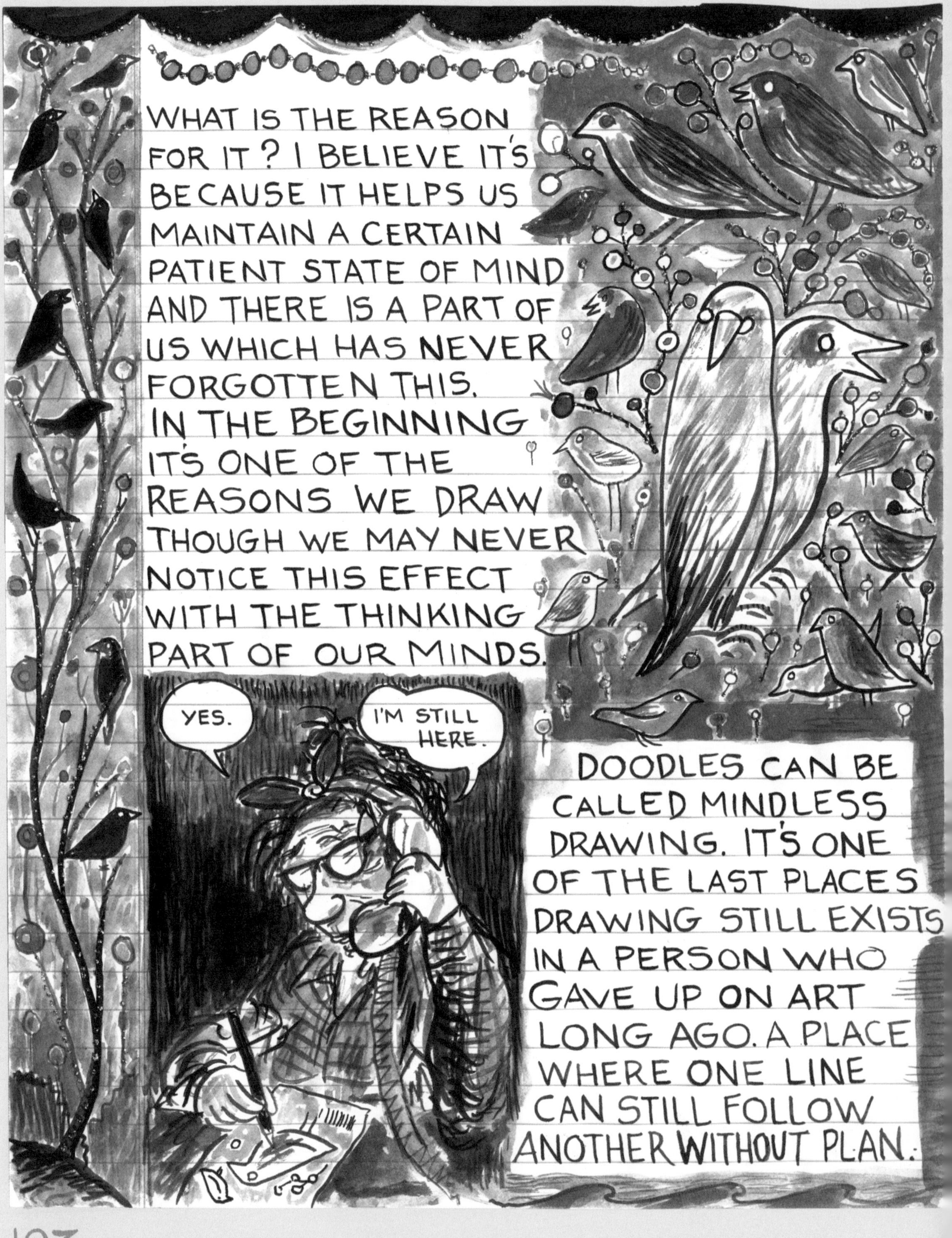
WHAT IS THE REASON FOR IT? I BELIEVE IT'S BECAUSE IT HELPS US MAINTAIN A CERTAIN PATIENT STATE OF MIND AND THERE IS A PART OF US WHICH HAS NEVER FORGOTTEN THIS.
IN THE BEGINNING IT'S ONE OF THE REASONS WE DRAW THOUGH WE MAY NEVER NOTICE THIS EFFECT WITH THE THINKING PART OF OUR MINDS.
YES.
I'M STILL HERE.
DOODLES CAN BE CALLED MINDLESS DRAWING. IT'S ONE OF THE LAST PLACES DRAWING STILL EXISTS IN A PERSON WHO GAVE UP ON ART LONG AGO. A PLACE WHERE ONE LINE CAN STILL FOLLOW ANOTHER WITHOUT PLAN.

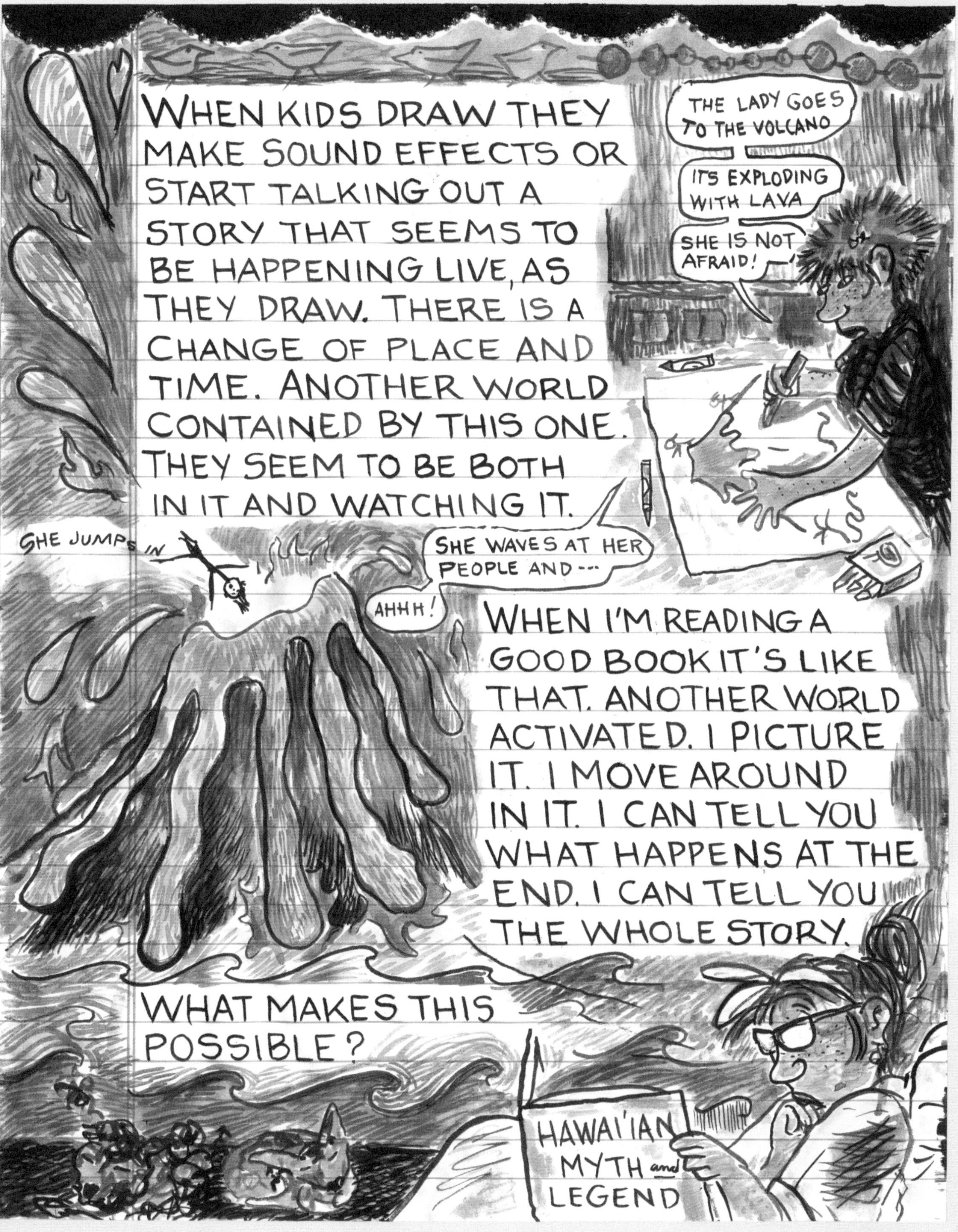

WHEN KIDS DRAW THEY MAKE SOUND EFFECTS OR START TALKING OUT A STORY THAT SEEMS TO BE HAPPENING LIVE, AS THEY DRAW. THERE IS A CHANGE OF PLACE AND TIME. ANOTHER WORLD CONTAINED BY THIS ONE. THEY SEEM TO BE BOTH IN IT AND WATCHING IT.
THE LADY GOES TO THE VOLCANO
ITS EXPLODING WITH LAVA
SHE IS NOT AFRAID!
SHE JUMPS IN
SHE WAVES AT HER PEOPLE AND---
AHHH!
WHEN I'M READING A GOOD BOOK IT'S LIKE THAT. ANOTHER WORLD ACTIVATED. I PICTURE IT. I MOVE AROUND IN IT. I CAN TELL YOU WHAT HAPPENS AT THE END. I CAN TELL YOU THE WHOLE STORY.
WHAT MAKES THIS POSSIBLE?
HAWAI'IAN MYTH and LEGEND

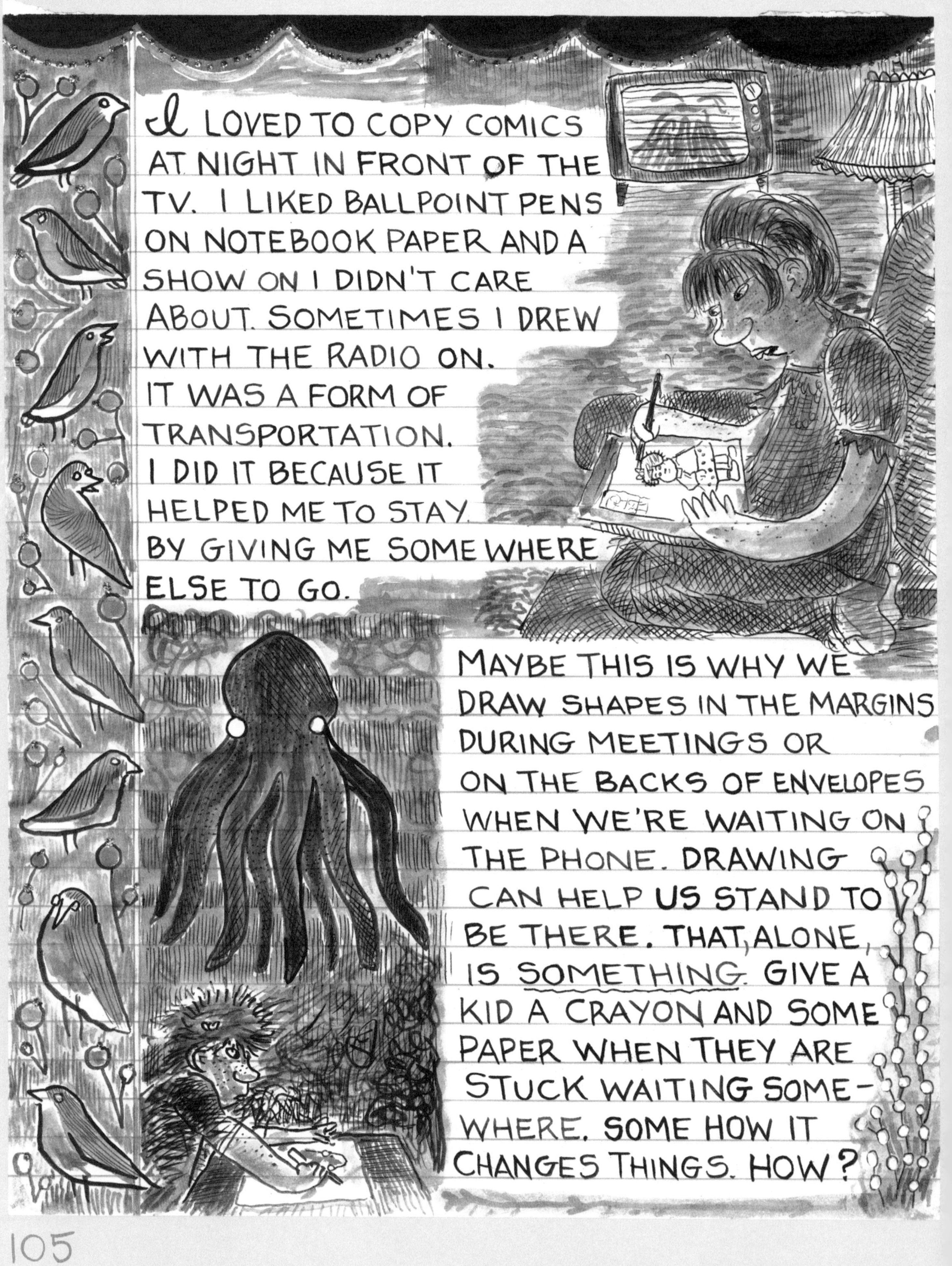
I LOVED TO COPY COMICS AT NIGHT IN FRONT OF THE TV. I LIKED BALLPOINT PENS ON NOTEBOOK PAPER AND A SHOW ON I DIDN'T CARE ABOUT. SOMETIMES I DREW WITH THE RADIO ON. IT WAS A FORM OF TRANSPORTATION. I DID IT BECAUSE IT HELPED ME TO STAY BY GIVING ME SOME WHERE ELSE TO GO.
MAYBE THIS IS WHY WE DRAW SHAPES IN THE MARGINS DURING MEETINGS OR ON THE BACKS OF ENVELOPES WHEN WE'RE WAITING ON THE PHONE. DRAWING CAN HELP US STAND TO BE THERE. THAT, ALONE, IS SOMETHING. GIVE A KID A CRAYON AND SOME PAPER WHEN THEY ARE STUCK WAITING SOME-WHERE. SOME HOW IT CHANGES THINGS. HOW?

Fire or Lightning · Windstorm or Hail · Explosion · Riot or Civil Commotion · Sinkhole Collapse

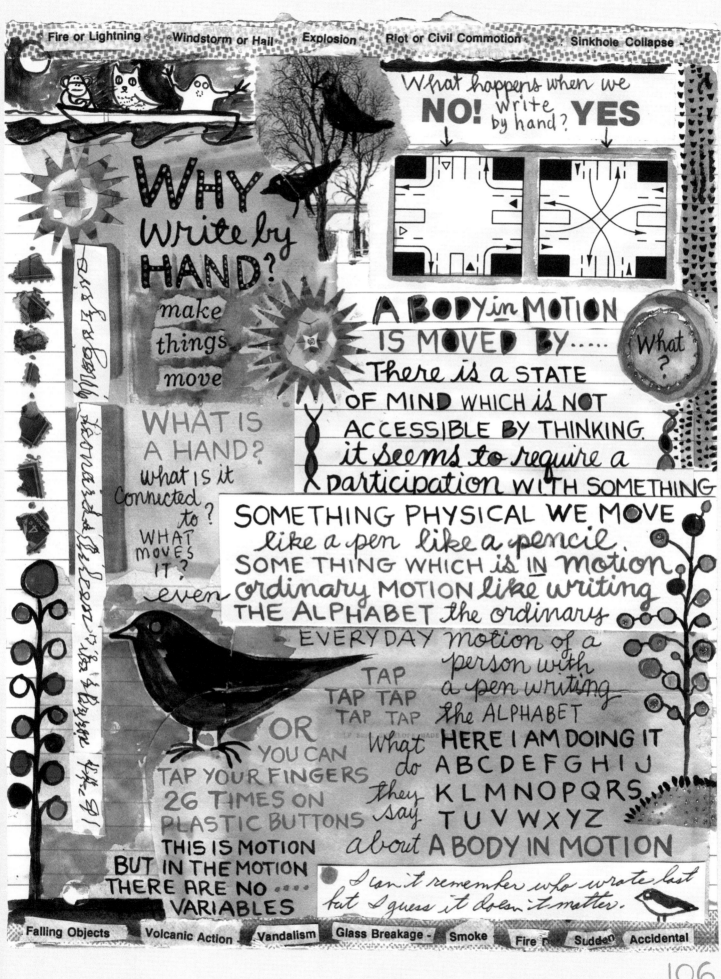

What happens when we write by hand?

NO! YES

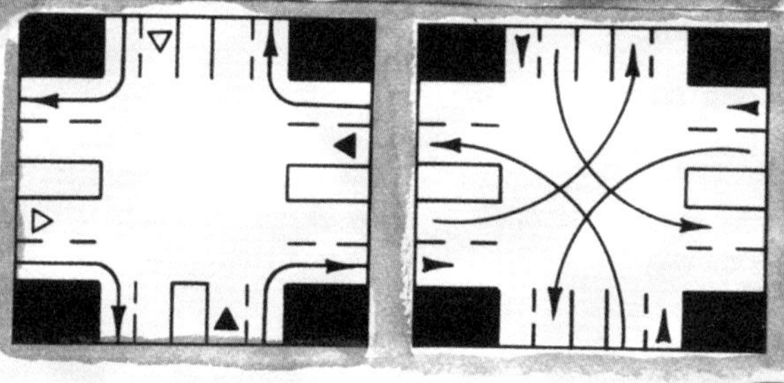

WHY Write by HAND?

make things move

A BODY in MOTION IS MOVED BY.....

What?

There is a STATE OF MIND WHICH is NOT ACCESSIBLE BY THINKING. it seems to require a participation WITH SOMETHING

WHAT IS A HAND? what is it Connected to? WHAT MOVES IT?

SOMETHING PHYSICAL WE MOVE like a pen like a pencil SOME THING WHICH is IN motion even ordinary MOTION like writing THE ALPHABET the ordinary EVERYDAY motion of a person with a pen writing the ALPHABET

TAP TAP TAP TAP TAP

What do they say about

HERE I AM DOING IT
ABCDEFGHIJ
KLMNOPQRS
TUVWXYZ

A BODY IN MOTION

OR YOU CAN TAP YOUR FINGERS 26 TIMES ON PLASTIC BUTTONS THIS IS MOTION BUT IN THE MOTION THERE ARE NO.... VARIABLES

I can't remember who wrote last but I guess it doesn't matter.

Falling Objects · Volcanic Action · Vandalism · Glass Breakage · Smoke · Fire · Sudden · Accidental

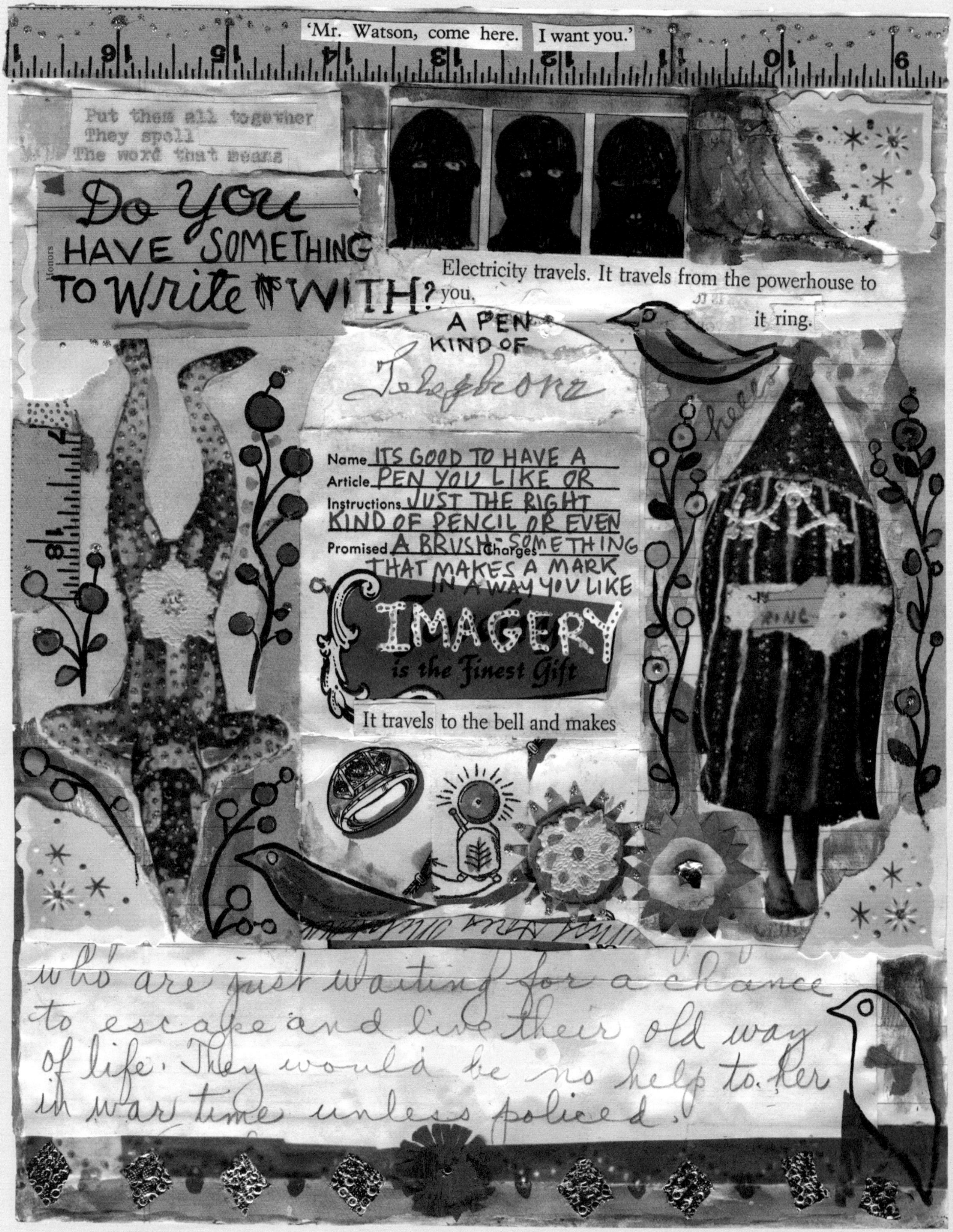
'Mr. Watson, come here. I want you.'
Put them all together
They spell
The word that means
Do you HAVE SOMETHING TO Write WITH?
Electricity travels. It travels from the powerhouse to you,
it ring.
A PEN KIND OF
Telephone
Name ITS GOOD TO HAVE A
Article PEN YOU LIKE OR
Instructions JUST THE RIGHT
KIND OF PENCIL OR EVEN
Promised A BRUSH Charges SOMETHING
THAT MAKES A MARK
IN A WAY YOU LIKE
IMAGERY
is the Finest Gift
It travels to the bell and makes
who are just waiting for a chance
to escape and live their old way
of life. They would be no help to her
in war time unless policed.

Why do things move?

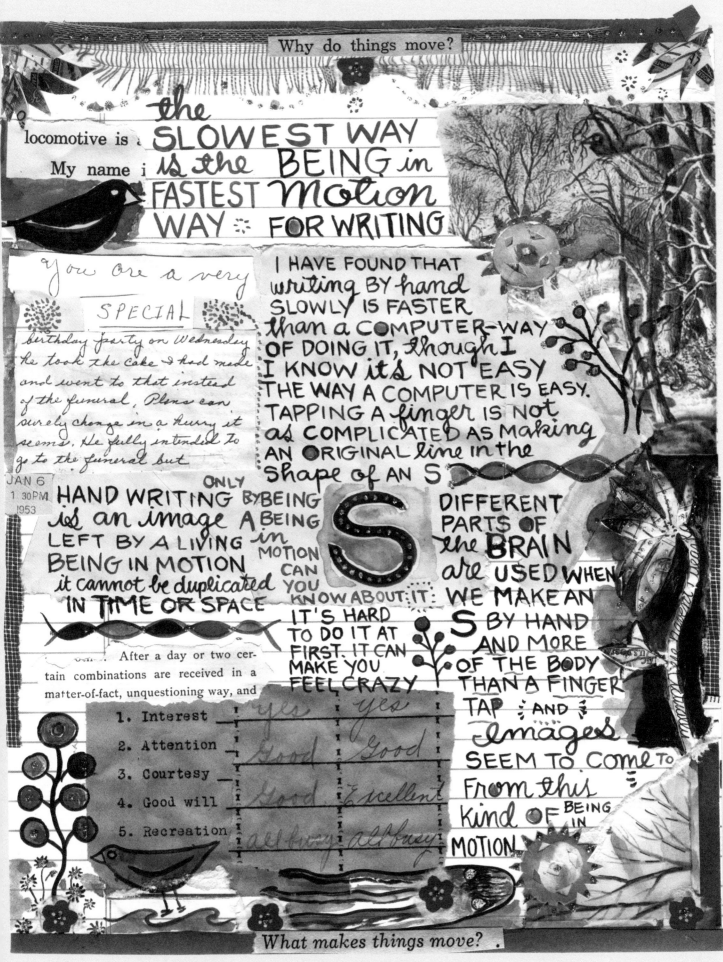

locomotive is

My name i

the SLOWEST WAY is the FASTEST WAY

BEING in Motion FOR WRITING

you are a very

SPECIAL

birthday party on Wednesday he took the cake I had made and went to that instead of the funeral. Plans can surely change in a hurry it seems. He fully intended to go to the funeral but

I HAVE FOUND THAT writing BY hand SLOWLY IS FASTER than a COMPUTER-WAY OF DOING IT, though I KNOW it's NOT EASY THE WAY A COMPUTER IS EASY. TAPPING A finger IS NOT as COMPLICATED AS making AN ORIGINAL line in the shape of AN S

JAN 6
1 30PM
1953

HAND WRITING is an image LEFT BY A LIVING BEING IN MOTION it cannot be duplicated IN TIME OR SPACE

ONLY BY BEING A BEING in MOTION CAN YOU KNOW ABOUT IT

S

DIFFERENT PARTS OF the BRAIN are USED WHEN WE MAKE AN S BY HAND AND MORE OF THE BODY THAN A FINGER TAP AND Images SEEM TO COME TO From this Kind OF BEING IN MOTION

IT'S HARD TO DO IT AT FIRST. IT CAN MAKE YOU FEEL CRAZY

...on. After a day or two certain combinations are received in a matter-of-fact, unquestioning way, and

1. Interest	yes	yes
2. Attention	Good	Good
3. Courtesy		
4. Good will	Good	Excellent
5. Recreation	all busy	all busy

What makes things move?

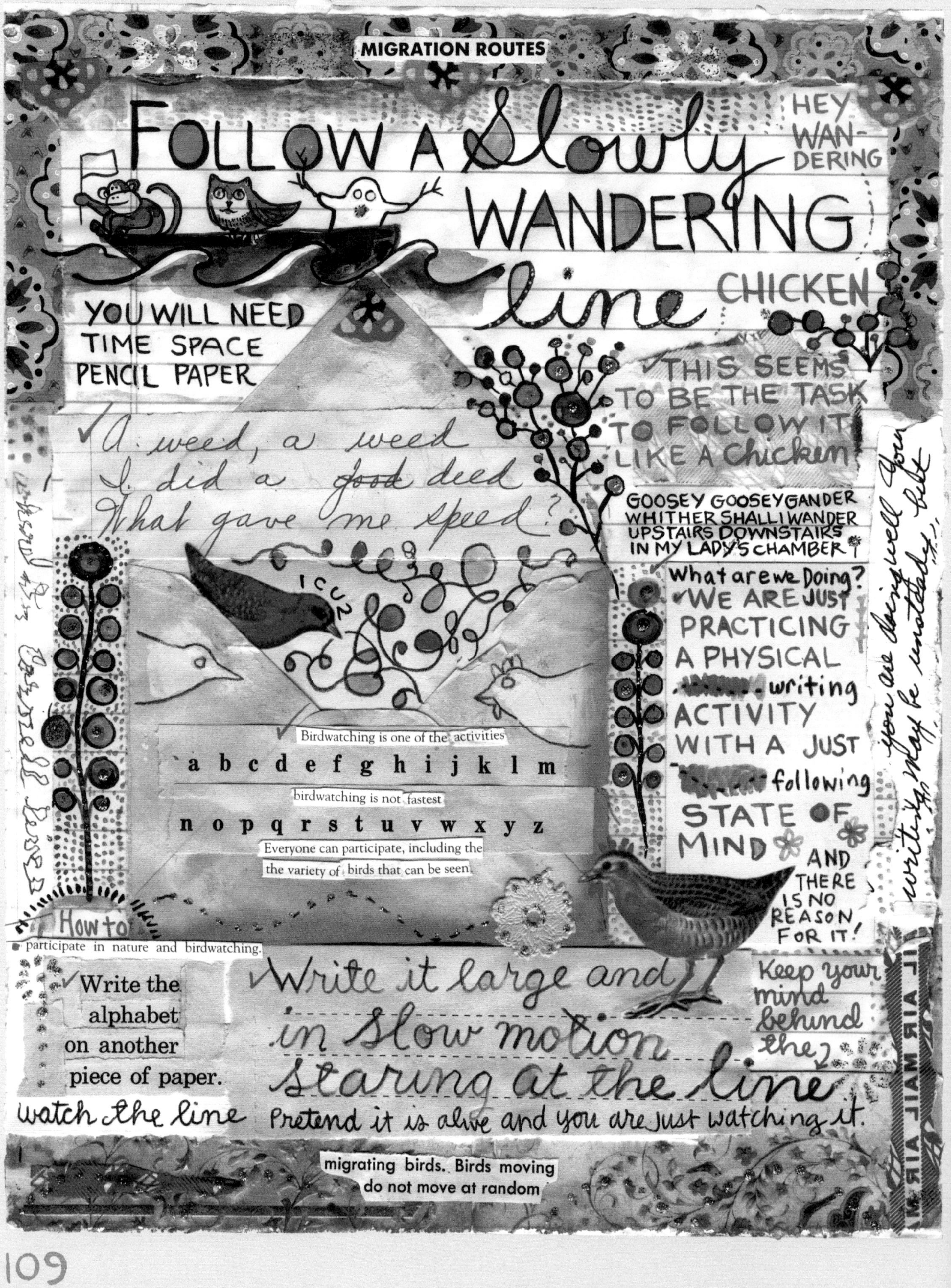

MIGRATION ROUTES
FOLLOW A Slowly WANDERING line
HEY WAN-DERING
CHICKEN
YOU WILL NEED TIME SPACE PENCIL PAPER
THIS SEEMS TO BE THE TASK TO FOLLOW IT LIKE A Chicken
A weed, a weed
I did a good deed
What gave me speed?
GOOSEY GOOSEY GANDER WHITHER SHALL I WANDER UPSTAIRS DOWNSTAIRS IN MY LADY'S CHAMBER
ICU2
What are we Doing?
WE ARE JUST PRACTICING A PHYSICAL [redacted] writing ACTIVITY WITH A JUST [redacted] following STATE OF MIND
AND THERE IS NO REASON FOR IT!
Birdwatching is one of the activities
a b c d e f g h i j k l m
birdwatching is not fastest
n o p q r s t u v w x y z
Everyone can participate, including the
the variety of birds that can be seen
How to
participate in nature and birdwatching.
Write the alphabet on another piece of paper.
watch the line
Write it large and in Slow motion staring at the line
Pretend it is alive and you are just watching it.
Keep your mind behind the
you are doing well your writing may be unsteady but
migrating birds. Birds moving do not move at random

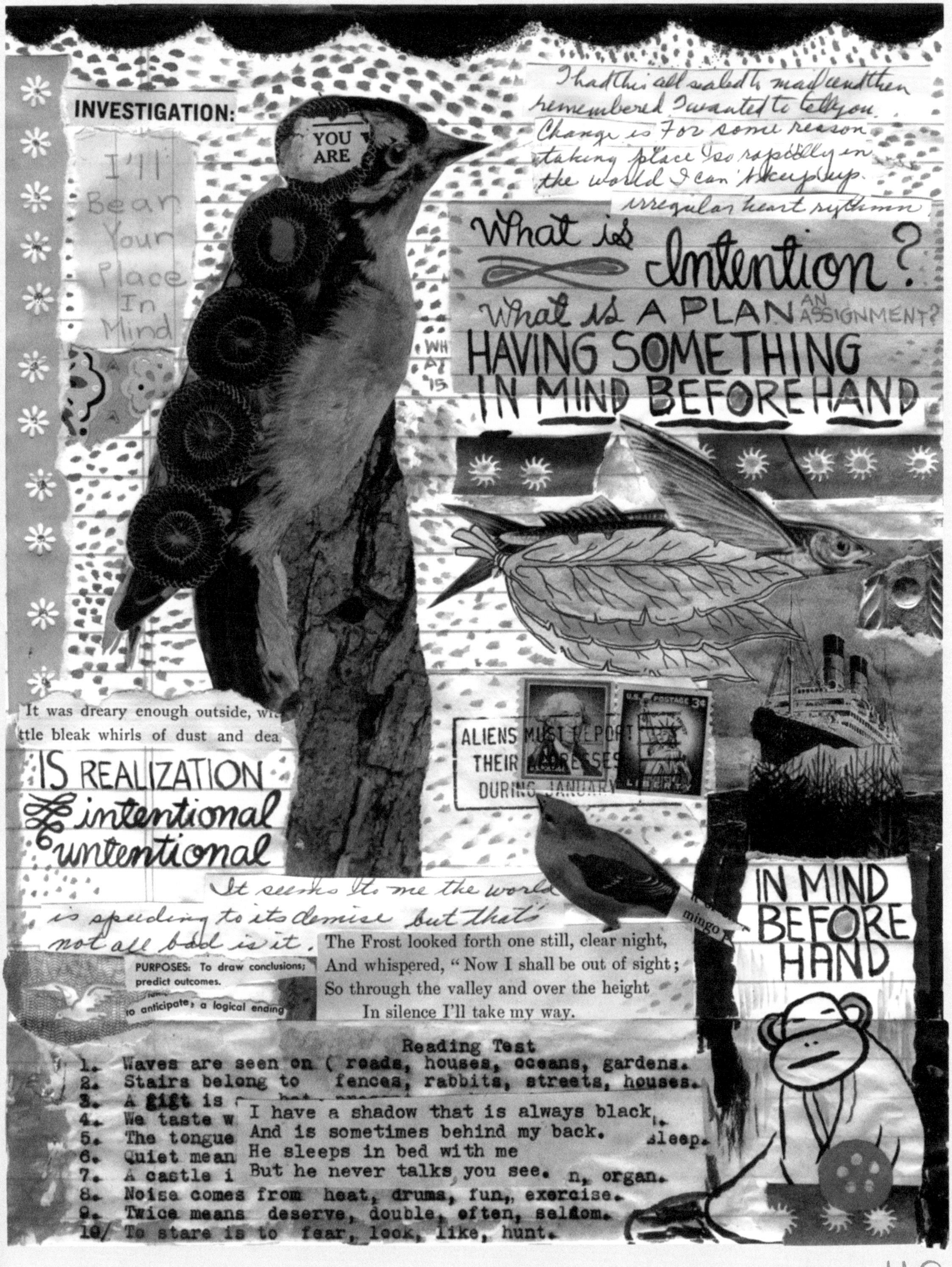

INVESTIGATION:
YOU ARE
I'll Bear Your Place In Mind
I had this all sealed to mail and then remembered I wanted to tell you.
Change is for some reason taking place so rapidly in the world I can't keep up.
irregular heart rythmn
What is Intention?
What is A PLAN AN ASSIGNMENT?
HAVING SOMETHING IN MIND BEFOREHAND
It was dreary enough outside, wi
ttle bleak whirls of dust and dea
IS REALIZATION
intentional
unintentional
ALIENS MUST REPORT THEIR ADDRESSES DURING JANUARY
It seems to me the world is speeding to its demise but that's not all bad is it.
mingo
IN MIND BEFORE HAND
PURPOSES: To draw conclusions; predict outcomes.
to anticipate, a logical ending
The Frost looked forth one still, clear night,
And whispered, "Now I shall be out of sight;
So through the valley and over the height
In silence I'll take my way.
Reading Test
1. Waves are seen on (roads, houses, oceans, gardens.
2. Stairs belong to fences, rabbits, streets, houses.
3. A gift is
4. We taste w
5. The tongue
6. Quiet mean
7. A castle i
8. Noise comes from heat, drums, fun, exercise.
9. Twice means deserve, double, often, seldom.
10/ To stare is to fear, look, like, hunt.
I have a shadow that is always black,
And is sometimes behind my back.
He sleeps in bed with me
But he never talks you see.

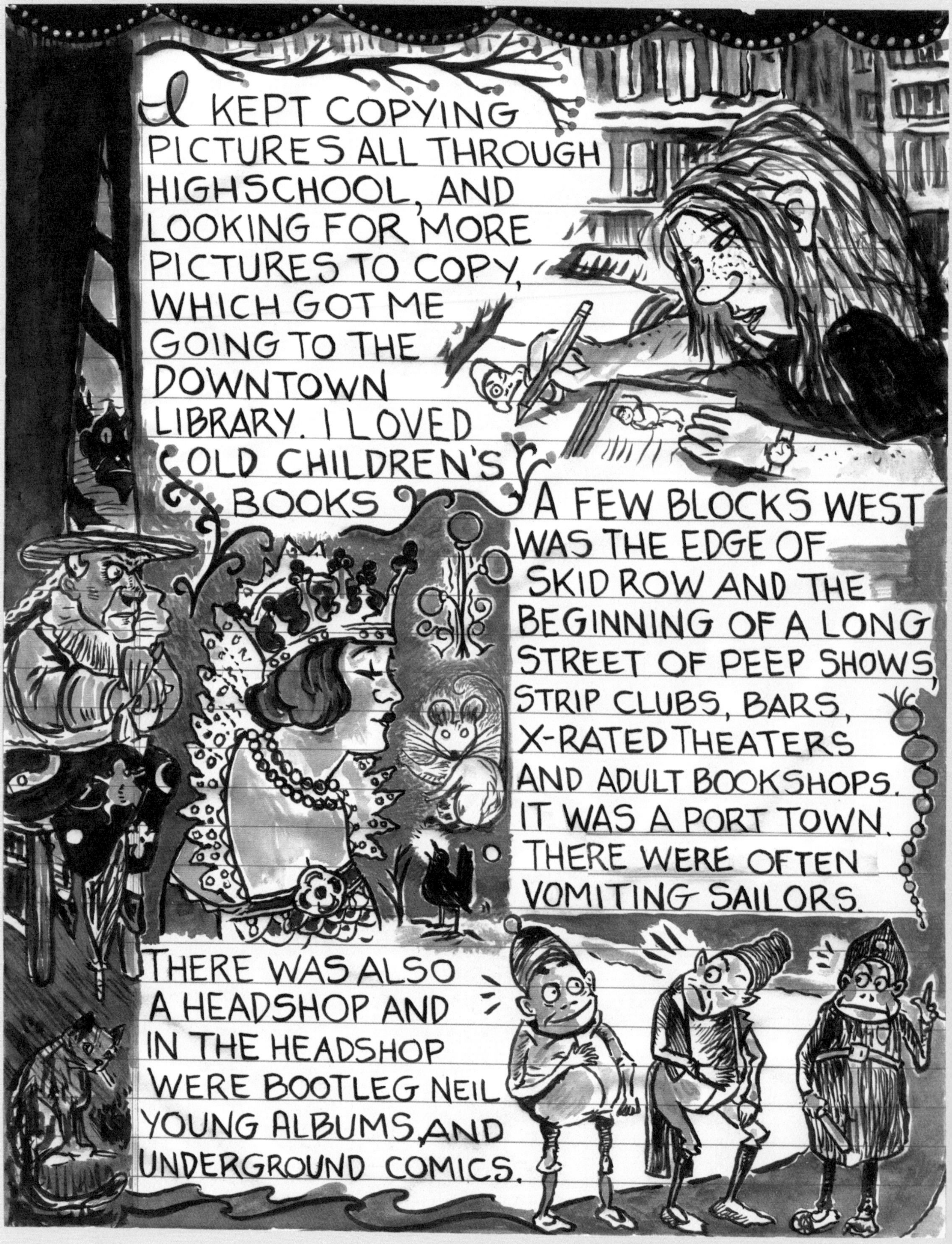
I KEPT COPYING PICTURES ALL THROUGH HIGHSCHOOL, AND LOOKING FOR MORE PICTURES TO COPY, WHICH GOT ME GOING TO THE DOWNTOWN LIBRARY. I LOVED OLD CHILDREN'S BOOKS
A FEW BLOCKS WEST WAS THE EDGE OF SKID ROW AND THE BEGINNING OF A LONG STREET OF PEEP SHOWS, STRIP CLUBS, BARS, X-RATED THEATERS AND ADULT BOOKSHOPS. IT WAS A PORT TOWN. THERE WERE OFTEN VOMITING SAILORS.
THERE WAS ALSO A HEADSHOP AND IN THE HEADSHOP WERE BOOTLEG NEIL YOUNG ALBUMS, AND UNDERGROUND COMICS.

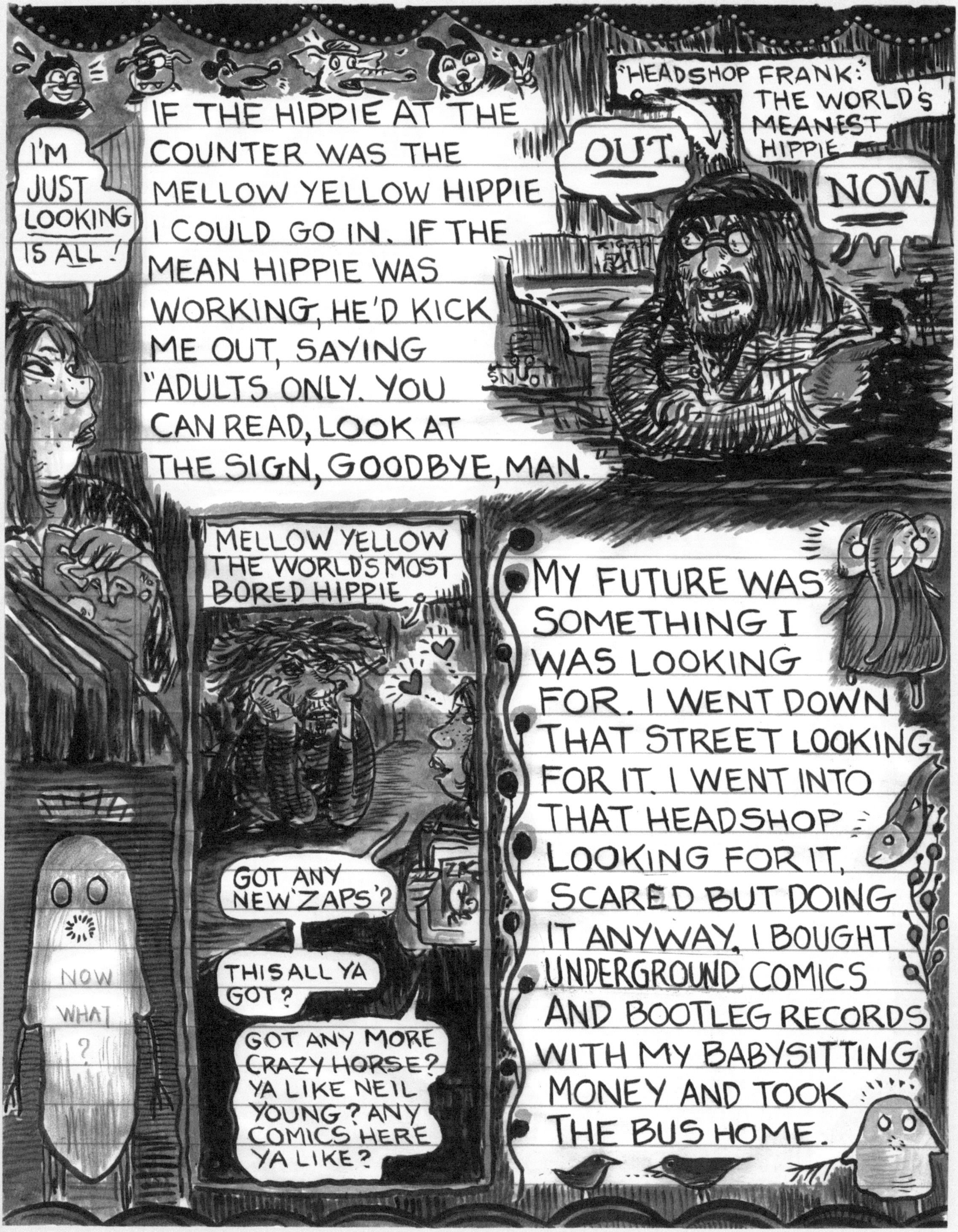
I'M JUST LOOKING IS ALL!
IF THE HIPPIE AT THE COUNTER WAS THE MELLOW YELLOW HIPPIE I COULD GO IN. IF THE MEAN HIPPIE WAS WORKING, HE'D KICK ME OUT, SAYING "ADULTS ONLY. YOU CAN READ, LOOK AT THE SIGN, GOODBYE, MAN."
HEADSHOP FRANK: THE WORLD'S MEANEST HIPPIE
OUT.
NOW.
MELLOW YELLOW THE WORLD'S MOST BORED HIPPIE
GOT ANY NEW 'ZAPS'?
THIS ALL YA GOT?
GOT ANY MORE CRAZY HORSE? YA LIKE NEIL YOUNG? ANY COMICS HERE YA LIKE?
NOW WHAT ?
MY FUTURE WAS SOMETHING I WAS LOOKING FOR. I WENT DOWN THAT STREET LOOKING FOR IT. I WENT INTO THAT HEADSHOP LOOKING FOR IT, SCARED BUT DOING IT ANYWAY. I BOUGHT UNDERGROUND COMICS AND BOOTLEG RECORDS WITH MY BABYSITTING MONEY AND TOOK THE BUS HOME.

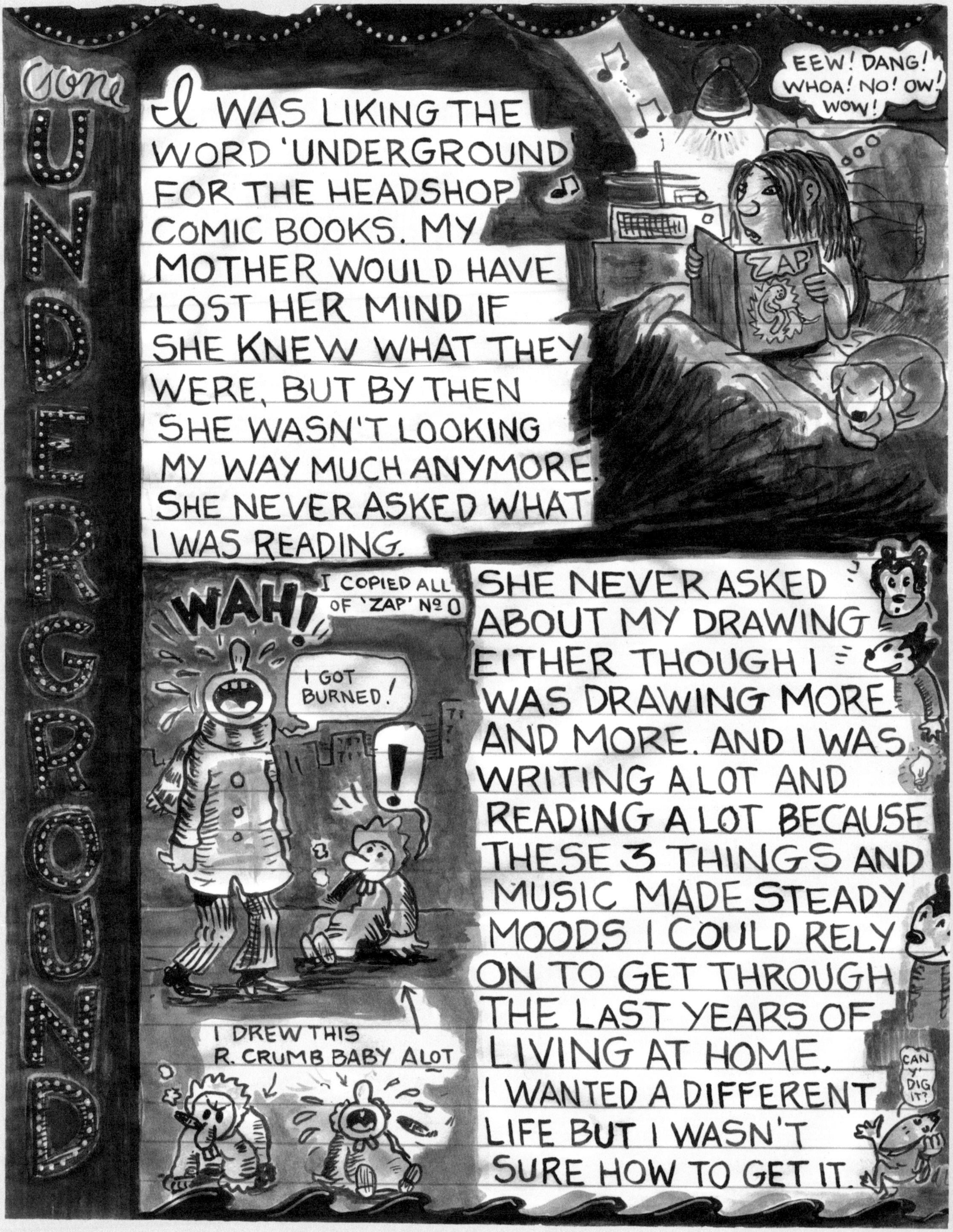
Gone UNDERGROUND
I WAS LIKING THE WORD 'UNDERGROUND' FOR THE HEADSHOP COMIC BOOKS. MY MOTHER WOULD HAVE LOST HER MIND IF SHE KNEW WHAT THEY WERE, BUT BY THEN SHE WASN'T LOOKING MY WAY MUCH ANYMORE. SHE NEVER ASKED WHAT I WAS READING.
EEW! DANG! WHOA! NO! OW! WOW!
ZAP
WAH!
I COPIED ALL OF 'ZAP' № 0
I GOT BURNED!
!
I DREW THIS R. CRUMB BABY ALOT
SHE NEVER ASKED ABOUT MY DRAWING EITHER THOUGH I WAS DRAWING MORE AND MORE. AND I WAS WRITING ALOT AND READING ALOT BECAUSE THESE 3 THINGS AND MUSIC MADE STEADY MOODS I COULD RELY ON TO GET THROUGH THE LAST YEARS OF LIVING AT HOME. I WANTED A DIFFERENT LIFE BUT I WASN'T SURE HOW TO GET IT.
CAN Y' DIG IT?

I CAN REMEMBER NOT BEING A TEENAGER AND THEN BEING ONE. BEING CATAPULTED INTO A NEW WORLD CONTAINED BY THE OLD ONE, JUST BY WALKING TO SCHOOL.

BUILDING A

REGISTRATION ORIENTATION

BUILDING A 8:00 AM

KIDS BURN UP IN THIS ATMOSPHERE. FRIENDSHIPS ATOMIZE. BUT THE TEEN PART IS SMELTERING ITSELF TOGETHER ALL ALONG, AND SOON YOU CAN THINK OF YOURSELF NO OTHER WAY.

SOMETHING WAS GONE, BUT I DIDN'T MISS IT. I DIDN'T MISS IT AT ALL.

LAST NAME?

A-G

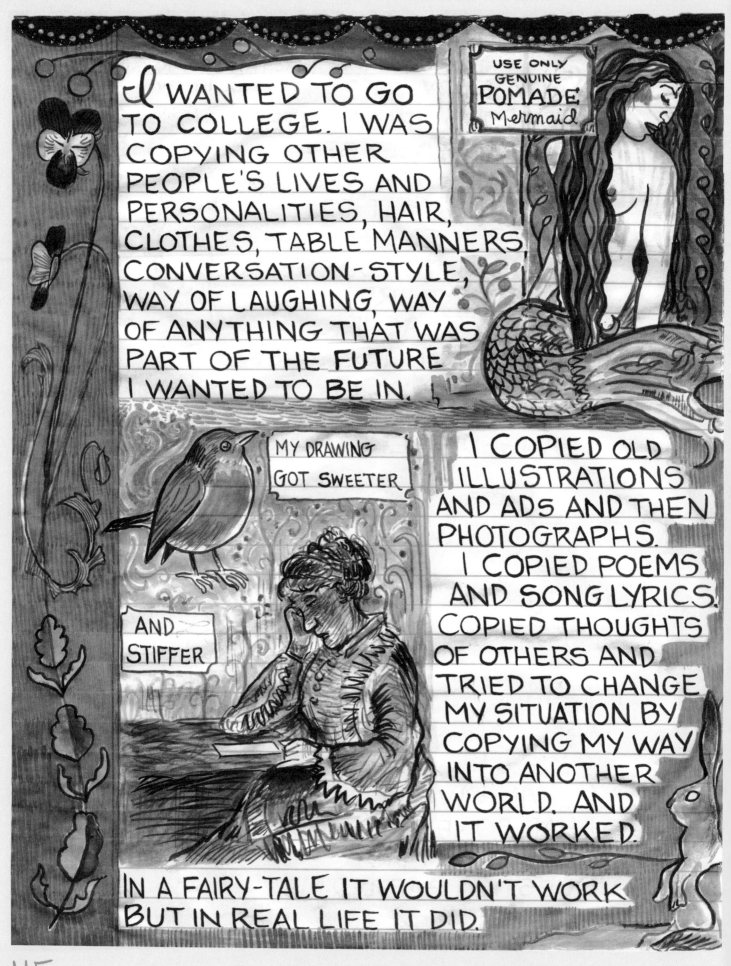

I WANTED TO GO TO COLLEGE. I WAS COPYING OTHER PEOPLE'S LIVES AND PERSONALITIES, HAIR, CLOTHES, TABLE MANNERS, CONVERSATION-STYLE, WAY OF LAUGHING, WAY OF ANYTHING THAT WAS PART OF THE FUTURE I WANTED TO BE IN.

USE ONLY GENUINE POMADE Mermaid

MY DRAWING GOT SWEETER

AND STIFFER

I COPIED OLD ILLUSTRATIONS AND ADS AND THEN PHOTOGRAPHS. I COPIED POEMS AND SONG LYRICS. COPIED THOUGHTS OF OTHERS AND TRIED TO CHANGE MY SITUATION BY COPYING MY WAY INTO ANOTHER WORLD. AND IT WORKED.

IN A FAIRY-TALE IT WOULDN'T WORK BUT IN REAL LIFE IT DID.

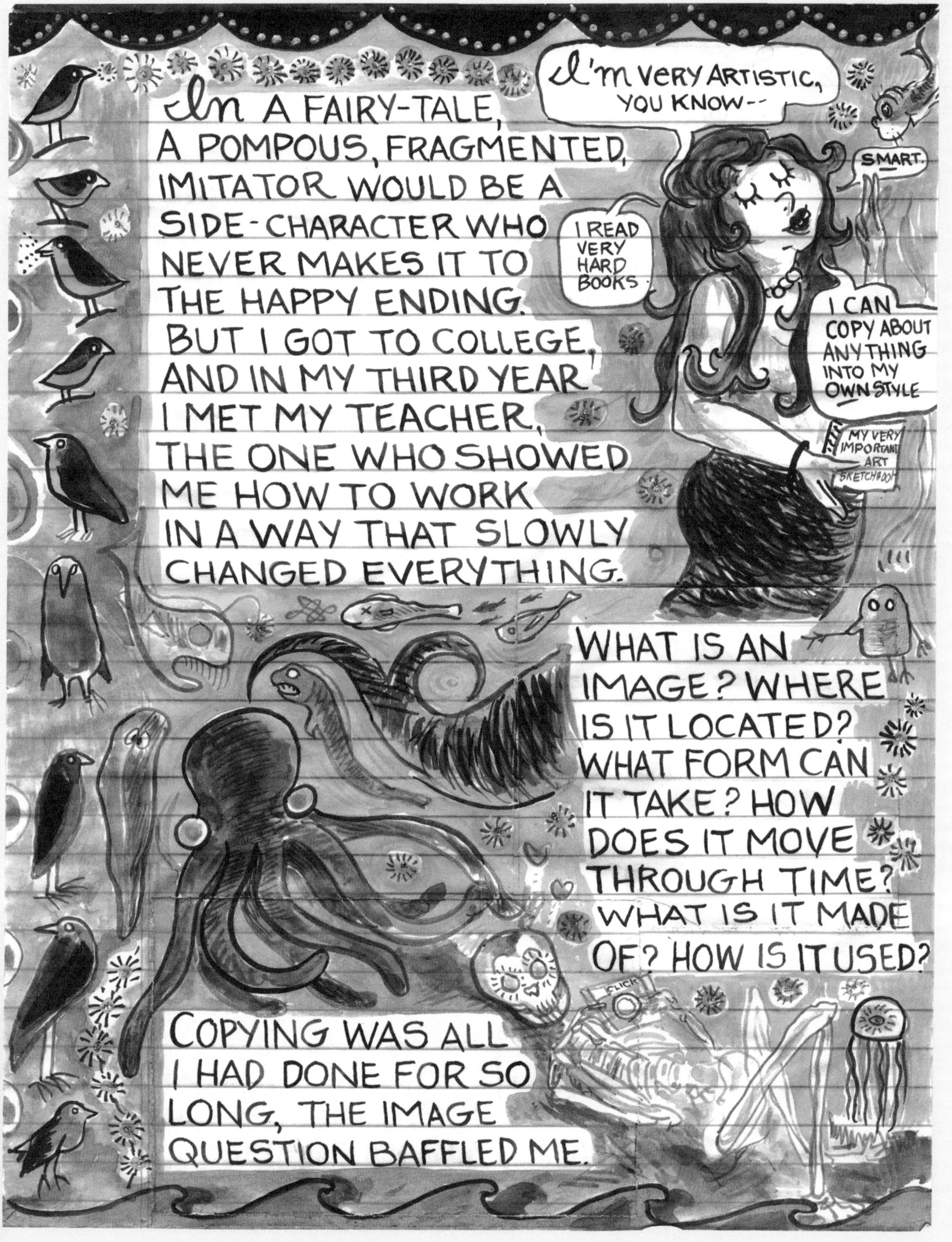
In A FAIRY-TALE, A POMPOUS, FRAGMENTED, IMITATOR WOULD BE A SIDE-CHARACTER WHO NEVER MAKES IT TO THE HAPPY ENDING.
BUT I GOT TO COLLEGE, AND IN MY THIRD YEAR I MET MY TEACHER, THE ONE WHO SHOWED ME HOW TO WORK IN A WAY THAT SLOWLY CHANGED EVERYTHING.
I'm VERY ARTISTIC, YOU KNOW--
SMART.
I READ VERY HARD BOOKS.
I CAN COPY ABOUT ANYTHING INTO MY OWN STYLE
MY VERY IMPORTANT ART SKETCHBOOK
WHAT IS AN IMAGE? WHERE IS IT LOCATED? WHAT FORM CAN IT TAKE? HOW DOES IT MOVE THROUGH TIME? WHAT IS IT MADE OF? HOW IS IT USED?
CLICK
COPYING WAS ALL I HAD DONE FOR SO LONG, THE IMAGE QUESTION BAFFLED ME.

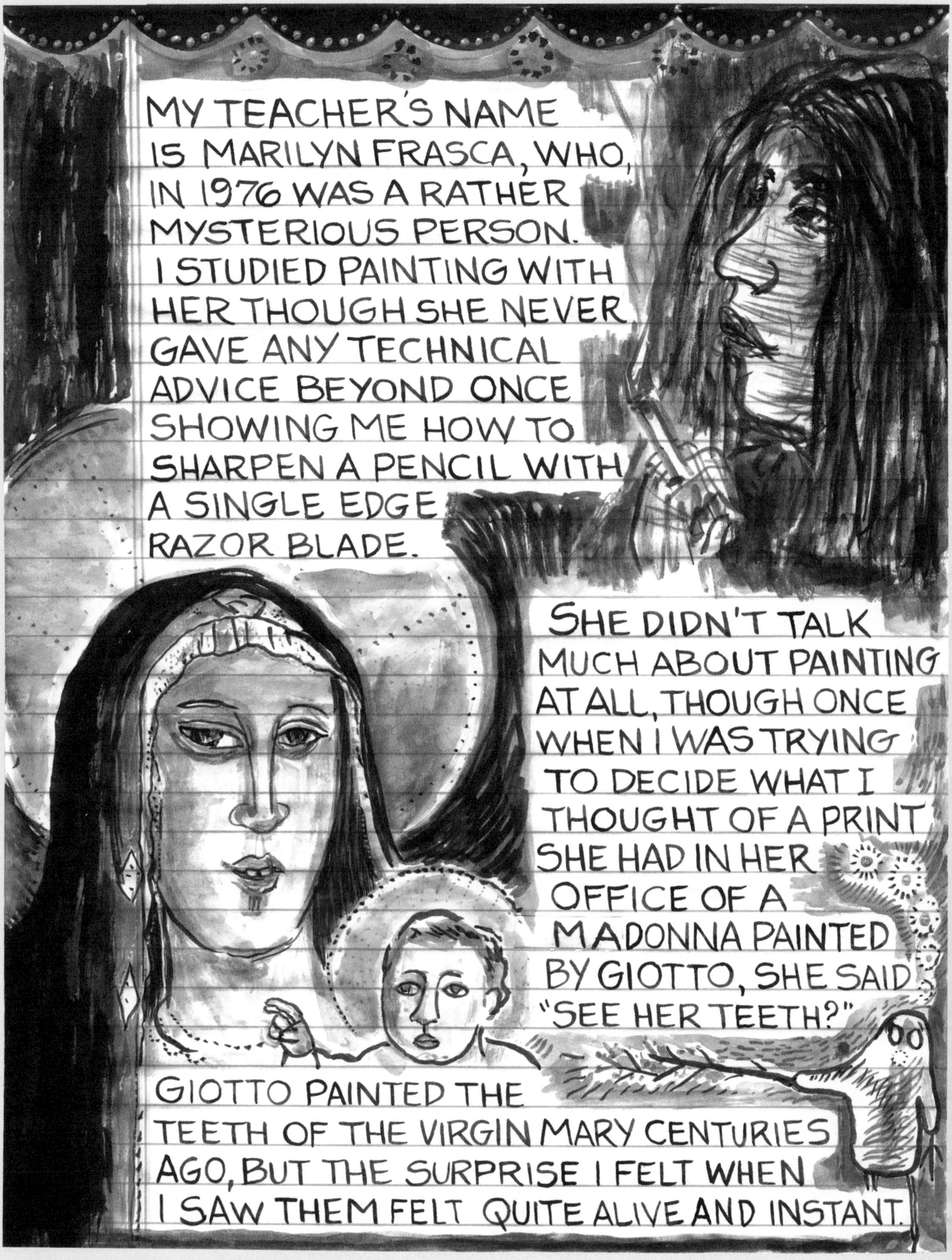
MY TEACHER'S NAME IS MARILYN FRASCA, WHO, IN 1976 WAS A RATHER MYSTERIOUS PERSON. I STUDIED PAINTING WITH HER THOUGH SHE NEVER GAVE ANY TECHNICAL ADVICE BEYOND ONCE SHOWING ME HOW TO SHARPEN A PENCIL WITH A SINGLE EDGE RAZOR BLADE.
SHE DIDN'T TALK MUCH ABOUT PAINTING AT ALL, THOUGH ONCE WHEN I WAS TRYING TO DECIDE WHAT I THOUGHT OF A PRINT SHE HAD IN HER OFFICE OF A MADONNA PAINTED BY GIOTTO, SHE SAID "SEE HER TEETH?"
GIOTTO PAINTED THE TEETH OF THE VIRGIN MARY CENTURIES AGO, BUT THE SURPRISE I FELT WHEN I SAW THEM FELT QUITE ALIVE AND INSTANT.

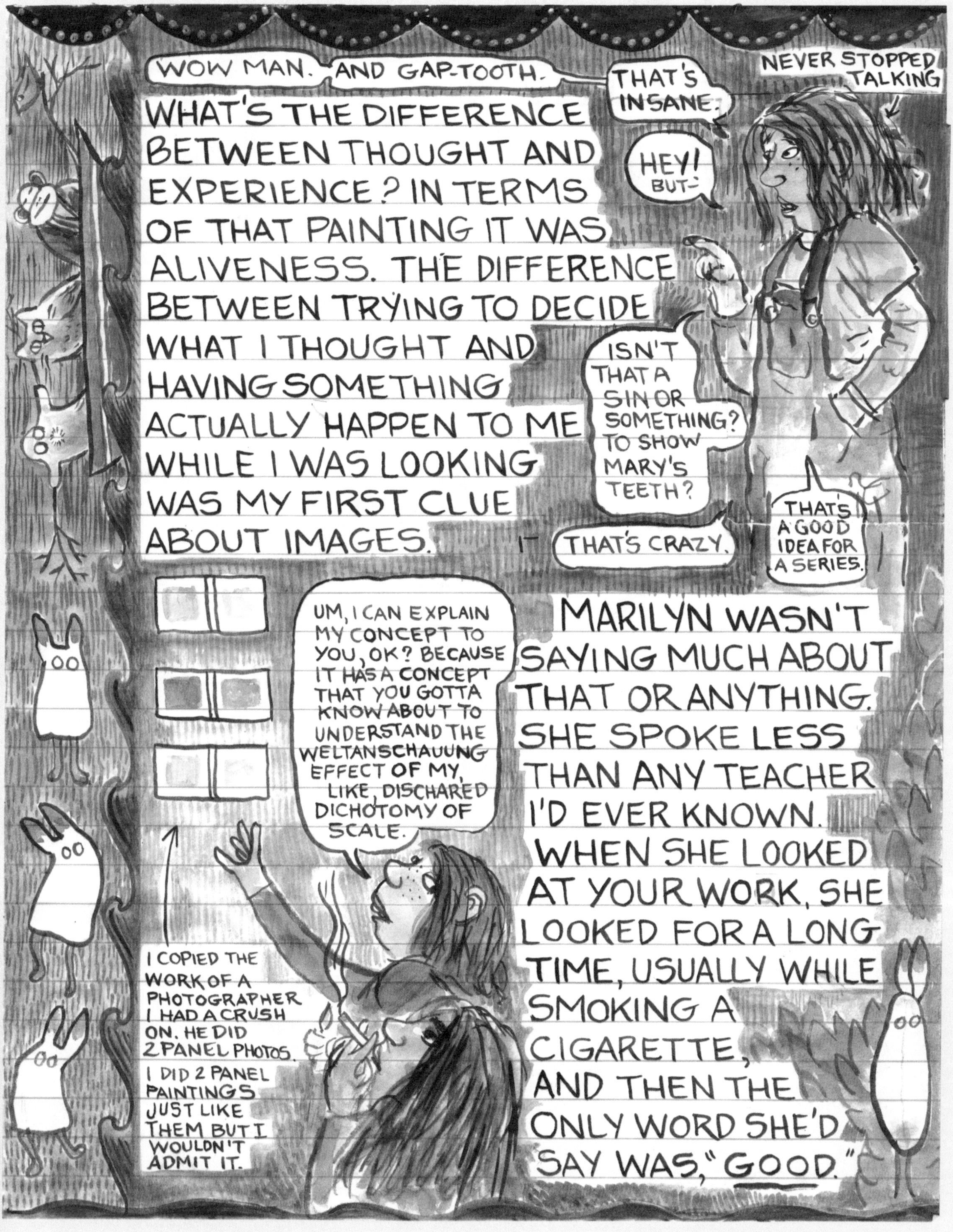
WOW MAN.
AND GAP-TOOTH.
THAT'S INSANE.
NEVER STOPPED TALKING
WHAT'S THE DIFFERENCE BETWEEN THOUGHT AND EXPERIENCE? IN TERMS OF THAT PAINTING IT WAS ALIVENESS. THE DIFFERENCE BETWEEN TRYING TO DECIDE WHAT I THOUGHT AND HAVING SOMETHING ACTUALLY HAPPEN TO ME WHILE I WAS LOOKING WAS MY FIRST CLUE ABOUT IMAGES.
HEY! BUT-
ISN'T THAT A SIN OR SOMETHING? TO SHOW MARY'S TEETH?
THAT'S CRAZY.
THAT'S A GOOD IDEA FOR A SERIES.
UM, I CAN EXPLAIN MY CONCEPT TO YOU, OK? BECAUSE IT HAS A CONCEPT THAT YOU GOTTA KNOW ABOUT TO UNDERSTAND THE WELTANSCHAUUNG EFFECT OF MY, LIKE, DISCHARED DICHOTOMY OF SCALE.
I COPIED THE WORK OF A PHOTOGRAPHER I HAD A CRUSH ON. HE DID 2 PANEL PHOTOS.
I DID 2 PANEL PAINTINGS JUST LIKE THEM BUT I WOULDN'T ADMIT IT.
MARILYN WASN'T SAYING MUCH ABOUT THAT OR ANYTHING. SHE SPOKE LESS THAN ANY TEACHER I'D EVER KNOWN. WHEN SHE LOOKED AT YOUR WORK, SHE LOOKED FOR A LONG TIME, USUALLY WHILE SMOKING A CIGARETTE, AND THEN THE ONLY WORD SHE'D SAY WAS, "GOOD."

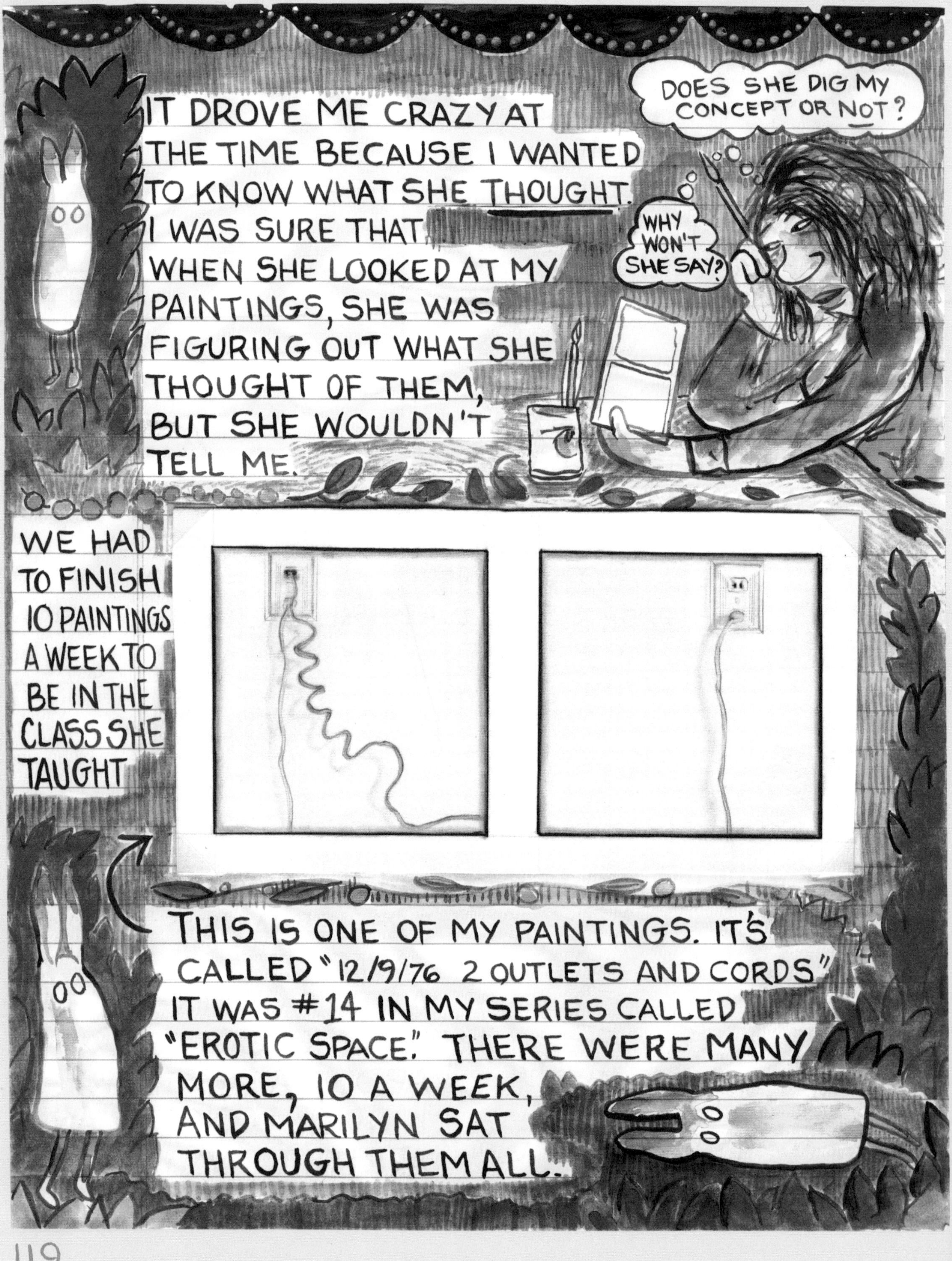

IT DROVE ME CRAZY AT THE TIME BECAUSE I WANTED TO KNOW WHAT SHE THOUGHT. I WAS SURE THAT WHEN SHE LOOKED AT MY PAINTINGS, SHE WAS FIGURING OUT WHAT SHE THOUGHT OF THEM, BUT SHE WOULDN'T TELL ME.
DOES SHE DIG MY CONCEPT OR NOT?
WHY WON'T SHE SAY?
WE HAD TO FINISH 10 PAINTINGS A WEEK TO BE IN THE CLASS SHE TAUGHT
THIS IS ONE OF MY PAINTINGS. IT'S CALLED "12/9/76 2 OUTLETS AND CORDS" IT WAS #14 IN MY SERIES CALLED "EROTIC SPACE." THERE WERE MANY MORE, 10 A WEEK, AND MARILYN SAT THROUGH THEM ALL.

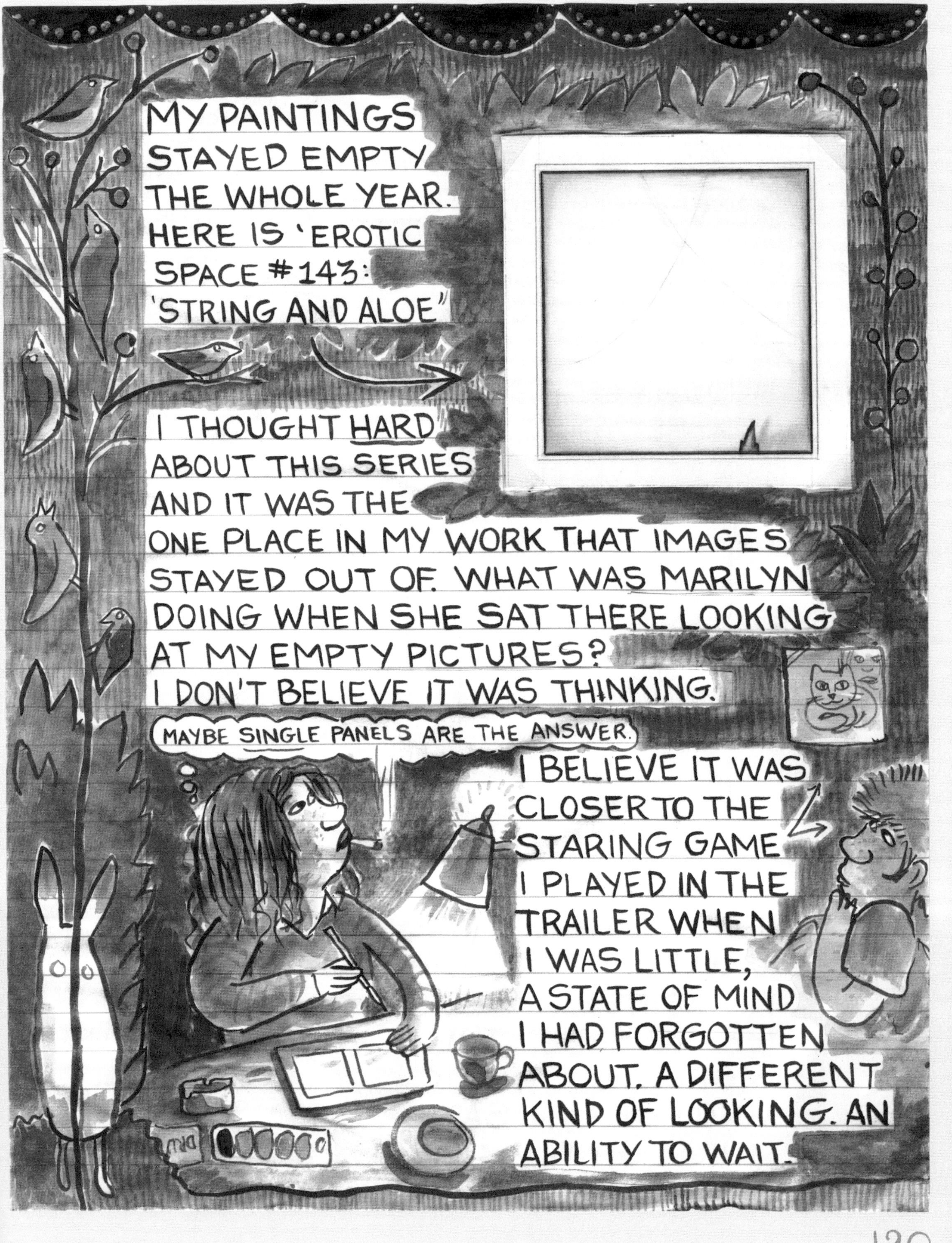
MY PAINTINGS STAYED EMPTY THE WHOLE YEAR. HERE IS 'EROTIC SPACE #143: 'STRING AND ALOE"
I THOUGHT HARD ABOUT THIS SERIES AND IT WAS THE ONE PLACE IN MY WORK THAT IMAGES STAYED OUT OF. WHAT WAS MARILYN DOING WHEN SHE SAT THERE LOOKING AT MY EMPTY PICTURES?
I DON'T BELIEVE IT WAS THINKING.
MAYBE SINGLE PANELS ARE THE ANSWER.
I BELIEVE IT WAS CLOSER TO THE STARING GAME I PLAYED IN THE TRAILER WHEN I WAS LITTLE, A STATE OF MIND I HAD FORGOTTEN ABOUT. A DIFFERENT KIND OF LOOKING. AN ABILITY TO WAIT.

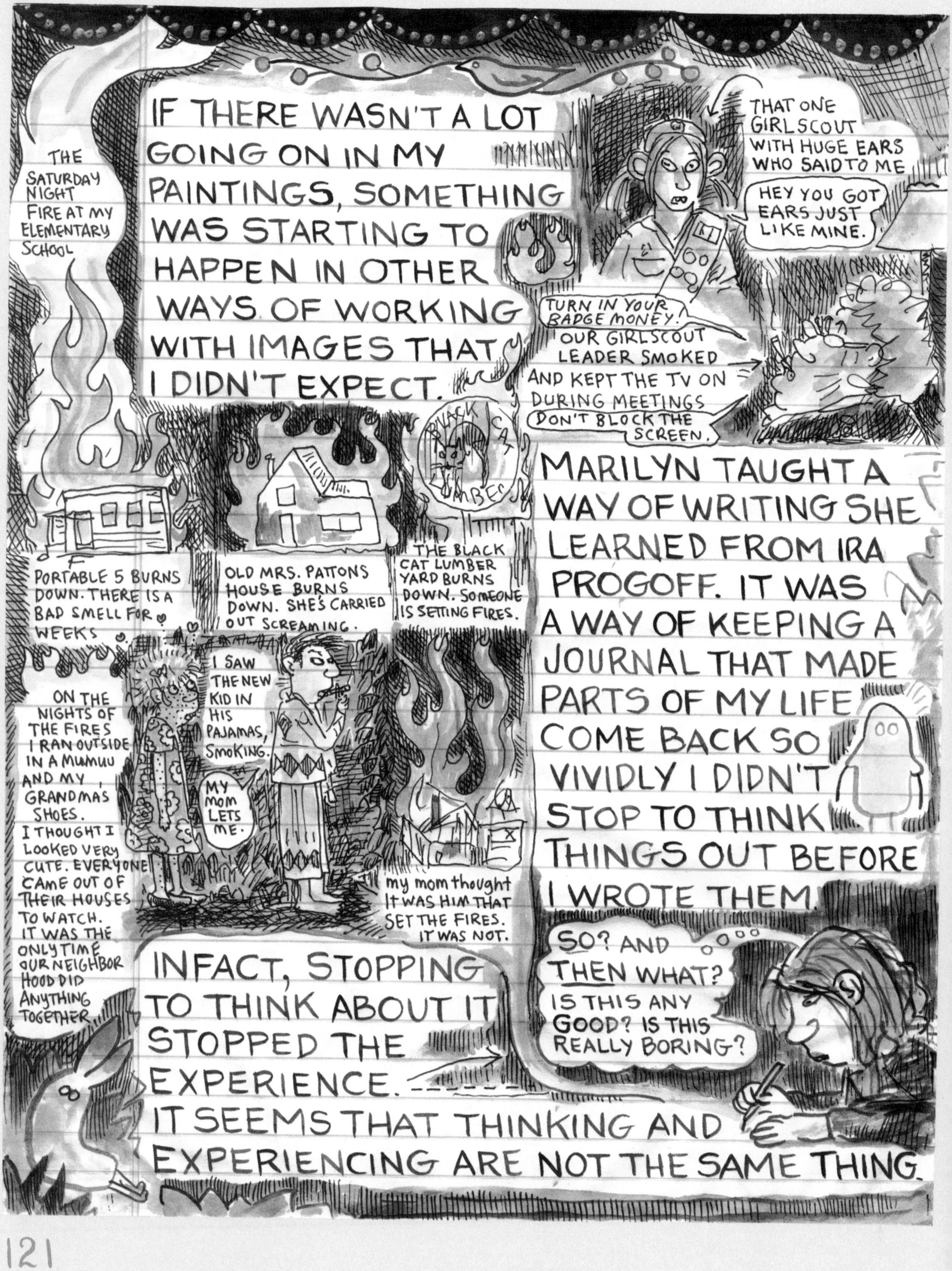
IF THERE WASN'T A LOT GOING ON IN MY PAINTINGS, SOMETHING WAS STARTING TO HAPPEN IN OTHER WAYS OF WORKING WITH IMAGES THAT I DIDN'T EXPECT.
THE SATURDAY NIGHT FIRE AT MY ELEMENTARY SCHOOL
THAT ONE GIRLSCOUT WITH HUGE EARS WHO SAID TO ME
HEY YOU GOT EARS JUST LIKE MINE.
TURN IN YOUR BADGE MONEY!
OUR GIRLSCOUT LEADER SMOKED AND KEPT THE TV ON DURING MEETINGS
DON'T BLOCK THE SCREEN.
BLACK CAT LUMBER
PORTABLE 5 BURNS DOWN. THERE IS A BAD SMELL FOR WEEKS
OLD MRS. PATTONS HOUSE BURNS DOWN. SHE'S CARRIED OUT SCREAMING.
THE BLACK CAT LUMBER YARD BURNS DOWN. SOMEONE IS SETTING FIRES.
MARILYN TAUGHT A WAY OF WRITING SHE LEARNED FROM IRA PROGOFF. IT WAS A WAY OF KEEPING A JOURNAL THAT MADE PARTS OF MY LIFE COME BACK SO VIVIDLY I DIDN'T STOP TO THINK THINGS OUT BEFORE I WROTE THEM.
ON THE NIGHTS OF THE FIRES I RAN OUTSIDE IN A MUMUU AND MY GRANDMA'S SHOES. I THOUGHT I LOOKED VERY CUTE. EVERYONE CAME OUT OF THEIR HOUSES TO WATCH. IT WAS THE ONLY TIME OUR NEIGHBORHOOD DID ANYTHING TOGETHER.
I SAW THE NEW KID IN HIS PAJAMAS, SMOKING.
MY MOM LETS ME.
my mom thought it was HIM THAT SET THE FIRES. IT WAS NOT.
SO? AND THEN WHAT? IS THIS ANY GOOD? IS THIS REALLY BORING?
INFACT, STOPPING TO THINK ABOUT IT STOPPED THE EXPERIENCE.
IT SEEMS THAT THINKING AND EXPERIENCING ARE NOT THE SAME THING.

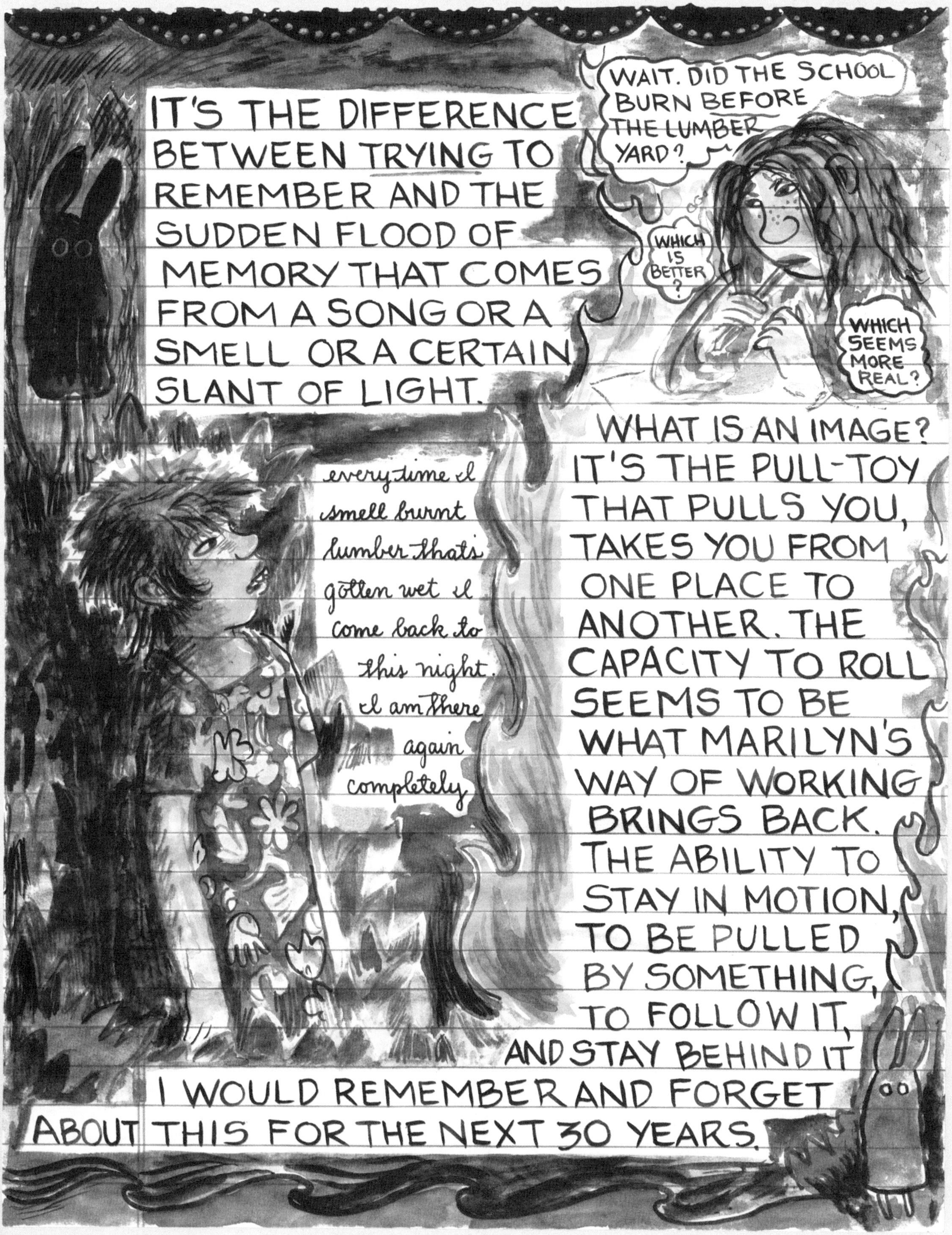
IT'S THE DIFFERENCE BETWEEN TRYING TO REMEMBER AND THE SUDDEN FLOOD OF MEMORY THAT COMES FROM A SONG OR A SMELL OR A CERTAIN SLANT OF LIGHT.
WAIT. DID THE SCHOOL BURN BEFORE THE LUMBER YARD?
WHICH IS BETTER?
WHICH SEEMS MORE REAL?
every time I smell burnt lumber that's gotten wet I come back to this night. I am there again completely.
WHAT IS AN IMAGE? IT'S THE PULL-TOY THAT PULLS YOU, TAKES YOU FROM ONE PLACE TO ANOTHER. THE CAPACITY TO ROLL SEEMS TO BE WHAT MARILYN'S WAY OF WORKING BRINGS BACK. THE ABILITY TO STAY IN MOTION, TO BE PULLED BY SOMETHING, TO FOLLOW IT, AND STAY BEHIND IT
I WOULD REMEMBER AND FORGET ABOUT THIS FOR THE NEXT 30 YEARS.

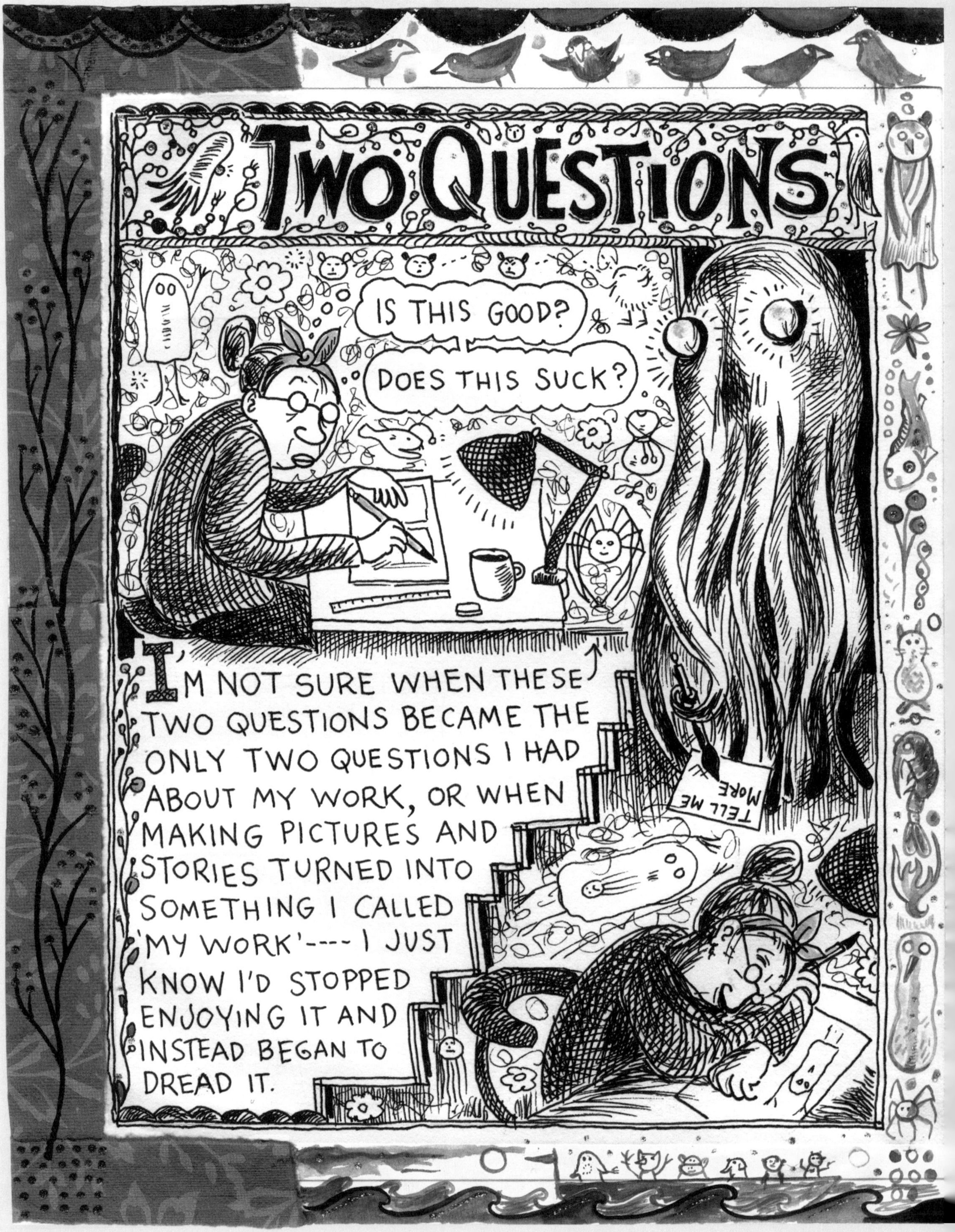
TWO QUESTIONS
IS THIS GOOD?
DOES THIS SUCK?
I'M NOT SURE WHEN THESE TWO QUESTIONS BECAME THE ONLY TWO QUESTIONS I HAD ABOUT MY WORK, OR WHEN MAKING PICTURES AND STORIES TURNED INTO SOMETHING I CALLED 'MY WORK'---- I JUST KNOW I'D STOPPED ENJOYING IT AND INSTEAD BEGAN TO DREAD IT.
TELL ME MORE

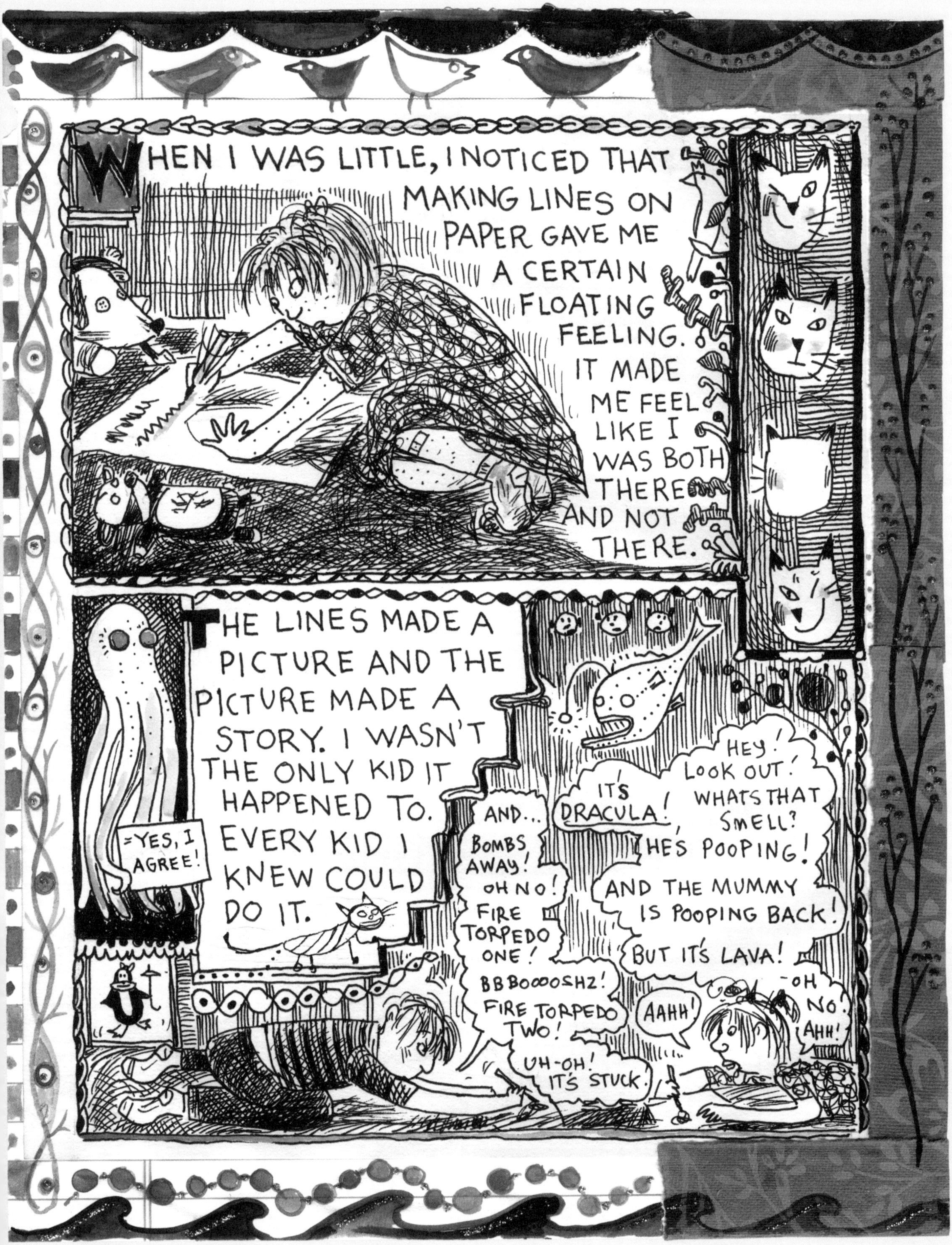
WHEN I WAS LITTLE, I NOTICED THAT MAKING LINES ON PAPER GAVE ME A CERTAIN FLOATING FEELING. IT MADE ME FEEL LIKE I WAS BOTH THERE AND NOT THERE.
THE LINES MADE A PICTURE AND THE PICTURE MADE A STORY. I WASN'T THE ONLY KID IT HAPPENED TO. EVERY KID I KNEW COULD DO IT.
YES, I AGREE!
AND...
BOMBS AWAY!
OH NO!
FIRE TORPEDO ONE!
BBBOOOOSHZ!
FIRE TORPEDO TWO!
UH-OH! IT'S STUCK.
IT'S DRACULA!
HEY! LOOK OUT!
WHATS THAT SMELL?
HE'S POOPING!
AND THE MUMMY IS POOPING BACK!
BUT IT'S LAVA!
AAHH!
OH NO. AHH!

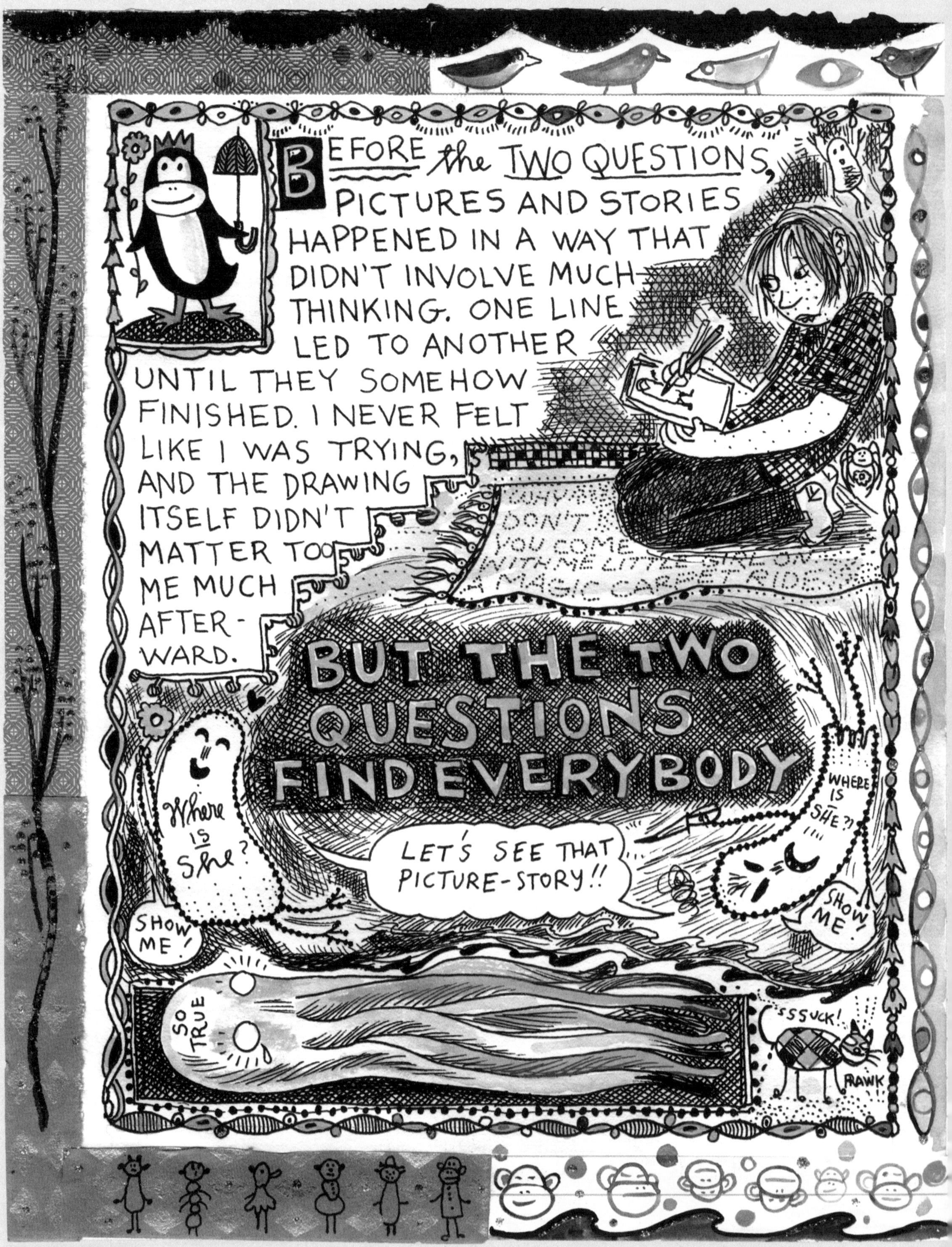
BEFORE the TWO QUESTIONS, PICTURES AND STORIES HAPPENED IN A WAY THAT DIDN'T INVOLVE MUCH THINKING. ONE LINE LED TO ANOTHER UNTIL THEY SOMEHOW FINISHED. I NEVER FELT LIKE I WAS TRYING, AND THE DRAWING ITSELF DIDN'T MATTER TOO ME MUCH AFTER-WARD.
WHY DON'T YOU COME WITH ME LITTLE GIRL ON A MAGIC CARPET RIDE
BUT THE TWO QUESTIONS FIND EVERYBODY
Where is She?
SHOW ME!
LET'S SEE THAT PICTURE-STORY!!
WHERE IS SHE?!
SHOW ME
SO TRUE
SSSUCK!
RAWK

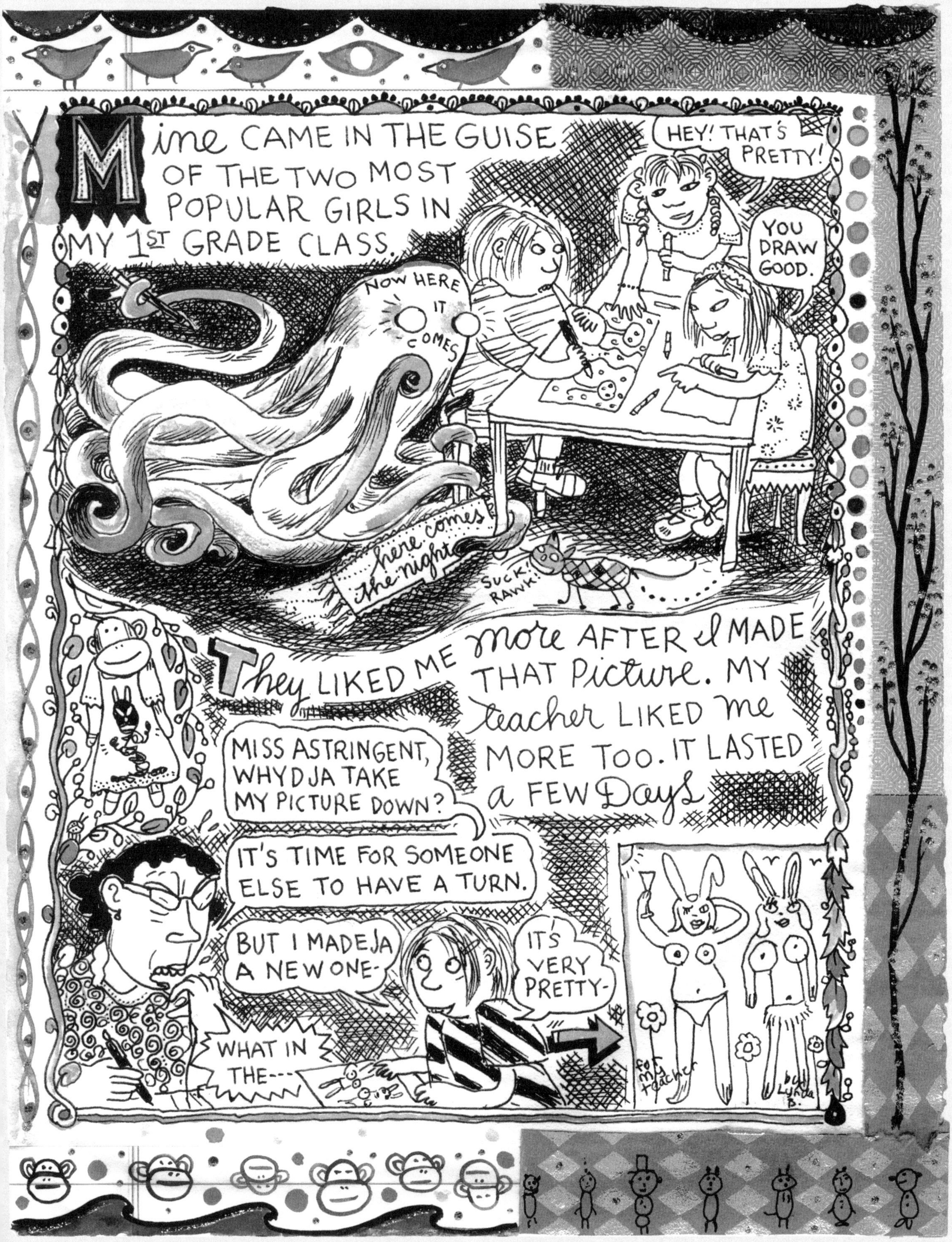
Mine CAME IN THE GUISE OF THE TWO MOST POPULAR GIRLS IN MY 1ST GRADE CLASS.
HEY! THAT'S PRETTY!
YOU DRAW GOOD.
NOW HERE IT COMES
here comes the night
SUCK! RAWK
They LIKED ME more AFTER I MADE THAT Picture. MY teacher LIKED me MORE TOO. IT LASTED a FEW Days
MISS ASTRINGENT, WHYDJA TAKE MY PICTURE DOWN?
IT'S TIME FOR SOMEONE ELSE TO HAVE A TURN.
BUT I MADEJA A NEW ONE-
IT'S VERY PRETTY-
WHAT IN THE---
for my teacher
by Lynda B.

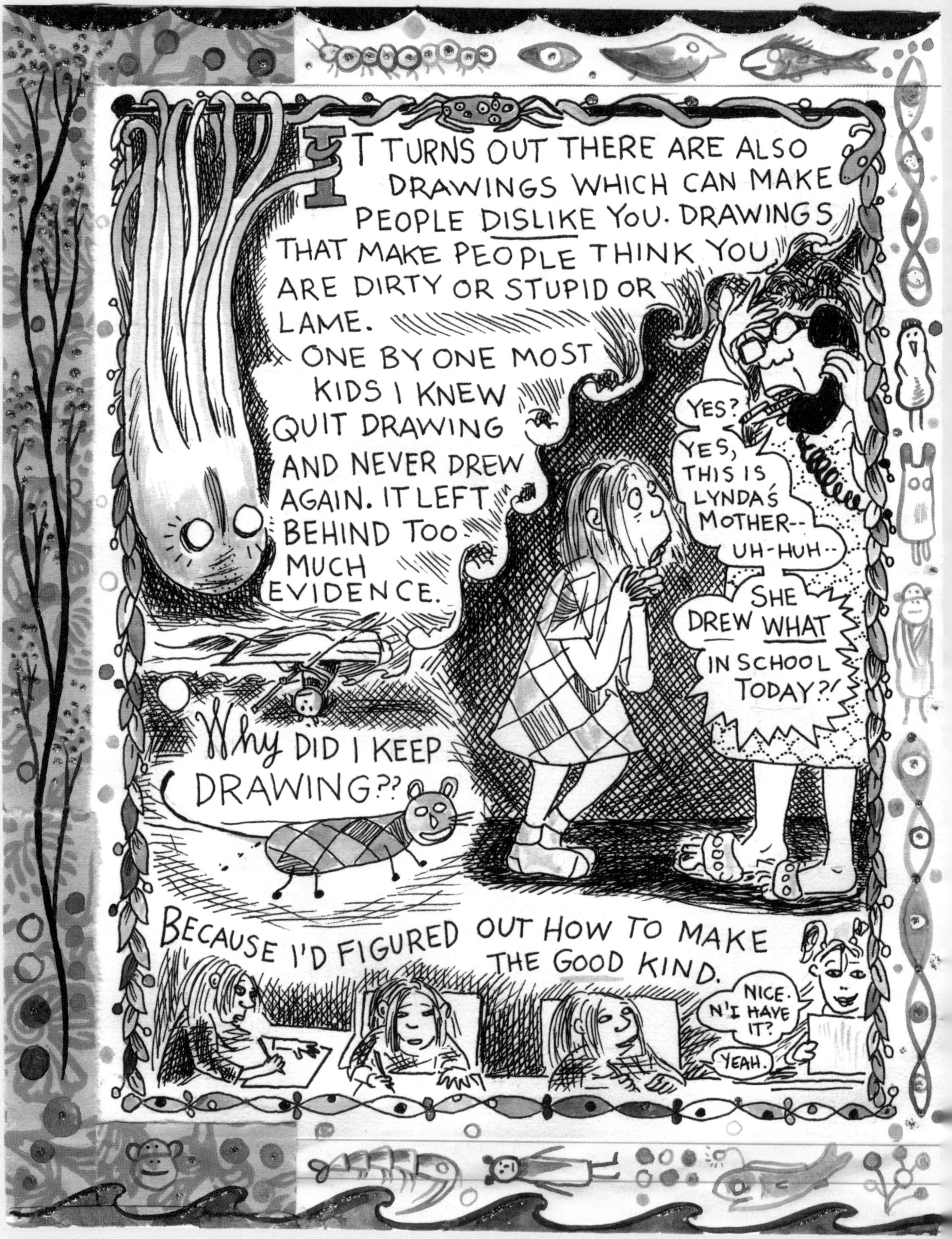
IT TURNS OUT THERE ARE ALSO DRAWINGS WHICH CAN MAKE PEOPLE DISLIKE YOU. DRAWINGS THAT MAKE PEOPLE THINK YOU ARE DIRTY OR STUPID OR LAME.
ONE BY ONE MOST KIDS I KNEW QUIT DRAWING AND NEVER DREW AGAIN. IT LEFT BEHIND TOO MUCH EVIDENCE.
YES?
YES, THIS IS LYNDA'S MOTHER-- UH-HUH--
SHE DREW WHAT IN SCHOOL TODAY?!
Why DID I KEEP DRAWING??
BECAUSE I'D FIGURED OUT HOW TO MAKE THE GOOD KIND.
NICE. N'I HAVE IT?
YEAH.

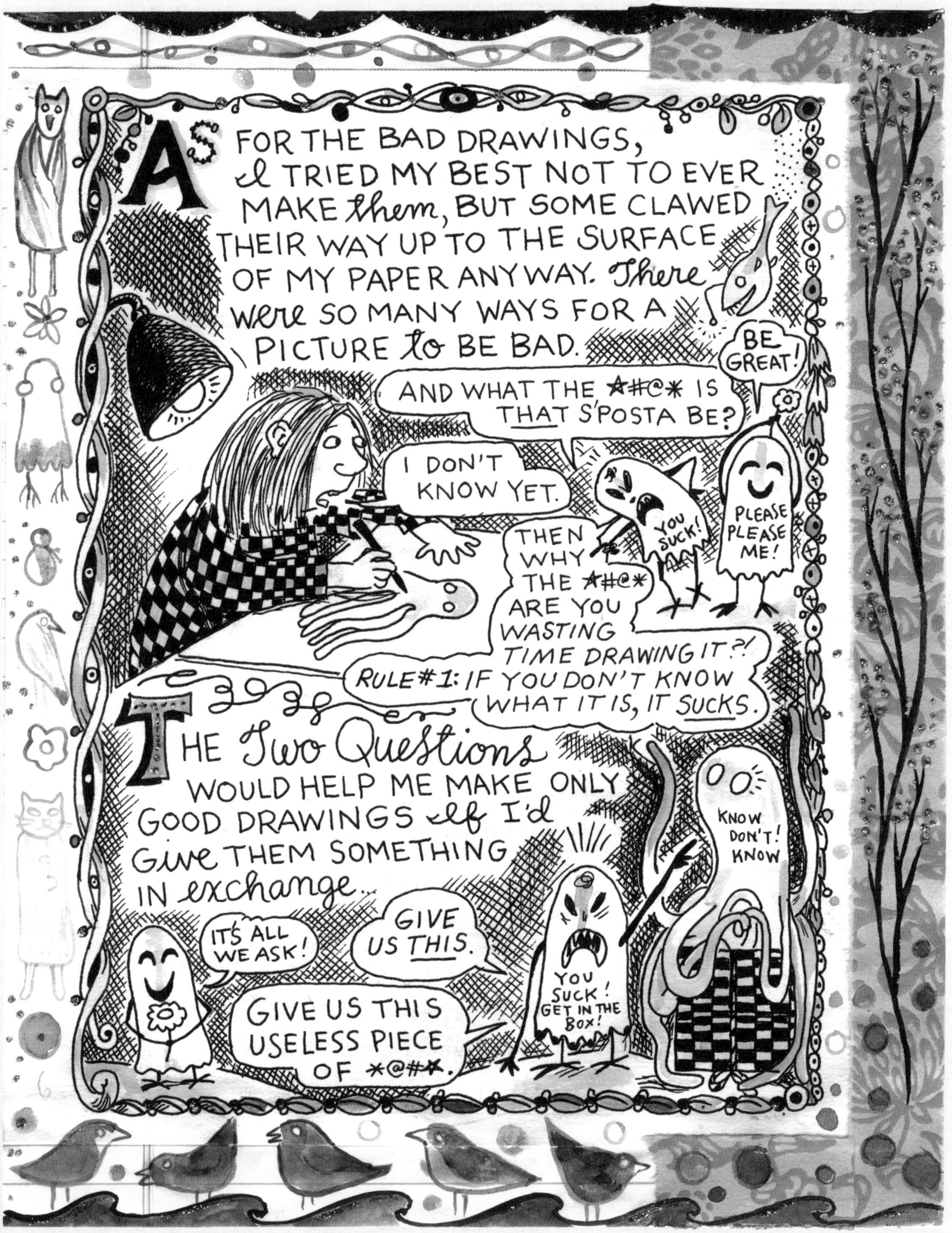

AS FOR THE BAD DRAWINGS, I TRIED MY BEST NOT TO EVER MAKE them, BUT SOME CLAWED THEIR WAY UP TO THE SURFACE OF MY PAPER ANYWAY. There were SO MANY WAYS FOR A PICTURE to BE BAD.
BE GREAT!
AND WHAT THE *#@* IS THAT S'POSTA BE?
I DON'T KNOW YET.
YOU SUCK!
PLEASE PLEASE ME!
THEN WHY THE *#@* ARE YOU WASTING TIME DRAWING IT?!
RULE #1: IF YOU DON'T KNOW WHAT IT IS, IT SUCKS.
THE Two Questions WOULD HELP ME MAKE ONLY GOOD DRAWINGS if I'd Give THEM SOMETHING IN exchange...
KNOW DON'T! KNOW
IT'S ALL WE ASK!
GIVE US THIS.
GIVE US THIS USELESS PIECE OF *@#*.
YOU SUCK! GET IN THE BOX!

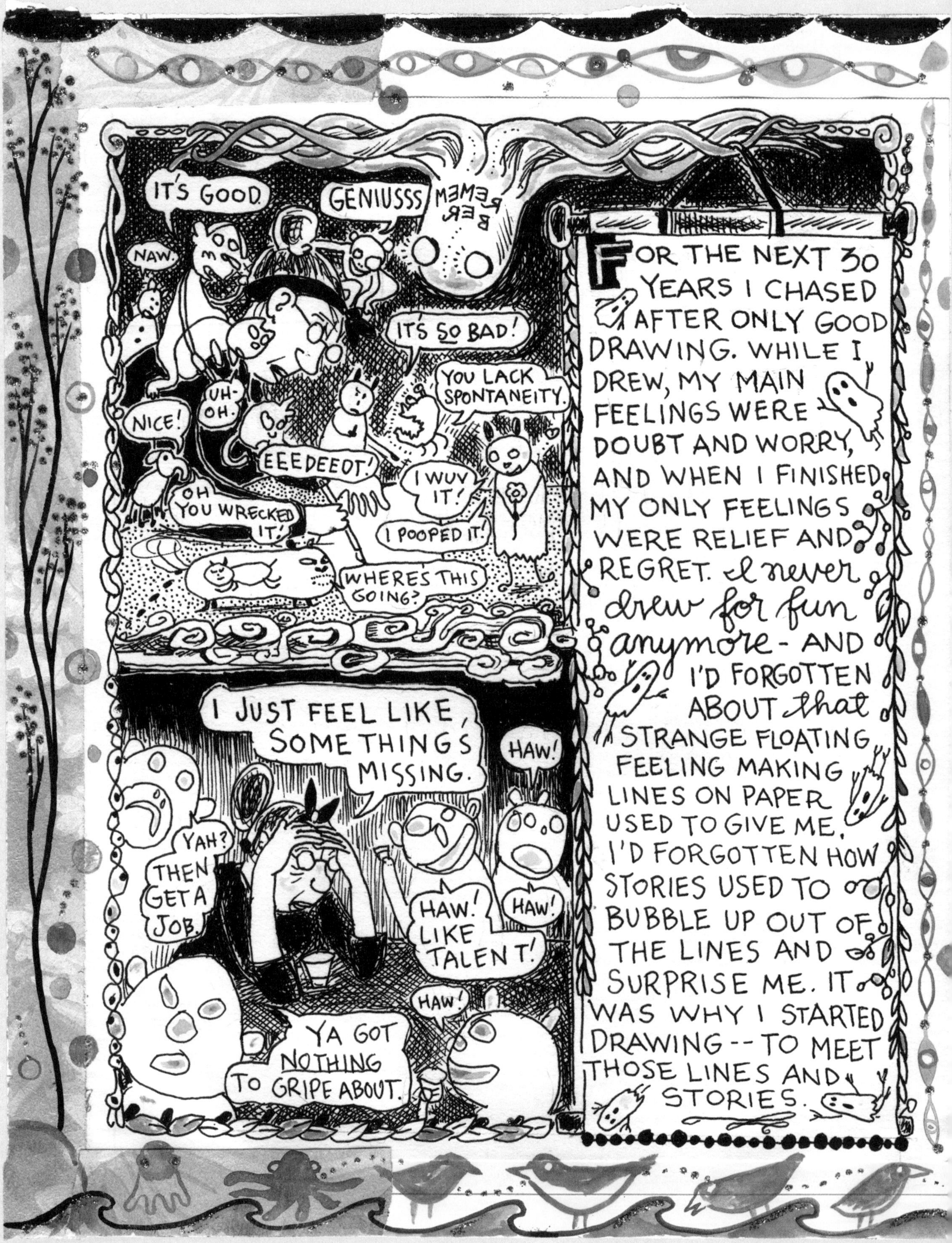
FOR THE NEXT 30 YEARS I CHASED AFTER ONLY GOOD DRAWING. WHILE I DREW, MY MAIN FEELINGS WERE DOUBT AND WORRY, AND WHEN I FINISHED MY ONLY FEELINGS WERE RELIEF AND REGRET. I never drew for fun anymore - AND I'D FORGOTTEN ABOUT that STRANGE FLOATING FEELING MAKING LINES ON PAPER USED TO GIVE ME. I'D FORGOTTEN HOW STORIES USED TO BUBBLE UP OUT OF THE LINES AND SURPRISE ME. IT WAS WHY I STARTED DRAWING -- TO MEET THOSE LINES AND STORIES.
IT'S GOOD.
GENIUSSS
NAW.
IT'S SO BAD!
YOU LACK SPONTANEITY.
UH-OH.
NICE!
EEEDEEOT!
I WUV IT!
OH YOU WRECKED IT!
I POOPED IT!
WHERE'S THIS GOING?
I JUST FEEL LIKE, SOMETHING'S MISSING.
HAW!
YAH? THEN GET A JOB.
HAW! LIKE TALENT!
HAW!
HAW!
YA GOT NOTHING TO GRIPE ABOUT.

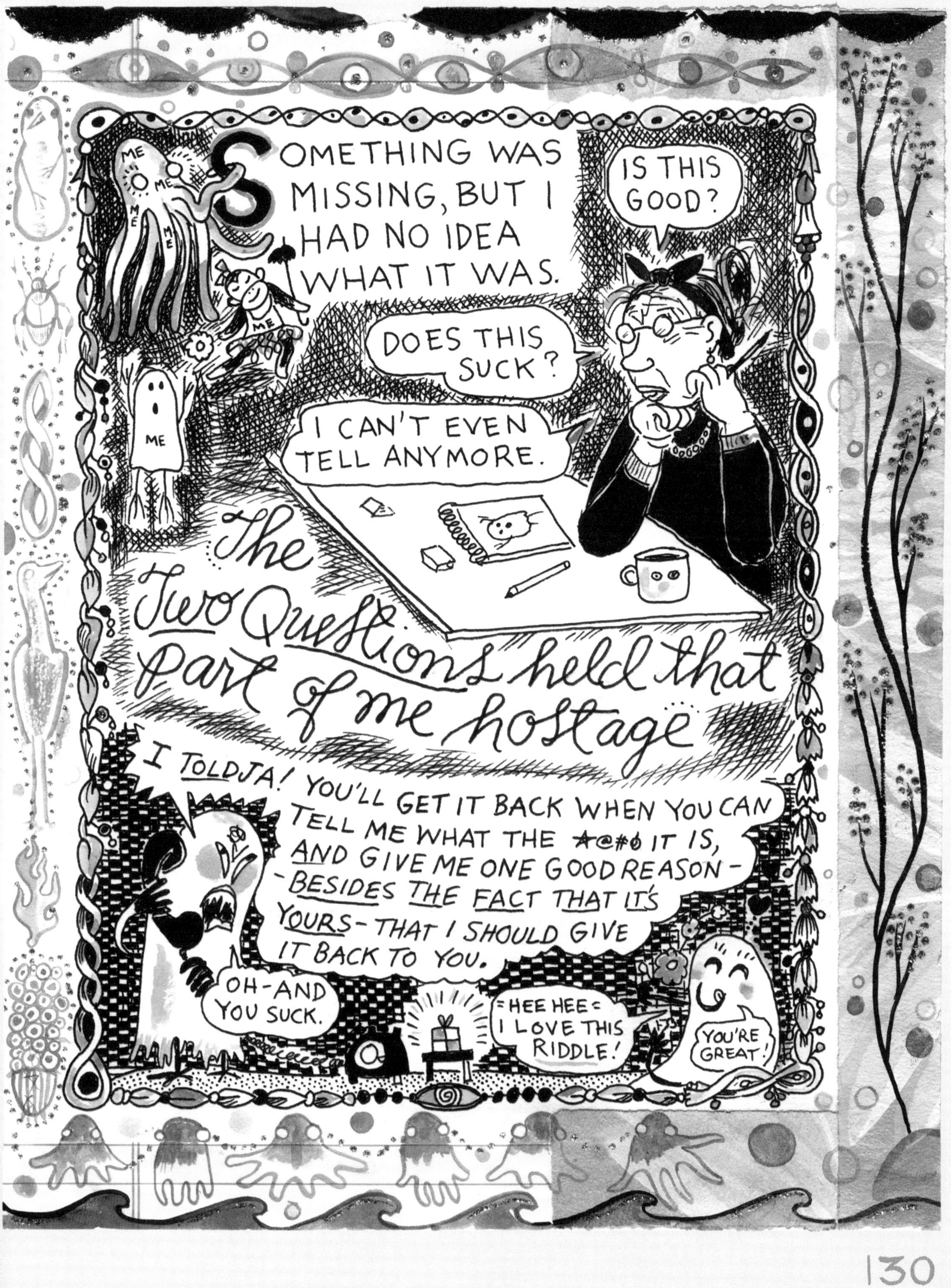
SOMETHING WAS MISSING, BUT I HAD NO IDEA WHAT IT WAS.
ME
IS THIS GOOD?
DOES THIS SUCK?
I CAN'T EVEN TELL ANYMORE.
The Two Questions held that part of me hostage
I TOLDJA! YOU'LL GET IT BACK WHEN YOU CAN TELL ME WHAT THE *@#$ IT IS, AND GIVE ME ONE GOOD REASON - BESIDES THE FACT THAT IT'S YOURS - THAT I SHOULD GIVE IT BACK TO YOU.
OH - AND YOU SUCK.
= HEE HEE = I LOVE THIS RIDDLE!
IT'S
YOU'RE GREAT!

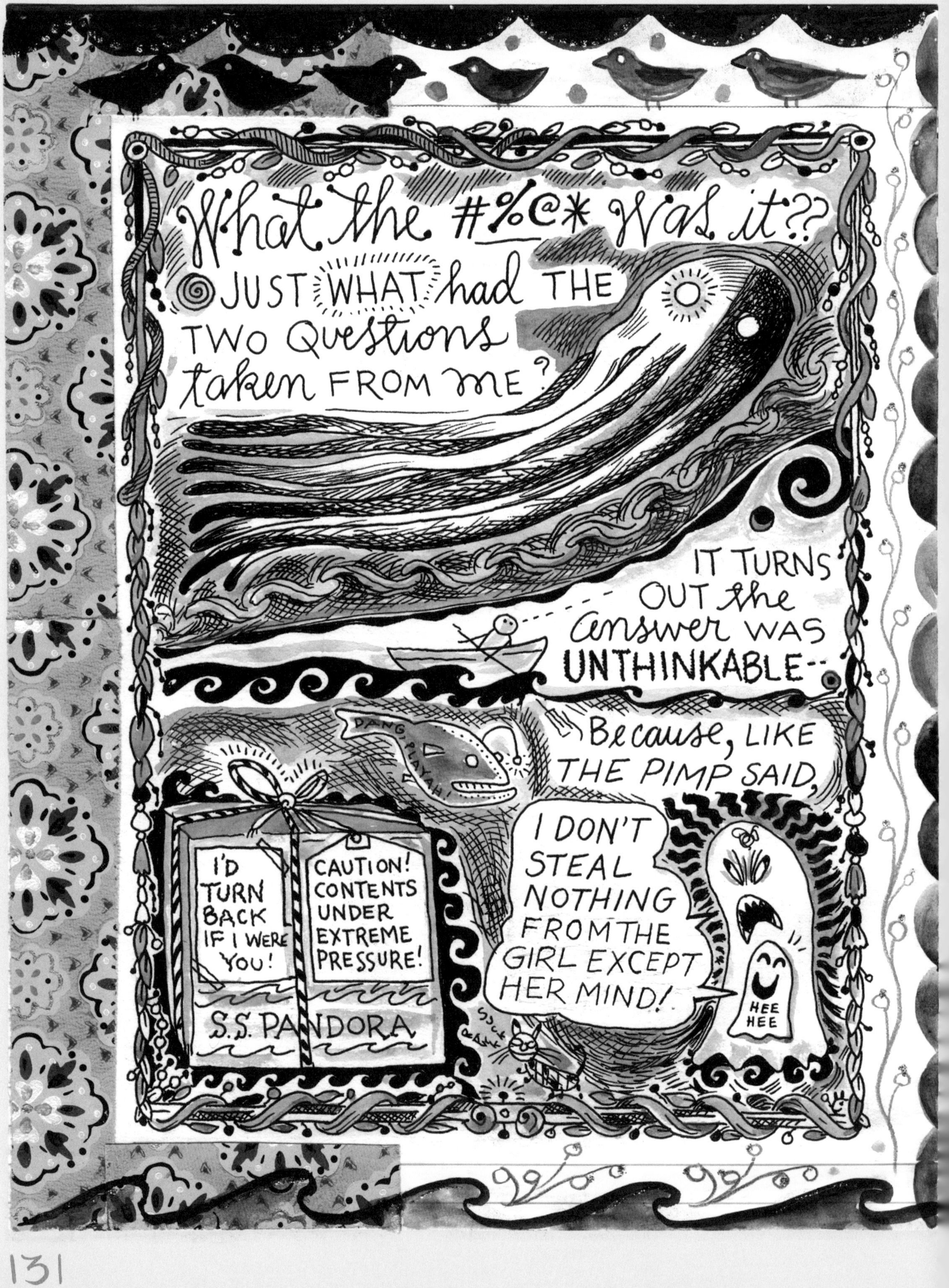
What the #%@* Was it??
JUST WHAT had THE TWO Questions taken FROM me?
IT TURNS OUT the answer WAS UNTHINKABLE--
Because, LIKE THE PIMP SAID,
I'D TURN BACK IF I WERE YOU!
CAUTION! CONTENTS UNDER EXTREME PRESSURE!
S.S. PANDORA
I DON'T STEAL NOTHING FROM THE GIRL EXCEPT HER MIND!
HEE HEE

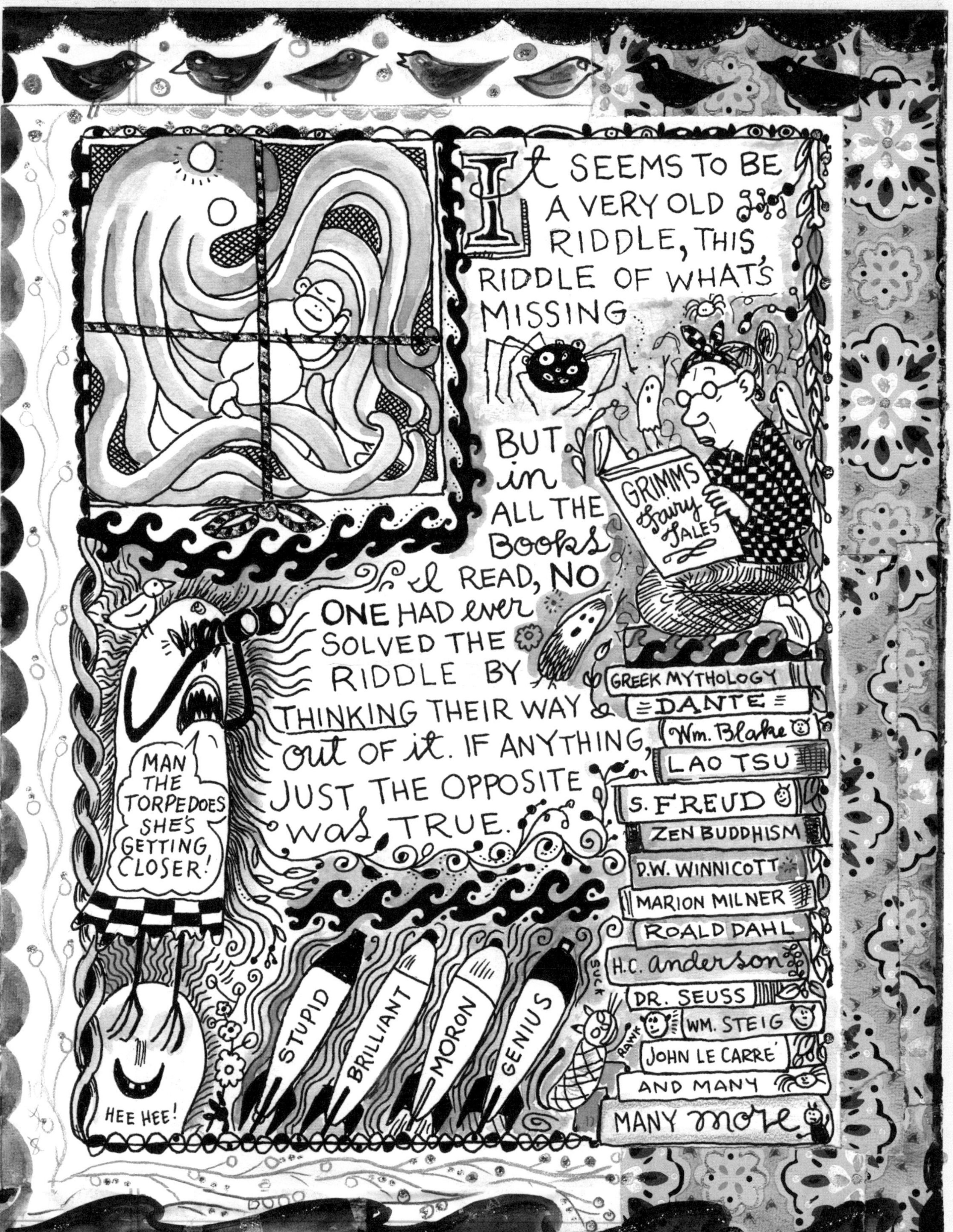
It SEEMS TO BE A VERY OLD RIDDLE, THIS RIDDLE OF WHAT'S MISSING
BUT in ALL THE Books I READ, NO ONE HAD ever SOLVED THE RIDDLE BY THINKING THEIR WAY out OF it. IF ANYTHING, JUST THE OPPOSITE was TRUE.
GRIMMS Fairy Tales
MAN THE TORPEDOES SHE'S GETTING CLOSER!
HEE HEE!
STUPID
BRILLIANT
MORON
GENIUS
SUCK
RAWK
GREEK MYTHOLOGY
DANTE
Wm. Blake
LAO TSU
S. FREUD
ZEN BUDDHISM
D.W. WINNICOTT
MARION MILNER
ROALD DAHL
H.C. anderson
DR. SEUSS
WM. STEIG
JOHN LE CARRE'
AND MANY
MANY more

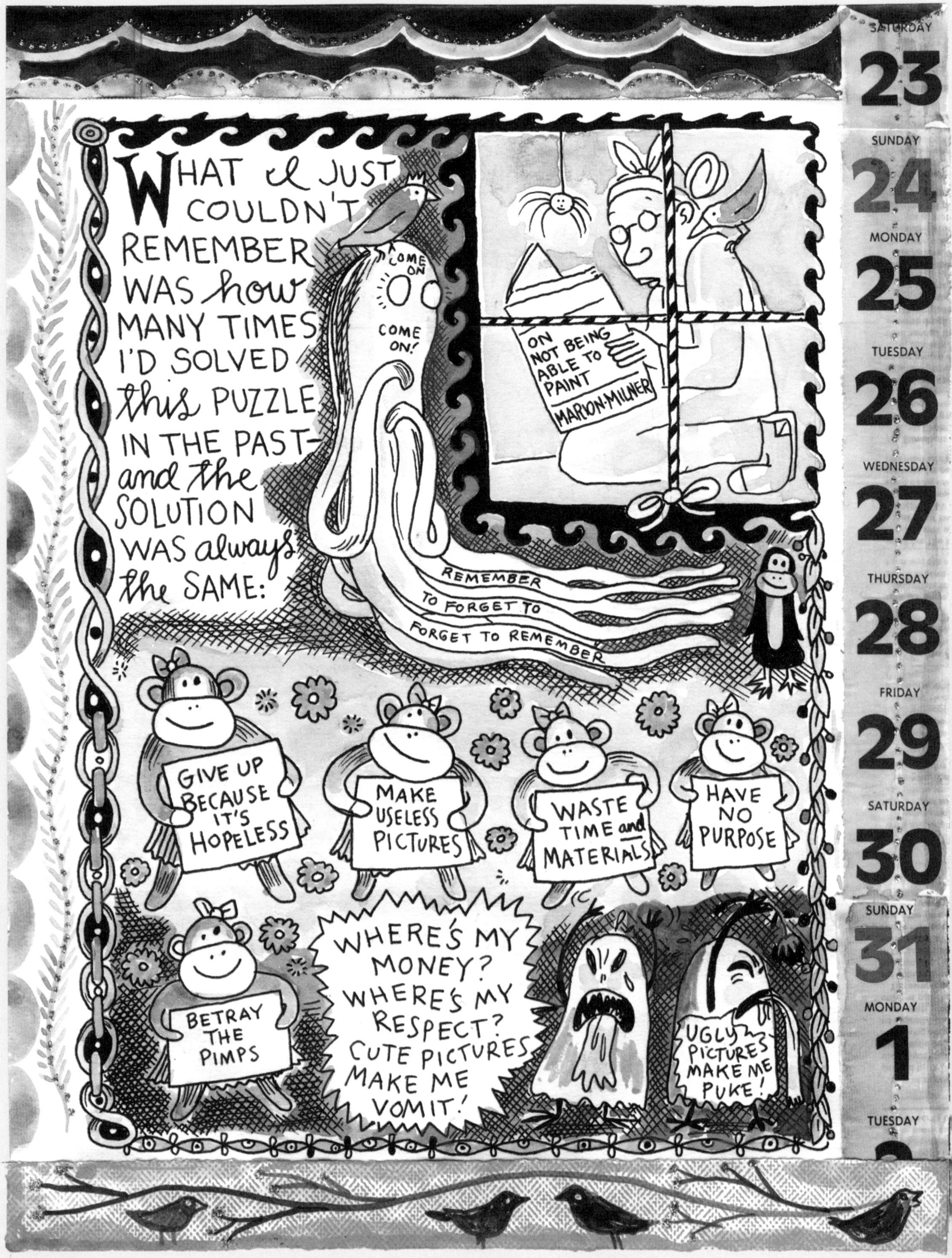
SATURDAY 23
SUNDAY 24
MONDAY 25
TUESDAY 26
WEDNESDAY 27
THURSDAY 28
FRIDAY 29
SATURDAY 30
SUNDAY 31
MONDAY 1
TUESDAY
WHAT I JUST COULDN'T REMEMBER WAS how MANY TIMES I'D SOLVED this PUZZLE IN THE PAST- and the SOLUTION WAS always the SAME:
COME ON
COME ON!
ON NOT BEING ABLE TO PAINT MARION MILNER
REMEMBER
TO FORGET TO
FORGET TO REMEMBER
GIVE UP BECAUSE IT'S HOPELESS
MAKE USELESS PICTURES
WASTE TIME and MATERIALS
HAVE NO PURPOSE
BETRAY THE PIMPS
WHERE'S MY MONEY? WHERE'S MY RESPECT? CUTE PICTURES MAKE ME VOMIT!
UGLY PICTURES MAKE ME PUKE!

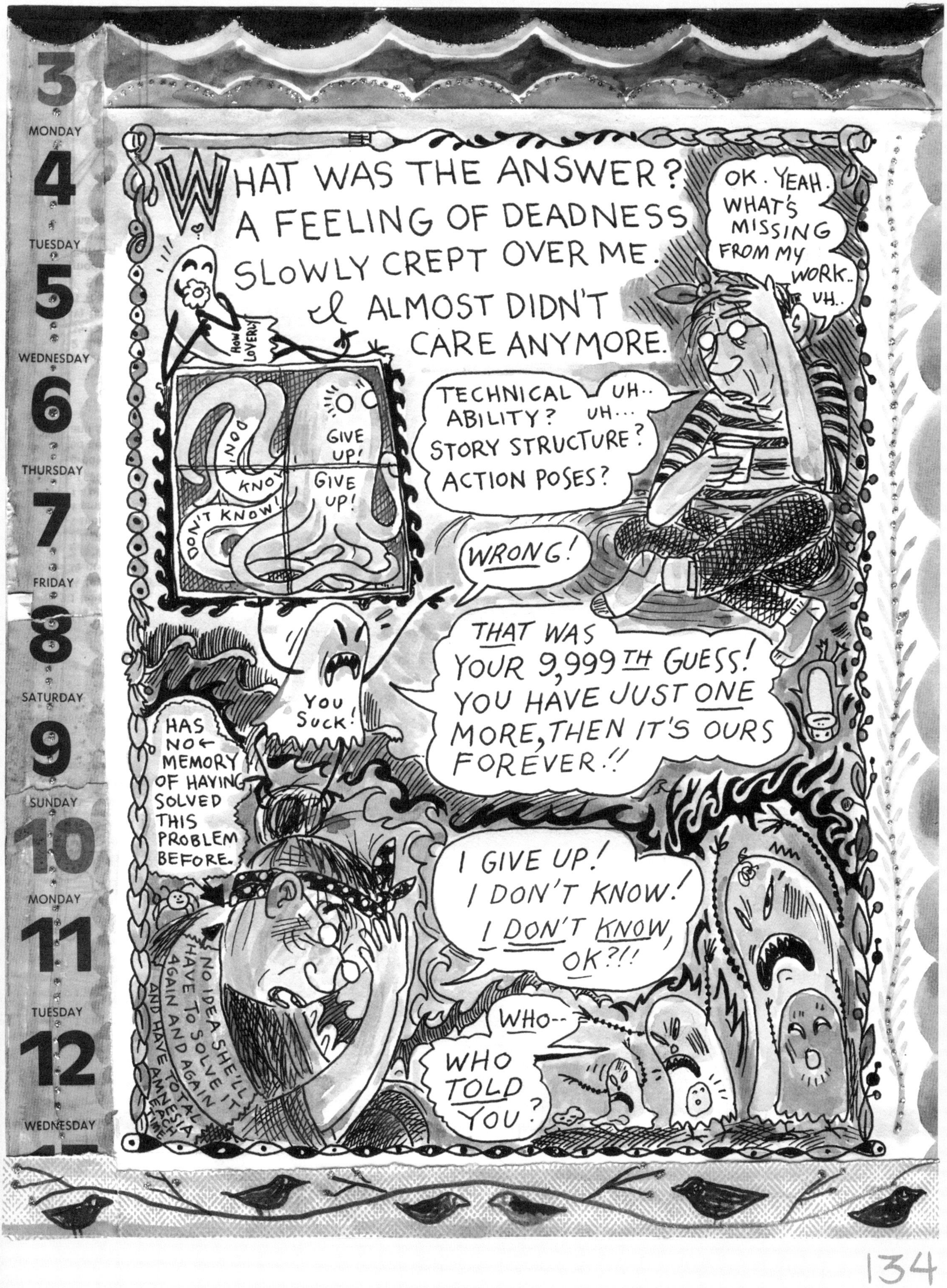
WHAT WAS THE ANSWER? A FEELING OF DEADNESS SLOWLY CREPT OVER ME. I ALMOST DIDN'T CARE ANYMORE.
OK. YEAH. WHAT'S MISSING FROM MY WORK.. UH..
HOW LOVERLY
DON'T KNOW
GIVE UP!
DON'T KNOW!
GIVE UP!
TECHNICAL ABILITY? UH... STORY STRUCTURE? ACTION POSES?
UH..
WRONG!
THAT WAS YOUR 9,999TH GUESS! YOU HAVE JUST ONE MORE, THEN IT'S OURS FOREVER!!
YOU SUCK!
HAS NO MEMORY OF HAVING SOLVED THIS PROBLEM BEFORE.
I GIVE UP! I DON'T KNOW! I DON'T KNOW, OK?!!
NO IDEA SHE'LL HAVE TO SOLVE IT AGAIN AND AGAIN AND HAVE TOTAL AMNESIA EACH TIME
WHO--
WHO TOLD YOU?
MONDAY
TUESDAY
WEDNESDAY
THURSDAY
FRIDAY
SATURDAY
SUNDAY
MONDAY
TUESDAY
WEDNESDAY

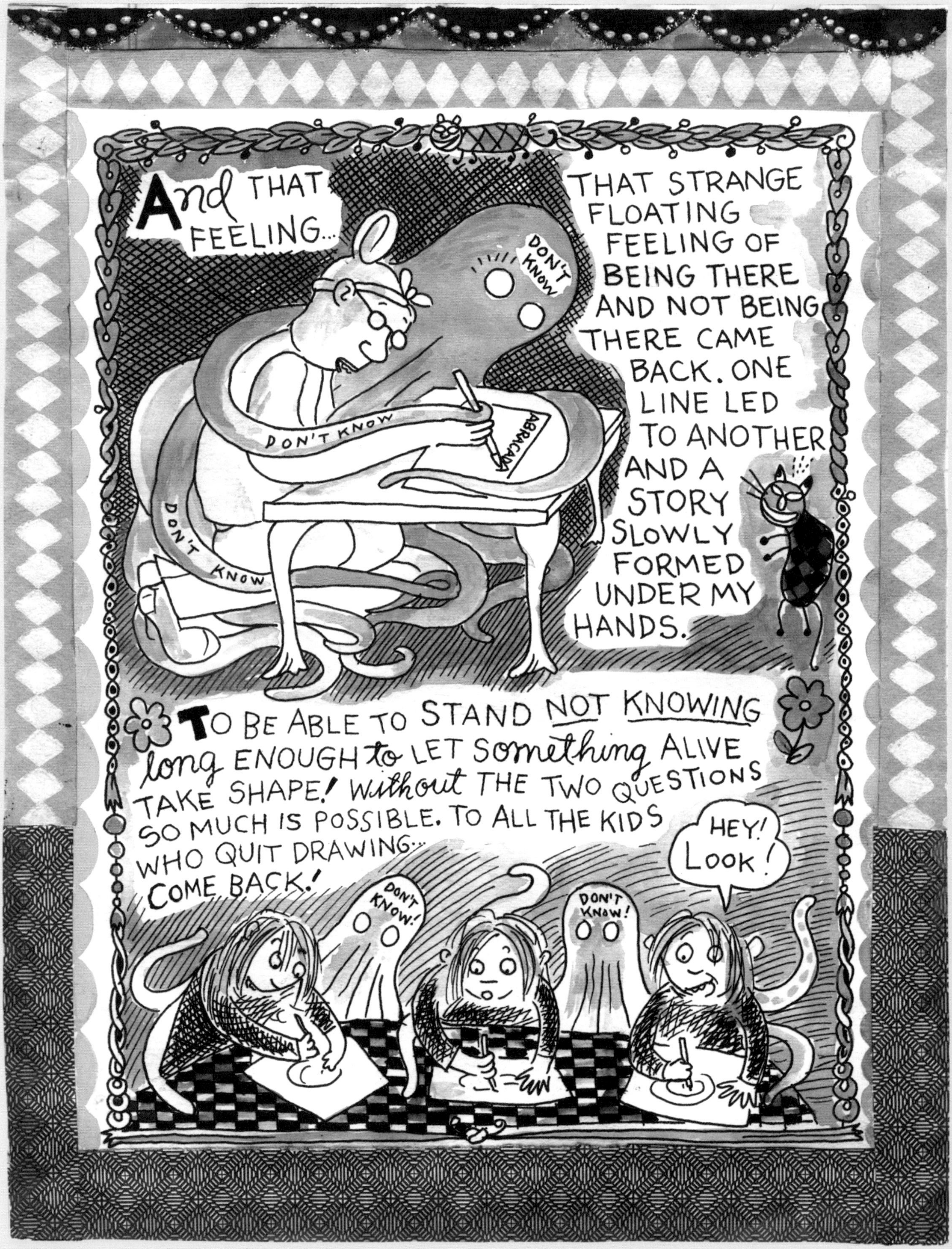
And THAT FEELING...
THAT STRANGE FLOATING FEELING OF BEING THERE AND NOT BEING THERE CAME BACK. ONE LINE LED TO ANOTHER AND A STORY SLOWLY FORMED UNDER MY HANDS.
DON'T KNOW
DON'T KNOW
DON'T KNOW
ABRACAD
TO BE ABLE TO STAND NOT KNOWING long ENOUGH to LET something ALIVE TAKE SHAPE! without THE TWO QUESTIONS SO MUCH IS POSSIBLE. TO ALL THE KIDS WHO QUIT DRAWING... COME BACK!
DON'T KNOW!
DON'T KNOW!
HEY! LOOK!

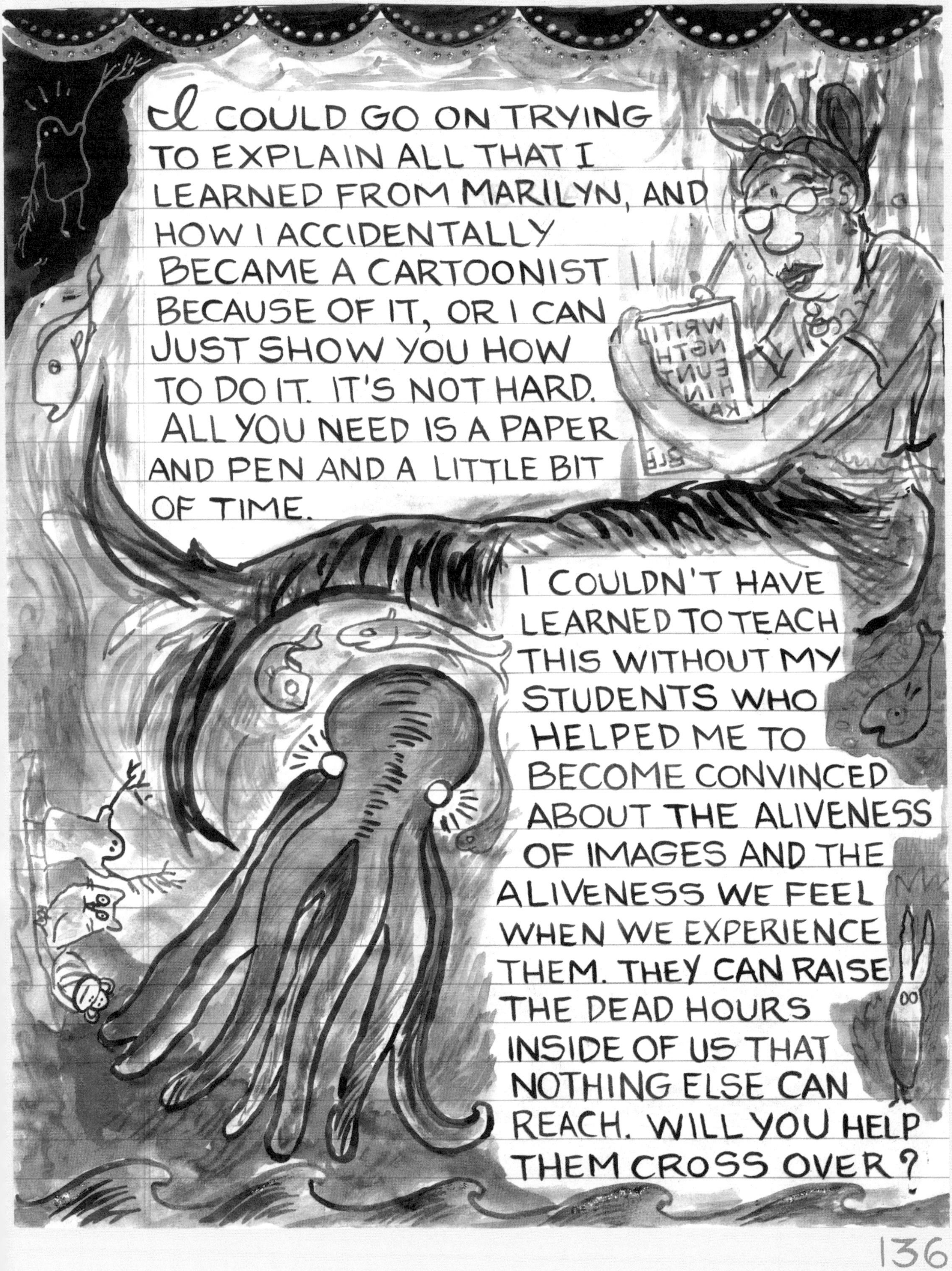
I COULD GO ON TRYING TO EXPLAIN ALL THAT I LEARNED FROM MARILYN, AND HOW I ACCIDENTALLY BECAME A CARTOONIST BECAUSE OF IT, OR I CAN JUST SHOW YOU HOW TO DO IT. IT'S NOT HARD. ALL YOU NEED IS A PAPER AND PEN AND A LITTLE BIT OF TIME.
I COULDN'T HAVE LEARNED TO TEACH THIS WITHOUT MY STUDENTS WHO HELPED ME TO BECOME CONVINCED ABOUT THE ALIVENESS OF IMAGES AND THE ALIVENESS WE FEEL WHEN WE EXPERIENCE THEM. THEY CAN RAISE THE DEAD HOURS INSIDE OF US THAT NOTHING ELSE CAN REACH. WILL YOU HELP THEM CROSS OVER?

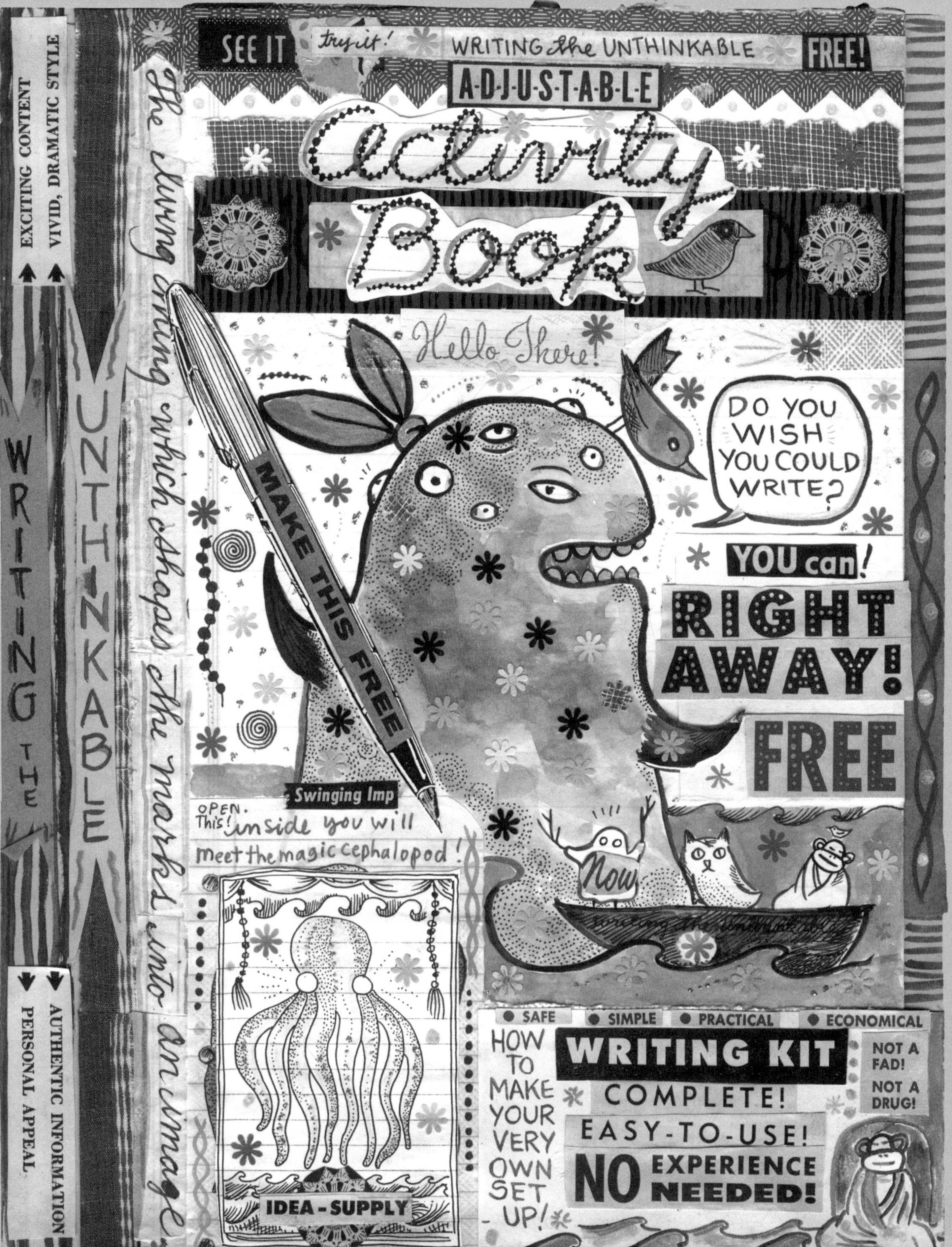

SEE IT
try it!
WRITING the UNTHINKABLE
FREE!
A-D-J-U-S-T-A-B-L-E
Activity Book
EXCITING CONTENT
VIVID, DRAMATIC STYLE
The living writing which shapes the marks into an image
WRITING THE UNTHINKABLE
Hello There!
MAKE THIS FREE
DO YOU WISH YOU COULD WRITE?
YOU can!
RIGHT AWAY!
FREE
Swinging Imp
OPEN. This! inside you will meet the magic cephalopod!
Now
IDEA - SUPPLY
AUTHENTIC INFORMATION
PERSONAL APPEAL
SAFE
SIMPLE
PRACTICAL
ECONOMICAL
HOW TO MAKE YOUR VERY OWN SET UP!
WRITING KIT
COMPLETE!
EASY-TO-USE!
NO EXPERIENCE NEEDED!
NOT A FAD!
NOT A DRUG!

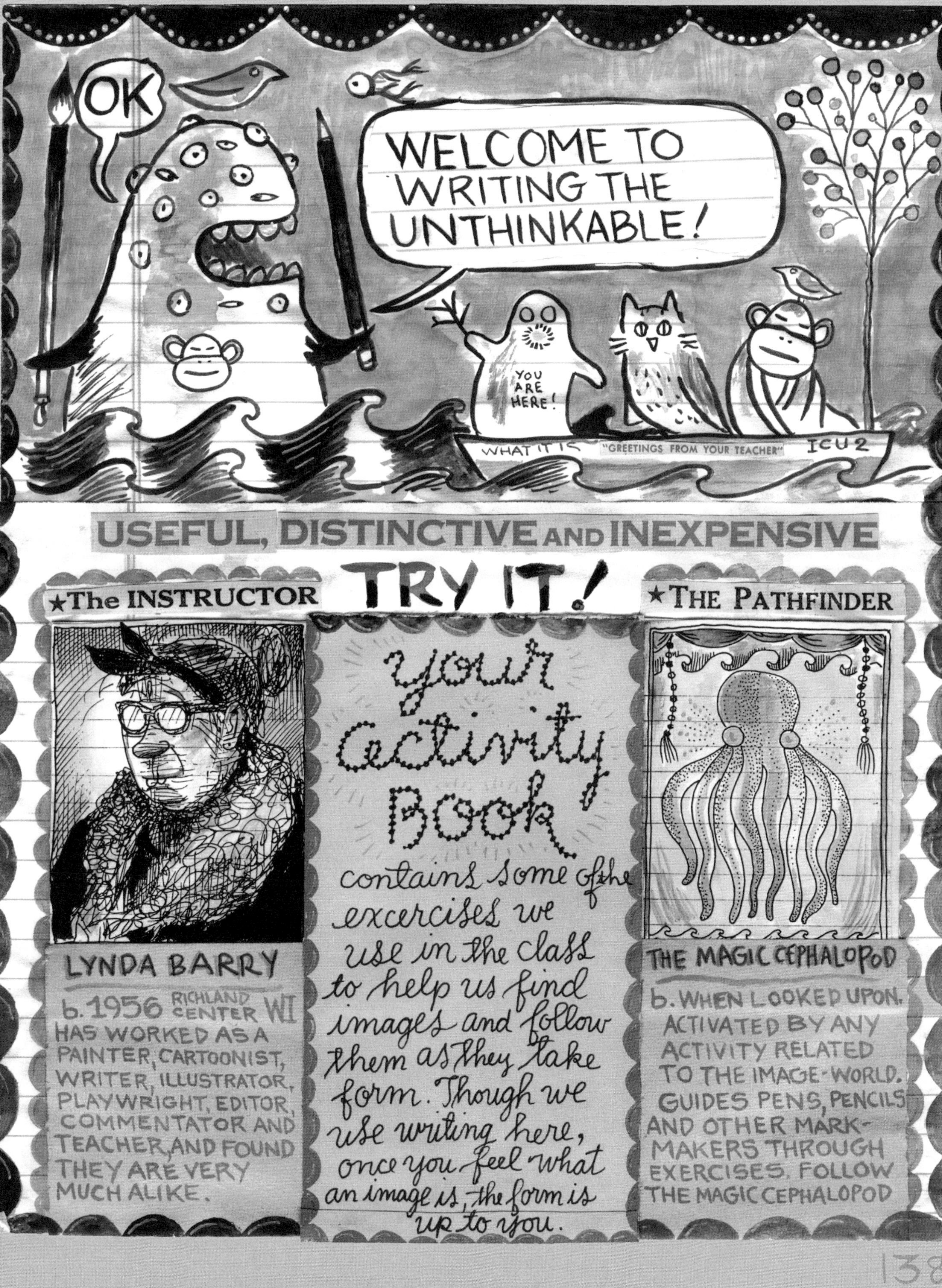
OK
WELCOME TO WRITING THE UNTHINKABLE!
YOU ARE HERE!
WHAT IT IS
"GREETINGS FROM YOUR TEACHER"
ICU 2
USEFUL, DISTINCTIVE AND INEXPENSIVE
TRY IT!
★The INSTRUCTOR
★THE PATHFINDER
your activity Book
contains some of the excercises we use in the class to help us find images and follow them as they take form. Though we use writing here, once you feel what an image is, the form is up to you.
LYNDA BARRY
b. 1956 RICHLAND CENTER WI
HAS WORKED AS A PAINTER, CARTOONIST, WRITER, ILLUSTRATOR, PLAYWRIGHT, EDITOR, COMMENTATOR AND TEACHER, AND FOUND THEY ARE VERY MUCH ALIKE.
THE MAGIC CEPHALOPOD
b. WHEN LOOKED UPON. ACTIVATED BY ANY ACTIVITY RELATED TO THE IMAGE-WORLD. GUIDES PENS, PENCILS AND OTHER MARK-MAKERS THROUGH EXERCISES. FOLLOW THE MAGIC CEPHALOPOD

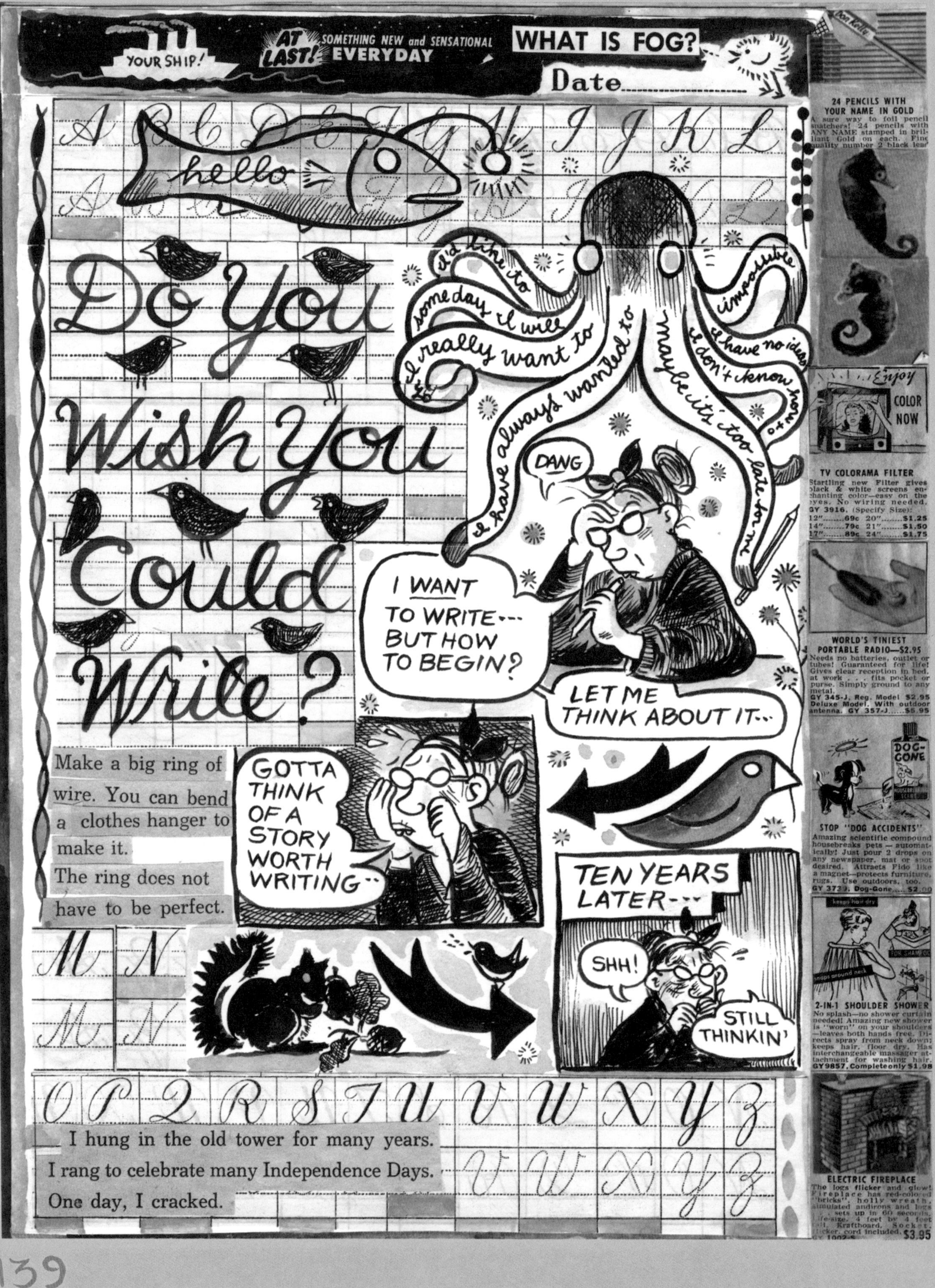
YOUR SHIP!
AT LAST!
SOMETHING NEW and SENSATIONAL
EVERYDAY
WHAT IS FOG?
Date
hello
Do You Wish You Could Write?
i'd like to
some day i will
i really want to
i have always wanted to
maybe it's too late for me
i don't know how to
i have no idea
impossible
DANG
I WANT TO WRITE--- BUT HOW TO BEGIN?
LET ME THINK ABOUT IT--
GOTTA THINK OF A STORY WORTH WRITING--
TEN YEARS LATER---
SHH!
STILL THINKIN'
Make a big ring of wire. You can bend a clothes hanger to make it.
The ring does not have to be perfect.
I hung in the old tower for many years.
I rang to celebrate many Independence Days.
One day, I cracked.
24 PENCILS WITH YOUR NAME IN GOLD
A sure way to foil pencil snatchers! 24 pencils with ANY NAME stamped in brilliant Gold on each. Fine quality number 2 black lead
Enjoy COLOR NOW
TV COLORAMA FILTER
Startling new Filter gives black & white screens enchanting color—easy on the eyes. No wiring needed. GY 3916. (Specify Size): 12"........69c 20"........$1.25 14"........79c 21"........$1.50 17"........89c 24"........$1.75
WORLD'S TINIEST PORTABLE RADIO—$2.95
Needs no batteries, outlet or tubes! Guaranteed for life! Gives clear reception in bed, at work . . . fits pocket or purse. Simply ground to any metal.
GY 345-J, Reg. Model $2.95
Deluxe Model. With outdoor antenna. GY 357-J......$5.95
DOG-GONE
STOP "DOG ACCIDENTS"
Amazing scientific compound housebreaks pets — automatically! Just pour 2 drops on any newspaper, mat or spot desired. Attracts Fido like a magnet—protects furniture, rugs. Use outdoors, too.
keeps hair dry
snaps around neck
FOR SHAMPOO
2-IN-1 SHOULDER SHOWER
No splash—no shower curtain needed! Amazing new shower is "worn" on your shoulders—leaves both hands free. Directs spray from neck down; keeps hair, floor dry. Has interchangeable massager attachment for washing hair.
GY9857, Completeonly $1.98
ELECTRIC FIREPLACE
The logs flicker and glow! Fireplace has red-colored "bricks", holly wreath, simulated andirons and logs . . . sets up in 60 seconds. Life-size. 4 feet by 4 feet tall. Kraftboard. Socket, flicker, cord included. $3.95

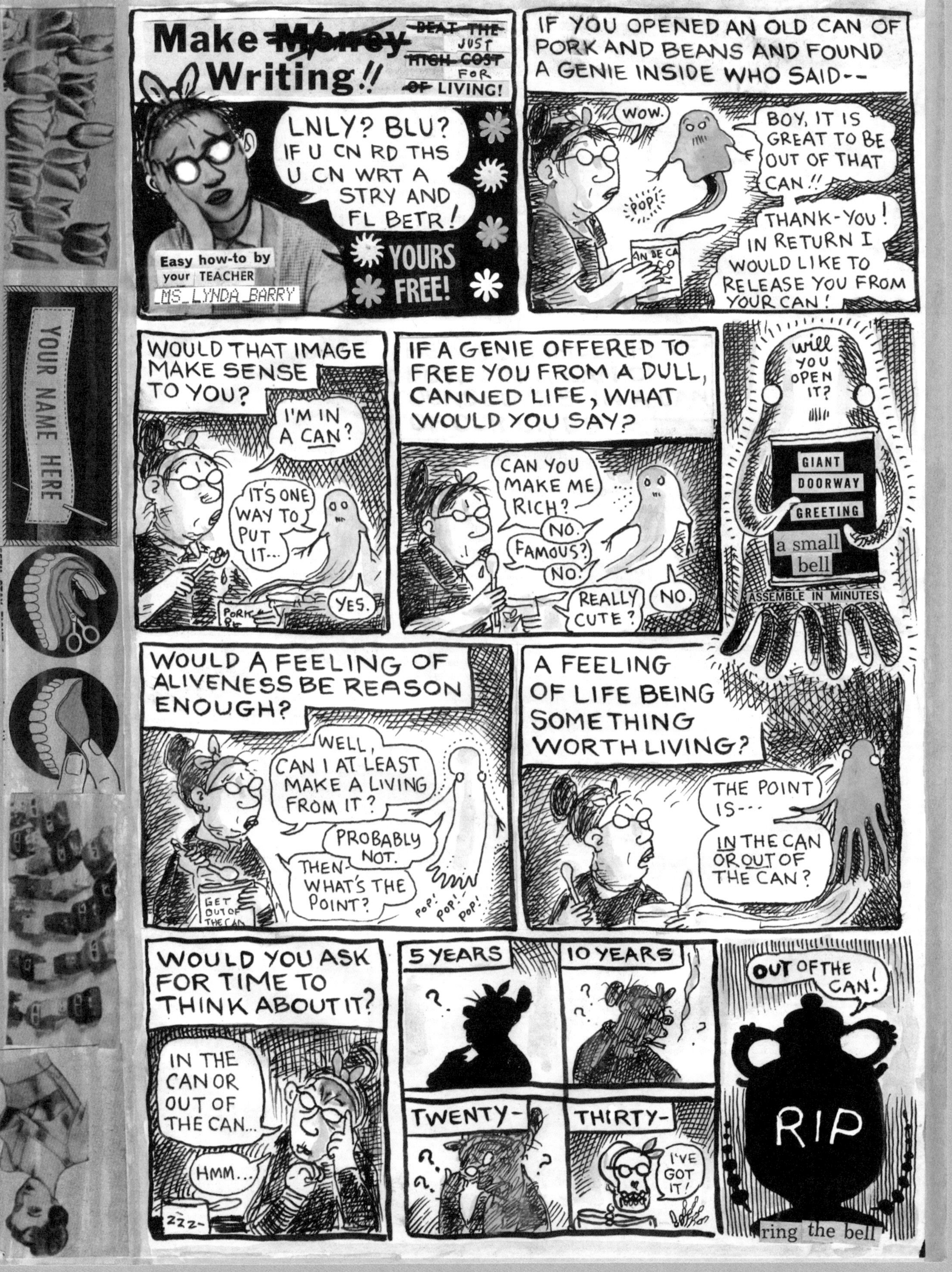

YOUR NAME HERE
Make ~~Money~~ Writing!!
~~BEAT THE~~ JUST ~~HIGH COST~~ FOR ~~OF~~ LIVING!
LNLY? BLU? IF U CN RD THS U CN WRT A STRY AND FL BETR!
Easy how-to by your TEACHER MS. LYNDA BARRY
YOURS FREE!
IF YOU OPENED AN OLD CAN OF PORK AND BEANS AND FOUND A GENIE INSIDE WHO SAID--
WOW.
POP!
AN BE CA
BOY, IT IS GREAT TO BE OUT OF THAT CAN!!
THANK-YOU! IN RETURN I WOULD LIKE TO RELEASE YOU FROM YOUR CAN!
WOULD THAT IMAGE MAKE SENSE TO YOU?
I'M IN A CAN?
IT'S ONE WAY TO PUT IT...
YES.
IF A GENIE OFFERED TO FREE YOU FROM A DULL, CANNED LIFE, WHAT WOULD YOU SAY?
CAN YOU MAKE ME RICH?
NO.
FAMOUS?
NO.
REALLY CUTE?
NO.
will YOU OPEN IT?
GIANT DOORWAY GREETING a small bell
ASSEMBLE IN MINUTES
WOULD A FEELING OF ALIVENESS BE REASON ENOUGH?
WELL, CAN I AT LEAST MAKE A LIVING FROM IT?
PROBABLY NOT.
THEN-WHAT'S THE POINT?
GET OUT OF THE CAN
POP! POP! POP!
A FEELING OF LIFE BEING SOMETHING WORTH LIVING?
THE POINT IS---
IN THE CAN OR OUT OF THE CAN?
WOULD YOU ASK FOR TIME TO THINK ABOUT IT?
IN THE CAN OR OUT OF THE CAN...
HMM...
ZZZ-
5 YEARS
10 YEARS
TWENTY-
THIRTY-
I'VE GOT IT!
OUT OF THE CAN!
RIP
ring the bell

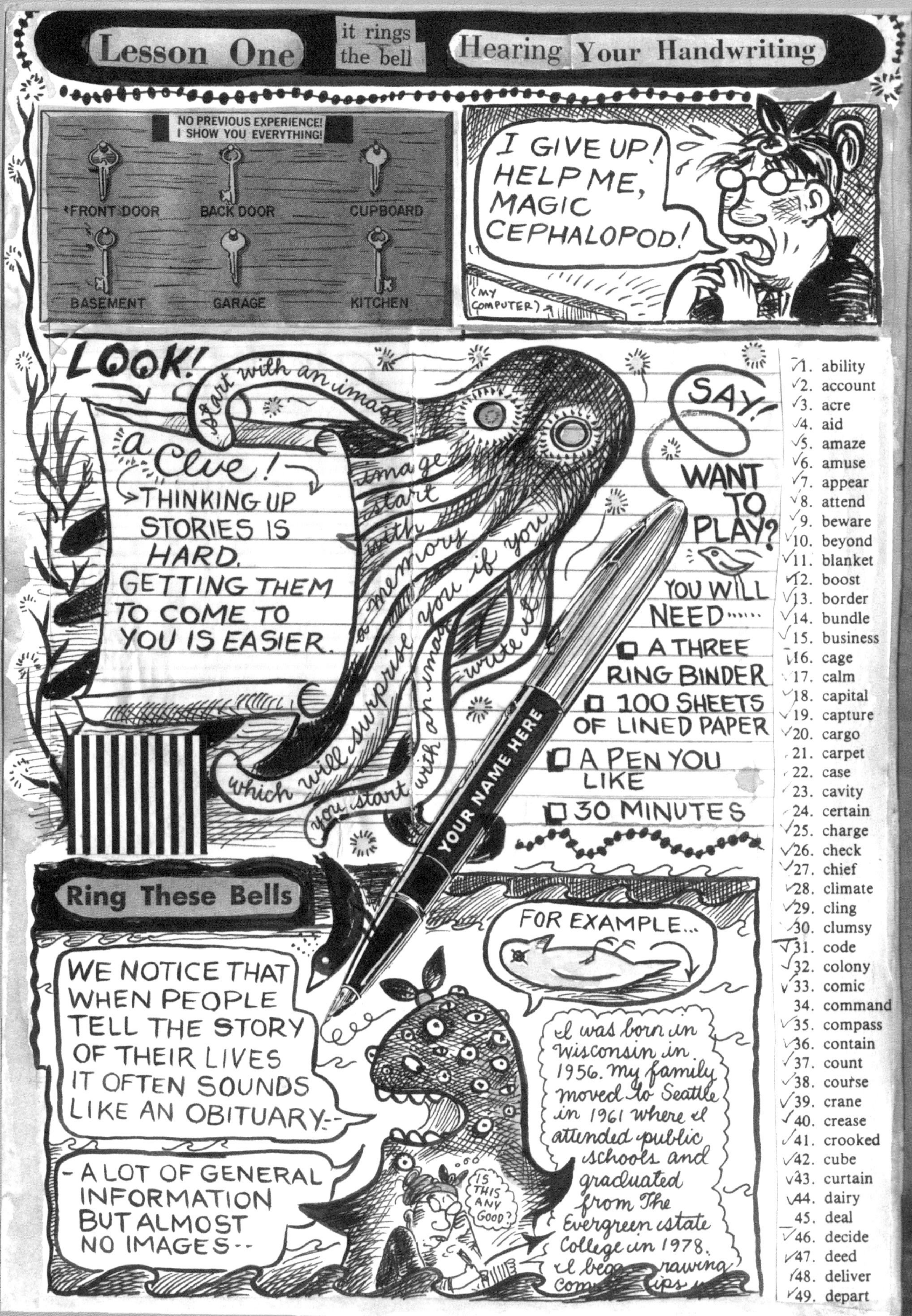

Lesson One
it rings the bell
Hearing Your Handwriting
NO PREVIOUS EXPERIENCE! I SHOW YOU EVERYTHING!
FRONT DOOR
BACK DOOR
CUPBOARD
BASEMENT
GARAGE
KITCHEN
I GIVE UP! HELP ME, MAGIC CEPHALOPOD!
(MY COMPUTER)
LOOK!
Start with an image
a Clue!
THINKING UP STORIES IS HARD. GETTING THEM TO COME TO YOU IS EASIER.
image start with memory
write it you if you
which will surprise you
you start with an image
YOUR NAME HERE
SAY!
WANT TO PLAY?
YOU WILL NEED......
A THREE RING BINDER
100 SHEETS OF LINED PAPER
A PEN YOU LIKE
30 MINUTES
1. ability
2. account
3. acre
4. aid
5. amaze
6. amuse
7. appear
8. attend
9. beware
10. beyond
11. blanket
12. boost
13. border
14. bundle
15. business
16. cage
17. calm
18. capital
19. capture
20. cargo
21. carpet
22. case
23. cavity
24. certain
25. charge
26. check
27. chief
28. climate
29. cling
30. clumsy
31. code
32. colony
33. comic
34. command
35. compass
36. contain
37. count
38. course
39. crane
40. crease
41. crooked
42. cube
43. curtain
44. dairy
45. deal
46. decide
47. deed
48. deliver
49. depart
Ring These Bells
FOR EXAMPLE...
WE NOTICE THAT WHEN PEOPLE TELL THE STORY OF THEIR LIVES IT OFTEN SOUNDS LIKE AN OBITUARY--
- A LOT OF GENERAL INFORMATION BUT ALMOST NO IMAGES--
IS THIS ANY GOOD?
I was born in Wisconsin in 1956. My family moved to Seattle in 1961 where I attended public schools and graduated from The Evergreen State College in 1978.

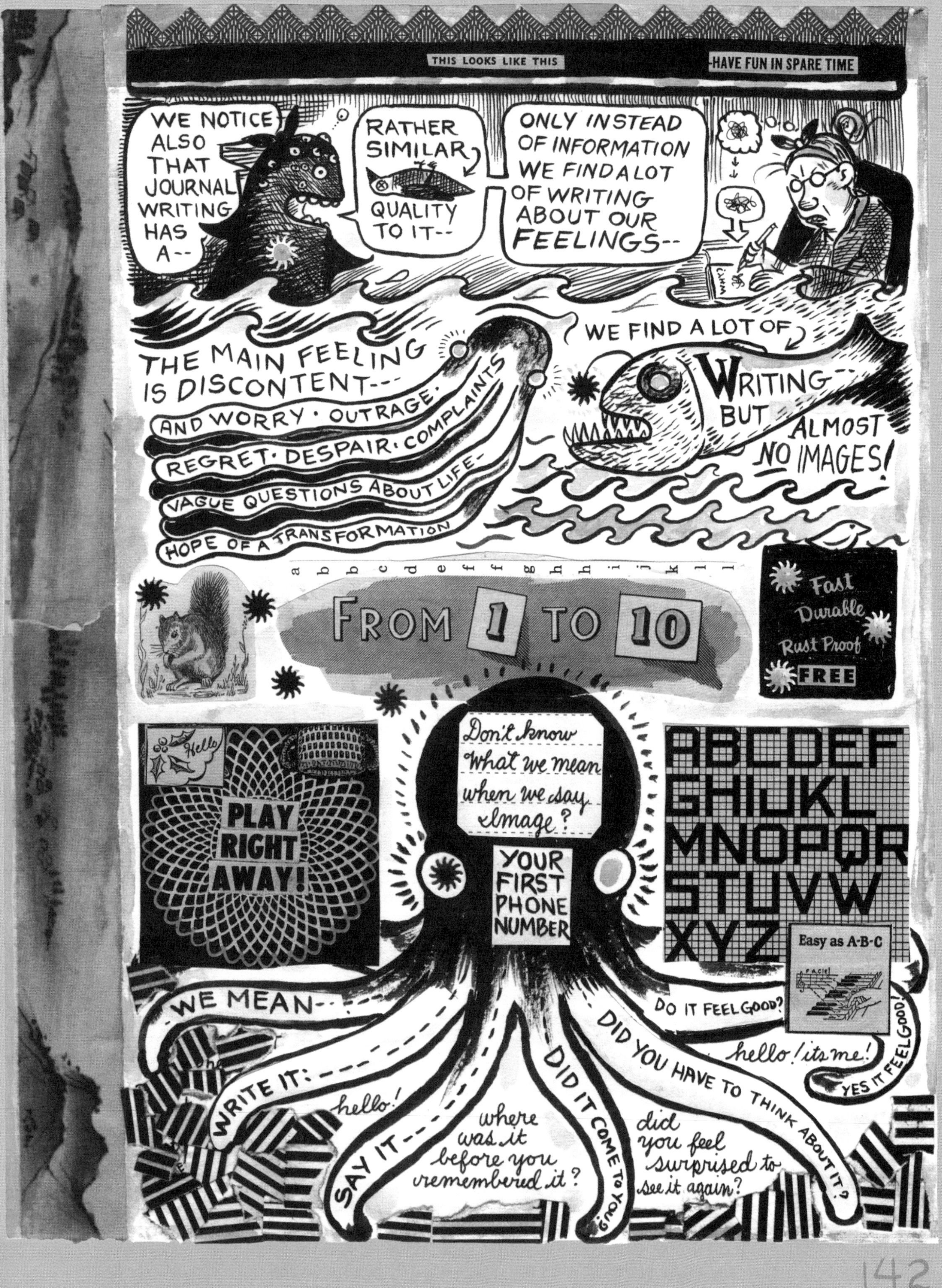

THIS LOOKS LIKE THIS
HAVE FUN IN SPARE TIME
WE NOTICE ALSO THAT JOURNAL WRITING HAS A--
RATHER SIMILAR QUALITY TO IT--
ONLY INSTEAD OF INFORMATION WE FIND A LOT OF WRITING ABOUT OUR FEELINGS--
THE MAIN FEELING IS DISCONTENT---
AND WORRY · OUTRAGE ·
REGRET · DESPAIR · COMPLAINTS
VAGUE QUESTIONS ABOUT LIFE-
HOPE OF A TRANSFORMATION
WE FIND A LOT OF WRITING-- BUT ALMOST NO IMAGES!
a b b c d e f f g h h i j k l l
FROM 1 TO 10
Fast
Durable
Rust Proof
FREE
PLAY RIGHT AWAY!
Don't know What we mean when we say Image?
YOUR FIRST PHONE NUMBER
ABCDEF
GHIJKL
MNOPQR
STUVW
XYZ
Easy as A-B-C
WE MEAN--
WRITE IT: ---
SAY IT---
DID IT COME TO YOU?
DID YOU HAVE TO THINK ABOUT IT?
DO IT FEEL GOOD?
YES IT FEEL GOOD!
hello! its me!
hello!
where was it before you remembered it?
did you feel surprised to see it again?

A SPECIAL GIFT * **What is an iceberg?** * A SPECIAL FRIEND

FOR MOST OF US, JUST SAYING OUR FIRST PHONE NUMBER GIVES US A KIND OF FEELING WE DO NOT FIND IN OTHER PHONE NUMBERS.

IT SEEMS TO JUMP AT THE CHANCE TO COME BACK TO US- WE DON'T HAVE TO THINK IT UP. IT'S THE OPPOSITE OF THIS ⟶ IT FEELS SOMEHOW ALIVE. THIS IS ONE THING WE MEAN WHEN WE SAY AN IMAGE

"LIVING FORM"

Most remarkable form ever made!

The GREATEST *Value Ever Offered*

10 CARS and TRUCK IMAGES

DIP CURLER — PLACE IN HAIR — LIKE MAGIC!

I WEAR THIS SUIT IN HONOR OF A VERY GOOD POEM ABOUT THE NATURE OF IMAGES BY - RUMI -

: THE DIVER'S CLOTHES LYING EMPTY ON THE BEACH :

30 minutes

all you need — the images are there — all you need

MAKE ~~MONEY~~ WRITING

..right away!

You don't have to be a trained author to make ~~money~~ writing. Hundreds now making ~~money~~ every day ~~on~~ short paragraphs. I tell you ~~what~~ to write, where and how ~~to sell~~; and supply big list ~~of editors who buy from beginners~~. Lots of small checks in a hurry ~~bring cash that~~ adds up quickly. No tedious study. Write ~~to sell~~, right away. ~~Send~~ for free ~~facts~~.

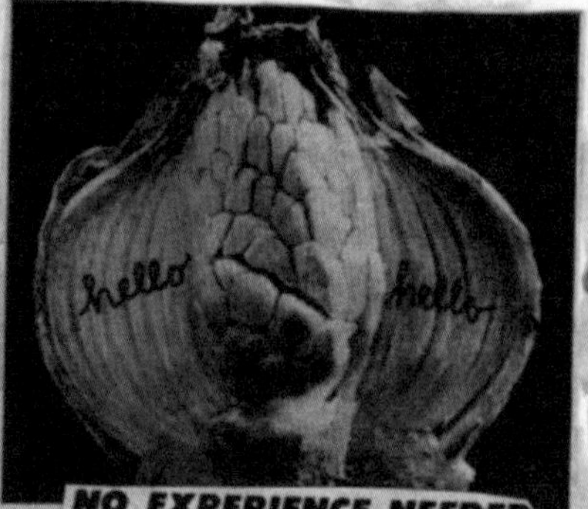

hello
hello

NO EXPERIENCE NEEDED

The flower is already formed within the hyacinth bulb, as this unusual photo of a cut-open bulb shows. Tulips and all other true bulbs have the same quality of forming the embryo blossom within the bulb. This is why, unless badly mistreated somehow, mature bulbs will never fail to produce blooms.

MAKE A LIST OF THE FIRST 10 CARS THAT COME TO YOU FROM EARLY-ON IN YOUR LIFE:

Write * now

1. number
2. your page
3. from one
4. to ten
5.
6. write down
7. the First 10
8. cars you
9. remember
10.

NOW CHOOSE ONE THAT SEEMS VIVID TO YOU - - - -

Uncle Raymond's Station wagon

icebergs are of enormous size and only a part shows above the water

TIP: DON'T SPEND MORE THAN 3 MINUTES ON YOUR LIST. DON'T SPEND LESS THAN 3 MINUTES ON YOUR LIST. IF YOU GET STUCK, WRITE THE ALPHABET OR DRAW IN THE MARGINS.

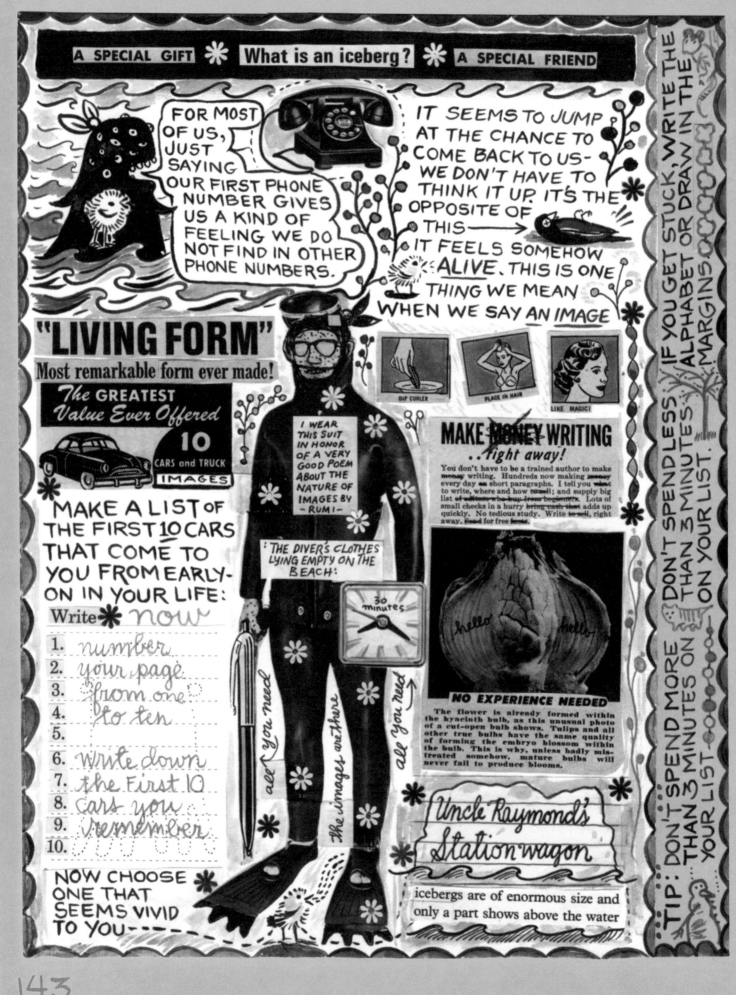

PICTURE THE CAR

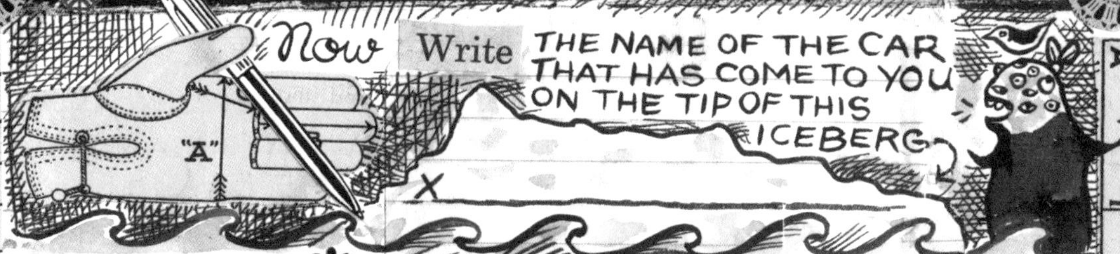
Now Write THE NAME OF THE CAR THAT HAS COME TO YOU ON THE TIP OF THIS ICEBERG
"A"
X

RIGHT EYE	20/200	20/100	20/70	20/50	20/40	20/30	20/20
PILOT LINE	E	m	E	∃	∃	w	m
		1	2	3	4	5	6
20/50 (Blue)	A	∃	E	w	∃	m	w
20/40 (Red)	B	w	w	∃	m	w	E
20/30 (Yellow)	C	∃	m	E	E	∃	w
20/20 (Green)	D	E	w	E	∃	w	m

LEFT EYE	20/200	20/100	20/70	20/50	20/40	20/30	20/20
PILOT LINE	∃	w	m	∃	E	∃	w
		1	2	3	4	5	6
20/50 (Blue)	A	E	w	E	∃	w	m
20/40 (Red)	B	m	E	m	∃	∃	E
20/30 (Yellow)	C	∃	w	w	∃	E	m
20/20 (Green)	D	E	∃	w	∃	m	w

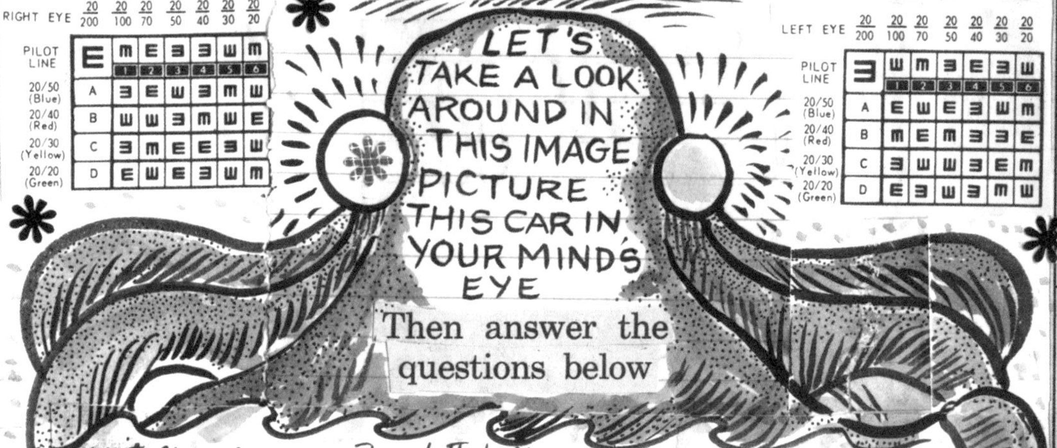
LET'S TAKE A LOOK AROUND IN THIS IMAGE PICTURE THIS CAR IN YOUR MIND'S EYE
Then answer the questions below

write your answers on the dotted lines

WHERE ARE YOU?

ARE YOU IN THE CAR OR OUT OF THE CAR?

IF YOU ARE INSIDE - WHICH SEAT ARE YOU IN?

WHAT ARE YOU DOING?

IF YOU ARE OUT OF THE CAR, WHAT PART OF IT ARE YOU FACING?

WHAT TIME OF DAY OR NIGHT DOES IT SEEM TO BE?

WHY ARE YOU THERE?

WHO ELSE IS THERE?

WHAT SEASON?

ABOUT HOW OLD ARE YOU?

N O P Q R S T U V W X Y

TIP: THIS PART SHOULD TAKE ABOUT 10 MINUTES

TIP: NOTICE THE DIFFERENCE BETWEEN WHEN THE ANSWERS COME TO YOU AND WHEN YOU HAVE TO THINK ABOUT IT

Place measure at "B" at base of middle finger, in front, take measurement TO THE NAIL.

Place measure at "C" in crotch of thumb, measure to fork of first and second finger.

Hold hand flat and rigid, place measure at "A" in palm, take measure CLOSE, but do not cramp bones of hand

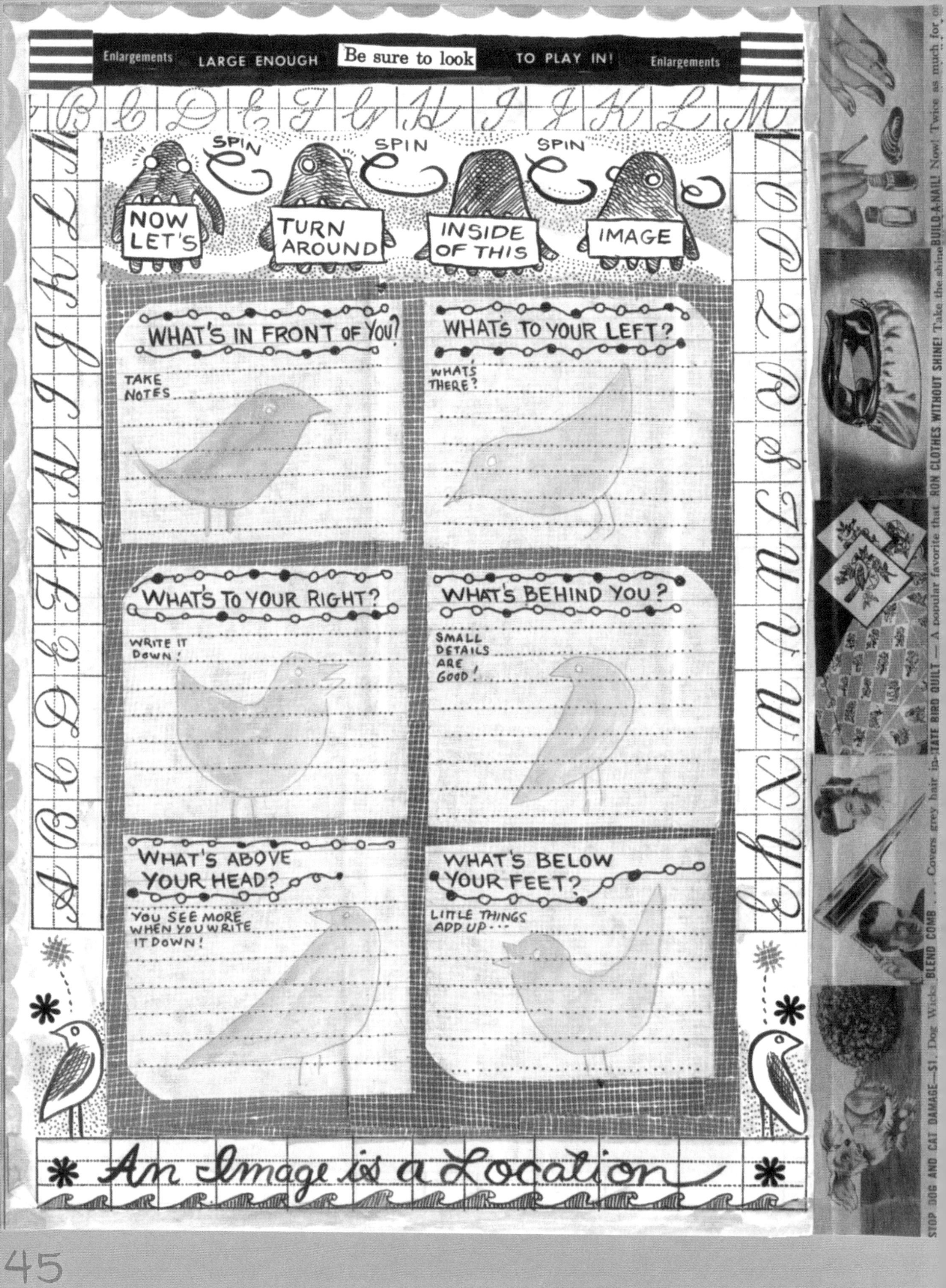
Enlargements
LARGE ENOUGH
Be sure to look
TO PLAY IN!
Enlargements
SPIN
SPIN
SPIN
NOW LET'S
TURN AROUND
INSIDE OF THIS
IMAGE
WHAT'S IN FRONT OF YOU?
TAKE NOTES
WHAT'S TO YOUR LEFT?
WHAT'S THERE?
WHAT'S TO YOUR RIGHT?
WRITE IT DOWN!
WHAT'S BEHIND YOU?
SMALL DETAILS ARE GOOD!
WHAT'S ABOVE YOUR HEAD?
YOU SEE MORE WHEN YOU WRITE IT DOWN!
WHAT'S BELOW YOUR FEET?
LITTLE THINGS ADD UP...
An Image is a Location

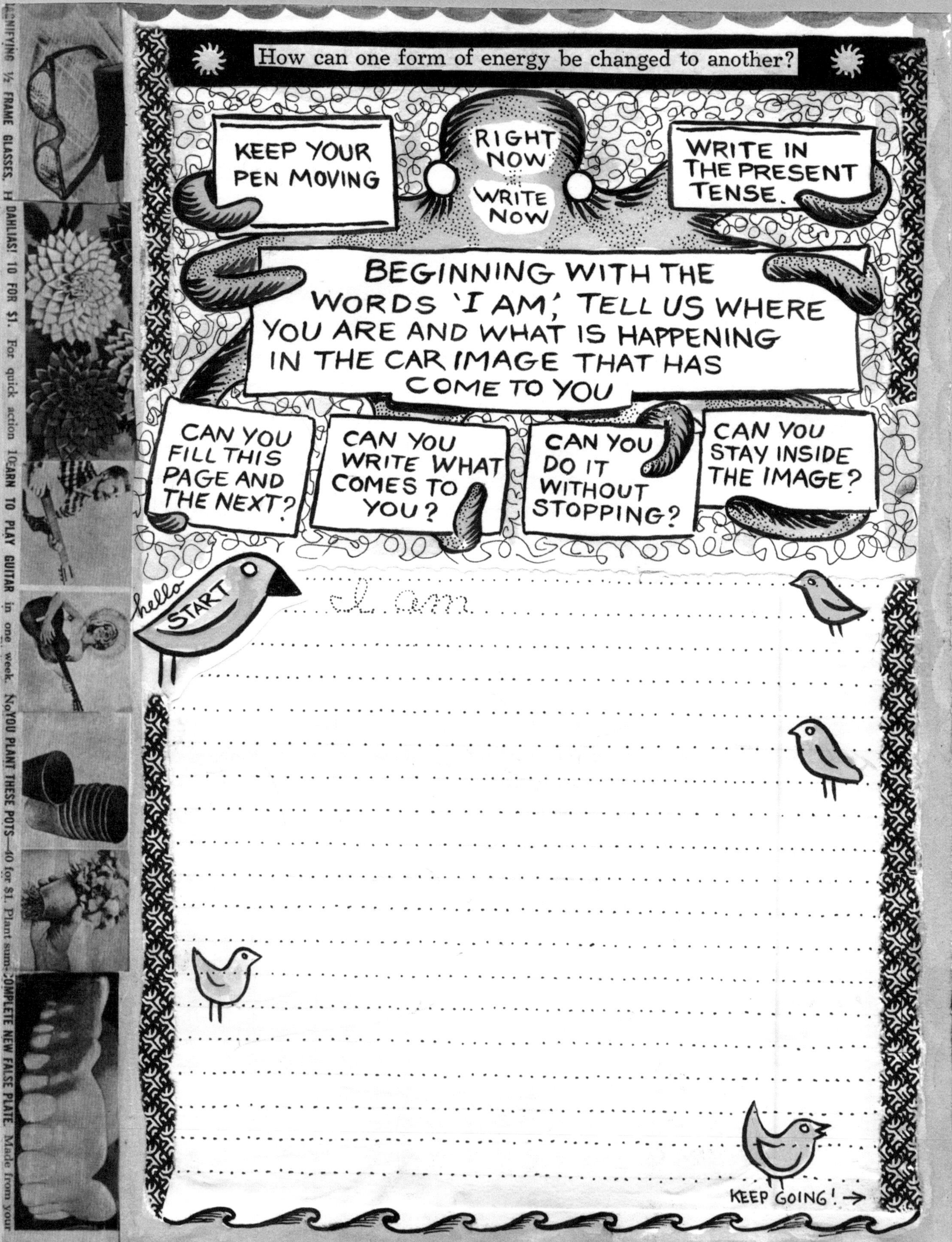
How can one form of energy be changed to another?
KEEP YOUR PEN MOVING
RIGHT NOW
WRITE NOW
WRITE IN THE PRESENT TENSE.
BEGINNING WITH THE WORDS 'I AM,' TELL US WHERE YOU ARE AND WHAT IS HAPPENING IN THE CAR IMAGE THAT HAS COME TO YOU
CAN YOU FILL THIS PAGE AND THE NEXT?
CAN YOU WRITE WHAT COMES TO YOU?
CAN YOU DO IT WITHOUT STOPPING?
CAN YOU STAY INSIDE THE IMAGE?
hello
START
I am
KEEP GOING! →
GNIFYING ½ FRAME GLASSES. H DAHLIAS! 10 FOR $1. For quick action LEARN TO PLAY GUITAR in one week. No YOU PLANT THESE POTS—40 for $1. Plant sun COMPLETE NEW FALSE PLATE. Made from your

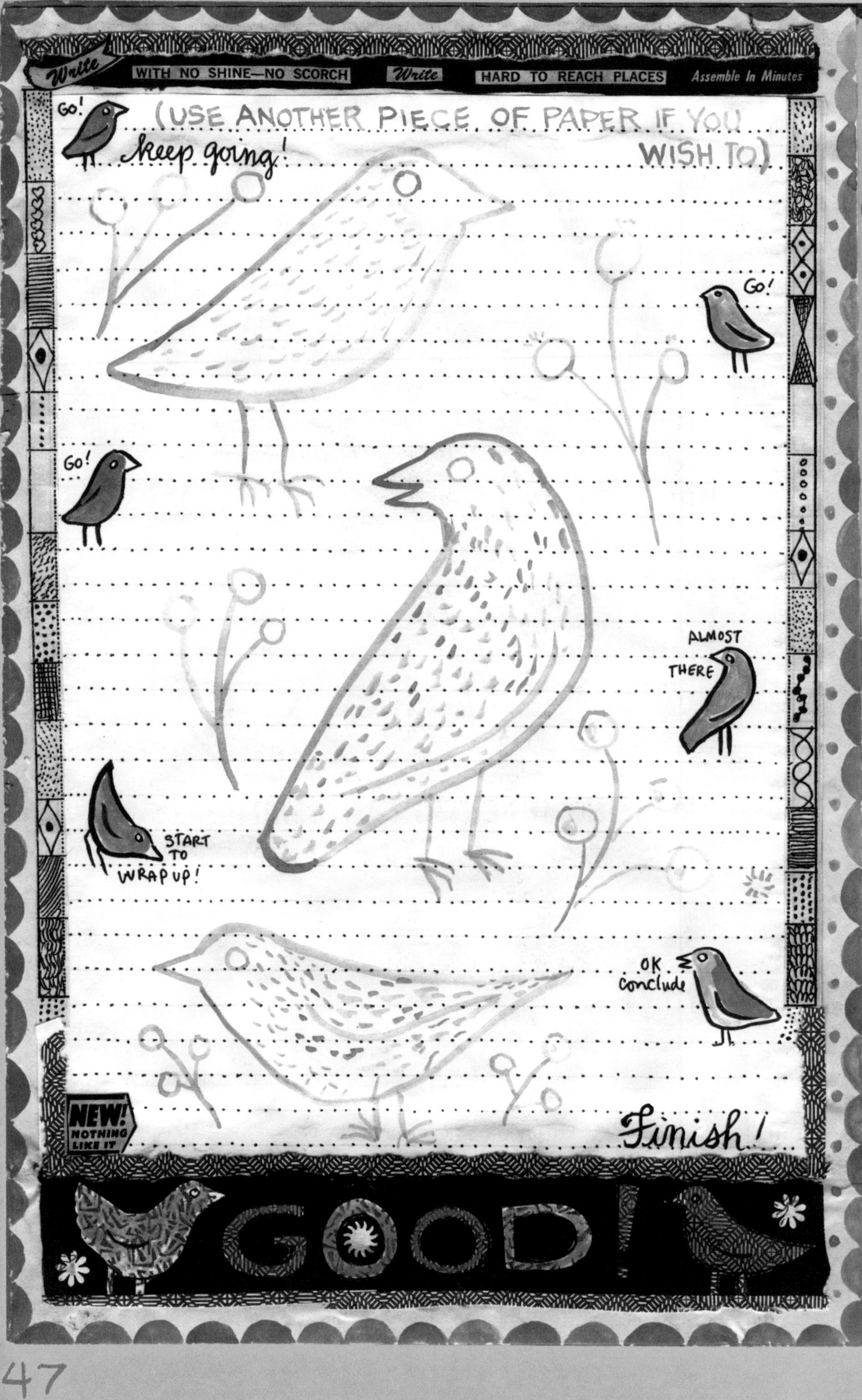
Write
WITH NO SHINE—NO SCORCH
Write
HARD TO REACH PLACES
Assemble In Minutes
Go!
(USE ANOTHER PIECE OF PAPER IF YOU WISH TO)
Keep going!
Go!
Go!
ALMOST THERE
START TO WRAP UP!
OK conclude
NEW! NOTHING LIKE IT
Finish!
GOOD!

TIP: TRY THIS AGAIN WITH ANOTHER CAR ON YOUR LIST BUT WHEN YOU GET TO THE WRITING PART, WRITE FOR 7 MINUTES STRAIGHT. USE TWO TIMERS. SET ONE FOR FOUR MINUTES AND THE OTHER FOR 7 MINUTES. WHEN THE FIRST ONE GOES OFF YOU'LL KNOW YOU HAVE 3 MINUTES TO FINISH YOUR STORY

DING!

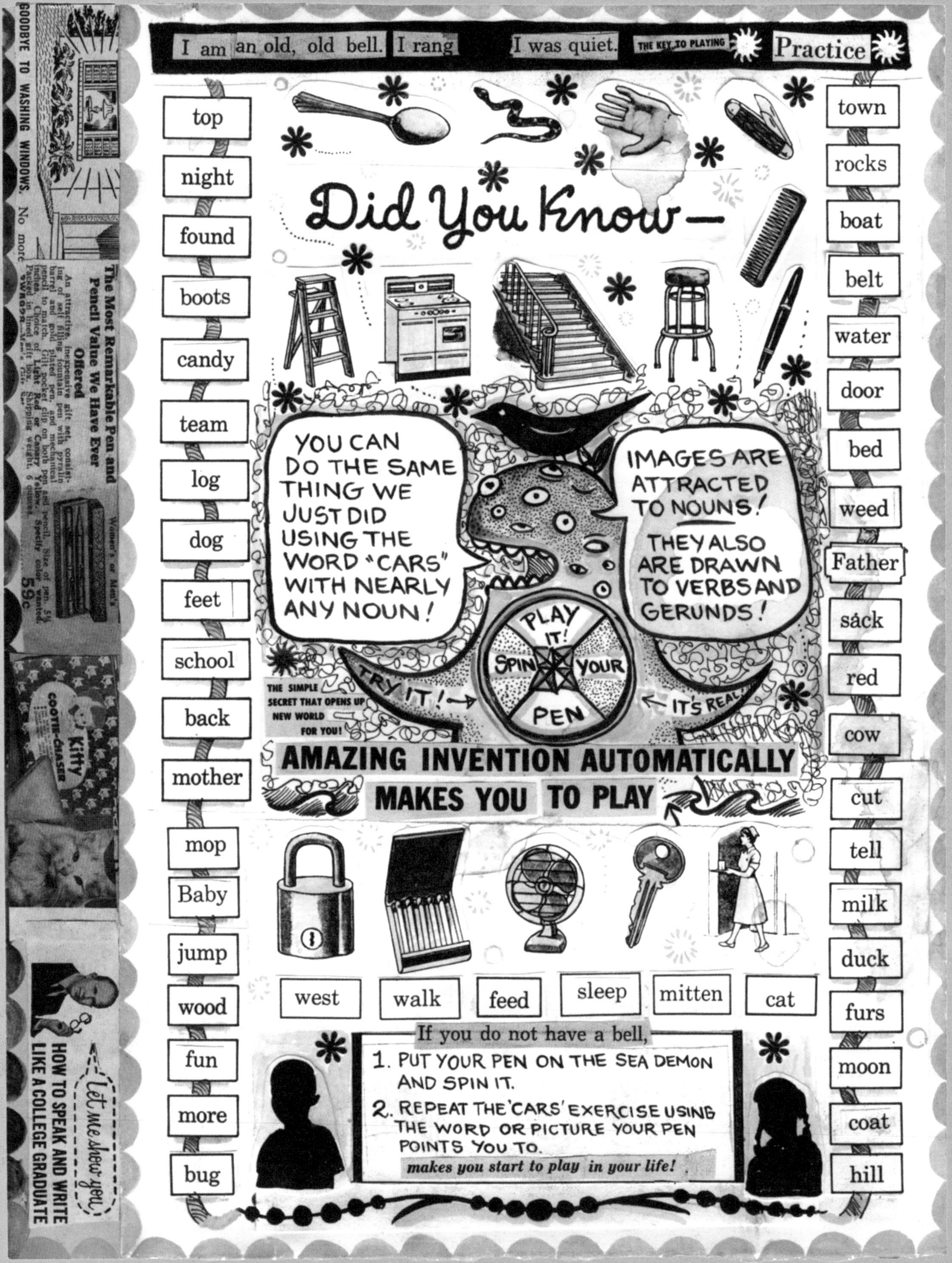

I am an old, old bell. I rang I was quiet.
THE KEY TO PLAYING
Practice
Did You Know—
YOU CAN DO THE SAME THING WE JUST DID USING THE WORD "CARS" WITH NEARLY ANY NOUN!
IMAGES ARE ATTRACTED TO NOUNS! THEY ALSO ARE DRAWN TO VERBS AND GERUNDS!
PLAY IT! SPIN YOUR PEN
TRY IT!
IT'S REAL!
THE SIMPLE SECRET THAT OPENS UP NEW WORLD FOR YOU!
AMAZING INVENTION AUTOMATICALLY
MAKES YOU TO PLAY
top
night
found
boots
candy
team
log
dog
feet
school
back
mother
mop
Baby
jump
wood
fun
more
bug
town
rocks
boat
belt
water
door
bed
weed
Father
sack
red
cow
cut
tell
milk
duck
furs
moon
coat
hill
west
walk
feed
sleep
mitten
cat
If you do not have a bell,
1. PUT YOUR PEN ON THE SEA DEMON AND SPIN IT.
2. REPEAT THE 'CARS' EXERCISE USING THE WORD OR PICTURE YOUR PEN POINTS YOU TO.
makes you start to play in your life!
GOODBYE TO WASHING WINDOWS. No more
The Most Remarkable Pen and Pencil Value We Have Ever Offered
59c
Kitty
COOTIE-CHASER
HOW TO SPEAK AND WRITE LIKE A COLLEGE GRADUATE
Let me show you!

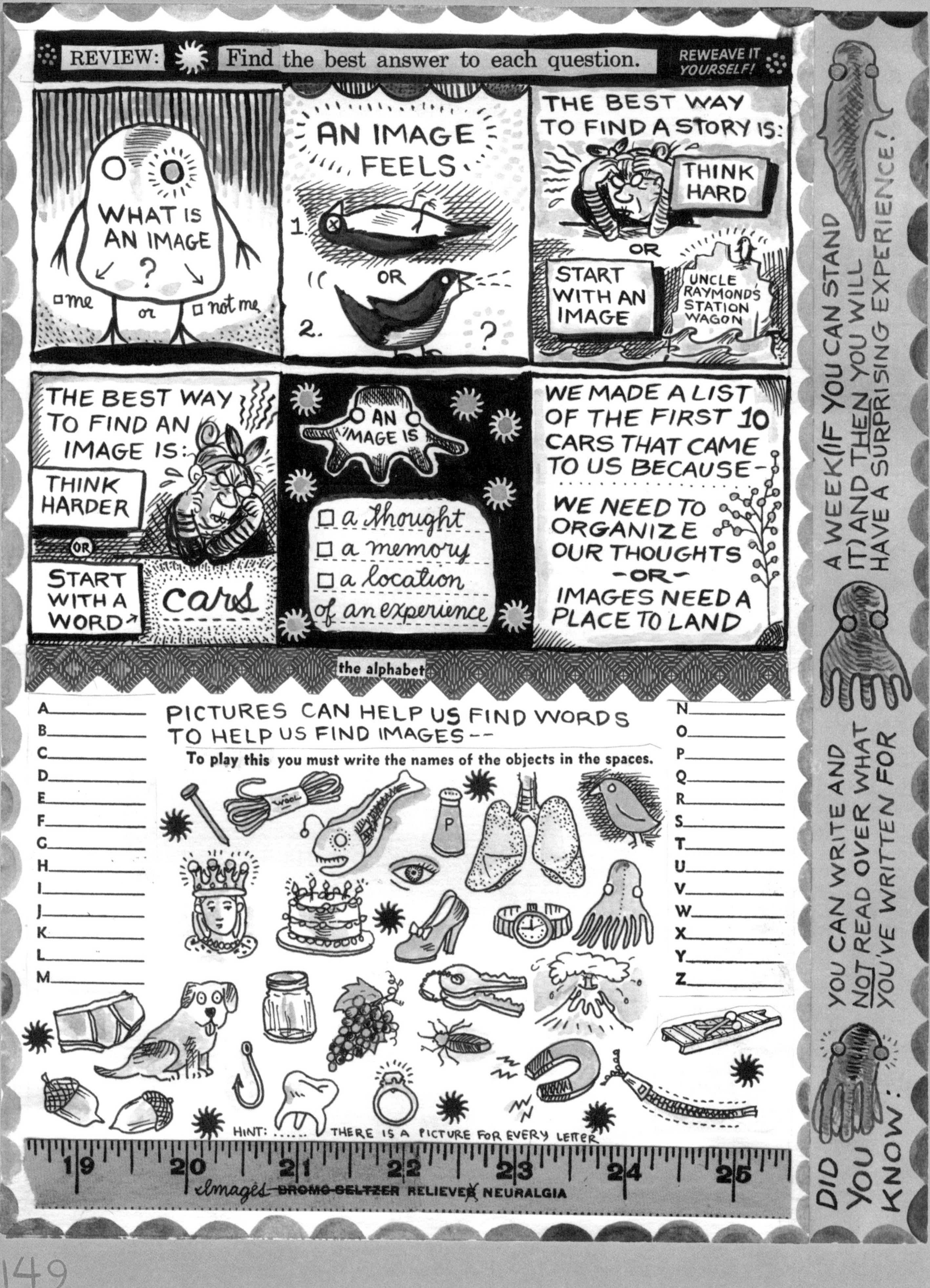
REVIEW:
Find the best answer to each question.
REWEAVE IT YOURSELF!
WHAT IS AN IMAGE ?
me or not me
AN IMAGE FEELS
1. OR 2. ?
THE BEST WAY TO FIND A STORY IS:
THINK HARD
OR
START WITH AN IMAGE
UNCLE RAYMOND'S STATION WAGON
THE BEST WAY TO FIND AN IMAGE IS:
THINK HARDER
OR
START WITH A WORD
cars
AN IMAGE IS
a thought
a memory
a location
of an experience
WE MADE A LIST OF THE FIRST 10 CARS THAT CAME TO US BECAUSE-
WE NEED TO ORGANIZE OUR THOUGHTS
-OR-
IMAGES NEED A PLACE TO LAND
the alphabet
PICTURES CAN HELP US FIND WORDS TO HELP US FIND IMAGES--
To play this you must write the names of the objects in the spaces.
A B C D E F G H I J K L M
N O P Q R S T U V W X Y Z
WOOL
P
HINT: ...... THERE IS A PICTURE FOR EVERY LETTER
19 20 21 22 23 24 25
Images ~~BROMO-SELTZER~~ RELIEVE~~S~~ NEURALGIA
DID YOU KNOW:
YOU CAN WRITE AND NOT READ OVER WHAT YOU'VE WRITTEN FOR A WEEK (IF YOU CAN STAND IT) AND THEN YOU WILL HAVE A SURPRISING EXPERIENCE!

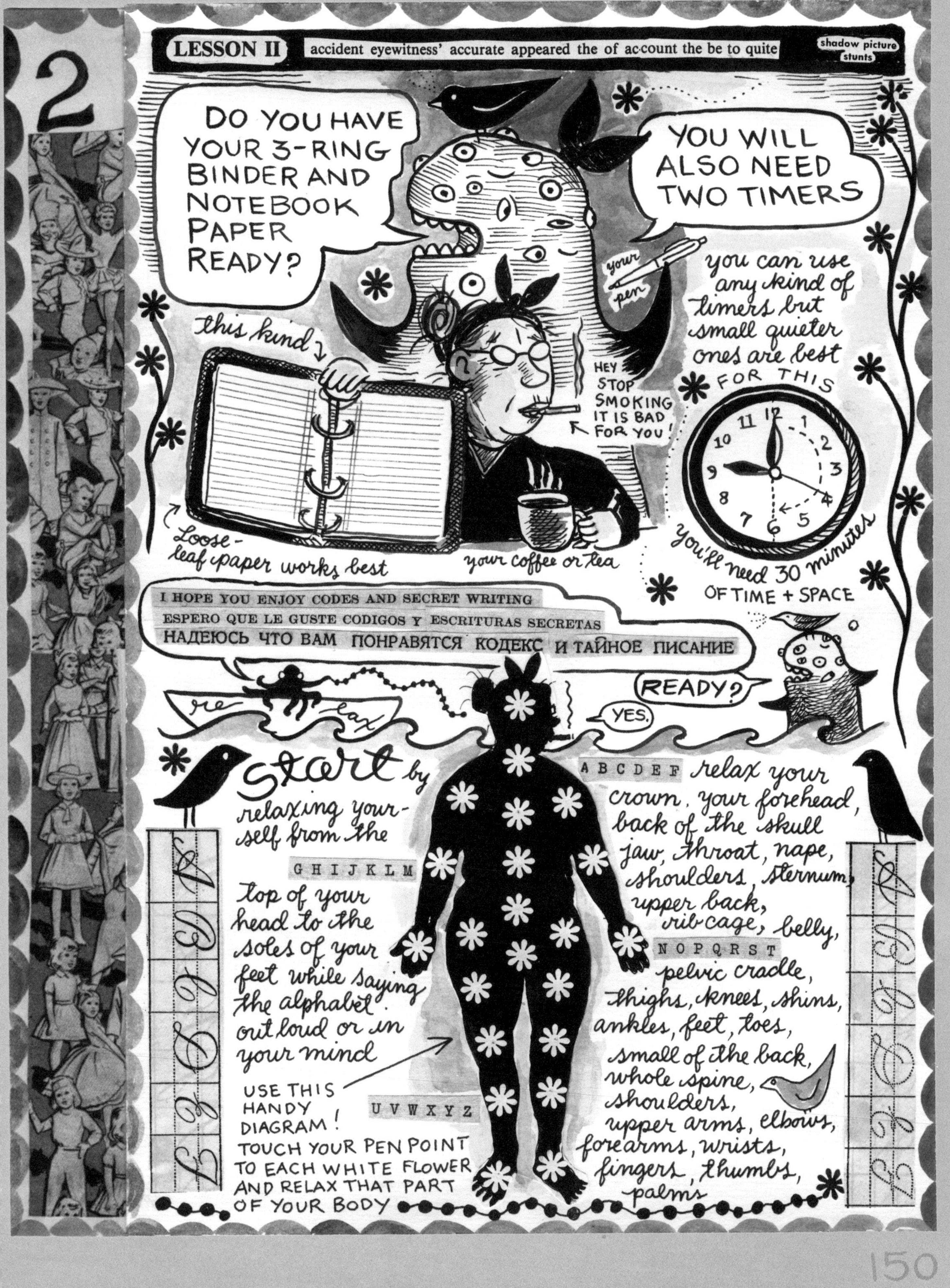
2
LESSON II
accident eyewitness' accurate appeared the of ac·count the be to quite
shadow picture stunts
DO YOU HAVE YOUR 3-RING BINDER AND NOTEBOOK PAPER READY?
YOU WILL ALSO NEED TWO TIMERS
your pen
you can use any kind of timers but small quieter ones are best FOR THIS
this kind ↓
HEY STOP SMOKING IT IS BAD FOR YOU!
Loose-leaf paper works best
your coffee or tea
12 1 2 3 4 5 6 7 8 9 10 11
You'll need 30 minutes OF TIME + SPACE
I HOPE YOU ENJOY CODES AND SECRET WRITING
ESPERO QUE LE GUSTE CODIGOS Y ESCRITURAS SECRETAS
НАДЕЮСЬ ЧТО ВАМ ПОНРАВЯТСЯ КОДЕКС И ТАЙНОЕ ПИСАНИЕ
READY?
YES.
re-lax
start by relaxing yourself from the
GHIJKLM
top of your head to the soles of your feet while saying the alphabet out loud or in your mind
USE THIS HANDY DIAGRAM!
UVWXYZ
TOUCH YOUR PEN POINT TO EACH WHITE FLOWER AND RELAX THAT PART OF YOUR BODY
ABCDEF
relax your crown, your forehead, back of the skull jaw, throat, nape, shoulders, sternum, upper back, rib cage, belly,
NOPQRST
pelvic cradle, thighs, knees, shins, ankles, feet, toes, small of the back, whole spine, shoulders, upper arms, elbows, forearms, wrists, fingers, thumbs, palms

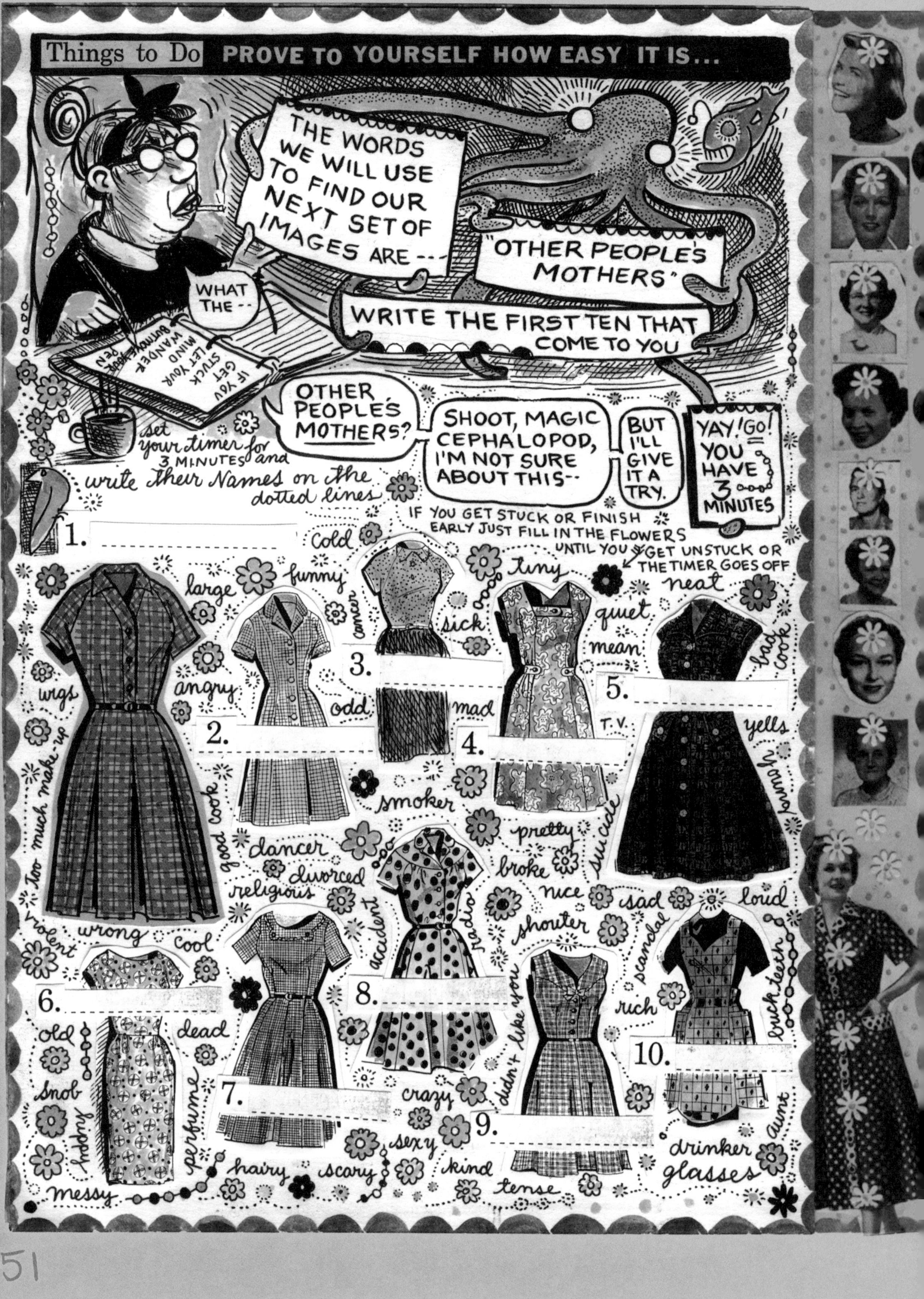

Things to Do
PROVE TO YOURSELF HOW EASY IT IS...
THE WORDS WE WILL USE TO FIND OUR NEXT SET OF IMAGES ARE---
"OTHER PEOPLE'S MOTHERS"
WRITE THE FIRST TEN THAT COME TO YOU
WHAT THE--
IF YOU GET STUCK LET YOUR MIND WANDER
OTHER PEOPLE'S MOTHERS?
SHOOT, MAGIC CEPHALOPOD, I'M NOT SURE ABOUT THIS--
BUT I'LL GIVE IT A TRY.
YAY! GO! YOU HAVE 3 MINUTES
set your timer for 3 MINUTES and write their Names on the dotted lines
IF YOU GET STUCK OR FINISH EARLY JUST FILL IN THE FLOWERS UNTIL YOU GET UNSTUCK OR THE TIMER GOES OFF
1.
2.
3.
4.
5.
6.
7.
8.
9.
10.
cold
large
funny
cancer
sick
tiny
neat
quiet
mean
bad cook
wigs
angry
odd
mad
T.V.
yells
too much make-up
good cook
smoker
dancer
divorced
religious
pretty
broke
suicide
violent
wrong
cool
accident
radio
nice
sad
loud
shouter
scandal
buck teeth
rich
old
dead
didn't like you
crazy
snob
hobby
perfume
sexy
hairy
scary
kind
tense
drinker
glasses
aunt
messy

down to the bottom of the sea. have gone Many ships with treasure

LOOK OVER YOUR LIST AND CHOOSE ONE —

WRITE IT. NOW

HINT: PICK ONE THAT CAME TO YOU, RATHER THAN ONE YOU THOUGHT UP

AND OF COURSE YOU CAN USE ADDITIONAL PAPER IF YOU NEED TO!

Please SET YOUR TIMER FOR ANOTHER 3 MINUTES

TIP: YOU ONLY NEED TO WRITE A SENTENCE OR TWO IN RESPONSE TO THESE QUESTIONS

PICTURE THE SCENE AND WRITE DOWN WHAT YOU SEE WITH YOUR MIND'S EYE

IF YOU DON'T KNOW THE ANSWER TO A QUESTION, GUESS — -OR- WRITE "DON'T KNOW"

1. Picture this person in a place where you have seen her before—

2. where are you?

(THIS SPACE IS TOO SMALL USE YOUR NOTEBOOK PAPER! OK!)

3. what are you doing?

4. what is she doing?

5. What time of day does it seem to be?

6. What season?

7. about how old are you? about how old is she?

8. Why are you there? Why is she there?

9. Is there any one else in this image? If so, who?

10. Is there anyone who just left or who may be coming?

11. what kind of mood does this mother seem to be in?

12. what does she look like?

with a weird light in the deep-sea darkness glow

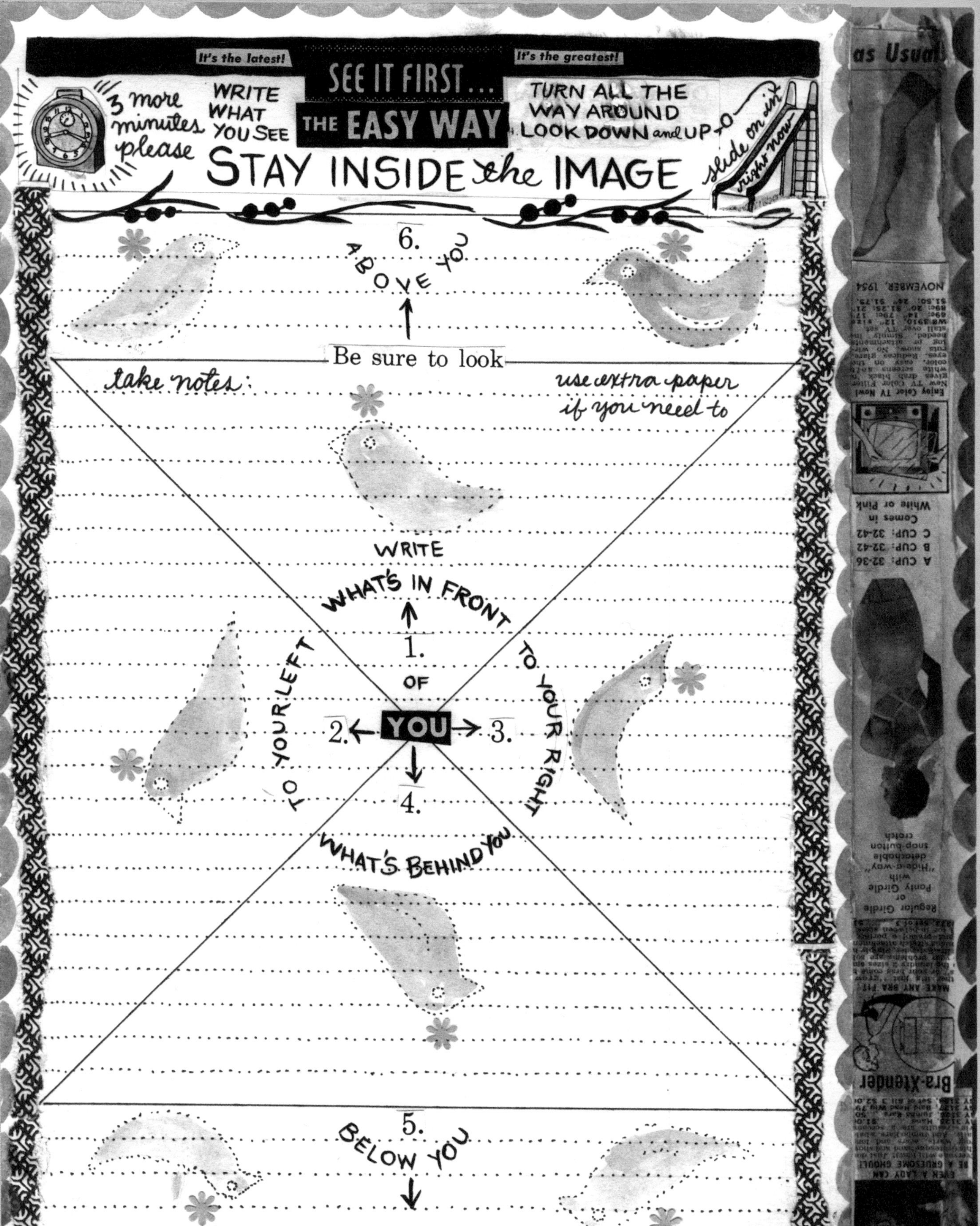
It's the latest!
It's the greatest!
SEE IT FIRST...
THE EASY WAY
3 more minutes please
WRITE WHAT YOU SEE
TURN ALL THE WAY AROUND LOOK DOWN and UP
slide on in right now
STAY INSIDE the IMAGE
6. ABOVE YOU
Be sure to look
take notes:
use extra paper if you need to
WRITE
WHAT'S IN FRONT
1.
OF
YOU
2.
3.
TO YOUR LEFT
TO YOUR RIGHT
4.
WHAT'S BEHIND YOU
5. BELOW YOU
as Usual

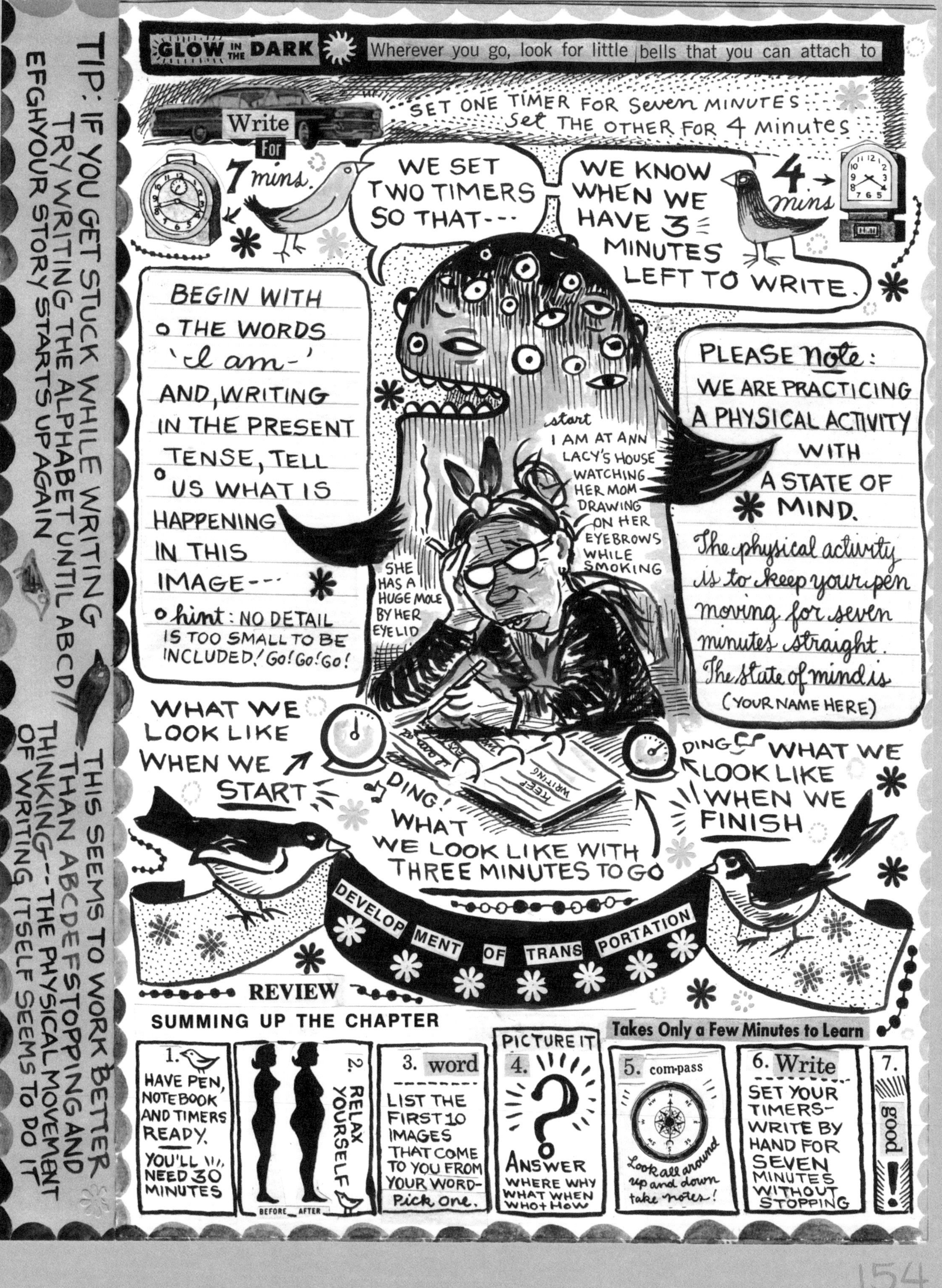
TIP: IF YOU GET STUCK WHILE WRITING TRY WRITING THE ALPHABET UNTIL ABCD EFGHYOUR STORY STARTS UP AGAIN
THIS SEEMS TO WORK BETTER THAN ABCDEFSTOPPING AND THINKING-- THE PHYSICAL MOVEMENT OF WRITING ITSELF SEEMS TO DO IT
GLOW IN THE DARK
Wherever you go, look for little bells that you can attach to
Write For 7 mins.
SET ONE TIMER FOR Seven MINUTES
Set THE OTHER FOR 4 Minutes
4 → mins
WE SET TWO TIMERS SO THAT---
WE KNOW WHEN WE HAVE 3 MINUTES LEFT TO WRITE.
BEGIN WITH
THE WORDS 'I am-'
AND, WRITING IN THE PRESENT TENSE, TELL
US WHAT IS HAPPENING IN THIS IMAGE---
hint: NO DETAIL IS TOO SMALL TO BE INCLUDED! GO! GO! GO!
start I AM AT ANN LACY'S HOUSE WATCHING HER MOM DRAWING ON HER EYEBROWS WHILE SMOKING
SHE HAS A HUGE MOLE BY HER EYELID
PLEASE note: WE ARE PRACTICING A PHYSICAL ACTIVITY WITH A STATE OF MIND.
The physical activity is to keep your pen moving for seven minutes straight. The state of mind is (YOUR NAME HERE)
WHAT WE LOOK LIKE WHEN WE START
DING!
WHAT WE LOOK LIKE WITH THREE MINUTES TO GO
DING
WHAT WE LOOK LIKE WHEN WE FINISH
KEEP WRITING
DEVELOPMENT OF TRANSPORTATION
REVIEW
SUMMING UP THE CHAPTER
Takes Only a Few Minutes to Learn
1. HAVE PEN, NOTEBOOK AND TIMERS READY. YOU'LL NEED 30 MINUTES
2. RELAX YOURSELF
BEFORE AFTER
3. word LIST THE FIRST 10 IMAGES THAT COME TO YOU FROM YOUR WORD- Pick One.
PICTURE IT 4. ? ANSWER WHERE WHY WHAT WHEN WHO + HOW
5. com·pass Look all around up and down take notes!
6. Write SET YOUR TIMERS- WRITE BY HAND FOR SEVEN MINUTES WITHOUT STOPPING
7. good !

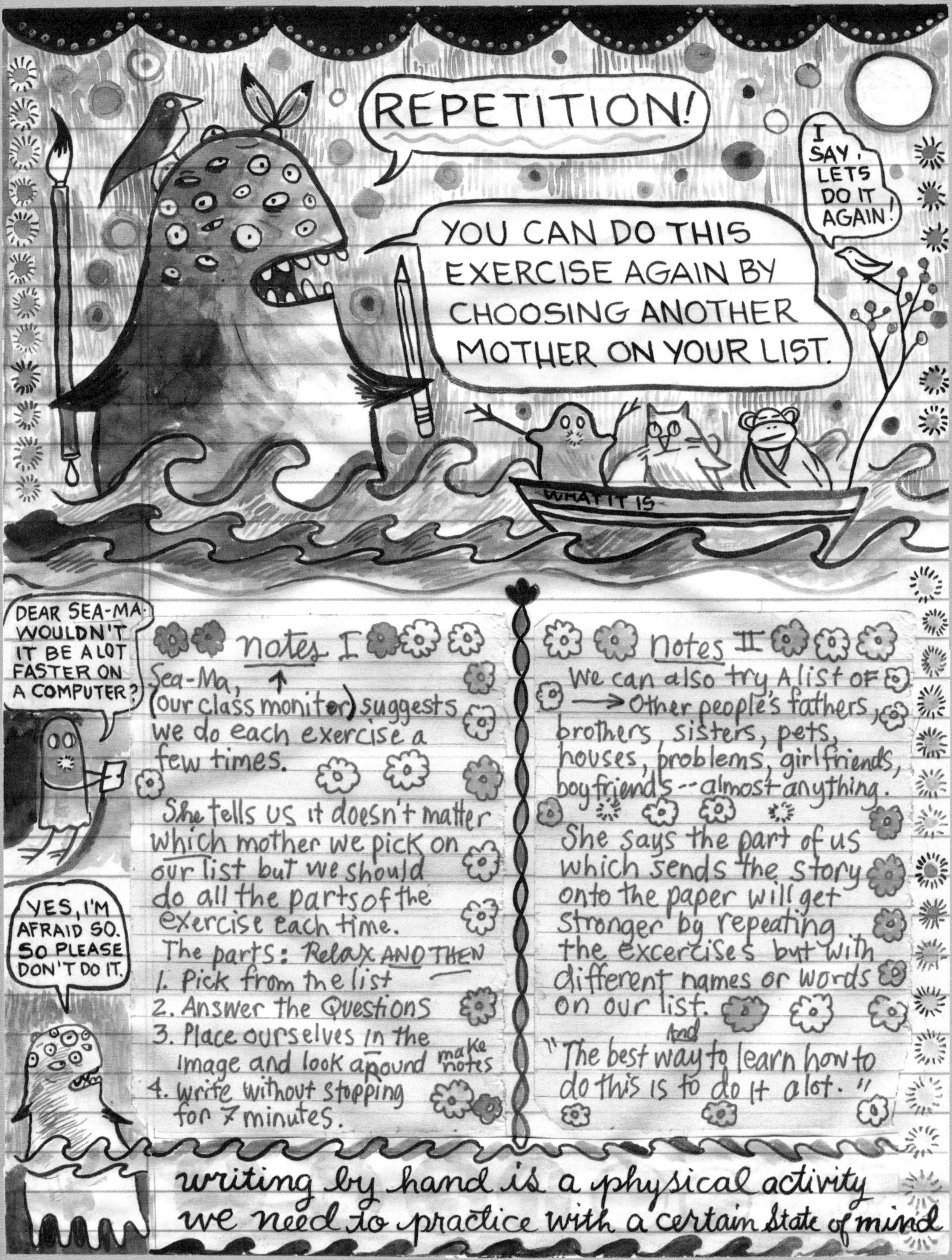
REPETITION!
YOU CAN DO THIS EXERCISE AGAIN BY CHOOSING ANOTHER MOTHER ON YOUR LIST.
I SAY, LETS DO IT AGAIN!
WHAT IT IS
DEAR SEA-MA. WOULDN'T IT BE A LOT FASTER ON A COMPUTER?
YES, I'M AFRAID SO. SO PLEASE DON'T DO IT.
notes I
Sea-Ma, (our class monitor) suggests we do each exercise a few times.
She tells us it doesn't matter which mother we pick on our list but we should do all the parts of the exercise each time.
The parts: Relax AND THEN
1. Pick from the list
2. Answer the Questions
3. Place ourselves in the image and look around make notes
4. write without stopping for 7 minutes.
Notes II
We can also try A list of → Other people's fathers, brothers, sisters, pets, houses, problems, girlfriends, boyfriends -- almost anything.
She says the part of us which sends the story onto the paper will get stronger by repeating the excercises but with different names or words on our list. And
"The best way to learn how to do this is to do it alot."
writing by hand is a physical activity we need to practice with a certain state of mind

"LEARNING IS NOT A TRAJECTORY, BUT A SLOWLY ASCENDING SPIRAL *"

* here Seama paraphrases MARION MILNER

Left margin panels (top to bottom):
I KNOW
YOU WANT
TO READ IT OVER.
BUT YOU MUST WAIT.

NOTES III

I just noticed Sea Ma has a very slight lisp she is answering the question of why we are not supposed to read over what we wrote for a week at least:

Sea ma:

① "because the part of you that is reading it over is not the same as the part of you that wrote it. All the part of you that is reading it over wants to know is IS IT ANY GOOD. Wait one week and you will have a different experience."

P.S. It will be a better one.

NOTES IV

"The Groove": By. Seama
There is something we fall in and out of when we are writing."

Sometimes the story comes very fast from your pen and all you have to do is keep writing.

Sometimes the story stops or falters and the urge is to also stop or falter your pen and think.

Sea-Ma says to keep your pen in motion by writing the abcdefal phabet.

NOTES V or draw in the margins

She says even if the story stops it will start back up if we keep our pens moving. She says another way to keep your pen moving when the story stops. Is to have another piece of paper nearby where you can work on a spiral or other kinds of pen moving

Don't stop and think

NOTES VI

you can even draw the eyes of Sea-Ma

SHE JUST KEEPS saying the same thing

"The goal is to stay in motion for seven minutes straight"

keep pen in motion   OK Sea-ma we GET IT!

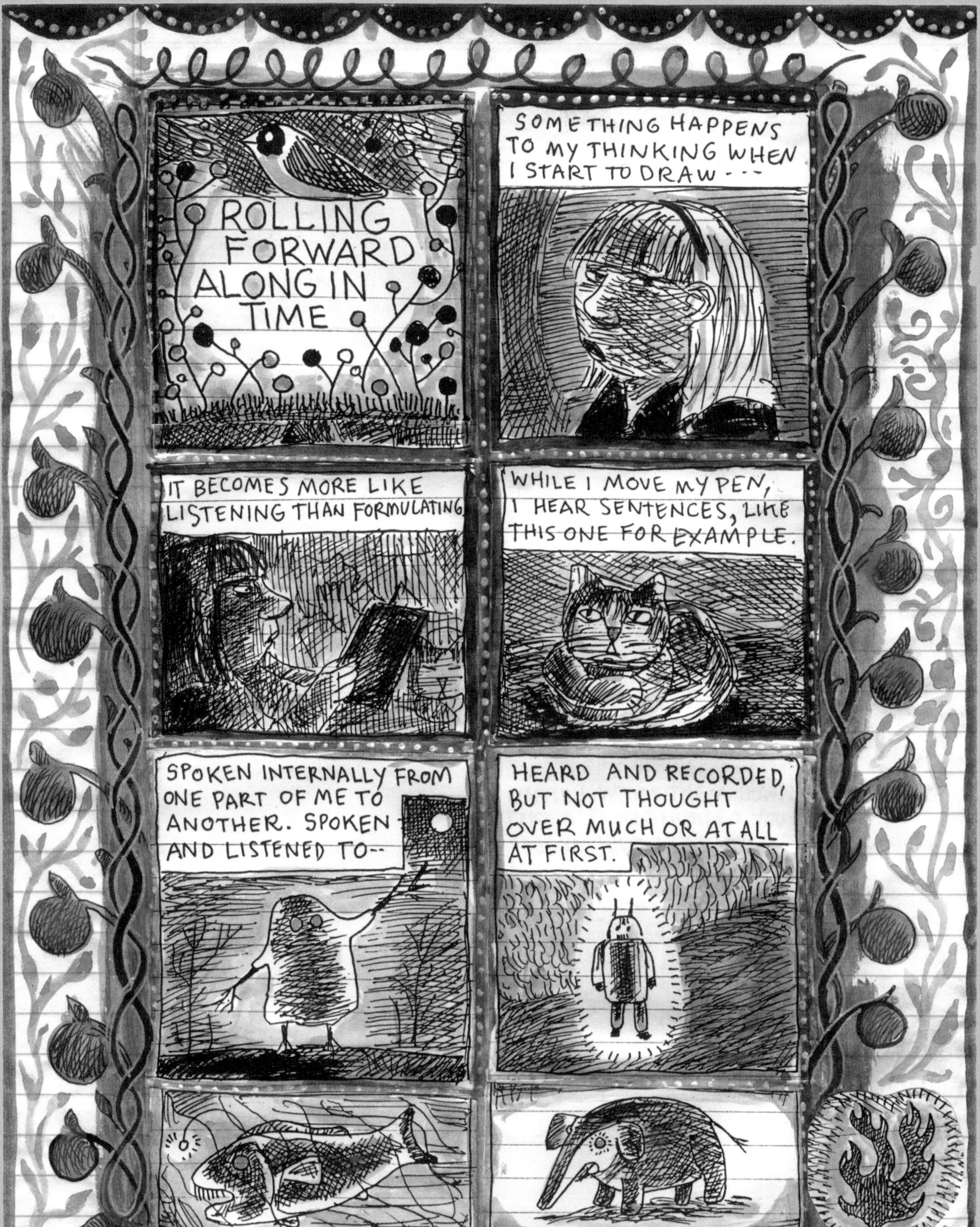
ROLLING FORWARD ALONG IN TIME
SOMETHING HAPPENS TO MY THINKING WHEN I START TO DRAW---
IT BECOMES MORE LIKE LISTENING THAN FORMULATING.
WHILE I MOVE MY PEN, I HEAR SENTENCES, LIKE THIS ONE FOR EXAMPLE.
SPOKEN INTERNALLY FROM ONE PART OF ME TO ANOTHER. SPOKEN AND LISTENED TO--
HEARD AND RECORDED, BUT NOT THOUGHT OVER MUCH OR AT ALL AT FIRST.
WHEN I KEEP MY PEN MOVING IT IS NOT A YES OR NO SITUATION.

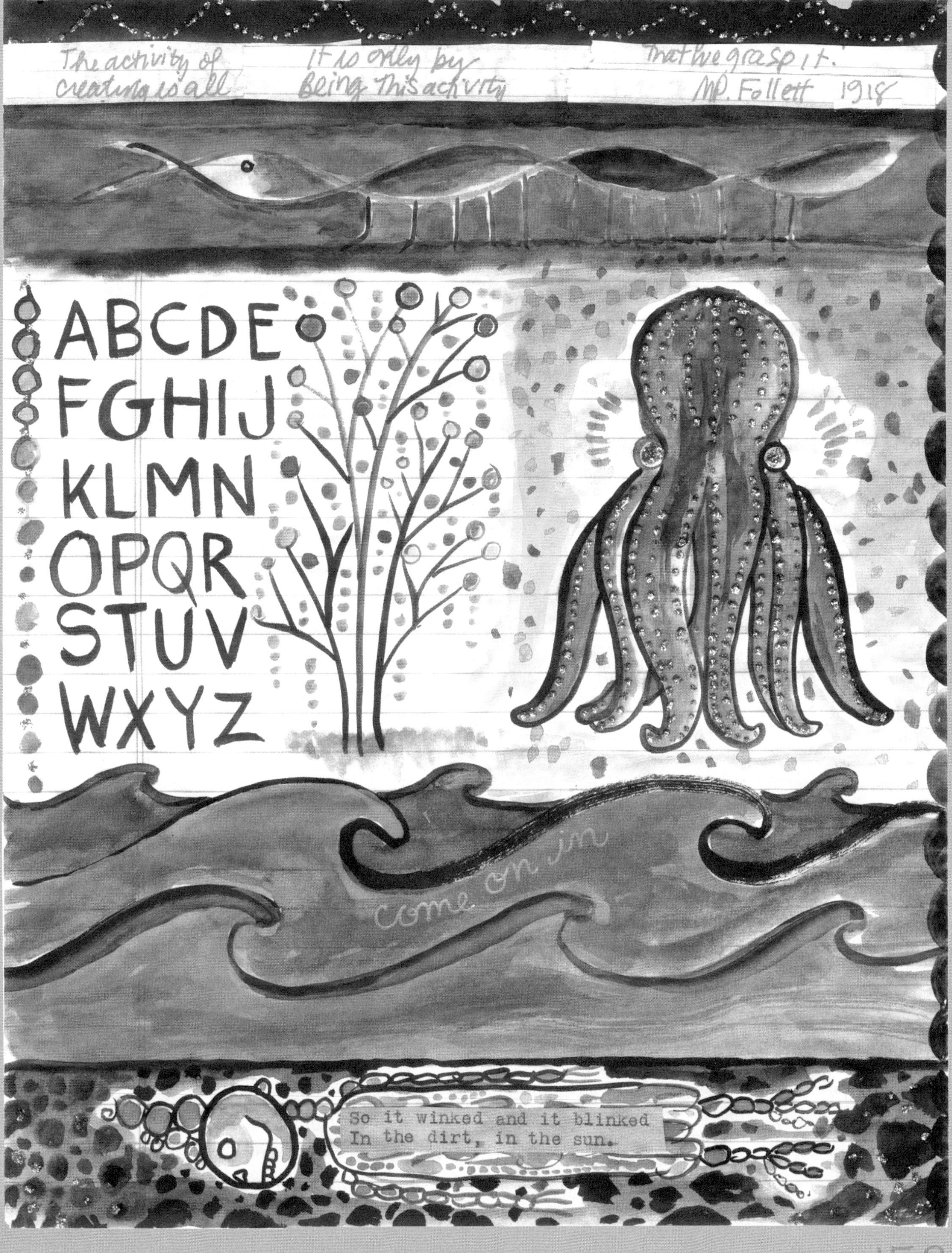
The activity of creating is all
It is only by being this activity
that we grasp it.
M.P. Follett 1918
ABCDE
FGHIJ
KLMN
OPQR
STUV
WXYZ
come on in
So it winked and it blinked
In the dirt, in the sun.

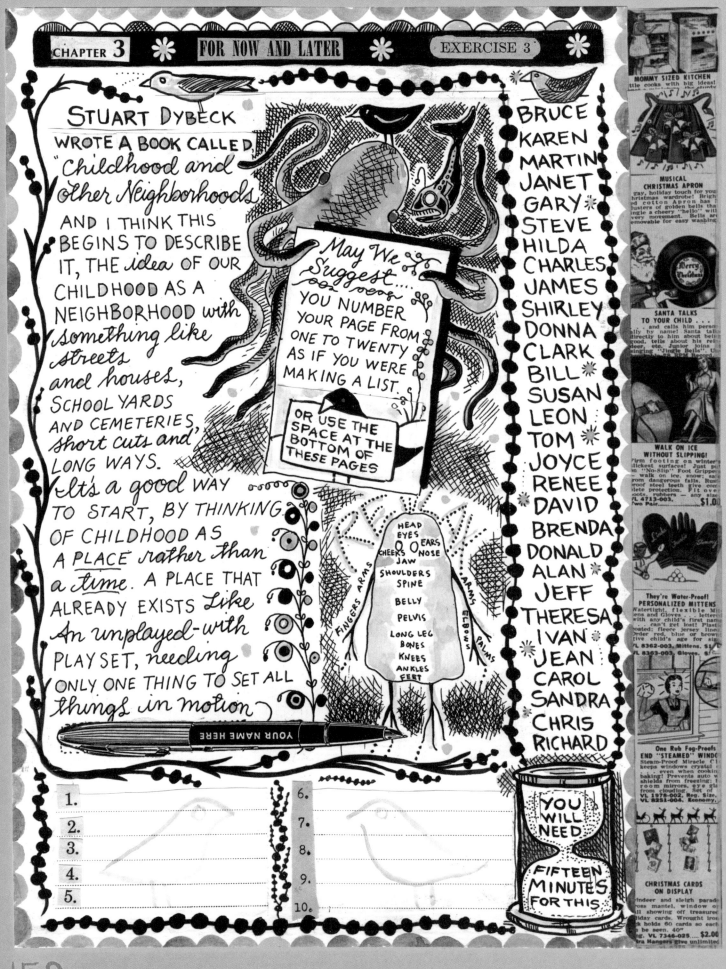

STUART DYBECK WROTE A BOOK CALLED, "*Childhood and Other Neighborhoods*" AND I THINK THIS BEGINS TO DESCRIBE IT, THE *idea* OF OUR CHILDHOOD AS A NEIGHBORHOOD *with something like streets and houses*, SCHOOL YARDS AND CEMETERIES, *short cuts and* LONG WAYS. *It's a good* WAY TO START, BY THINKING OF CHILDHOOD AS A PLACE *rather than* a *time*. A PLACE THAT ALREADY EXISTS *Like An unplayed-with* PLAYSET, *needing* ONLY ONE THING TO SET ALL *things in motion*

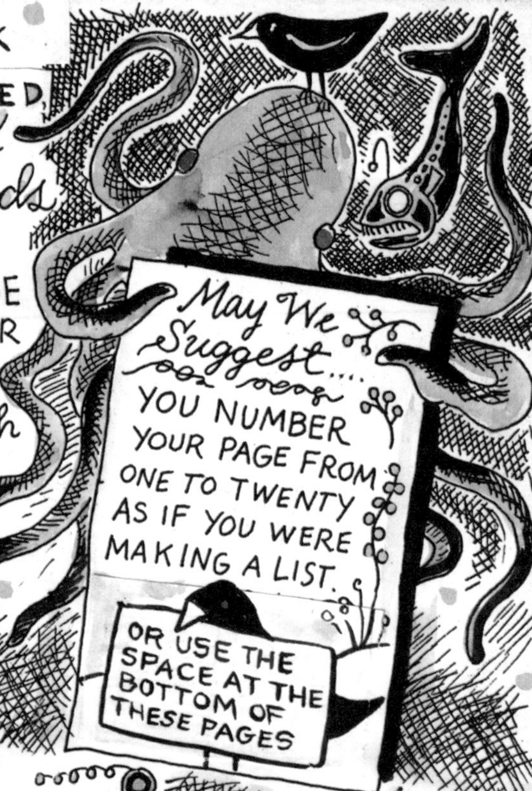
May We Suggest...
YOU NUMBER YOUR PAGE FROM ONE TO TWENTY AS IF YOU WERE MAKING A LIST.
OR USE THE SPACE AT THE BOTTOM OF THESE PAGES

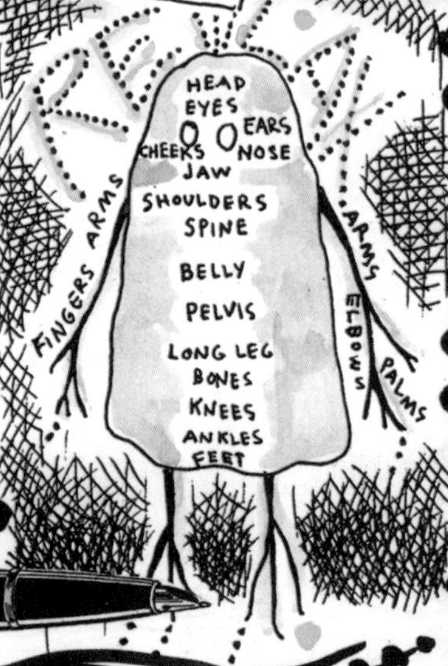
HEAD
EYES
EARS
CHEEKS
NOSE
JAW
SHOULDERS
SPINE
BELLY
PELVIS
LONG LEG BONES
KNEES
ANKLES
FEET
FINGERS
ARMS
ARMS
ELBOWS
PALMS

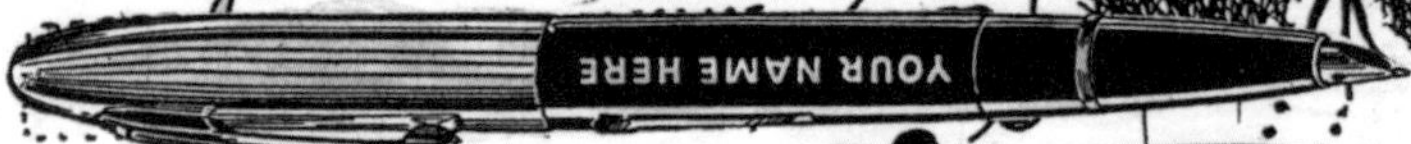
YOUR NAME HERE

BRUCE
KAREN
MARTIN
JANET
GARY
STEVE
HILDA
CHARLES
JAMES
SHIRLEY
DONNA
CLARK
BILL
SUSAN
LEON
TOM
JOYCE
RENEE
DAVID
BRENDA
DONALD
ALAN
JEFF
THERESA
IVAN
JEAN
CAROL
SANDRA
CHRIS
RICHARD

1.
2.
3.
4.
5.
6.
7.
8.
9.
10.

YOU WILL NEED FIFTEEN MINUTES FOR THIS

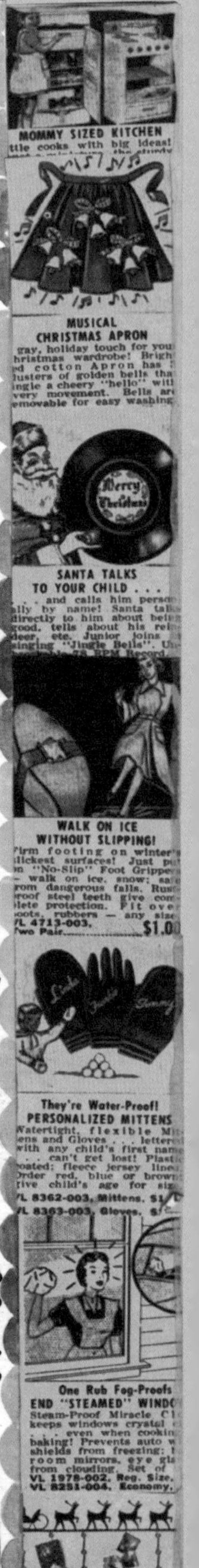
MOMMY SIZED KITCHEN
MUSICAL CHRISTMAS APRON
SANTA TALKS TO YOUR CHILD . . .
WALK ON ICE WITHOUT SLIPPING!
They're Water-Proof! PERSONALIZED MITTENS
One Rub Fog-Proofs END "STEAMED" WINDO
CHRISTMAS CARDS ON DISPLAY

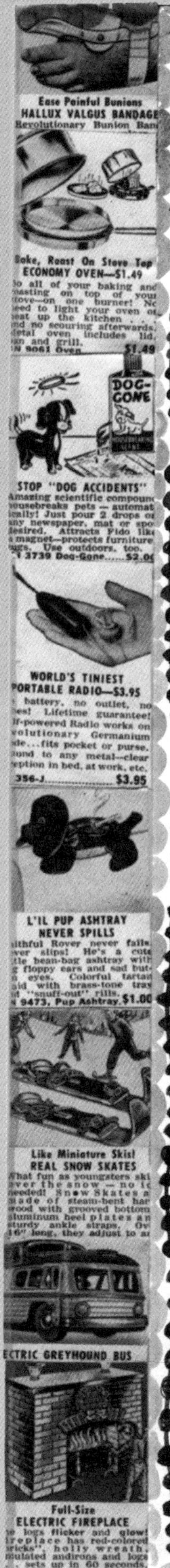

Ease Painful Bunions
HALLUX VALGUS BANDAGE
Revolutionary Bunion Ban
Bake, Roast On Stove Top
ECONOMY OVEN—$1.49
DOG-GONE
STOP "DOG ACCIDENTS"
WORLD'S TINIEST PORTABLE RADIO—$3.95
L'IL PUP ASHTRAY NEVER SPILLS
Like Miniature Skis!
REAL SNOW SKATES
ECTRIC GREYHOUND BUS
Full-Size
ELECTRIC FIREPLACE

Fast-Growing · **INVISIBLE THREAD** · **Ever-Blooming**

KATIE
RONALD
MARY
KEN
JIM
DIANE
NICK
SCOTT
DAN
PATRICIA
DENNIS
MATT
ANNE
TIM
CHERYL
JOAN
DUANE
ANDY
HOWARD
NANCY
DEAN
AMY
JANE
KEITH
JEN

There ARE other NEIGHBORHOODS OF images. NEIGHBORHOODS OF THINGS WE HAVE HATED, THINGS WE HAVE BROKEN, THINGS WE HAVE LOST. AND the opposite neighborhoods are all there, THINGS AND PEOPLE WE HAVE LOVED, LUCKY THINGS, THINGS TURNING OUT ALL RIGHT.

Things not forgotten but UNREMEMBERED UNTIL ---

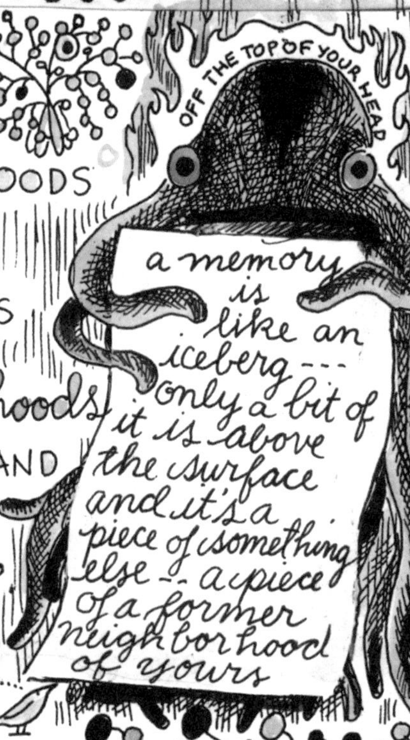

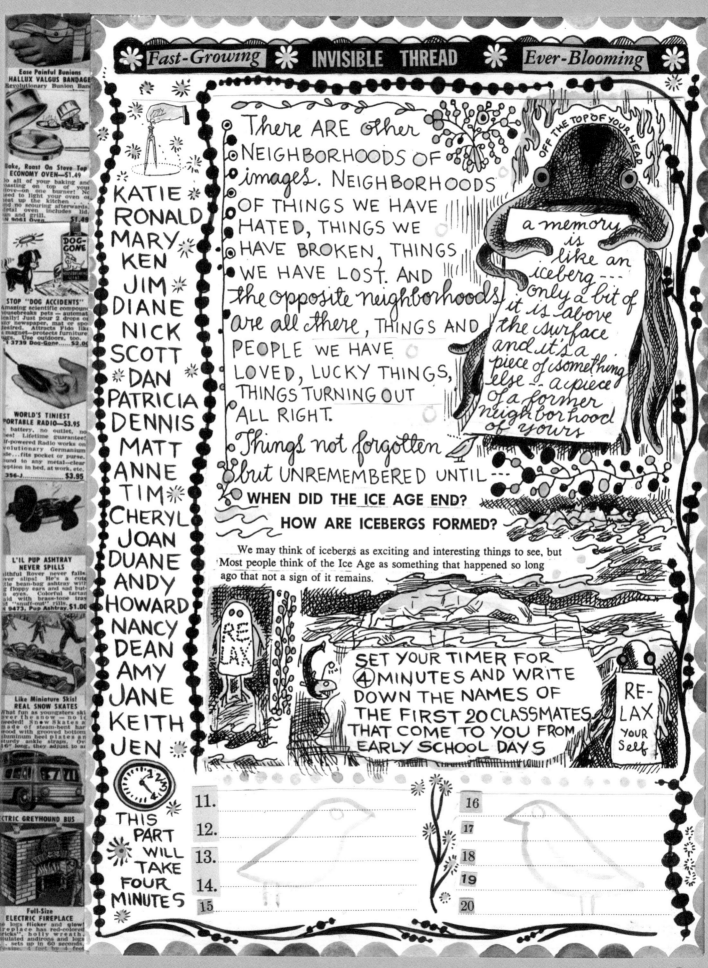

OFF THE TOP OF YOUR HEAD
a memory is like an iceberg --- only a bit of it is above the surface and it's a piece of something else -- a piece of a former neighborhood of yours

WHEN DID THE ICE AGE END?

HOW ARE ICEBERGS FORMED?

We may think of icebergs as exciting and interesting things to see, but Most people think of the Ice Age as something that happened so long ago that not a sign of it remains.

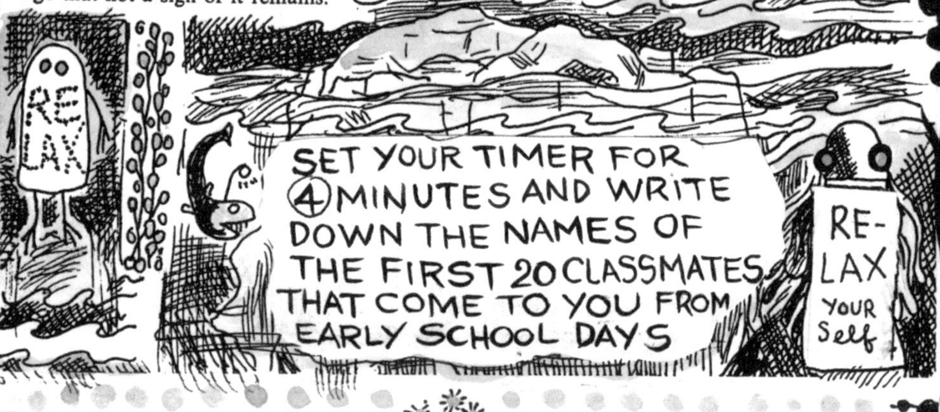

RE-LAX
SET YOUR TIMER FOR 4 MINUTES AND WRITE DOWN THE NAMES OF THE FIRST 20 CLASSMATES THAT COME TO YOU FROM EARLY SCHOOL DAYS
RE-LAX YOUR Self

THIS PART WILL TAKE FOUR MINUTES

11. ....
12. ....
13. ....
14. ....
15. ....
16. ....
17. ....
18. ....
19. ....
20. ....

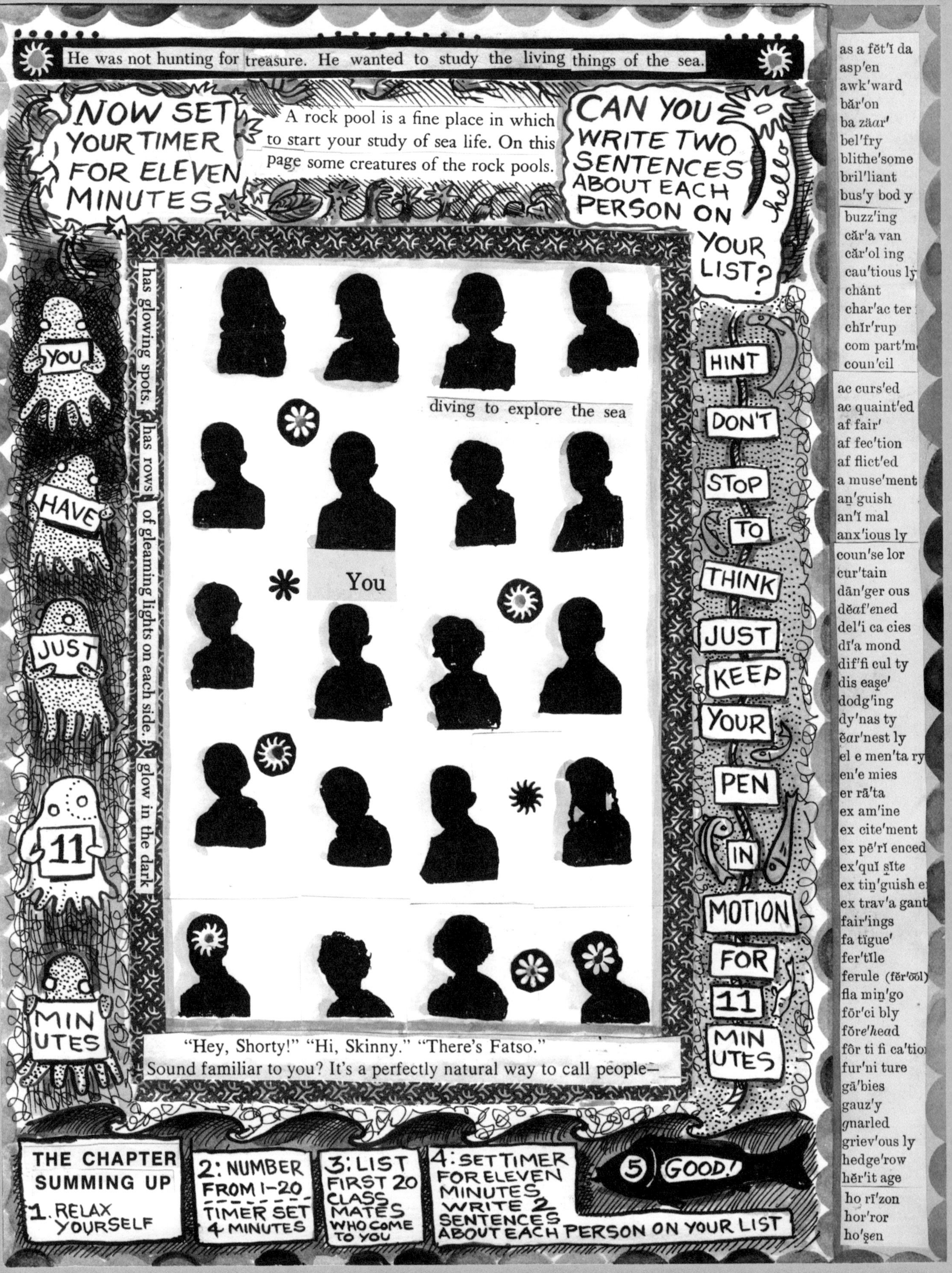
He was not hunting for treasure. He wanted to study the living things of the sea.
NOW SET YOUR TIMER FOR ELEVEN MINUTES
A rock pool is a fine place in which to start your study of sea life. On this page some creatures of the rock pools.
CAN YOU WRITE TWO SENTENCES ABOUT EACH PERSON ON YOUR LIST?
hello
YOU
HAVE
JUST
11
MIN UTES
has glowing spots.
has rows
of gleaming lights on each side.
glow in the dark
diving to explore the sea
You
"Hey, Shorty!" "Hi, Skinny." "There's Fatso."
Sound familiar to you? It's a perfectly natural way to call people—
HINT
DON'T
STOP
TO
THINK
JUST
KEEP
YOUR
PEN
IN
MOTION
FOR
11
MIN UTES
THE CHAPTER SUMMING UP
1. RELAX YOURSELF
2: NUMBER FROM 1-20
TIMER SET 4 MINUTES
3: LIST FIRST 20 CLASS MATES WHO COME TO YOU
4: SET TIMER FOR ELEVEN MINUTES WRITE 2 SENTENCES ABOUT EACH PERSON ON YOUR LIST
5 GOOD!
as a fĕt'ĭ da
asp'en
awk'ward
băr'on
ba zäar'
bel'fry
blithe'some
bril'liant
bus'y bod y
buzz'ing
căr'a van
căr'ol ing
cau'tious ly
chånt
char'ac ter
chĭr'rup
com part'm
coun'cil
ac curs'ed
ac quaint'ed
af fair'
af fec'tion
af flict'ed
a muse'ment
an'guish
an'ĭ mal
anx'ious ly
coun'se lor
cur'tain
dān'ger ous
dĕaf'ened
del'i ca cies
dī'a mond
dif'fi cul ty
dis ease'
dodg'ing
dy'nas ty
ĕar'nest ly
el e men'ta ry
en'e mies
er rā'ta
ex am'ine
ex cite'ment
ex pē'rĭ enced
ex'quĭ sīte
ex tin'guish
ex trav'a gant
fair'ings
fa tigue'
fer'tĭle
ferule (fĕr'ōōl)
fla min'go
fŏr'ci bly
fōre'head
fôr ti fi ca'tio
fur'ni ture
gā'bies
gauz'y
gnarled
griev'ous ly
hedge'row
hĕr'it age
ho rī'zon
hor'ror
ho'sen

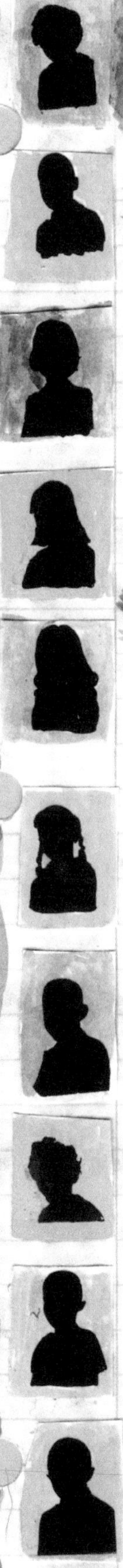

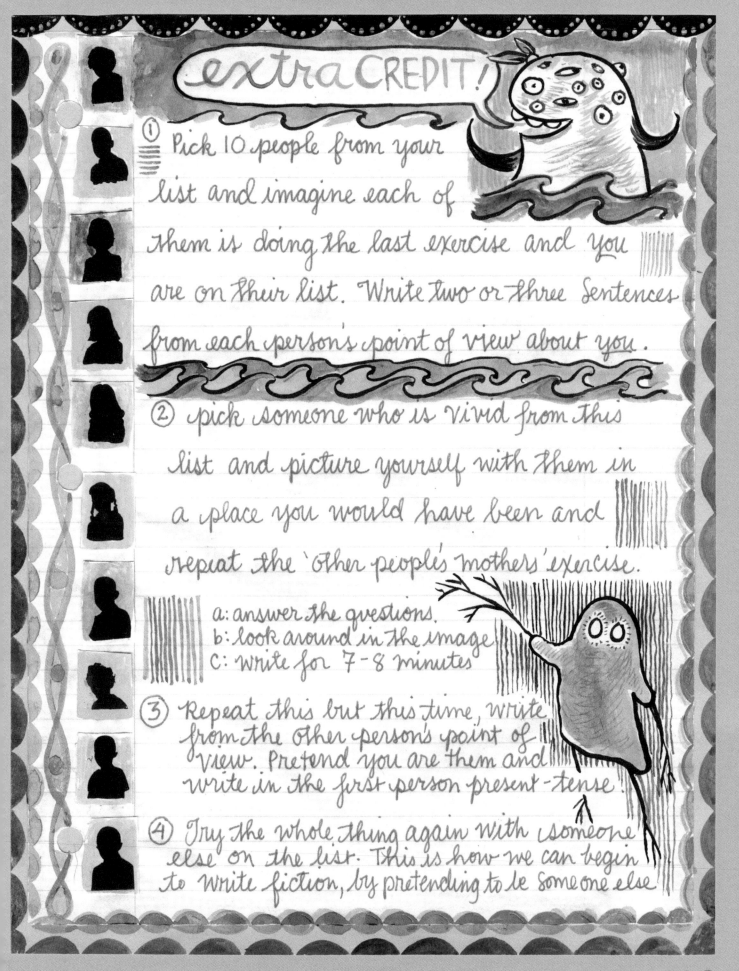

extra CREDIT!

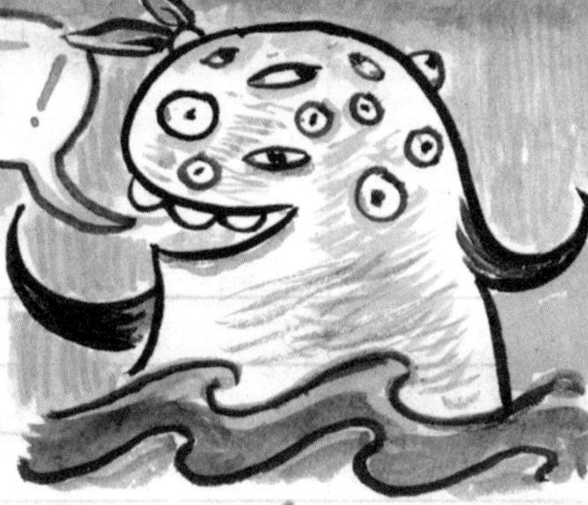

① Pick 10 people from your list and imagine each of them is doing the last exercise and you are on their list. Write two or three sentences from each person's point of view about you.

② pick someone who is vivid from this list and picture yourself with them in a place you would have been and repeat the 'other people's mothers' exercise.

a: answer the questions.
b: look around in the image
c: write for 7-8 minutes

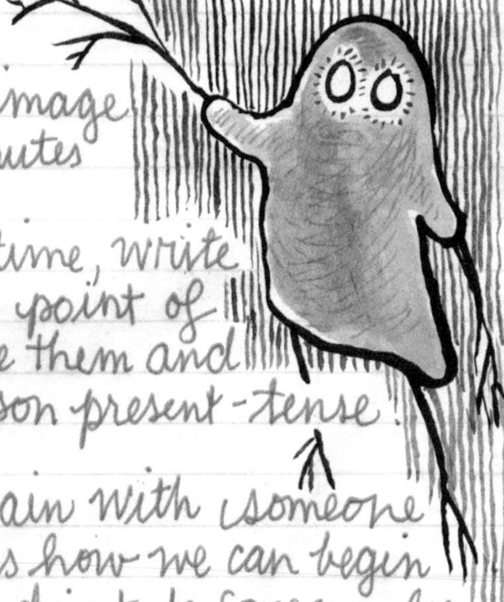

③ Repeat this but this time, write from the other person's point of view. Pretend you are them and write in the first person present-tense.

④ Try the whole thing again with someone else on the list. This is how we can begin to write fiction, by pretending to be someone else

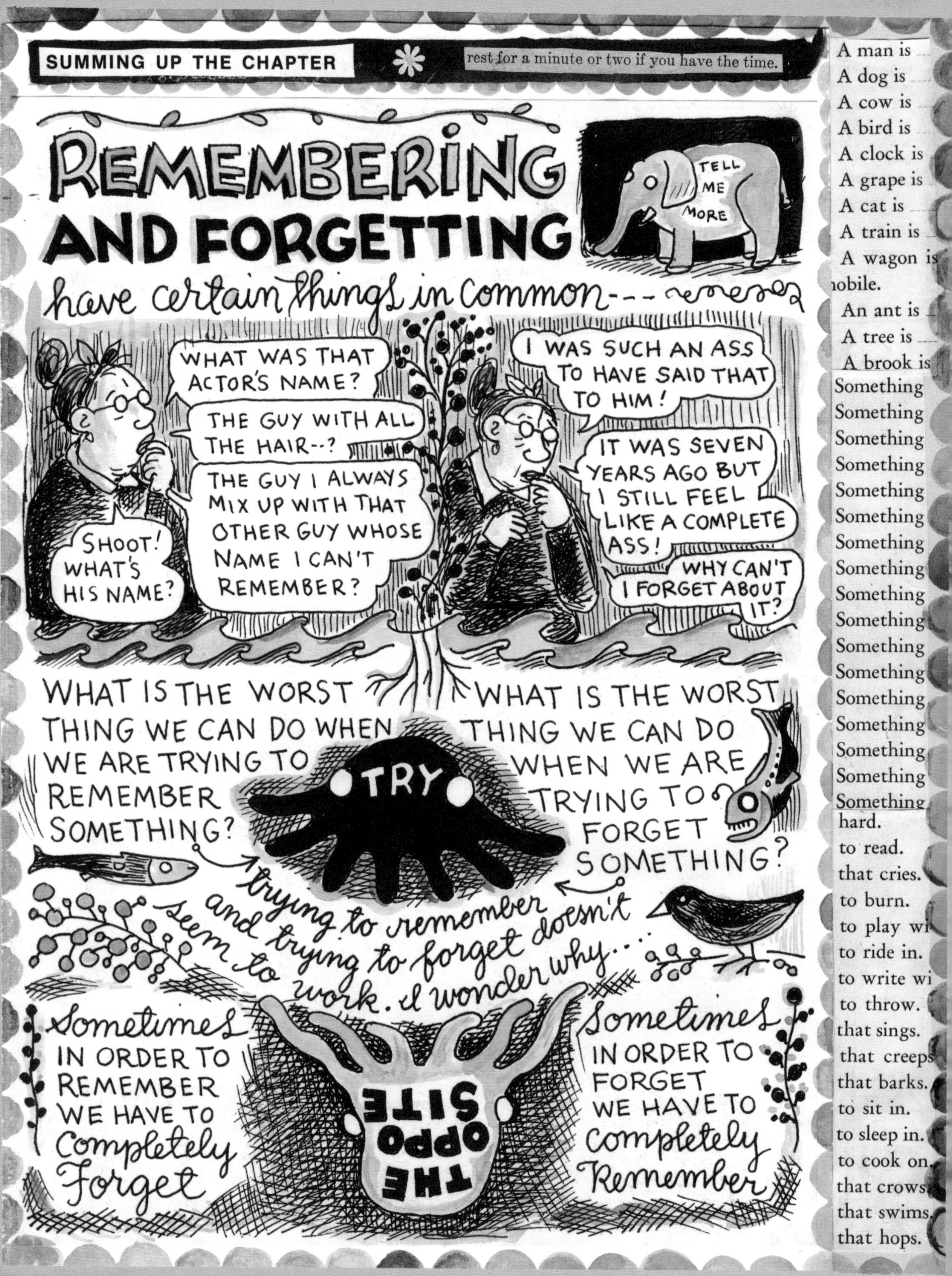
SUMMING UP THE CHAPTER
rest for a minute or two if you have the time.
REMEMBERING AND FORGETTING
TELL ME MORE
have certain things in common---
WHAT WAS THAT ACTOR'S NAME?
THE GUY WITH ALL THE HAIR--?
THE GUY I ALWAYS MIX UP WITH THAT OTHER GUY WHOSE NAME I CAN'T REMEMBER?
SHOOT! WHAT'S HIS NAME?
I WAS SUCH AN ASS TO HAVE SAID THAT TO HIM!
IT WAS SEVEN YEARS AGO BUT I STILL FEEL LIKE A COMPLETE ASS!
WHY CAN'T I FORGET ABOUT IT?
WHAT IS THE WORST THING WE CAN DO WHEN WE ARE TRYING TO REMEMBER SOMETHING?
TRY
WHAT IS THE WORST THING WE CAN DO WHEN WE ARE TRYING TO FORGET SOMETHING?
trying to remember and trying to forget doesn't seem to work. I wonder why....
Sometimes IN ORDER TO REMEMBER WE HAVE TO Completely Forget
THE OPPOSITE
Sometimes IN ORDER TO FORGET WE HAVE TO Completely Remember
A man is
A dog is
A cow is
A bird is
A clock is
A grape is
A cat is
A train is
A wagon is
nobile.
An ant is
A tree is
A brook is
Something
Something
Something
Something
Something
Something
Something
Something
Something
Something
Something
Something
Something
Something
Something
Something
Something
hard.
to read.
that cries.
to burn.
to play wi
to ride in.
to write wi
to throw.
that sings.
that creeps
that barks.
to sit in.
to sleep in.
to cook on.
that crows.
that swims.
that hops.

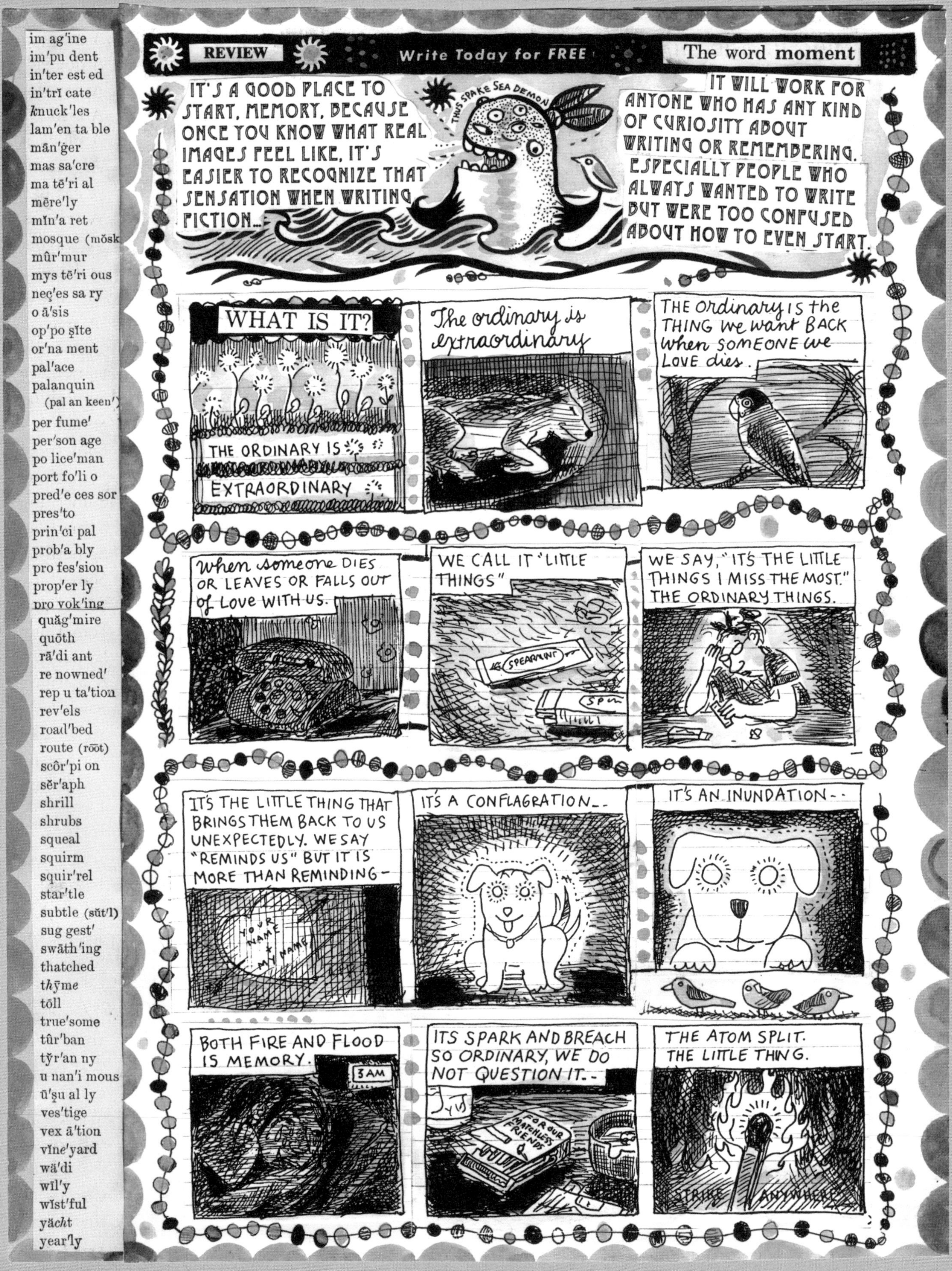

im ag'ine
im'pu dent
in'ter est ed
in'trĭ cate
knuck'les
lam'en ta ble
mān'ger
mas sa'cre
ma tē'ri al
mēre'ly
mĭn'a ret
mosque (mŏsk
mûr'mur
mys tē'ri ous
neç'es sa ry
o ā'sis
op'po şĭte
or'na ment
pal'ace
palanquin
(pal an keen')
per fume'
per'son age
po lice'man
port fo'li o
pred'e ces sor
pres'to
prin'ci pal
prob'a bly
pro fes'sion
prop'er ly
pro vok'ing
quăg'mire
quōth
rā'di ant
re nowned'
rep u ta'tion
rev'els
road'bed
route (rōōt)
scôr'pi on
sĕr'aph
shrill
shrubs
squeal
squirm
squir'rel
star'tle
subtle (sŭt'l)
sug gest'
swāth'ing
thatched
thȳme
tōll
true'some
tûr'ban
tȳr'an ny
u nan'i mous
ū'şu al ly
ves'tige
vex ā'tion
vīne'yard
wä'di
wīl'y
wīst'ful
yächt
year'ly
REVIEW
Write Today for FREE
The word moment
IT'S A GOOD PLACE TO START, MEMORY, BECAUSE ONCE YOU KNOW WHAT REAL IMAGES FEEL LIKE, IT'S EASIER TO RECOGNIZE THAT SENSATION WHEN WRITING FICTION...
THUS SPAKE SEA DEMON
IT WILL WORK FOR ANYONE WHO HAS ANY KIND OF CURIOSITY ABOUT WRITING OR REMEMBERING. ESPECIALLY PEOPLE WHO ALWAYS WANTED TO WRITE BUT WERE TOO CONFUSED ABOUT HOW TO EVEN START.
WHAT IS IT?
THE ORDINARY IS EXTRAORDINARY
The ordinary is extraordinary
THE ordinary is the THING we want BACK when SOMEONE we LOVE dies.
when someone DIES OR LEAVES OR FALLS OUT of LOVE WITH US.
WE CALL IT "LITTLE THINGS"
SPEARMINT
WE SAY, "IT'S THE LITTLE THINGS I MISS THE MOST." THE ORDINARY THINGS.
IT'S THE LITTLE THING THAT BRINGS THEM BACK TO US UNEXPECTEDLY. WE SAY "REMINDS US" BUT IT IS MORE THAN REMINDING-
YOUR NAME + MY NAME
IT'S A CONFLAGRATION--
IT'S AN INUNDATION--
BOTH FIRE AND FLOOD IS MEMORY.
3AM
ITS SPARK AND BREACH SO ORDINARY, WE DO NOT QUESTION IT.-
FOR OUR MATCHLESS FRIENDS
THE ATOM SPLIT. THE LITTLE THING.
STRIKE ANYWHERE

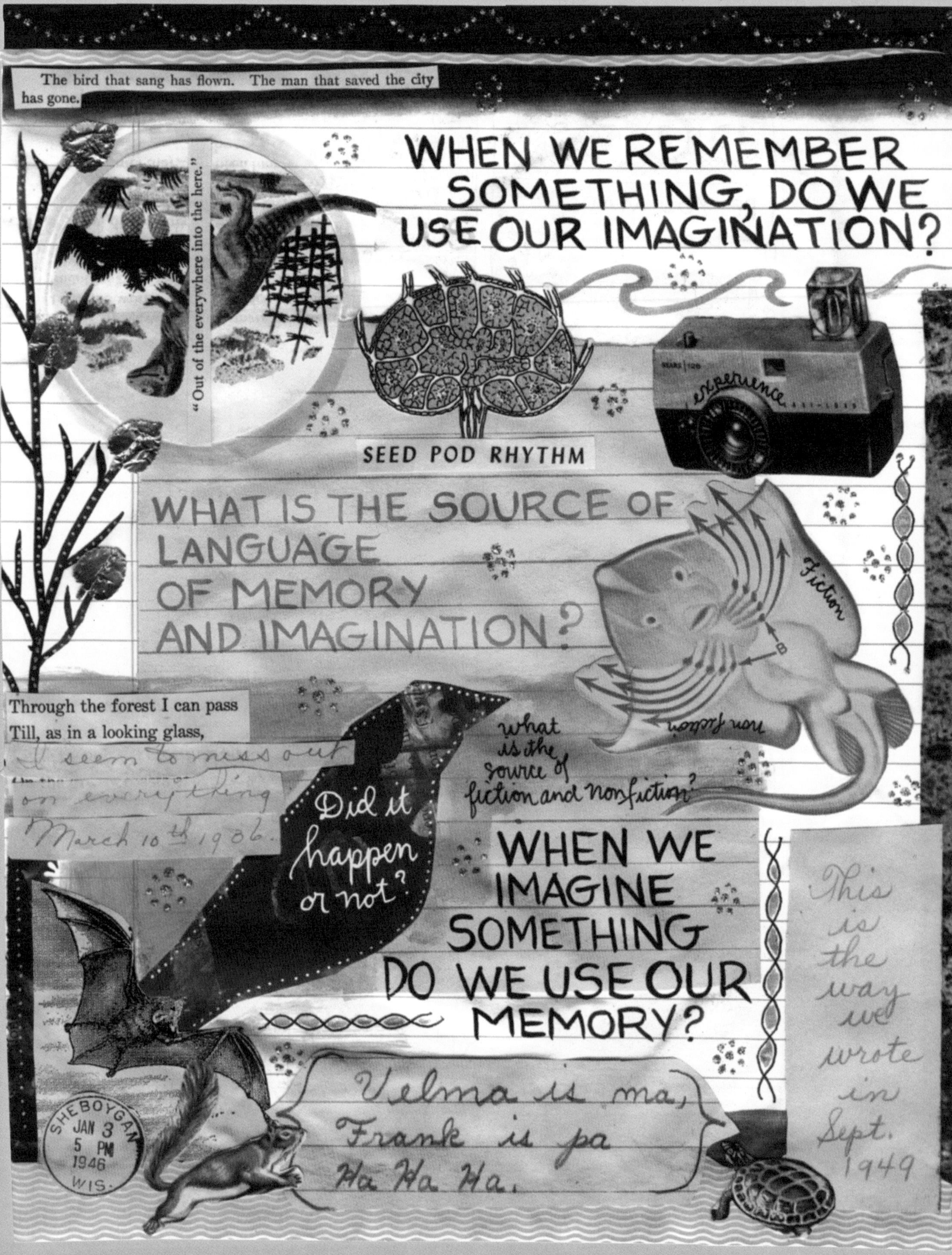
The bird that sang has flown. The man that saved the city has gone.
WHEN WE REMEMBER SOMETHING, DO WE USE OUR IMAGINATION?
"Out of the everywhere into the here."
SEED POD RHYTHM
experience
WHAT IS THE SOURCE OF LANGUAGE OF MEMORY AND IMAGINATION?
Fiction
non fiction
Through the forest I can pass
Till, as in a looking glass,
I seem to miss out on everything
March 10th 1936.
what is the source of fiction and nonfiction?
Did it happen or not?
WHEN WE IMAGINE SOMETHING DO WE USE OUR MEMORY?
This is the way we wrote in Sept. 1949
Velma is ma, Frank is pa Ha Ha Ha.
SHEBOYGAN JAN 3 5 PM 1946 WIS.

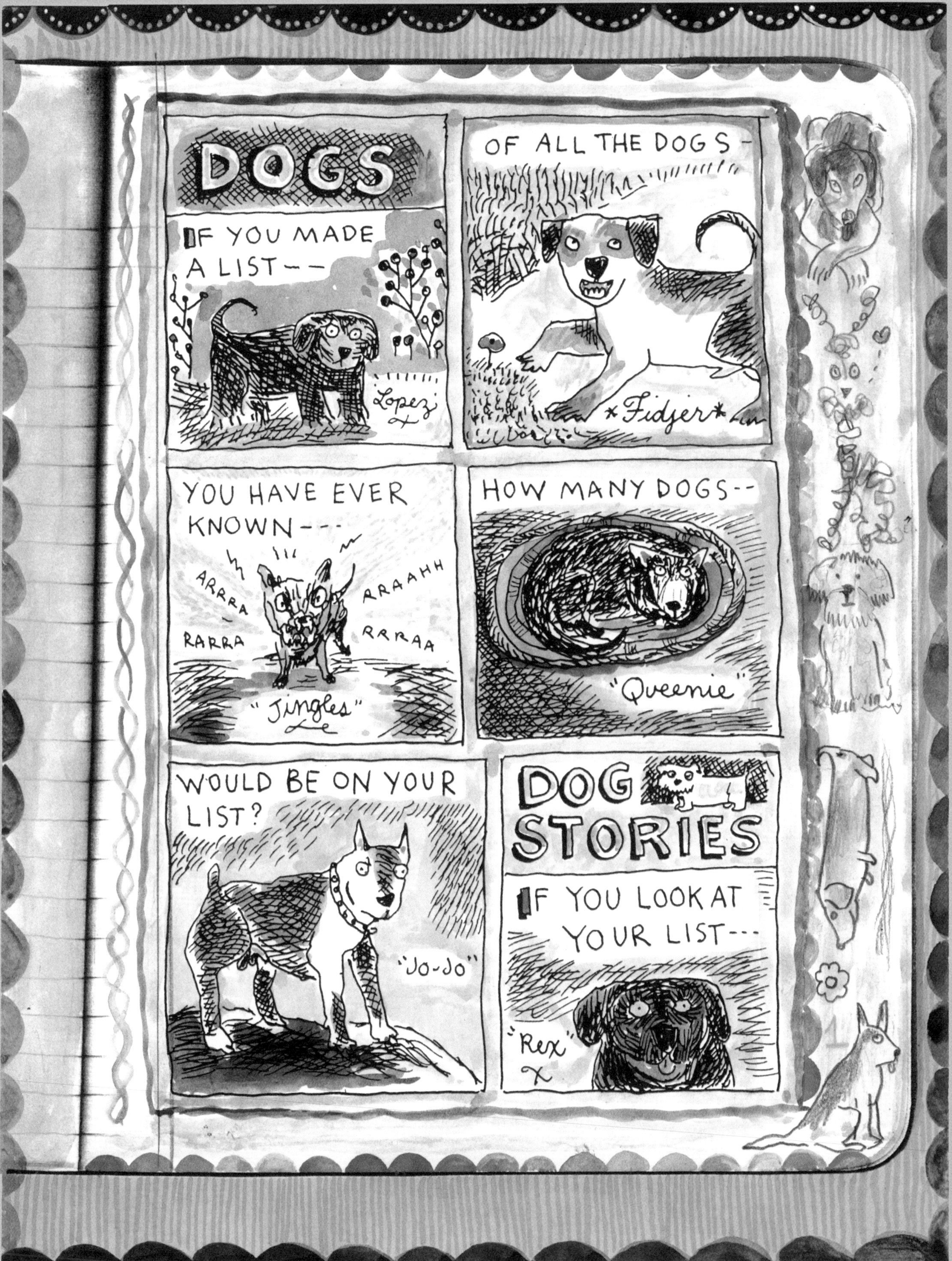
DOGS
IF YOU MADE A LIST--
Lopez
OF ALL THE DOGS -
Fidjer
YOU HAVE EVER KNOWN---
ARRRA
RARRA
RRAAHH
RRRAA
"Jingles"
HOW MANY DOGS--
"Queenie"
WOULD BE ON YOUR LIST?
"Jo-Jo"
DOG STORIES
IF YOU LOOK AT YOUR LIST---
"Rex"

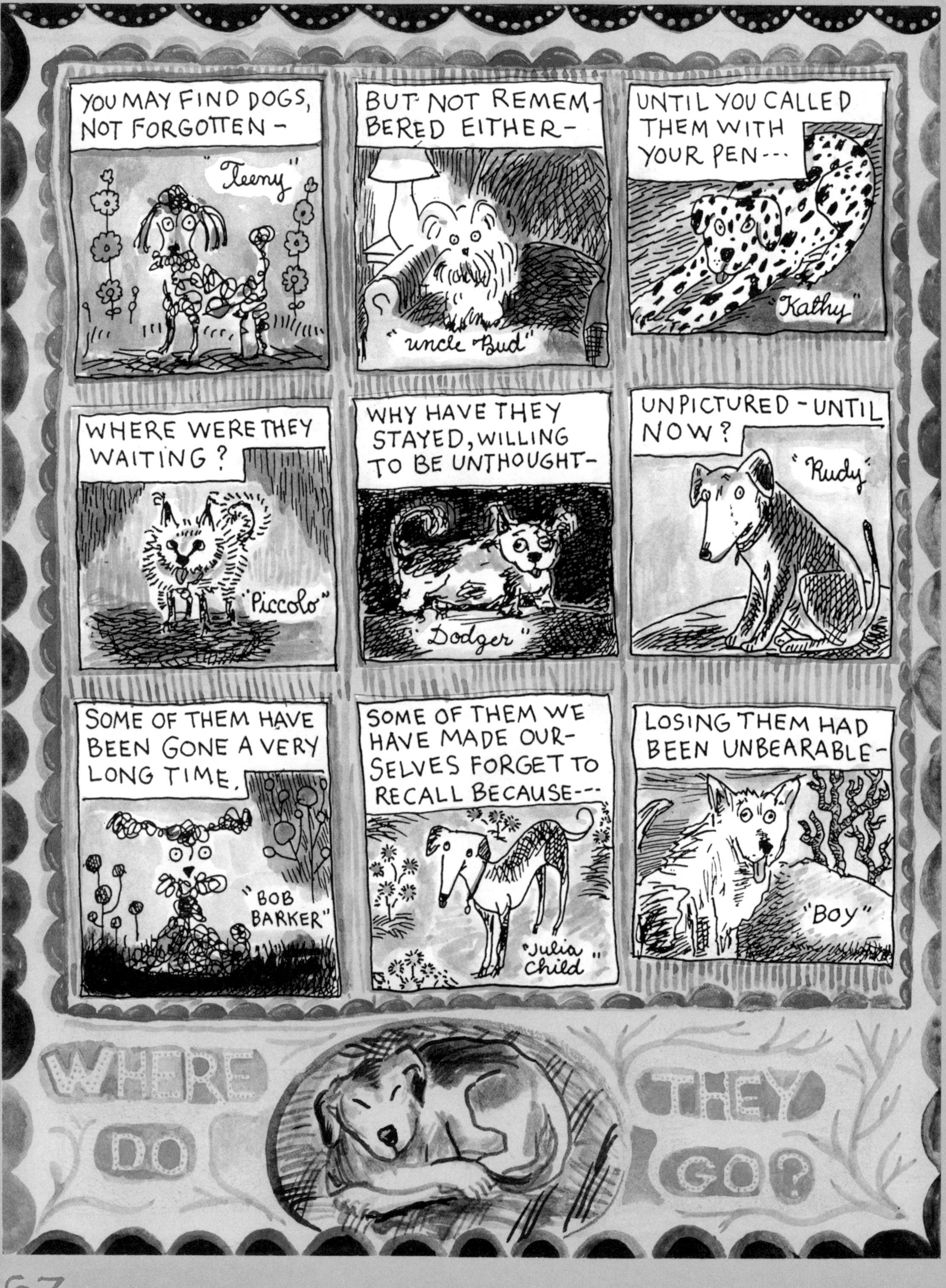
YOU MAY FIND DOGS, NOT FORGOTTEN -
"Teeny"
BUT NOT REMEMBERED EITHER -
"uncle Bud"
UNTIL YOU CALLED THEM WITH YOUR PEN - - -
"Kathy"
WHERE WERE THEY WAITING?
"Piccolo"
WHY HAVE THEY STAYED, WILLING TO BE UNTHOUGHT -
"Dodger"
UNPICTURED - UNTIL NOW?
"Rudy"
SOME OF THEM HAVE BEEN GONE A VERY LONG TIME.
"BOB BARKER"
SOME OF THEM WE HAVE MADE OURSELVES FORGET TO RECALL BECAUSE - - -
"Julia Child"
LOSING THEM HAD BEEN UNBEARABLE -
"Boy"
WHERE DO THEY GO?

AND BEING WITHOUT THEM, WORSE.

Nikki

AND SO THEY SEEM GONE FROM OUR THOUGHTS---

"Schneken"

AS A FAVOR TO US. A KIND OF MERCY--

"Helen OF TROY"

THEY DO NOT CROSS OUR MINDS UNTIL WE CAN STAND IT AGAIN.

BUT THEY ARE THERE INSIDE OF US IN THAT IMAGE-PLACE---

THEY HAPPENED TO US AND WE HAP- PENED TO THEM.

THIS CANNOT BE UNDONE BY FORGETTING--

WHO LIKES A BELLY SCRATCH? HUH? IS IT YOU? IS IT?

OR RE-MADE BY REMEMBERING---

WE CANNOT BRING THEM BACK AND WE CANNOT LOSE THEM --

WE KNOW THIS BECAUSE WE HAVE TRIED. DURING THE UNBEARABLE TIME -

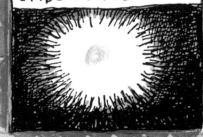

AND THE EMPTY TIME WHICH FOLLOWED-

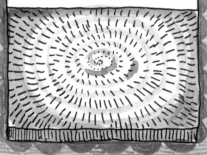

AND THE UNREMEM- BERED TIME THAT IS NOT FORGETTING, BUT A KIND OF FENCING-OFF;

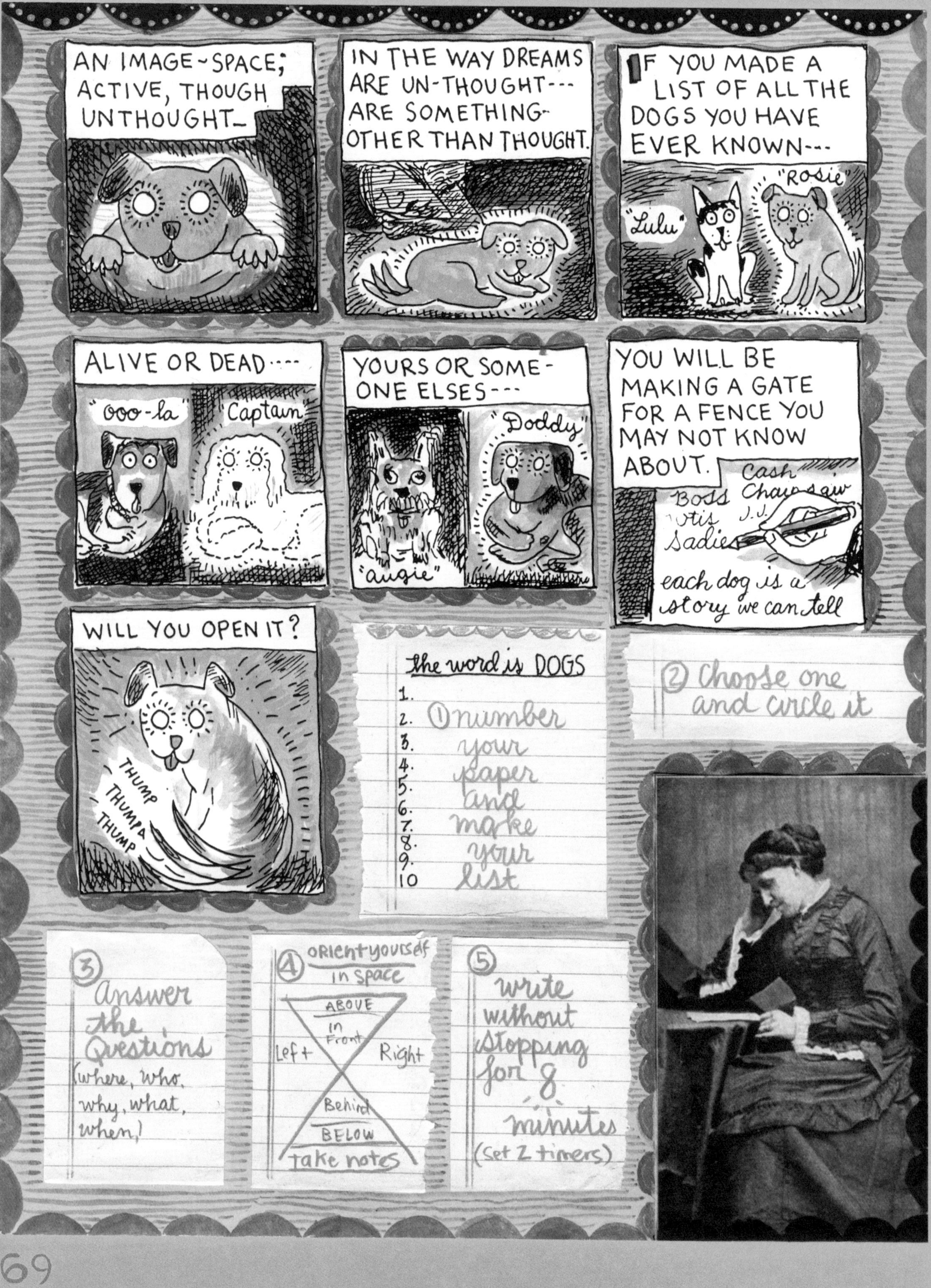
AN IMAGE-SPACE; ACTIVE, THOUGH UNTHOUGHT_
IN THE WAY DREAMS ARE UN-THOUGHT--- ARE SOMETHING-OTHER THAN THOUGHT.
IF YOU MADE A LIST OF ALL THE DOGS YOU HAVE EVER KNOWN---
"Lulu"
"Rosie"
ALIVE OR DEAD----
"ooo-la"
"Captain"
YOURS OR SOME-ONE ELSES---
"augie"
"Doddy"
YOU WILL BE MAKING A GATE FOR A FENCE YOU MAY NOT KNOW ABOUT.
Cash
Boss
J.J.
Sadie
each dog is a story we can tell
WILL YOU OPEN IT?
THUMP
THUMPA
THUMP
the word is DOGS
1.
2. ① number
3. your
4. paper
5. and
6. make
7. your
8. list
9.
10
② Choose one and circle it
③ Answer the Questions (where, who, why, what, when,)
④ ORIENT yourself in space
ABOVE
In Front
Left
Right
Behind
BELOW
Take notes
⑤ write without stopping for 8 minutes (set 2 timers)

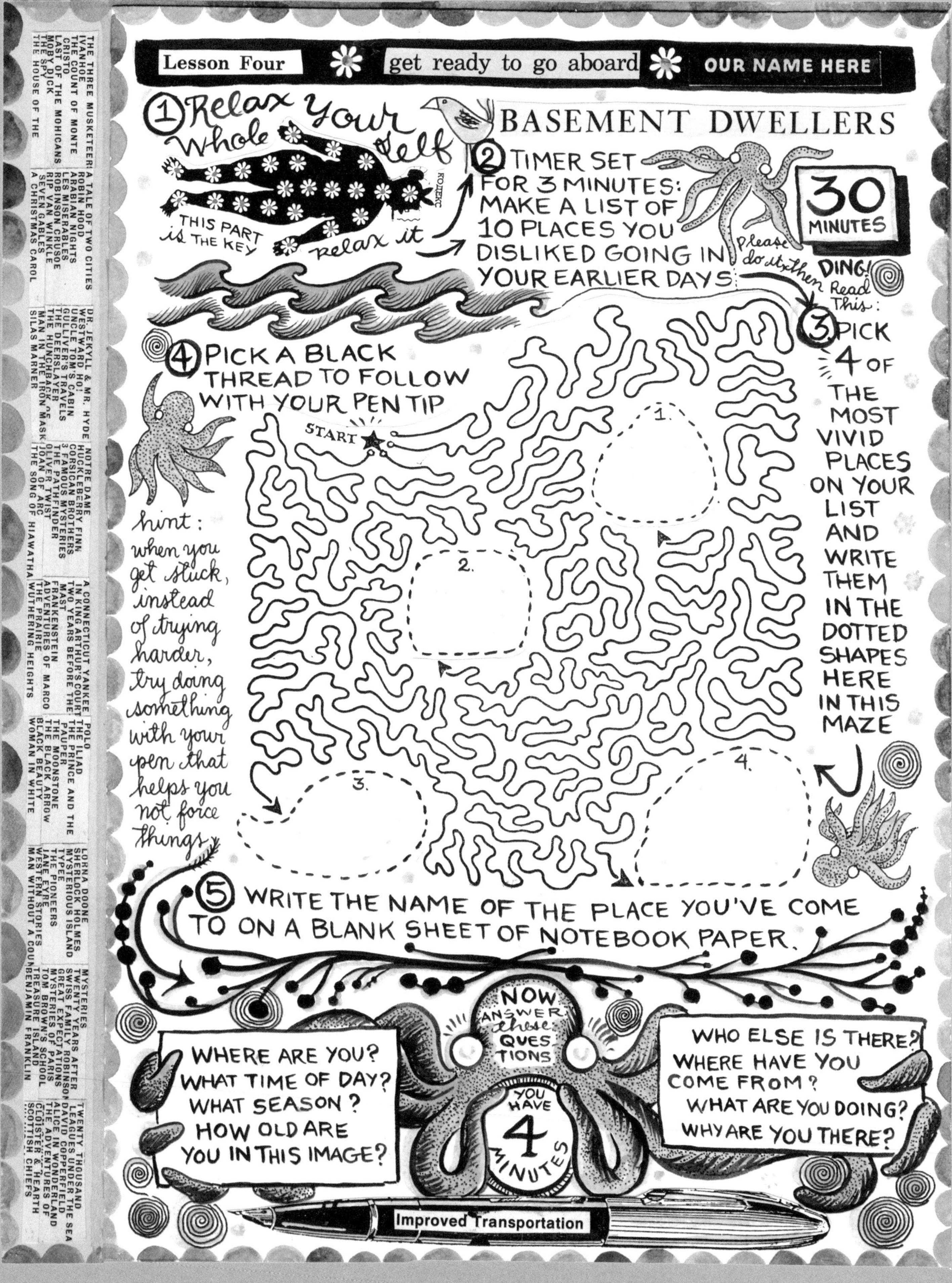

Lesson Four
get ready to go aboard
OUR NAME HERE
BASEMENT DWELLERS
1 Relax your whole self
THIS PART is THE KEY
relax it
2 TIMER SET FOR 3 MINUTES: MAKE A LIST OF 10 PLACES YOU DISLIKED GOING IN YOUR EARLIER DAYS
30 MINUTES
Please do it, then DING! Read This:
3 PICK 4 OF THE MOST VIVID PLACES ON YOUR LIST AND WRITE THEM IN THE DOTTED SHAPES HERE IN THIS MAZE
4 PICK A BLACK THREAD TO FOLLOW WITH YOUR PEN TIP
START
1.
2.
3.
4.
hint: when you get stuck, instead of trying harder, try doing something with your pen that helps you not force things
5 WRITE THE NAME OF THE PLACE YOU'VE COME TO ON A BLANK SHEET OF NOTEBOOK PAPER.
NOW ANSWER these QUESTIONS
YOU HAVE 4 MINUTES
WHERE ARE YOU?
WHAT TIME OF DAY?
WHAT SEASON?
HOW OLD ARE YOU IN THIS IMAGE?
WHO ELSE IS THERE?
WHERE HAVE YOU COME FROM?
WHAT ARE YOU DOING?
WHY ARE YOU THERE?
Improved Transportation

Draw the road travel it

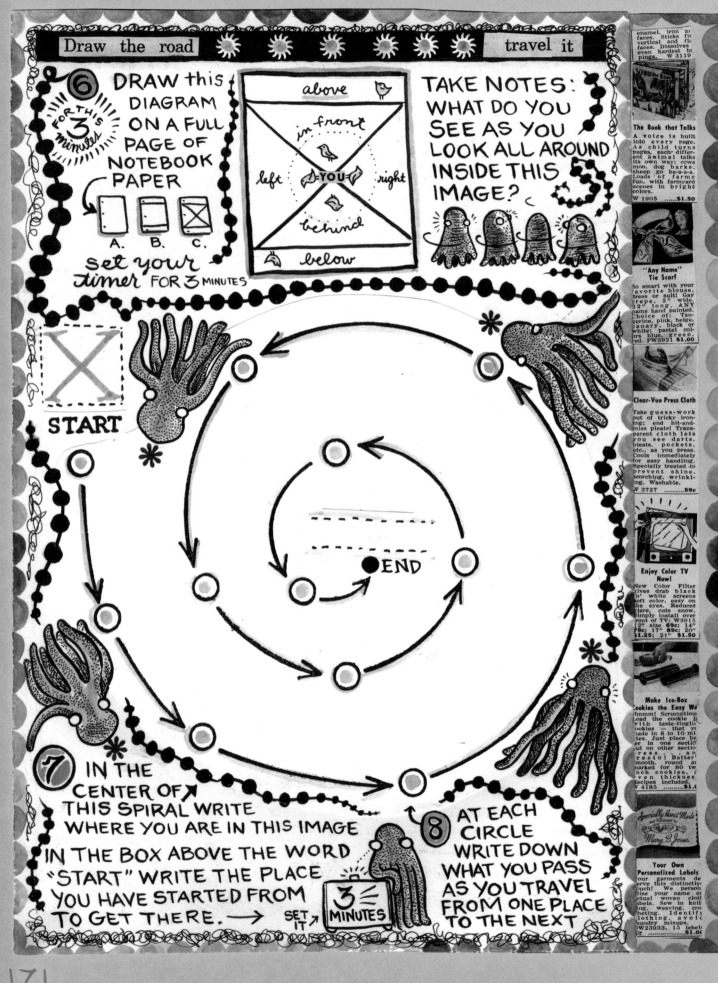

6 FOR THIS 3 minutes

DRAW this DIAGRAM ON A FULL PAGE OF NOTEBOOK PAPER

A. B. C.

set your timer FOR 3 MINUTES

above
in front
left
YOU
right
behind
below

TAKE NOTES: WHAT DO YOU SEE AS YOU LOOK ALL AROUND INSIDE THIS IMAGE?

START

END

7 IN THE CENTER OF THIS SPIRAL WRITE WHERE YOU ARE IN THIS IMAGE

IN THE BOX ABOVE THE WORD "START" WRITE THE PLACE YOU HAVE STARTED FROM TO GET THERE. →

SET IT → 3 MINUTES

8 AT EACH CIRCLE WRITE DOWN WHAT YOU PASS AS YOU TRAVEL FROM ONE PLACE TO THE NEXT

The Book that Talks
"Any Name" Tie Scarf
Clear-Vue Press Cloth
Enjoy Color TV Now!
Make Ice-Box Cookies the Easy Wa
Your Own Personalized Labels

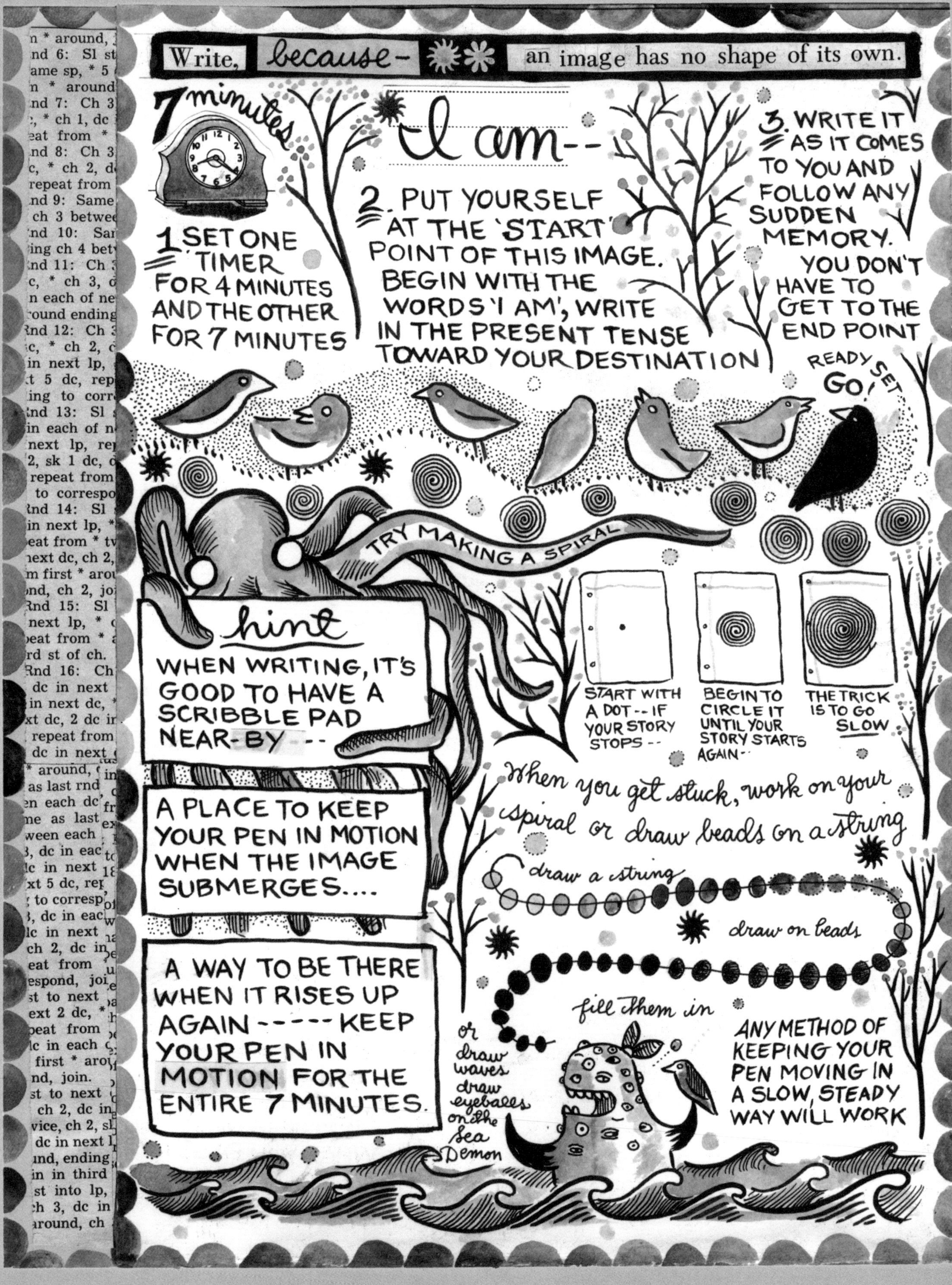

Write, because - an image has no shape of its own.
7 minutes
I am--
1 SET ONE TIMER FOR 4 MINUTES AND THE OTHER FOR 7 MINUTES
2. PUT YOURSELF AT THE 'START' POINT OF THIS IMAGE. BEGIN WITH THE WORDS 'I AM', WRITE IN THE PRESENT TENSE TOWARD YOUR DESTINATION
3. WRITE IT AS IT COMES TO YOU AND FOLLOW ANY SUDDEN MEMORY.
YOU DON'T HAVE TO GET TO THE END POINT
READY SET GO!
TRY MAKING A SPIRAL
hint
WHEN WRITING, IT'S GOOD TO HAVE A SCRIBBLE PAD NEAR-BY --
A PLACE TO KEEP YOUR PEN IN MOTION WHEN THE IMAGE SUBMERGES....
A WAY TO BE THERE WHEN IT RISES UP AGAIN ----- KEEP YOUR PEN IN MOTION FOR THE ENTIRE 7 MINUTES.
START WITH A DOT -- IF YOUR STORY STOPS --
BEGIN TO CIRCLE IT UNTIL YOUR STORY STARTS AGAIN--
THE TRICK IS TO GO SLOW
When you get stuck, work on your spiral or draw beads on a string
draw a string
draw on beads
fill them in
or draw waves draw eyeballs on the Sea Demon
ANY METHOD OF KEEPING YOUR PEN MOVING IN A SLOW, STEADY WAY WILL WORK

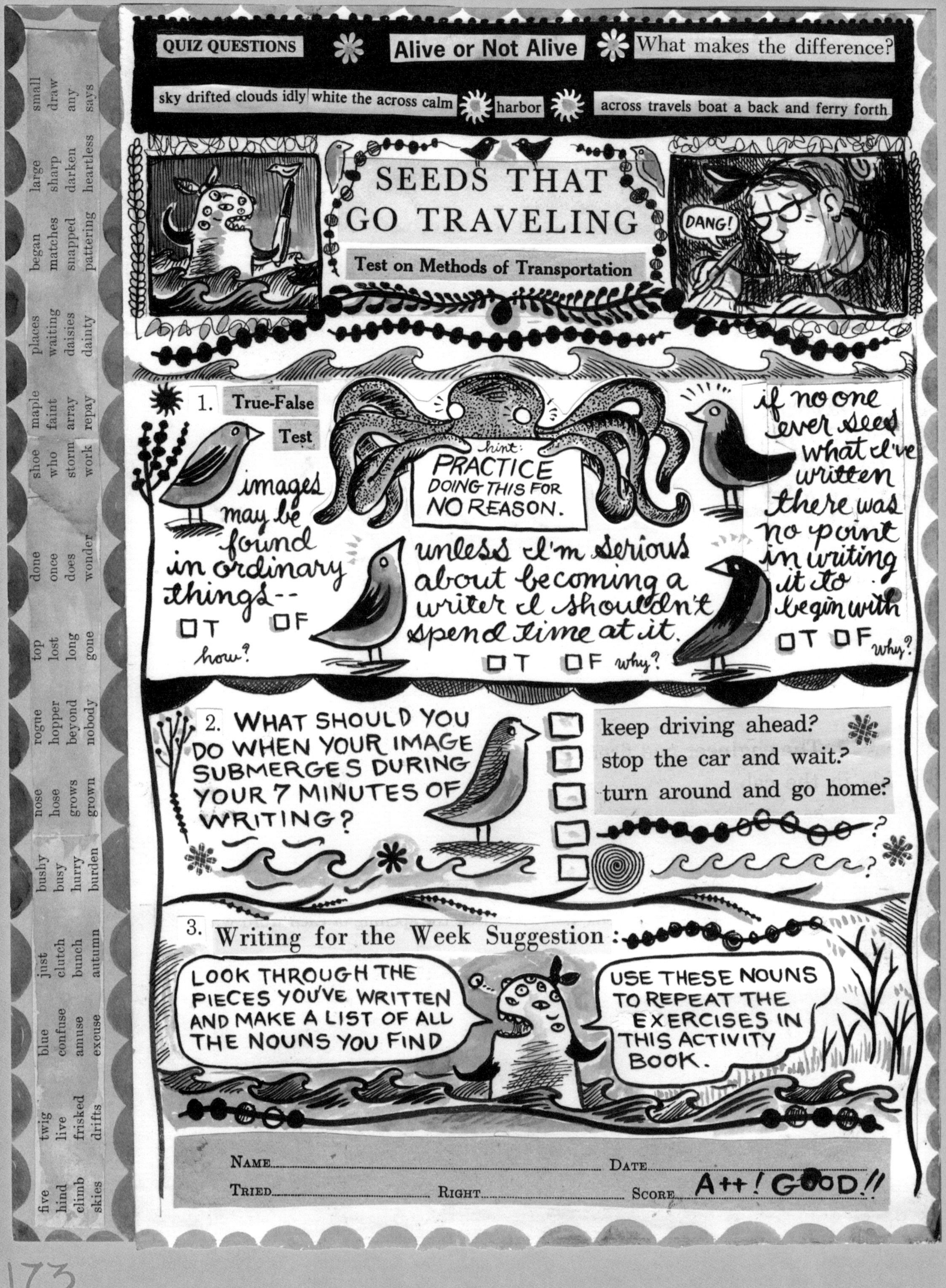
QUIZ QUESTIONS
Alive or Not Alive
What makes the difference?
sky drifted clouds idly white the across calm
harbor
across travels boat a back and ferry forth
SEEDS THAT GO TRAVELING
Test on Methods of Transportation
DANG!
1. True-False Test
hint: PRACTICE DOING THIS FOR NO REASON.
images may be found in ordinary things-- ☐T ☐F how?
unless I'm serious about becoming a writer I shouldn't spend time at it. ☐T ☐F why?
if no one ever sees what I've written there was no point in writing it to begin with ☐T ☐F why?
2. WHAT SHOULD YOU DO WHEN YOUR IMAGE SUBMERGES DURING YOUR 7 MINUTES OF WRITING?
☐ keep driving ahead?
☐ stop the car and wait?
☐ turn around and go home?
☐ ?
☐ ?
3. Writing for the Week Suggestion:
LOOK THROUGH THE PIECES YOU'VE WRITTEN AND MAKE A LIST OF ALL THE NOUNS YOU FIND
USE THESE NOUNS TO REPEAT THE EXERCISES IN THIS ACTIVITY BOOK.
NAME .... DATE ....
TRIED .... RIGHT .... SCORE .... A++! GOOD!!
small draw any says
large sharp darken heartless
began matches snapped pattering
places waiting daisies dainty
maple faint array repay
shoe who storm work
done once does wonder
top lost long gone
rogue hopper beyond nobody
nose hose grows grown
bushy busy hurry burden
just clutch bunch autumn
blue confuse amuse excuse
twig live frisked drifts
five hind climb skies

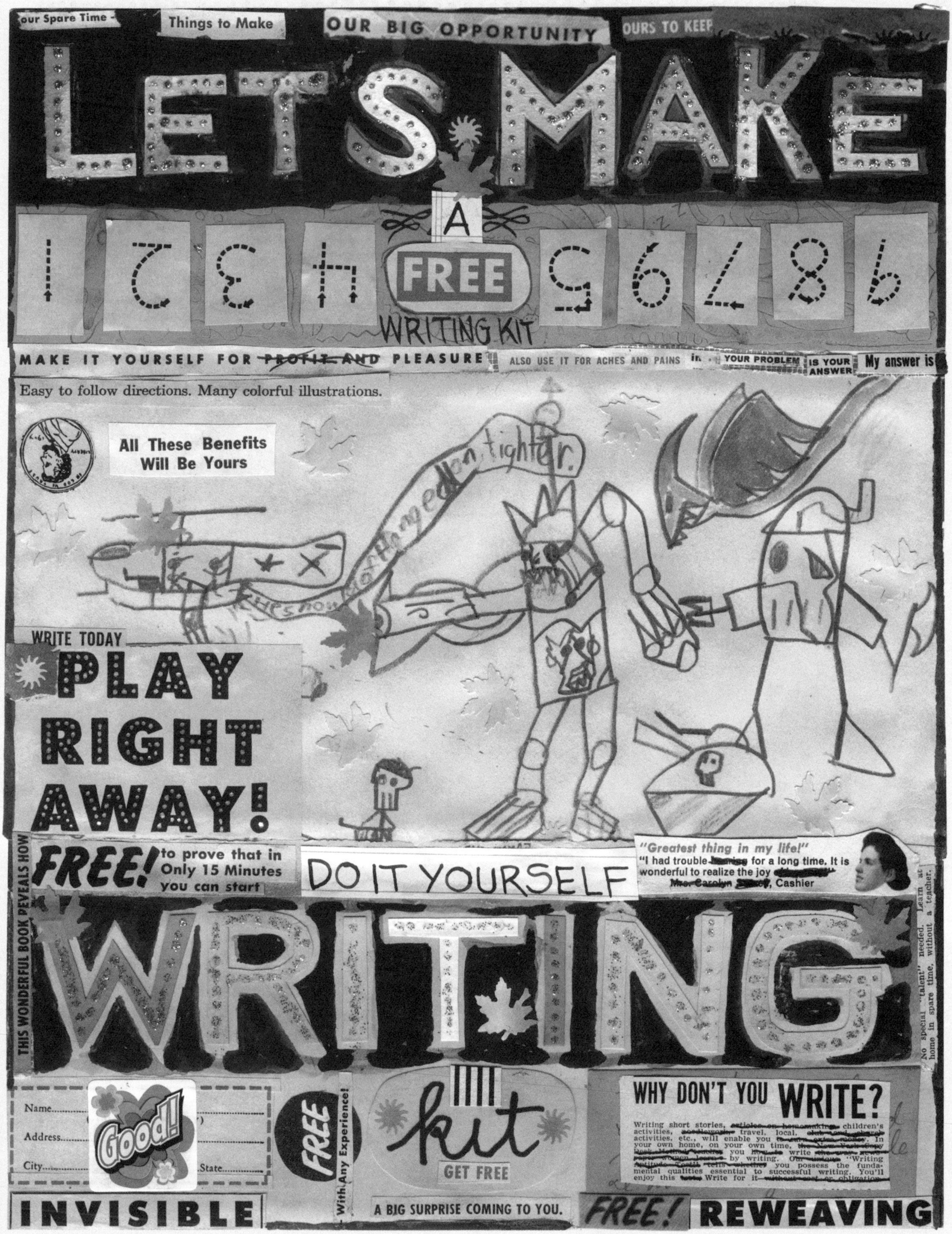
our Spare Time -
Things to Make
OUR BIG OPPORTUNITY
OURS TO KEEP
LET'S MAKE
A
FREE
WRITING KIT
MAKE IT YOURSELF FOR PROFIT AND PLEASURE
ALSO USE IT FOR ACHES AND PAINS
YOUR PROBLEM
IS YOUR ANSWER
My answer is
Easy to follow directions. Many colorful illustrations.
All These Benefits Will Be Yours
WRITE TODAY
PLAY RIGHT AWAY!
FREE! to prove that in Only 15 Minutes you can start
DO IT YOURSELF
"Greatest thing in my life!"
"I had trouble [redacted] for a long time. It is wonderful to realize the joy [redacted]"
Mrs. Carolyn [redacted], Cashier
THIS WONDERFUL BOOK REVEALS HOW
WRITING
No special "talent" needed. Learn at home in spare time, without a teacher.
Name
Address
City
State
Good!
FREE
With Any Experience!
kit
GET FREE
WHY DON'T YOU WRITE?
A BIG SURPRISE COMING TO YOU.
INVISIBLE
FREE!
REWEAVING

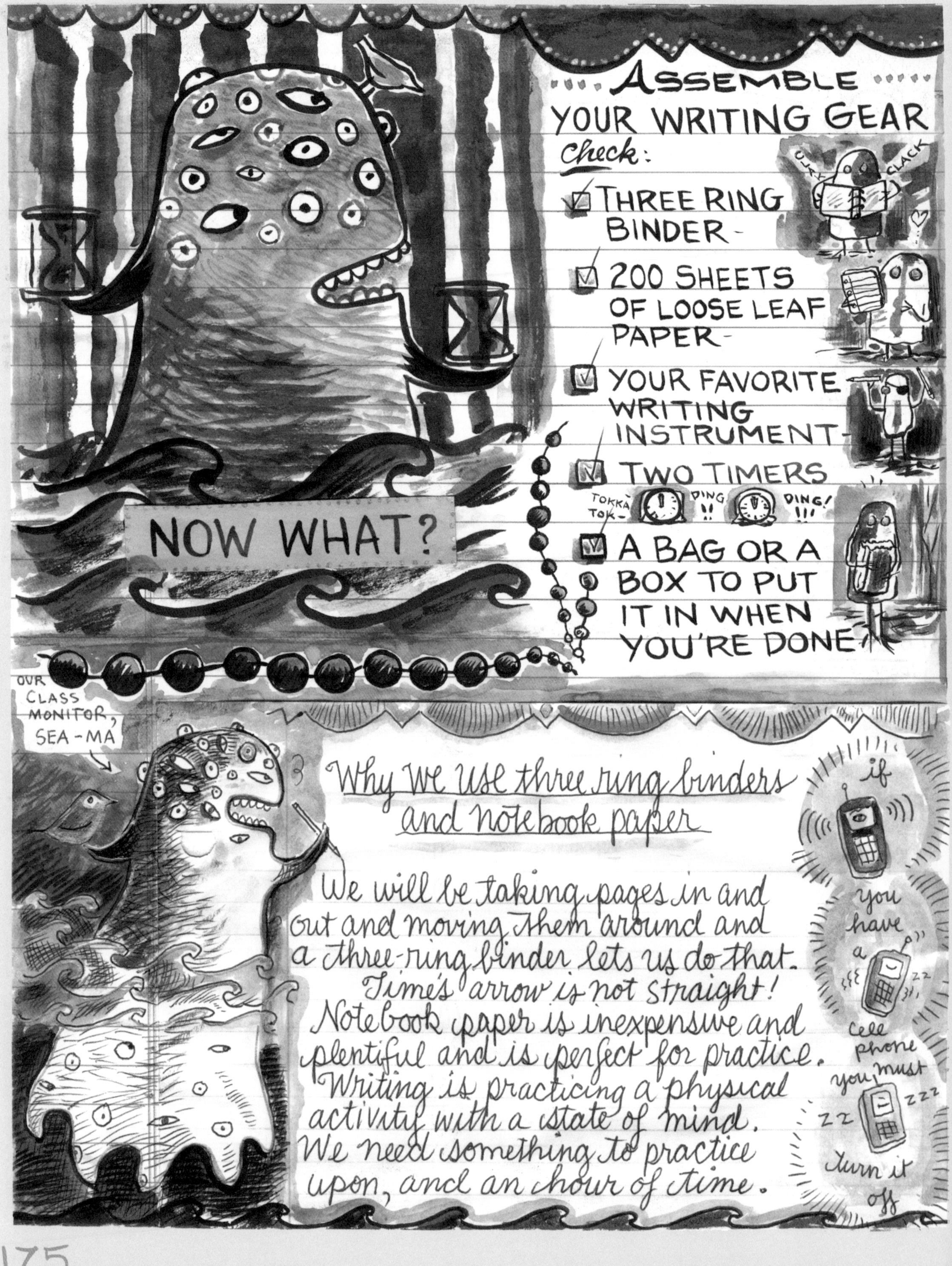
ASSEMBLE
YOUR WRITING GEAR
Check:
THREE RING BINDER
CLACK
200 SHEETS OF LOOSE LEAF PAPER
YOUR FAVORITE WRITING INSTRUMENT
TWO TIMERS
TOKKA TOK
DING !!
DING! !!!
A BAG OR A BOX TO PUT IT IN WHEN YOU'RE DONE
NOW WHAT?
OUR CLASS MONITOR, SEA-MA
Why we use three ring binders and notebook paper
We will be taking pages in and out and moving them around and a three-ring binder lets us do that.
Time's arrow is not straight!
Notebook paper is inexpensive and plentiful and is perfect for practice.
Writing is practicing a physical activity with a state of mind.
We need something to practice upon, and an hour of time.
if you have a cell phone you must turn it off

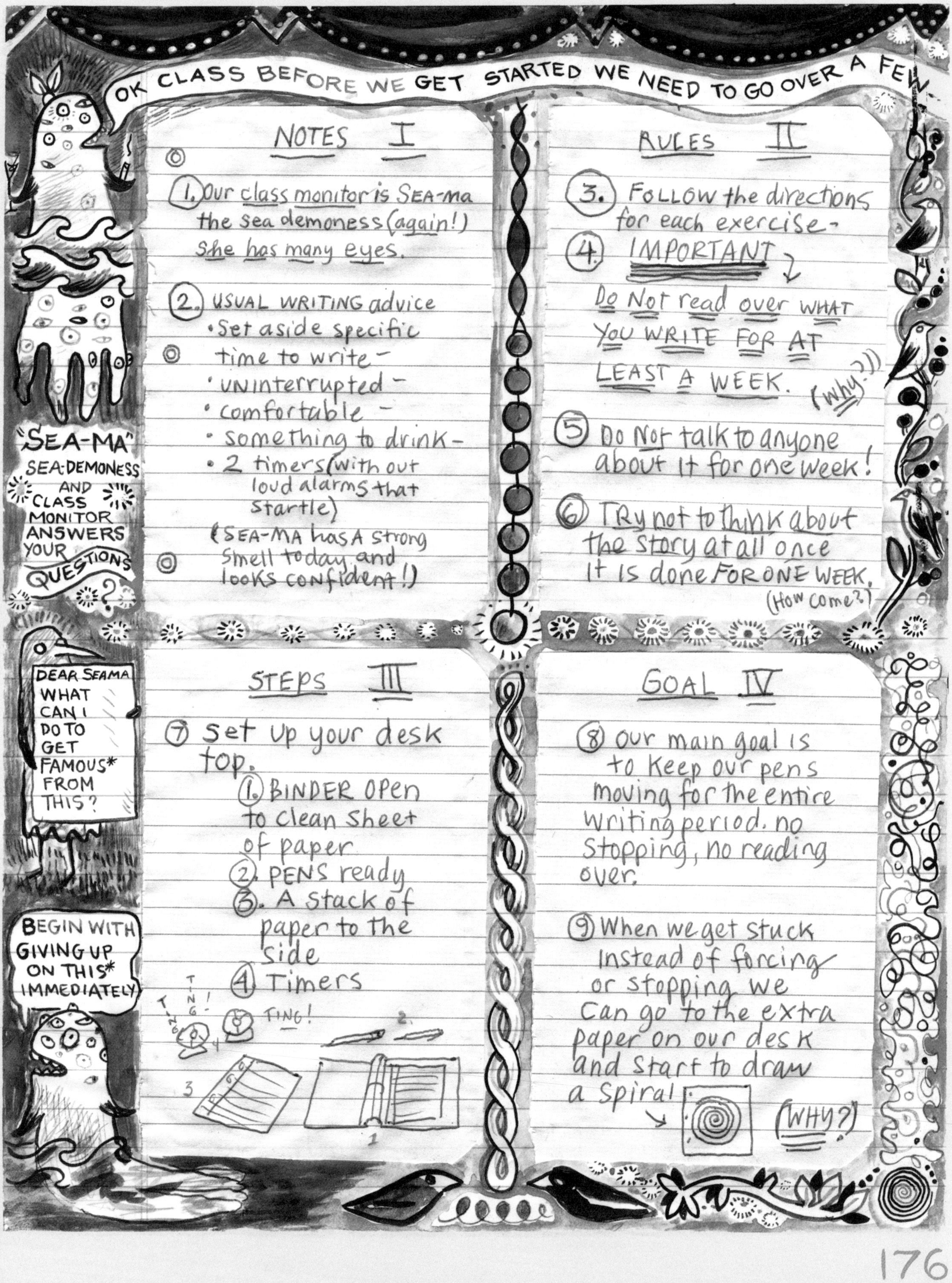
OK CLASS BEFORE WE GET STARTED WE NEED TO GO OVER A FEW...
NOTES I
1. Our class monitor is SEA-ma the sea demoness (again!) She has many eyes.
2. USUAL WRITING advice
• Set aside specific time to write –
• uninterrupted –
• comfortable –
• something to drink –
• 2 timers (with out loud alarms that startle)
(SEA-MA has A strong smell today and looks confident!)
RULES II
3. FOLLOW the directions for each exercise –
4. IMPORTANT
Do NOT read over WHAT YOU WRITE FOR AT LEAST A WEEK.
(why??)
5. Do NOT talk to anyone about it for one week!
6. TRy not to think about the story at all once it is done FOR ONE WEEK.
(How come?)
"SEA-MA" SEA-DEMONESS AND CLASS MONITOR ANSWERS YOUR QUESTIONS ?
DEAR SEAMA WHAT CAN I DO TO GET FAMOUS* FROM THIS?
BEGIN WITH GIVING UP ON THIS* IMMEDIATELY
STEPS III
7. Set up your desk top.
1. BINDER OPEN to clean sheet of paper
2. PENS ready
3. A stack of paper to the side
4. Timers
TING!
TING!
GOAL IV
8. our main goal is to keep our pens moving for the entire writing period. no stopping, no reading over.
9. When we get stuck instead of forcing or stopping we can go to the extra paper on our desk and start to draw a spiral
(WHY?)

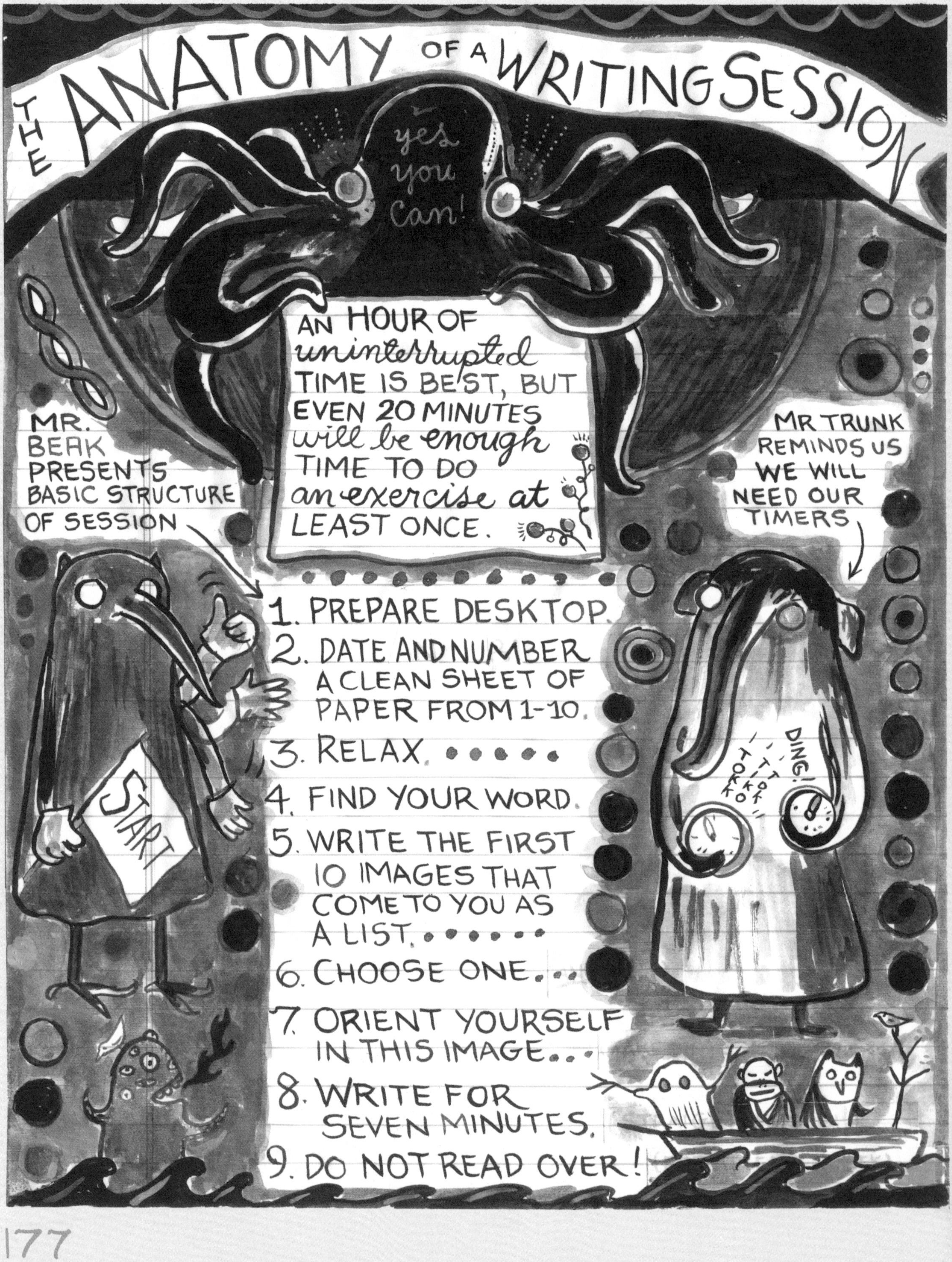

THE ANATOMY OF A WRITING SESSION
yes you can!
AN HOUR OF uninterrupted TIME IS BEST, BUT EVEN 20 MINUTES will be enough TIME TO DO an exercise at LEAST ONCE.
MR. BEAK PRESENTS BASIC STRUCTURE OF SESSION
MR TRUNK REMINDS US WE WILL NEED OUR TIMERS
1. PREPARE DESKTOP.
2. DATE AND NUMBER A CLEAN SHEET OF PAPER FROM 1-10.
3. RELAX.
4. FIND YOUR WORD.
5. WRITE THE FIRST 10 IMAGES THAT COME TO YOU AS A LIST.
6. CHOOSE ONE...
7. ORIENT YOURSELF IN THIS IMAGE...
8. WRITE FOR SEVEN MINUTES.
9. DO NOT READ OVER!
START
DING!

HOW TO MAKE A WORD BAG

① Our Word List

radio	monkey	running	park
too much	cook	airplane	dog
responsible	basement	skin	candy
wrap	carpet	fire	night time
stop	teeth	hat	lights
rope	winter	rip	sink
milk	telling	hanging	lie
missing	witch	call	hair
over with	keep out	winner	kitchen
tug-o'-war	garbage	telephone	downhill
lotion	president	broken	church
coffee	blood	upstairs	table
poke	adore	pig	glue

Q. What is a word bag?

A. A word bag is a bag with words inside of it. We will use the word bag when we write our stories.

Q. MATERIALS?

A. scissors
envelopes
medium sized paper bag
or even a grocery bag
or a Box if you like Boxes.

② cook, table, airplane, skin, candy, gone, basement, glue, upstairs, blood, broken, bop, adore, sink, garbage, telephone

① START by COPYING ALL 4 PAGES OF 'OUR WORD LIST' ONTO CARD STOCK OR TAGBOARD.

② CUT OUT ALL THE WORDS

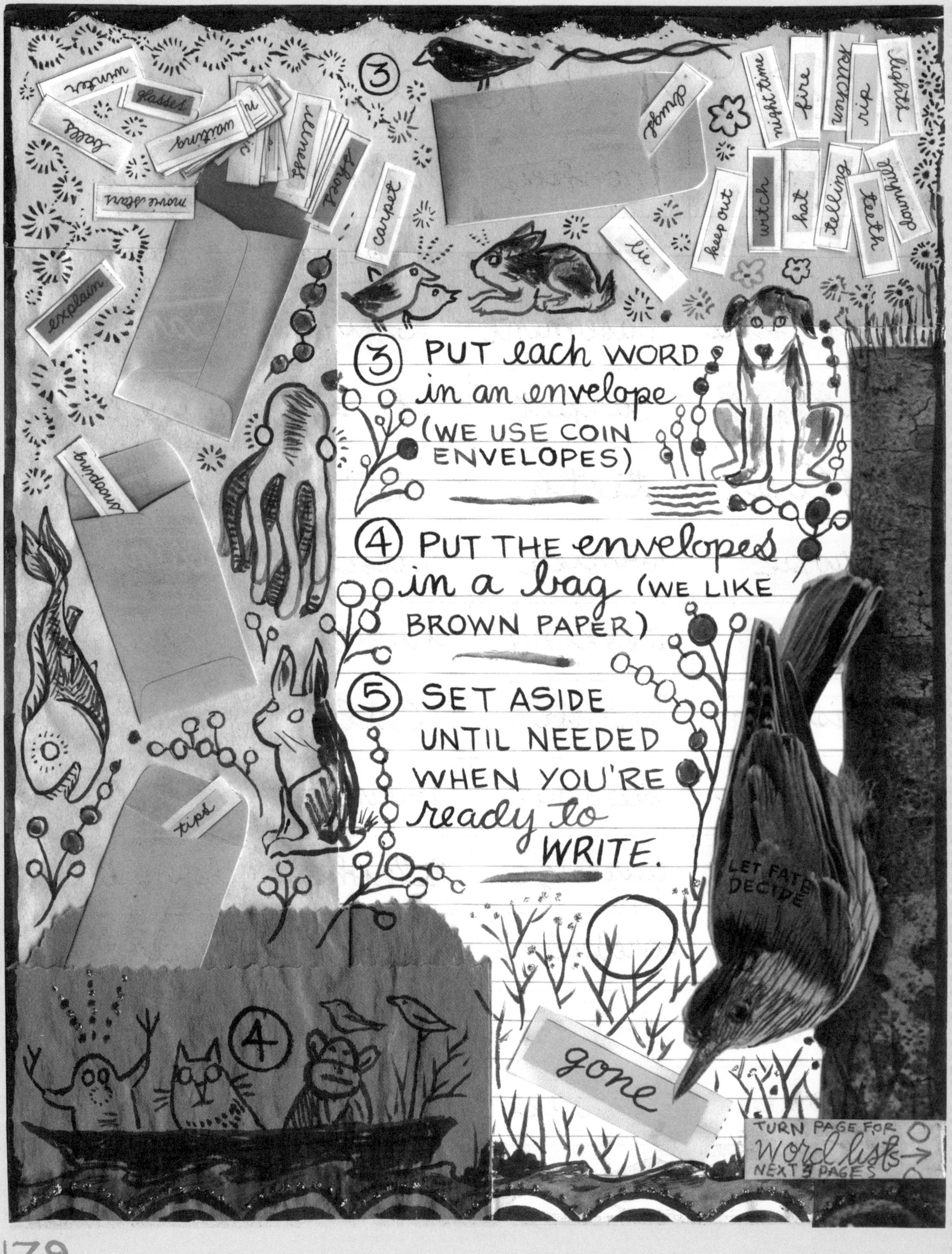
winter
glasses
bells
waiting
shoes
moved
move stars
carpet
laugh
night time
fire
kitchen
rip
lights
keep out
witch
hat
telling
teeth
lie
explain
snooping
tips
LET FATE DECIDE
gone

③ PUT each WORD in an envelope (WE USE COIN ENVELOPES)

④ PUT THE envelopes in a bag (WE LIKE BROWN PAPER)

⑤ SET ASIDE UNTIL NEEDED WHEN YOU'RE ready to WRITE.

TURN PAGE FOR word lists → NEXT 3 PAGES

Our Word List

radio	monkey	running	park
too much	cook	airplane	dog
responsible	basement	skin	candy
wrap	carpet	fire	night time
stop	teeth	hat	lights
rope	winter	rip	sink
milk	telling	hanging	lie
missing	witch	call	hair
over with	keep out	winner	kitchen
tug-o'-war	garbage	telephone	downhill
lotion	president	broken	church
coffee	blood	upstairs	table
poke	adore	pig	glue

shoes	neighbors	stitches	envy
chicken	illness	snooping	glasses
too soon	towels	tips	ugly
leather	substitute	balls	stung
relatives	mosquitoes	explain	eggs
fake	locked doors	movie stars	mad
monsters	refrigerator	blue eyes	rich
television	hallways	speeches	drums
music	groceries	waiting	boots
sugar	kissing	drugs	dirt
sweat	bread	sunglasses	bugs
lunch room	new clothes	gone	lose
feet	unexplained	money	caught

dishes	temperature	do-over	eating
spiders	costumes	paint	pickles
jail	red	popcorn	traps
camping	coffee	the dark	closed
worry	electricity	coming back	pets
movies	the zoo	beards	debt
bully	talking	loans	beer
smash	announcement	garage	police
bees	the beach	driving	parade
eyes	creep	cheese	smoke
dead	giant	train	cake
soap	clues	sandwiches	needles
buffalo	back yard	worn out	laundry

hiding	going away	bitten	crimes
funeral	purse	cut	falling
lakes	hangovers	guitars	stoves
bad food	make-up	straps	girls
ears	squatting	a visitor	bad luck
wall paper	heat	silverware	drug store
singing	wine	bars	turtle necks
empty	repair	soda pop	base ball
magazines	hatred	ladder	cheating
birthdays	underwear	sharing	living room
clouds	wrong	bedroom	smells
movies	hair cuts	water	boys
stealing	ink	tease	marshmallow

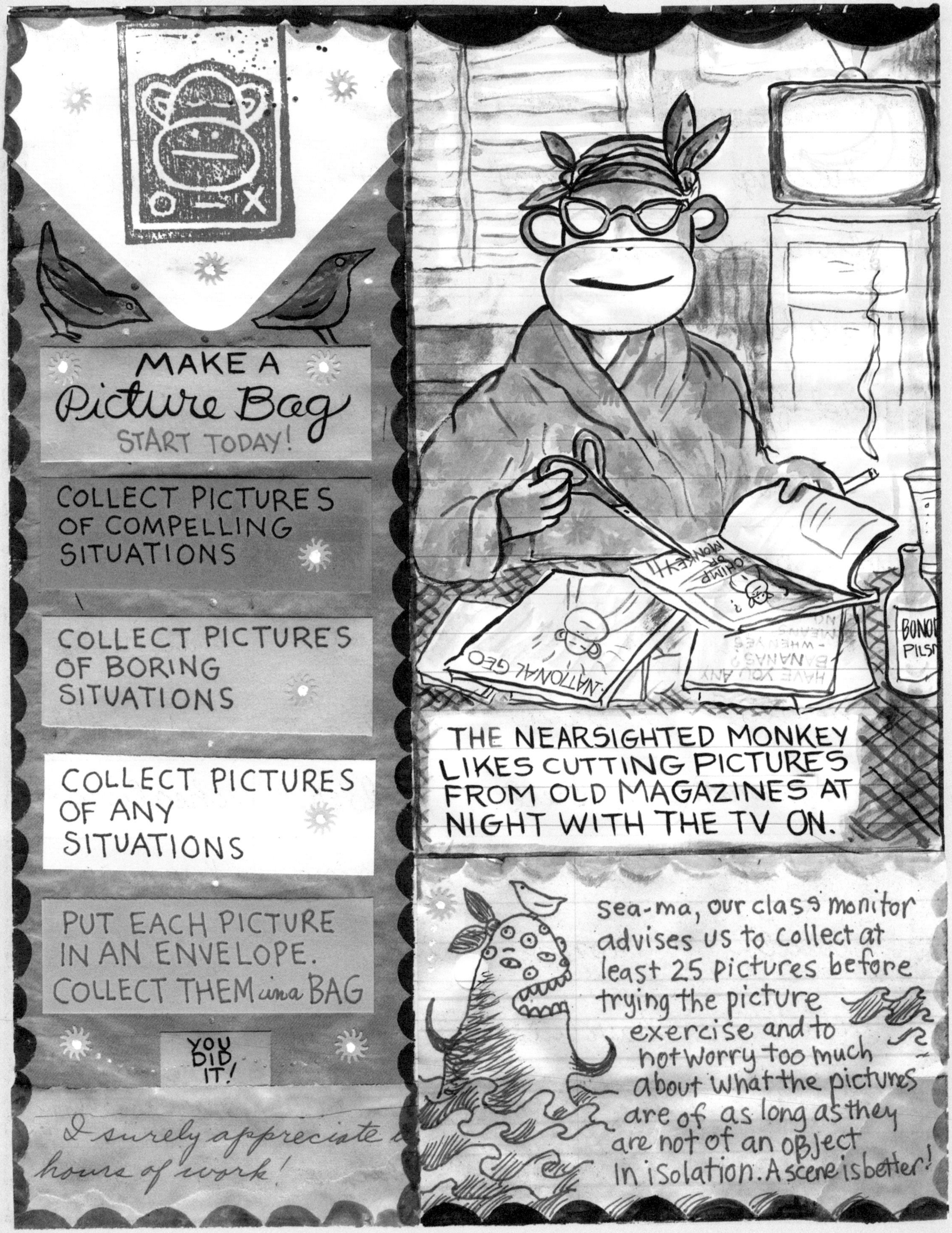
MAKE A
Picture Bag
START TODAY!
COLLECT PICTURES OF COMPELLING SITUATIONS
COLLECT PICTURES OF BORING SITUATIONS
COLLECT PICTURES OF ANY SITUATIONS
PUT EACH PICTURE IN AN ENVELOPE. COLLECT THEM in a BAG
YOU DID IT!
I surely appreciate
hours of work!
THE NEARSIGHTED MONKEY LIKES CUTTING PICTURES FROM OLD MAGAZINES AT NIGHT WITH THE TV ON.
sea-ma, our class monitor advises us to collect at least 25 pictures before trying the picture exercise and to not worry too much about what the pictures are of as long as they are not of an object in isolation. A scene is better!

Let's use the picture bag!

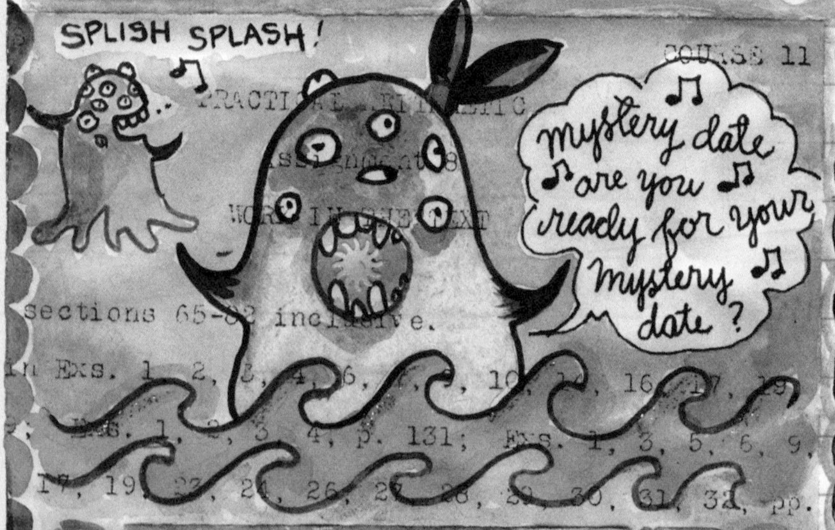
SPLISH SPLASH!
mystery date are you ready for your mystery date?
sections 65-82 inclusive.

DIG IT! E-Z INSTRUCTIONS! TRY IT!

NOTES ON Sea-Ma's instructions for the picture EXERCISES.

After an unecessary musical interlude of Sea Ma Singing (to "get us in the mood,") she said to open our notebooks to a blank page.

She said writing fiction is not that different from writing from your own experience, and this exercise is not that different from the ones we've been doing.

1. Secure 20 minutes of uninterrupted time
2. Relax yourself in front of your blank paper.
3. ~~Pull a MYSTERY envelope from your picture~~ ~~word~~ bag. (They are all mystery envelopes because you don't know what's inside!)
4. Before you open it, tell yourself that you are either in this picture, or this is what you see
5. Answer the same Questions we've used for previous exercises →
6. When you're ready, beginning with the words "I am", write what comes to you for 8 minutes
7. For some special sauce, try combining a picture from your picture bag and a word from your word bag!

1. where are you?
2. what time of day is it?
3. What season does it seem to be?
4. What are you doing?

5. why are you there?
6. who else is in this image?
7. what's the temperature like?
8. what sounds can you hear?

9. what does the air smell like?
10 what are some of the objects around you?

Now turn around in this image. WHAT IS in front, right, left behind, above, below you?

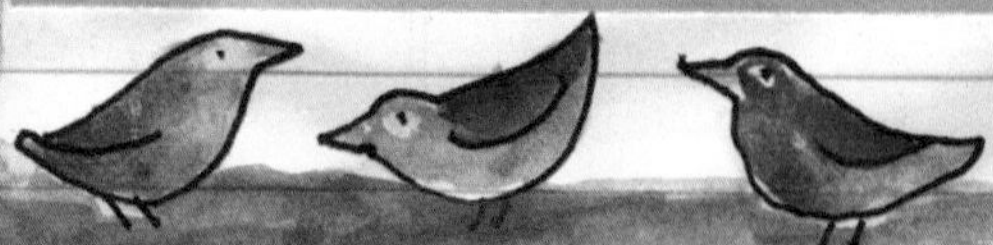

First copy these questions then cut them out now you can use them anytime!

where are you?	what time of day does it seem to be?	what season does it seem to be?	about how old are you in this image?
why are you there?	what are you doing?	is there anyone else in this image?	is there anyone who just left or who may be coming?
what is the temperature like in this image?	what does the air smell like?	what are some of the sounds in this image?	what are some of the objects in this image?
what's in front of you?	what's to your right?	what's to your left?	what's behind you?

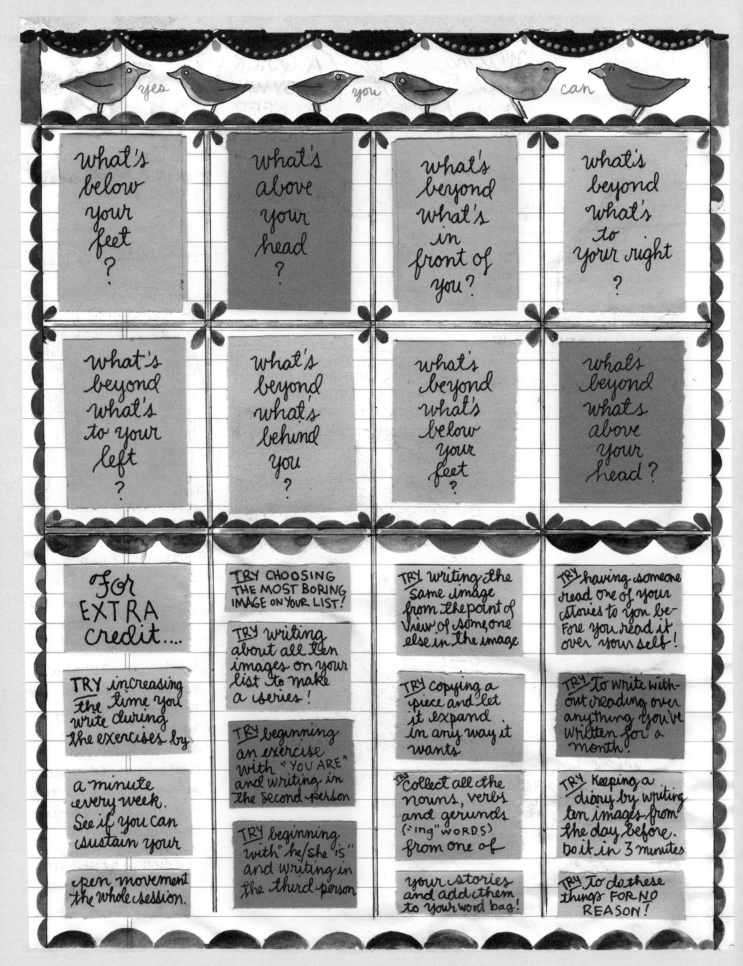

yes you can

what's below your feet?

what's above your head?

what's beyond what's in front of you?

what's beyond what's to your right?

what's beyond what's to your left?

what's beyond what's behind you?

what's beyond what's below your feet?

what's beyond what's above your head?

FOR EXTRA credit....

TRY increasing the time you write during the exercises by

a minute every week. See if you can sustain your

pen movement the whole session.

TRY CHOOSING THE MOST BORING IMAGE ON YOUR LIST!

TRY writing about all ten images on your list to make a series!

TRY beginning an exercise with "YOU ARE" and writing in the second person

TRY beginning with "he/she is" and writing in the third person

TRY writing the same image from the point of view of someone else in the image

TRY copying a piece and let it expand in any way it wants

TRY Collect all the nouns, verbs and gerunds ("ing" WORDS) from one of

your stories and add them to your word bag!

TRY having someone read one of your stories to you before you read it over yourself!

TRY to write without reading over anything you've written for a month!

TRY keeping a diary by writing ten images from the day before. Do it in 3 minutes

TRY to do these things FOR NO REASON!

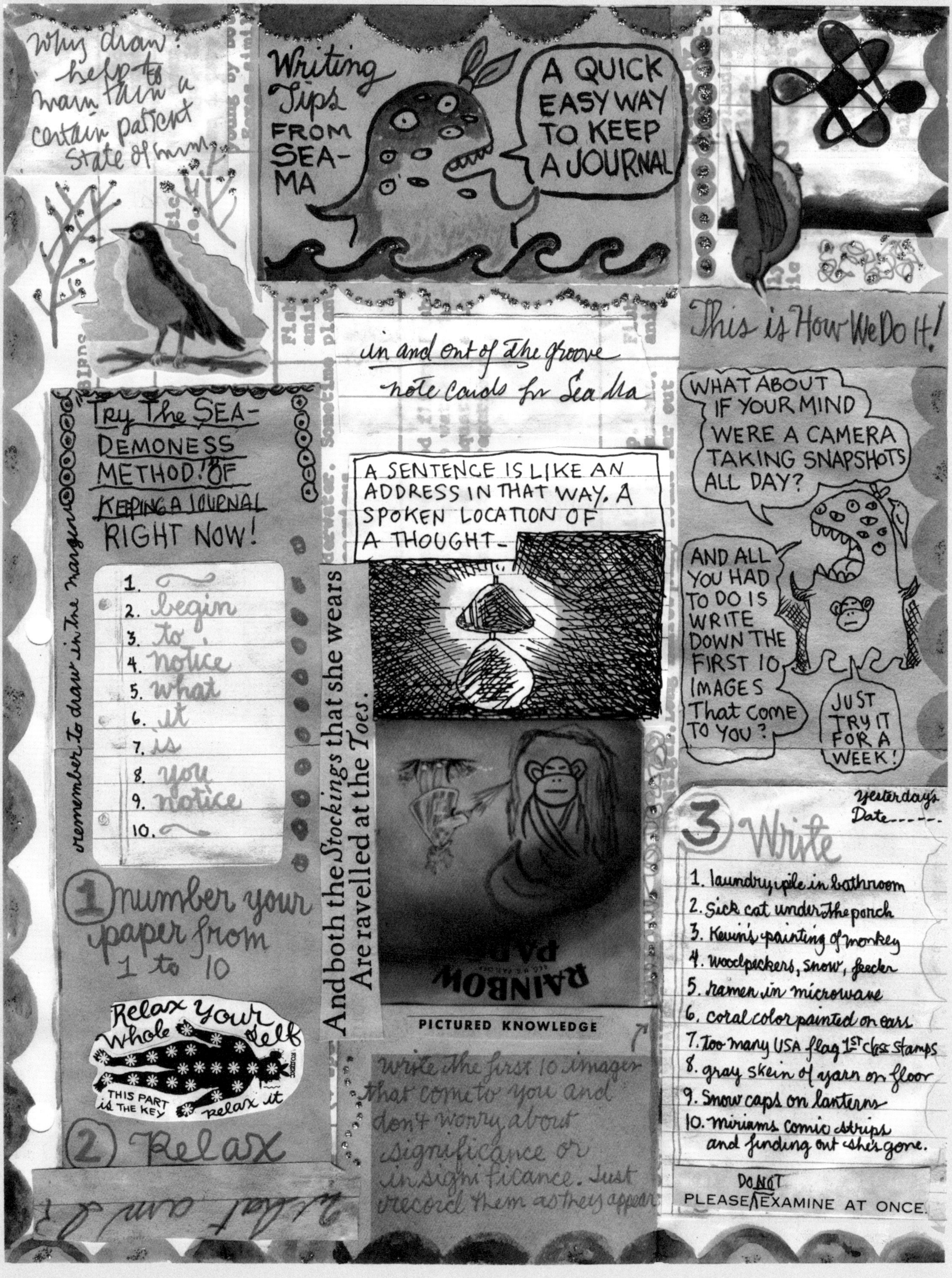

Why draw? helps to maintain a certain patient state of mind.
Writing Tips from Sea-Ma
A QUICK EASY WAY TO KEEP A JOURNAL
This is How We Do It!
in and out of the groove
note cards for Sea Ma
Try The SEA-DEMONESS METHOD! OF KEEPING A JOURNAL RIGHT NOW!
remember to draw in the margins
1.
2. begin
3. to
4. notice
5. what
6. it
7. is
8. you
9. notice
10.
① number your paper from 1 to 10
Relax your whole self
THIS PART is THE KEY
relax it
② Relax
A SENTENCE IS LIKE AN ADDRESS IN THAT WAY. A SPOKEN LOCATION OF A THOUGHT.
And both the Stockings that she wears Are ravelled at the Toes.
RAINBOW
PICTURED KNOWLEDGE
write the first 10 images that come to you and don't worry about significance or insignificance. Just record them as they appear
WHAT ABOUT IF YOUR MIND WERE A CAMERA TAKING SNAPSHOTS ALL DAY?
AND ALL YOU HAD TO DO IS WRITE DOWN THE FIRST 10 IMAGES That COME TO YOU?
JUST TRY IT FOR A WEEK!
Yesterday's Date-----
③ Write
1. laundry pile in bathroom
2. Sick cat under the porch
3. Kevin's painting of monkey
4. woodpeckers, snow, feeder
5. ramen in microwave
6. coral color painted on ears
7. Too many USA flag 1st class stamps
8. gray skein of yarn on floor
9. Snow caps on lanterns
10. miriams comic strips and finding out she's gone.
PLEASE DO NOT EXAMINE AT ONCE.

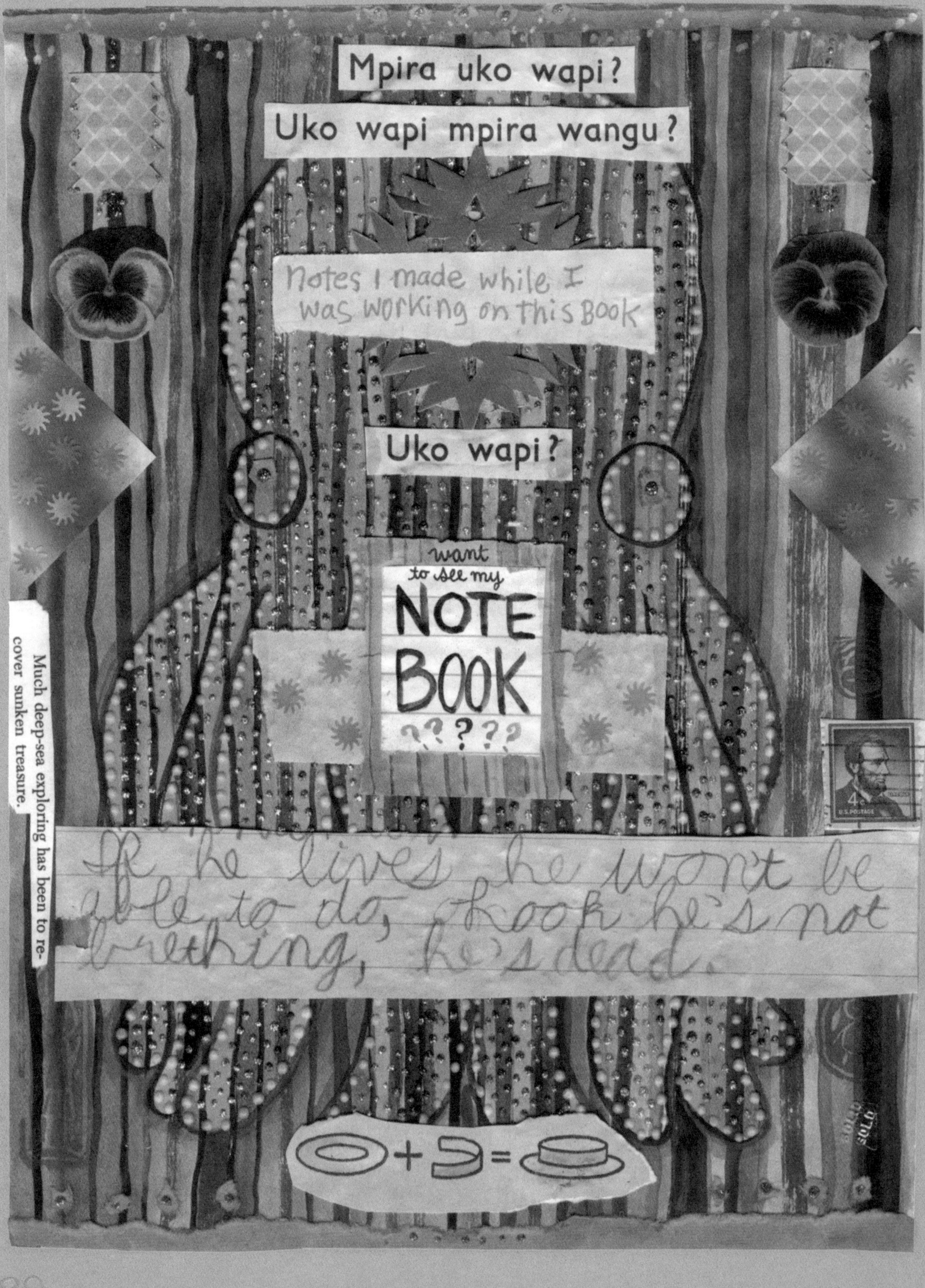
Mpira uko wapi?
Uko wapi mpira wangu?
Notes I made while I was working on this Book
Uko wapi?
want to see my NOTE BOOK ?????
If he lives he won't be able to do, look he's not brething, he's dead.
Much deep-sea exploring has been to re-cover sunken treasure.

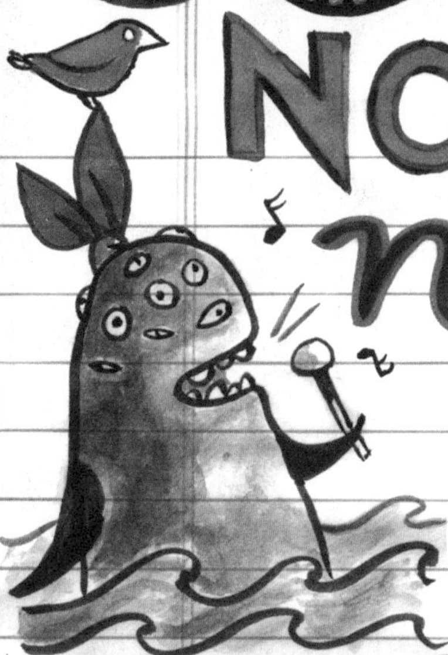

NOTES ON *notes*

ABCDEFGHIJ
KLMNOPQRS
TUVWXYZ

Sea-ma says notes can be just the alphabet, can be drawings, can be phrases in your head. It doesn't matter what you make, as long as your pen keeps moving and you follow.

WHILE I WORK, I ALWAYS KEEP A BLANK PAD BESIDE ME THAT I WORK ON ALL DAY, TURNING TO IT WHEN I GET STUCK. INSTEAD OF STOPPING TO THINK, I KEEP MY BRUSH IN MOTION BY MOVING IT TO MY NOTE PAD. I DON'T PLAN A PATH FOR MY BRUSH. I JUST MOVE IT UNTIL MY OTHER PAD OF PAPER CALLS ME BACK. IT SEEMS TO WORK.

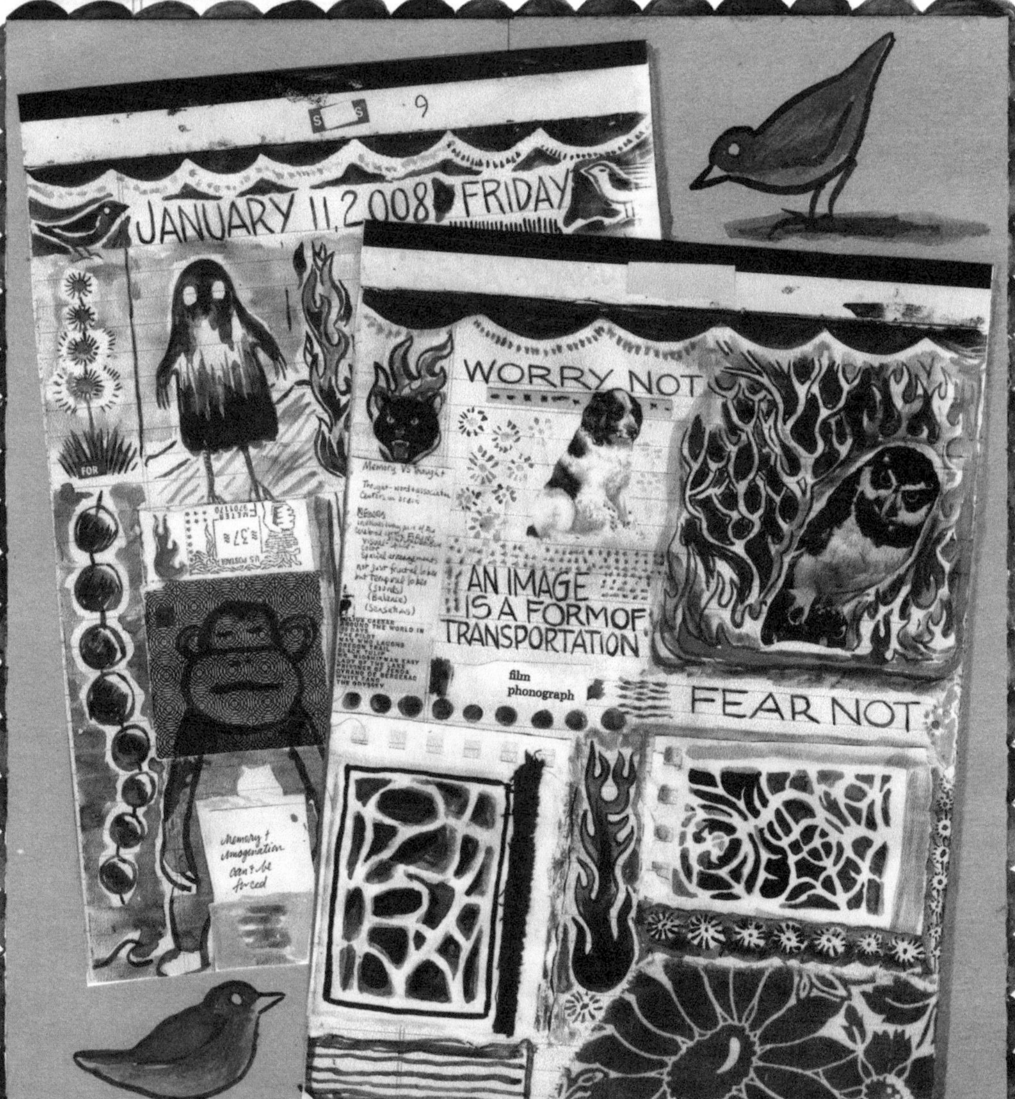

JANUARY 11, 2008 FRIDAY
WORRY NOT
AN IMAGE IS A FORM OF TRANSPORTATION
film
phonograph
FEAR NOT
Memory + imagination can't be forced

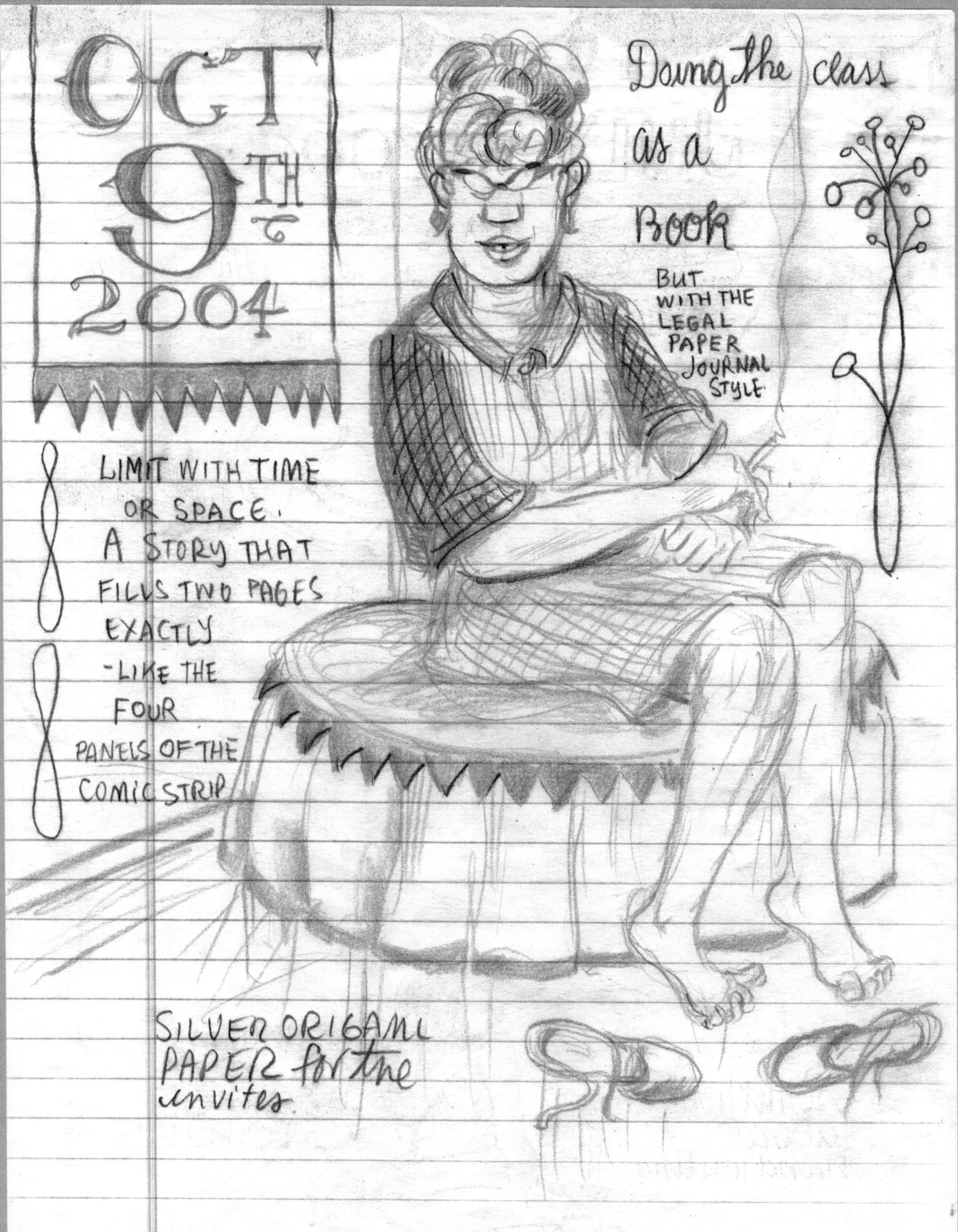
OCT 9TH 2004
Doing the class as a Book
BUT WITH THE LEGAL PAPER JOURNAL STYLE
LIMIT WITH TIME OR SPACE.
A STORY THAT FILLS TWO PAGES EXACTLY
-LIKE THE FOUR PANELS OF THE COMIC STRIP
SILVER ORIGAMI PAPER for the invites

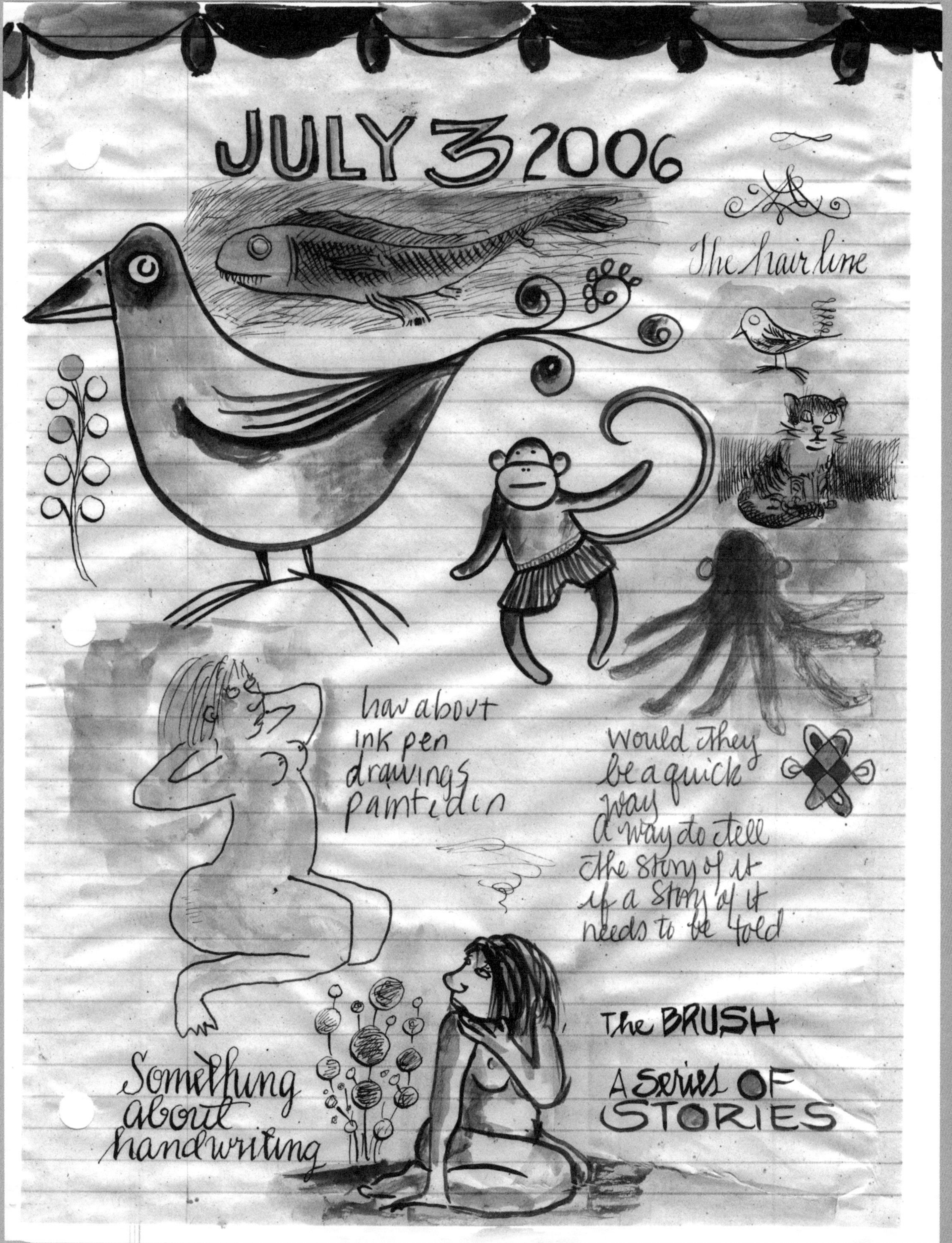
JULY 3 2006
The hair line
haw about
ink pen
drawings
pamtidin
would they
be a quick
way
a way do tell
the story of it
if a story of it
needs to be told
The BRUSH
Something
about
handwriting
A Series OF
STORIES

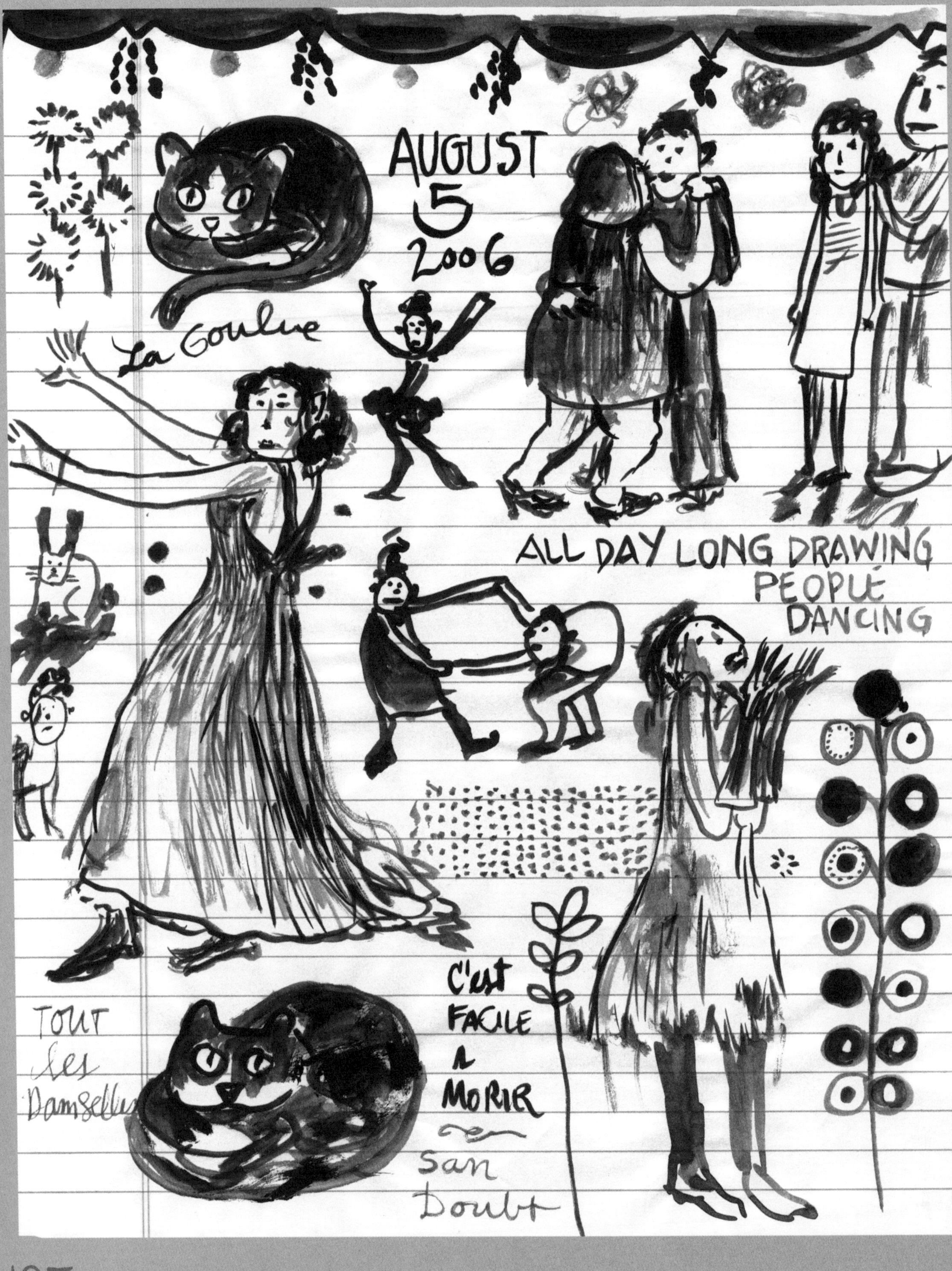
AUGUST 5 2006
La Goulue
ALL DAY LONG DRAWING PEOPLE DANCING
TOUT les Damselles
C'est FACILE A MORIR
San Doubt

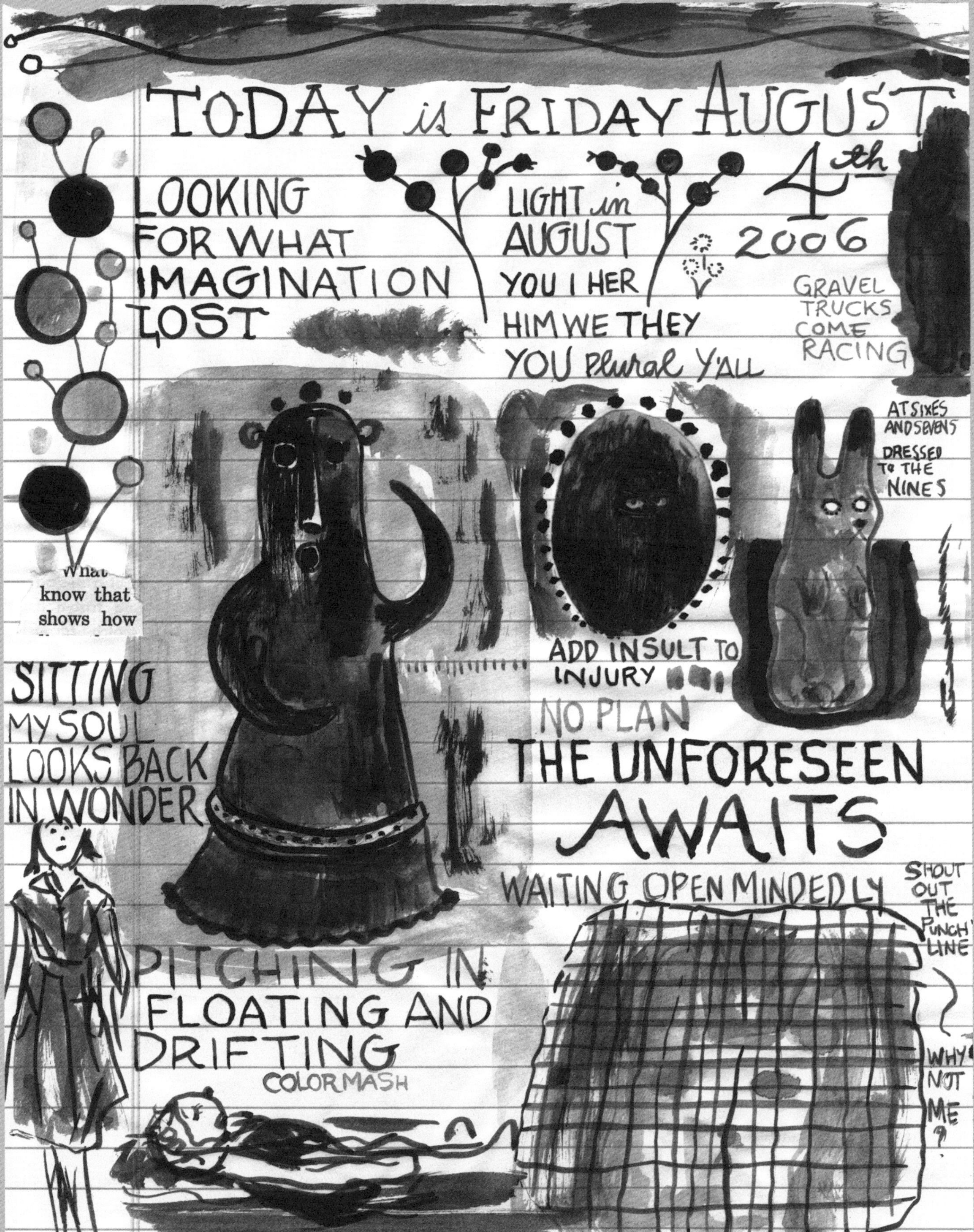
TODAY is FRIDAY AUGUST 4th 2006
LOOKING FOR WHAT IMAGINATION LOST
LIGHT in AUGUST
YOU I HER HIM WE THEY YOU plural Y'ALL
GRAVEL TRUCKS COME RACING
AT SIXES AND SEVENS
DRESSED TO THE NINES
know that
shows how
SITTING
MY SOUL LOOKS BACK IN WONDER
ADD INSULT TO INJURY
NO PLAN
THE UNFORESEEN AWAITS
WAITING OPEN MINDEDLY
SHOUT OUT THE PUNCH LINE
PITCHING IN
FLOATING AND DRIFTING
COLORMASH
WHY NOT ME ?

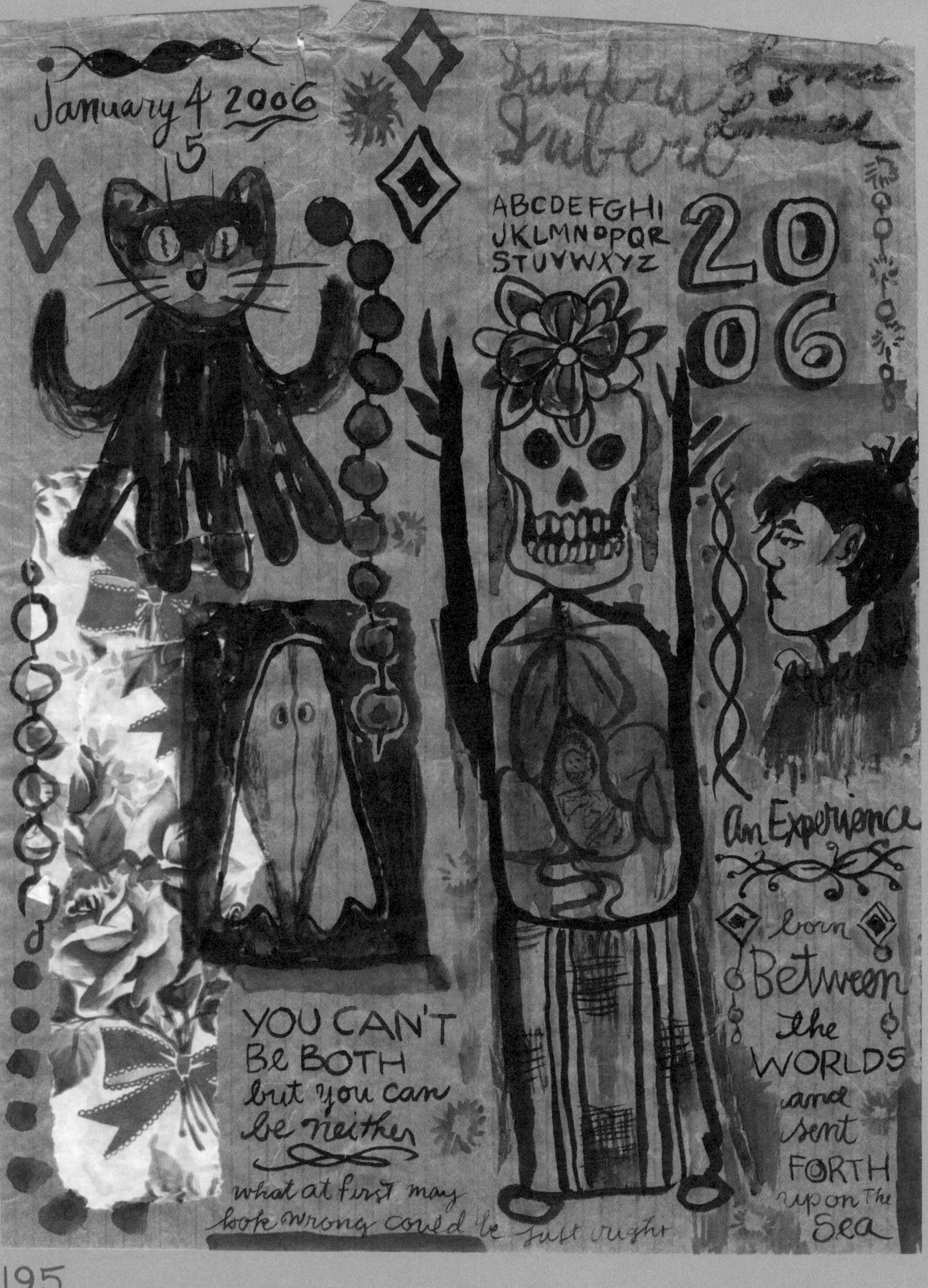
January 4 2006
5
ABCDEFGHI
JKLMNOPQR
STUVWXYZ
20
06
YOU CAN'T
Be BOTH
but you can
be neither
what at first may
look wrong could be just right
An Experience
born
Between
the
WORLDS
and
sent
FORTH
upon the
Sea

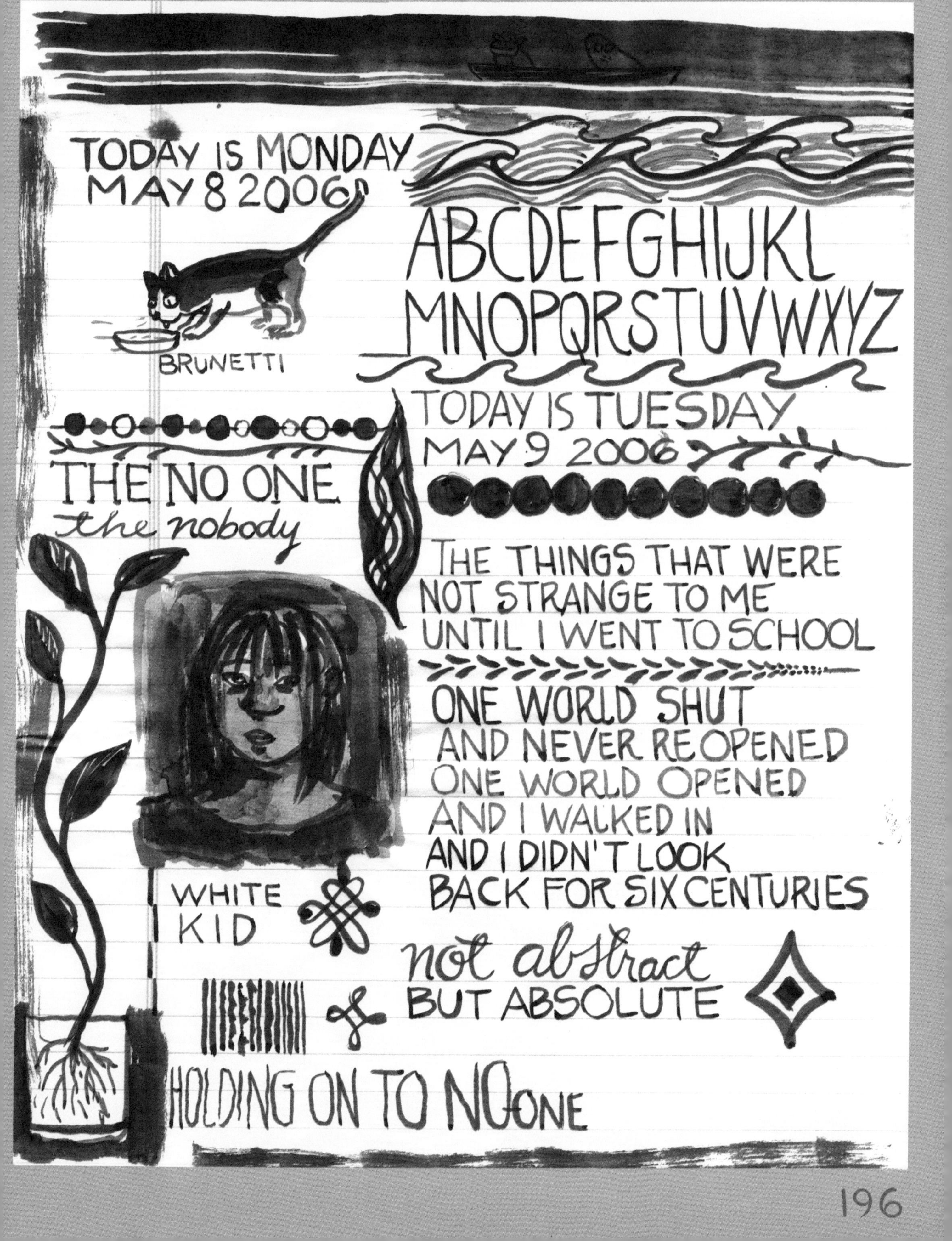
TODAY IS MONDAY
MAY 8 2006
BRUNETTI
ABCDEFGHIJKL
MNOPQRSTUVWXYZ
TODAY IS TUESDAY
MAY 9 2006
THE NO ONE
the nobody
THE THINGS THAT WERE
NOT STRANGE TO ME
UNTIL I WENT TO SCHOOL
ONE WORLD SHUT
AND NEVER REOPENED
ONE WORLD OPENED
AND I WALKED IN
AND I DIDN'T LOOK
BACK FOR SIX CENTURIES
WHITE
KID
not abstract
BUT ABSOLUTE
HOLDING ON TO NO ONE

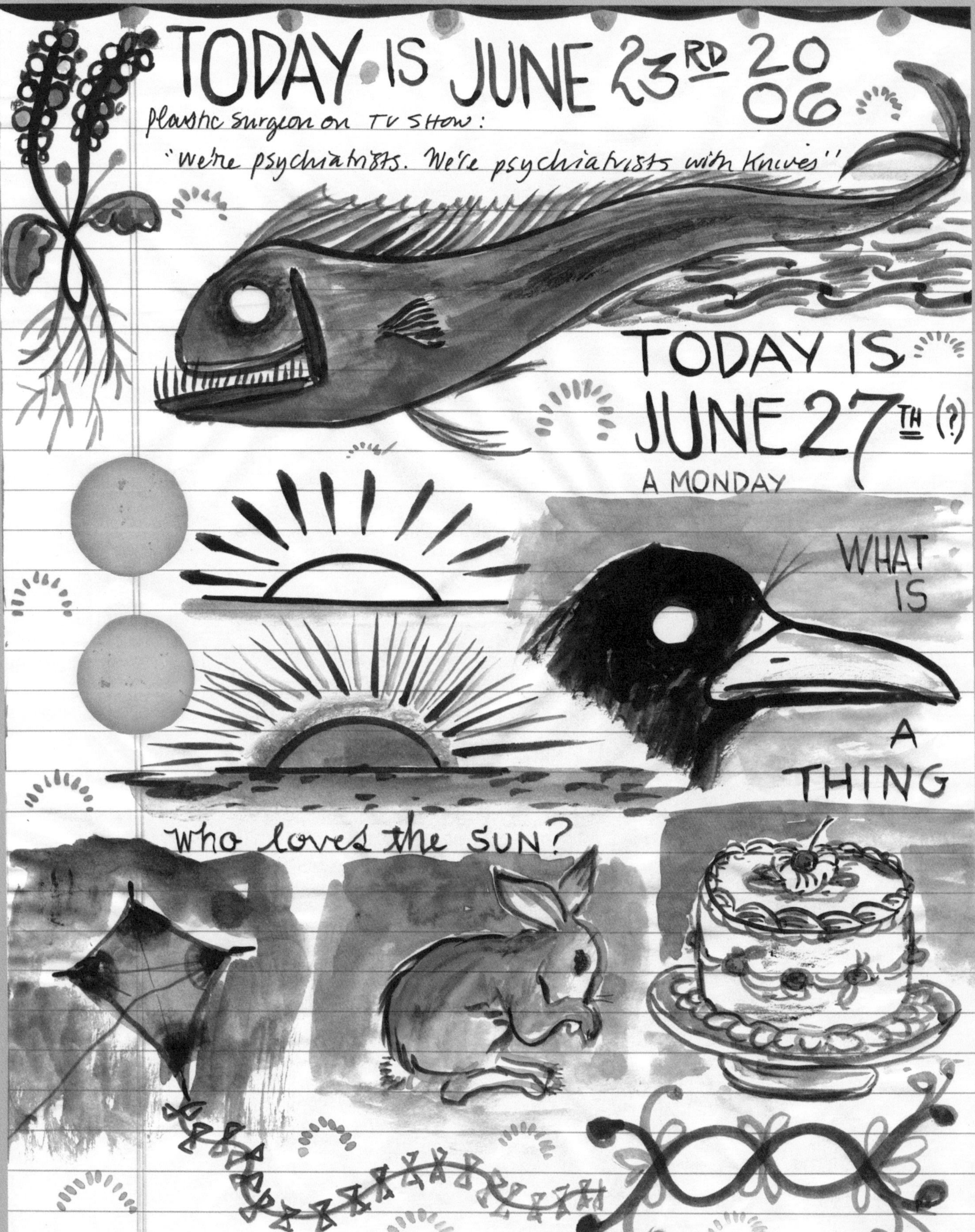
TODAY IS JUNE 23RD 2006
plastic surgeon on TV SHOW:
"We're psychiatrists. We're psychiatrists with knives"
TODAY IS JUNE 27TH (?)
A MONDAY
WHAT IS A THING
Who loves the SUN?

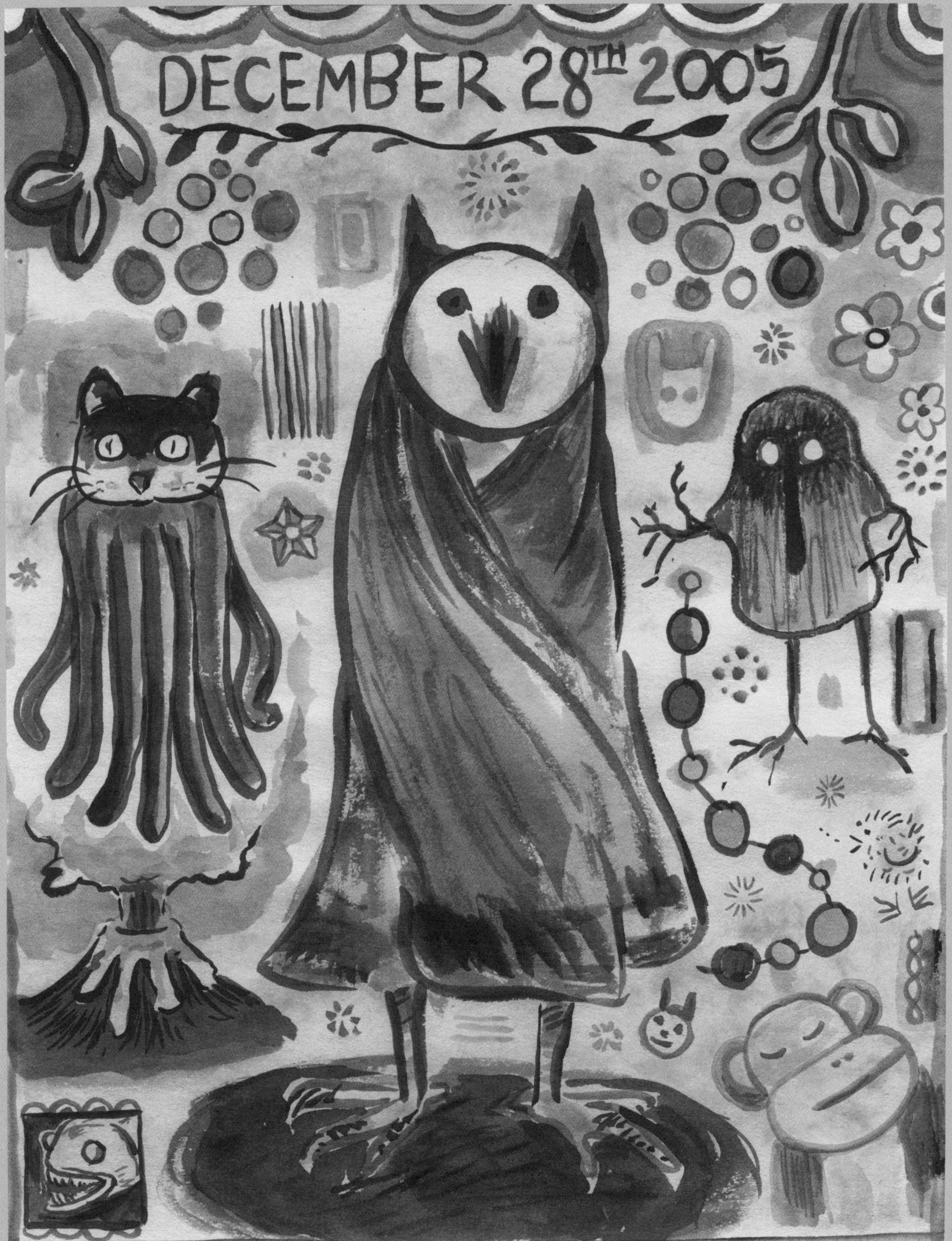
DECEMBER 28TH 2005

AUG 4
06

I thought imaginary meant unseen so this imaginary friend could be anywhere.
People who had them heard them speak but no one else could hear them.

I wanted one and tried to conjure one in different ways but none came.
Finally I just lied about having one. Which meant I had an Imaginary-Imaginary friend.

What is the difference
Between UNSEEN and UNREAL?

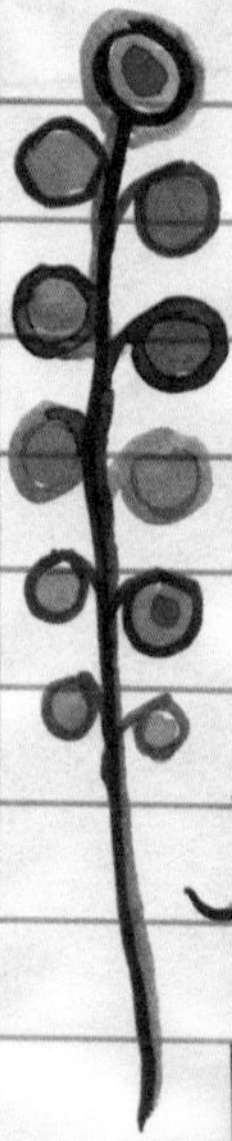

What is the Difference
between
A FAKE
imaginary
friend
and
A REAL
imaginary
friend

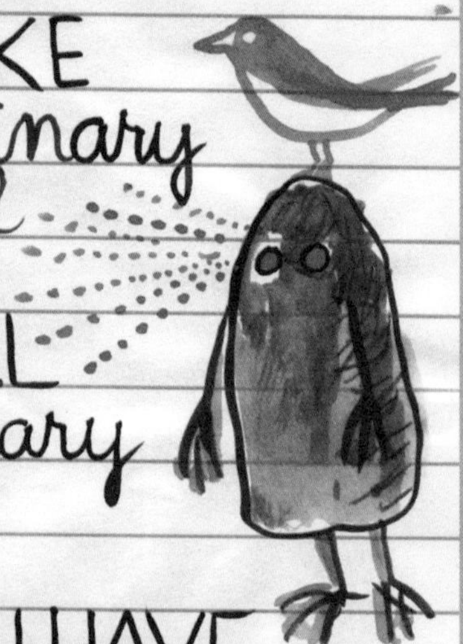

DO YOU HAVE
A FRIEND NO ONE
ELSE CAN SEE?

The Spirit of
the BLANKIE
IS
located
IN
the difference between

trying and not trying

A FAKE IMAGINARY FRIEND IS STILL YOU
A REAL IMAGINARY FRIEND FEELS LIKE
SOMEONE ELSE

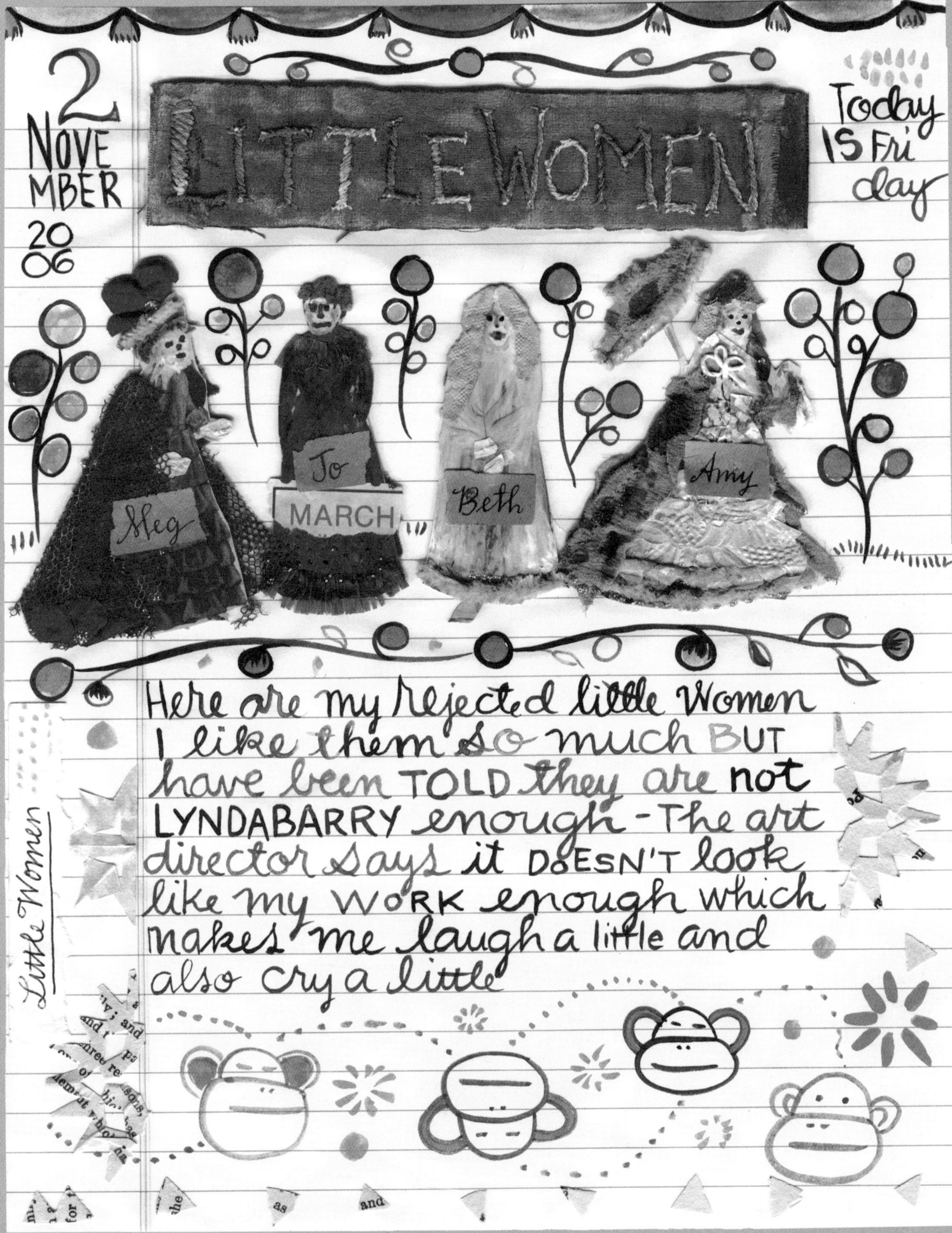
2
NOVEMBER
2006
LITTLE WOMEN
Today IS Friday
Meg
Jo
MARCH
Beth
Amy
Here are my Rejected little Women I like them SO much BUT have been TOLD they are not LYNDABARRY enough - The art director says it DOESN'T look like my WORK enough which makes me laugh a little and also cry a little
Little Women

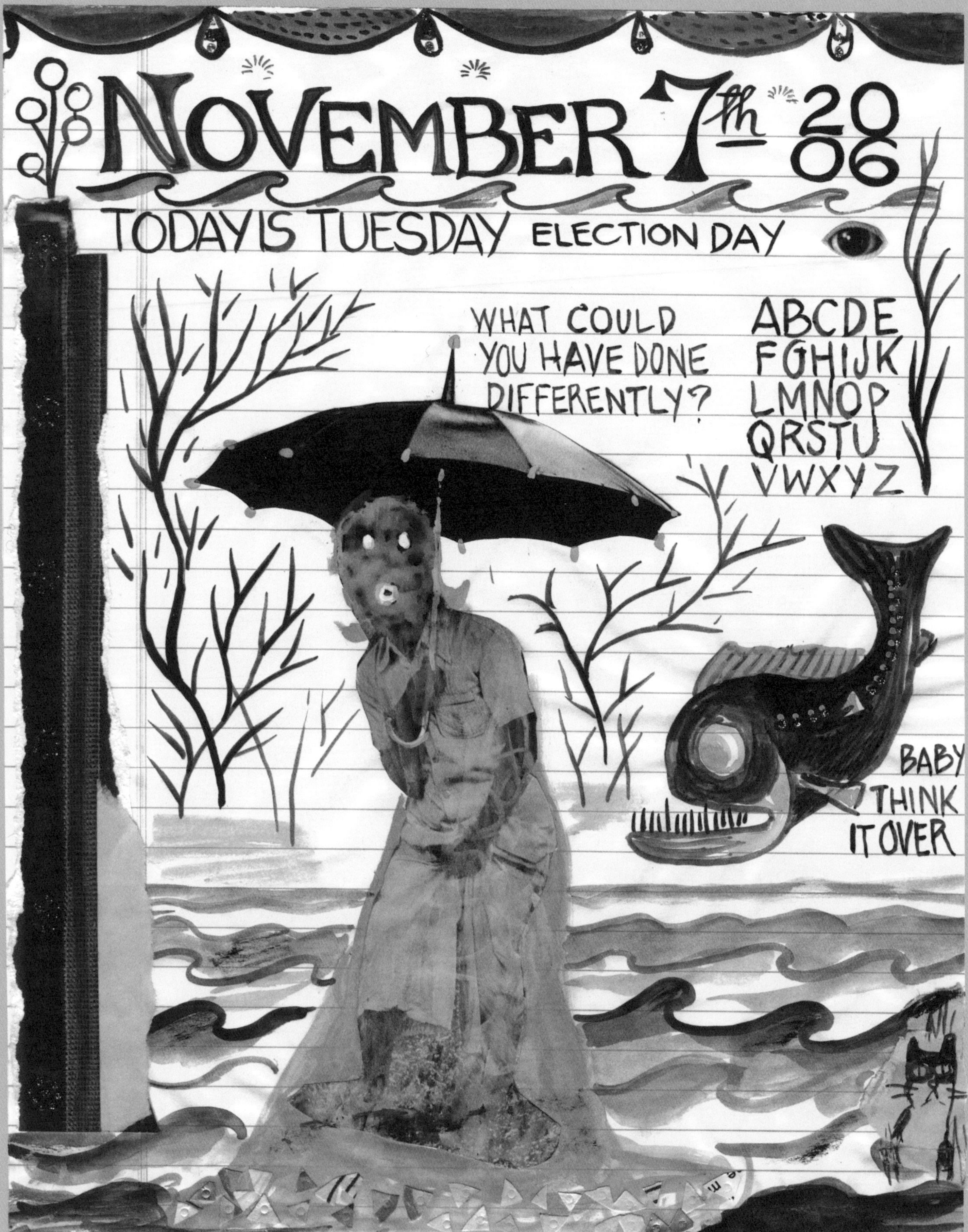
NOVEMBER 7th 2006
TODAY IS TUESDAY ELECTION DAY
WHAT COULD YOU HAVE DONE DIFFERENTLY?
ABCDE
FGHIJK
LMNOP
QRSTU
VWXYZ
BABY THINK IT OVER

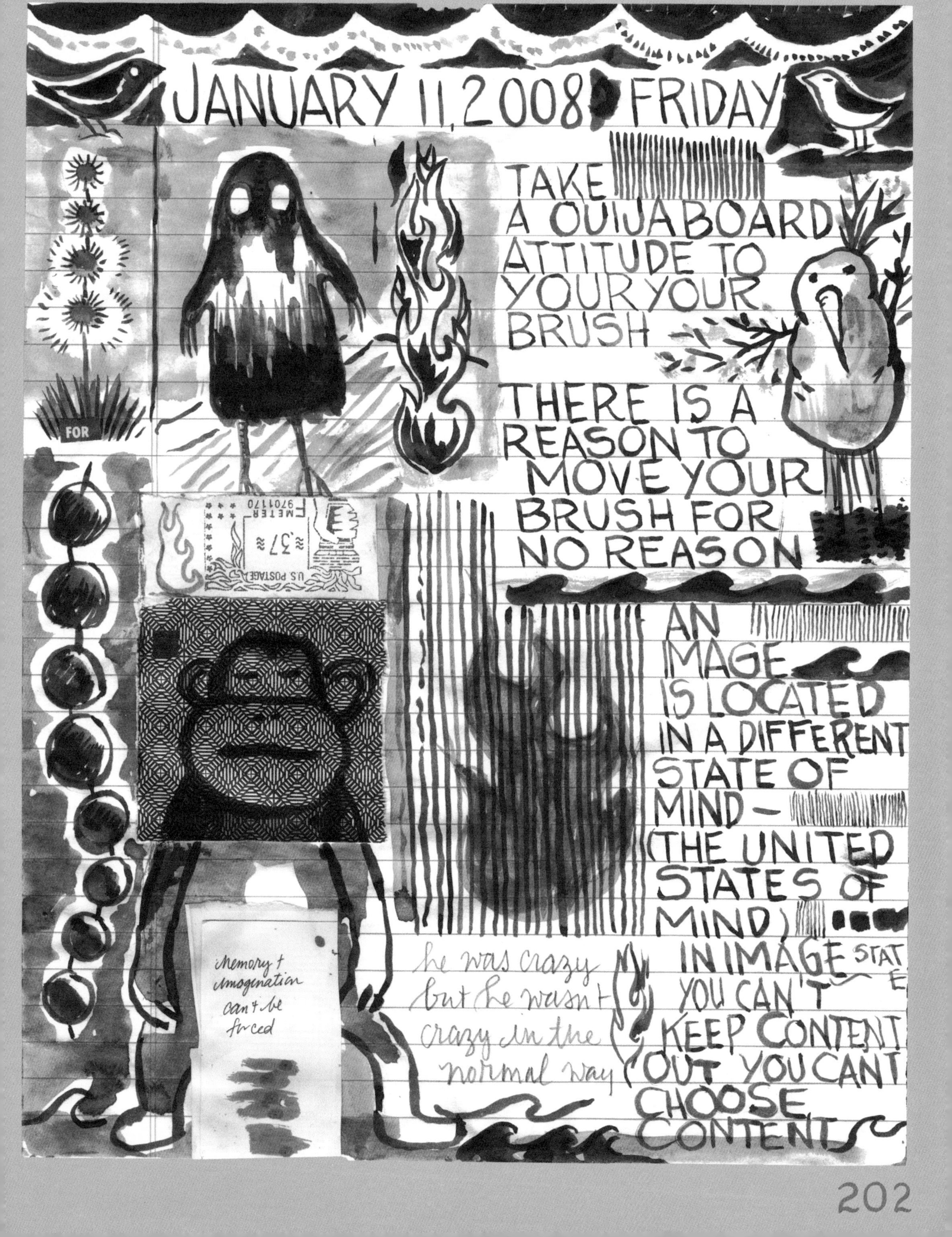
JANUARY 11, 2008 FRIDAY
TAKE A OUIJA BOARD ATTITUDE TO YOUR YOUR BRUSH
THERE IS A REASON TO MOVE YOUR BRUSH FOR NO REASON
AN IMAGE IS LOCATED IN A DIFFERENT STATE OF MIND — (THE UNITED STATES OF MIND)
IN IMAGE STATE YOU CAN'T KEEP CONTENT OUT YOU CANT CHOOSE CONTENT
he was crazy but he wasn't crazy in the normal way
memory + imagination can't be forced
FOR
U.S. POSTAGE
METER

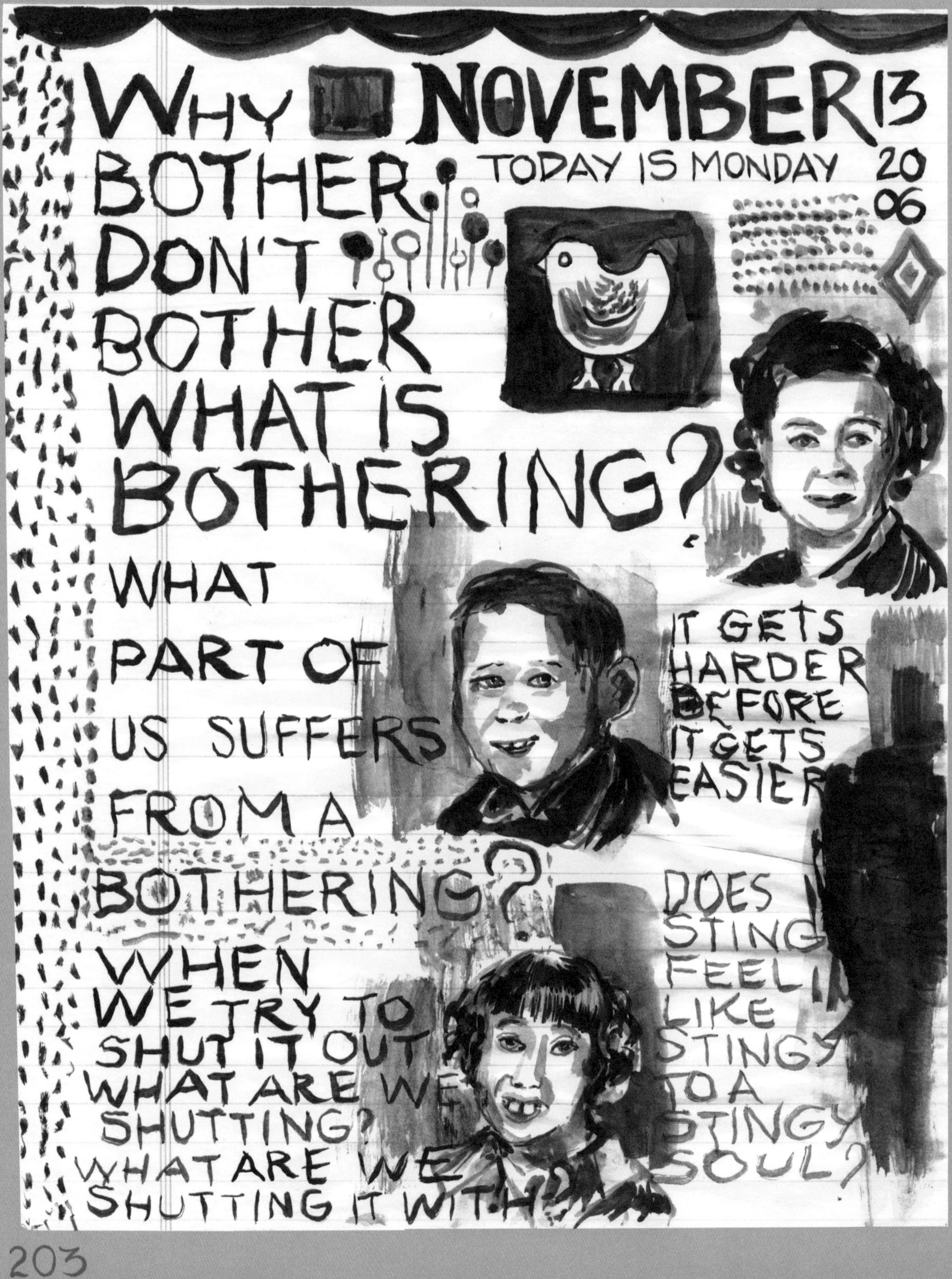
WHY
NOVEMBER 13
TODAY IS MONDAY
2006
BOTHER DON'T BOTHER WHAT IS BOTHERING?
WHAT PART OF US SUFFERS FROM A BOTHERING?
WHEN WE TRY TO SHUT IT OUT WHAT ARE WE SHUTTING? WHAT ARE WE SHUTTING IT WITH?
IT GETS HARDER BEFORE IT GETS EASIER
DOES STING FEEL LIKE STINGY TO A STINGY SOUL?

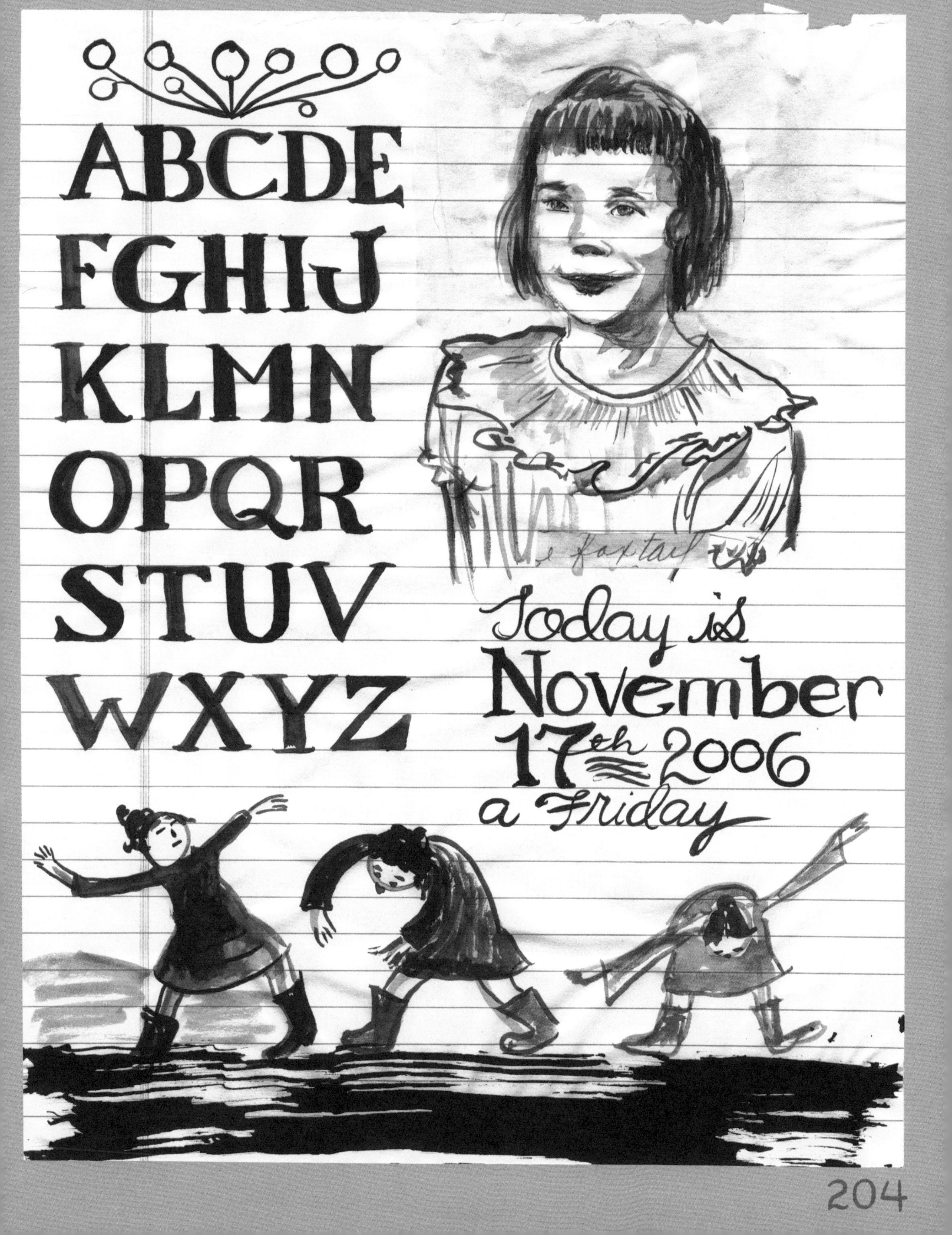
ABCDE
FGHIJ
KLMN
OPQR
STUV
WXYZ
Today is
November
17th 2006
a Friday

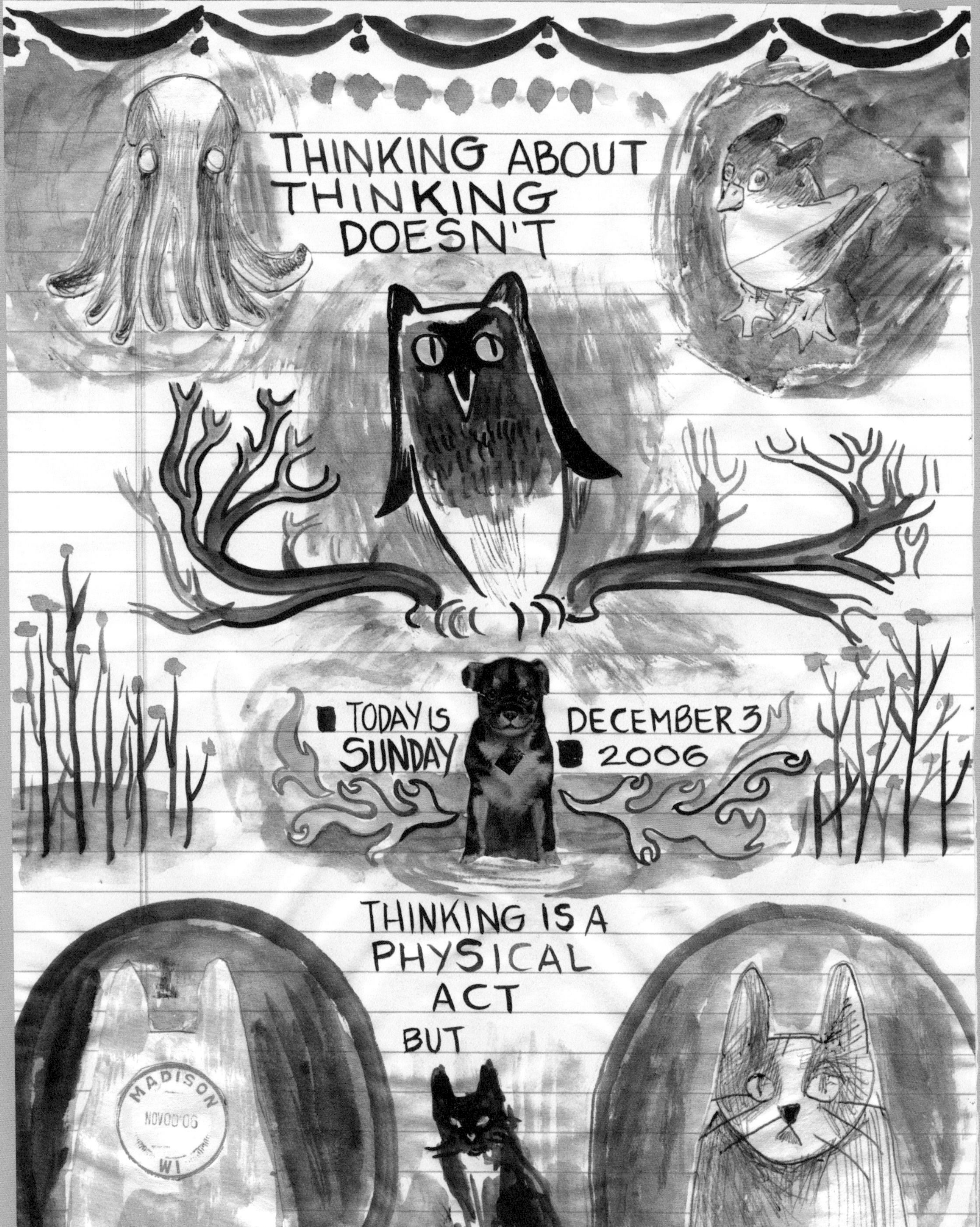
THINKING ABOUT THINKING DOESN'T
TODAY IS SUNDAY
DECEMBER 3 2006
THINKING IS A PHYSICAL ACT
BUT
MADISON NOV 00 06 WI

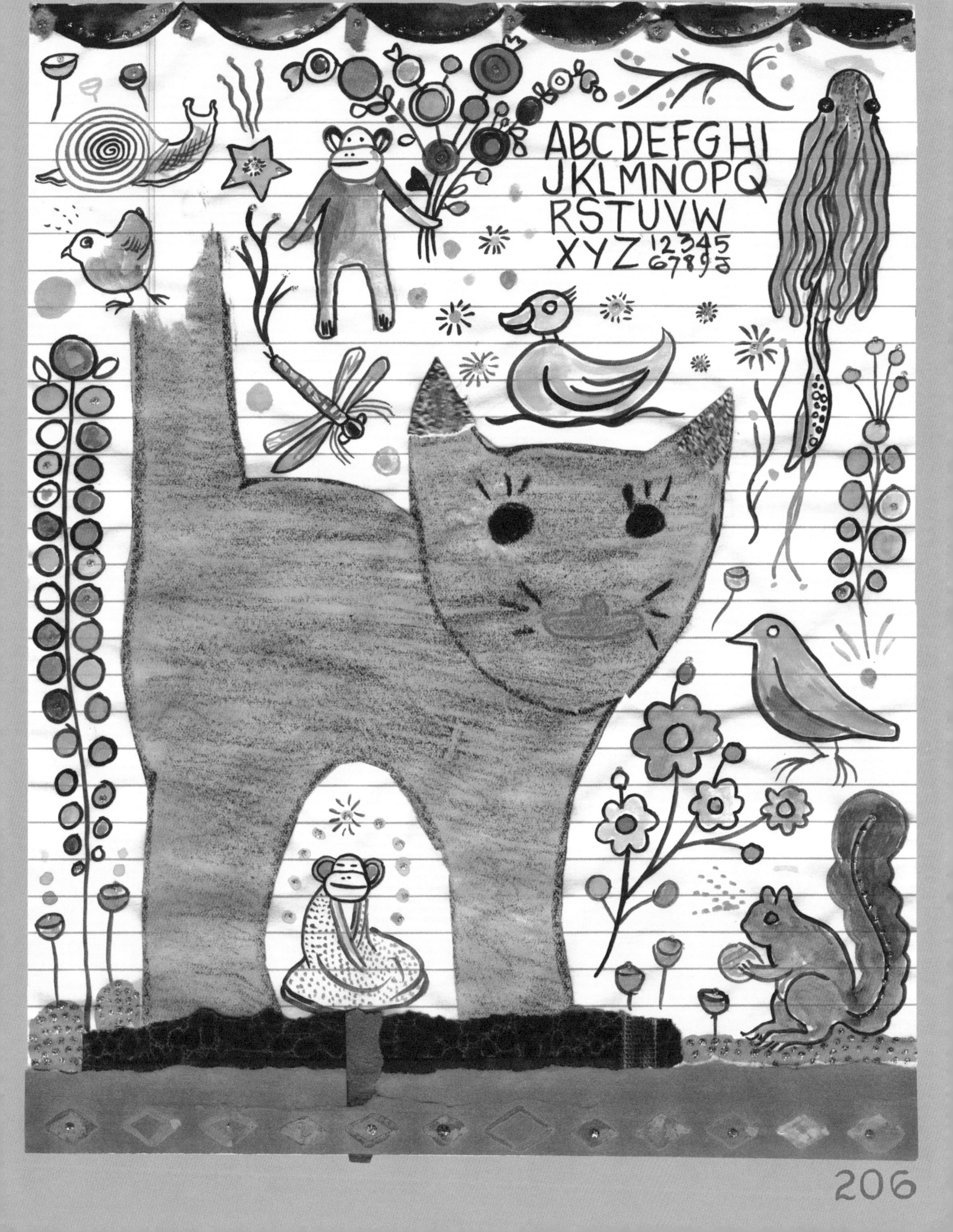
ABCDEFGHI
JKLMNOPQ
RSTUVW
XYZ 12345
6789

January 2nd 2007

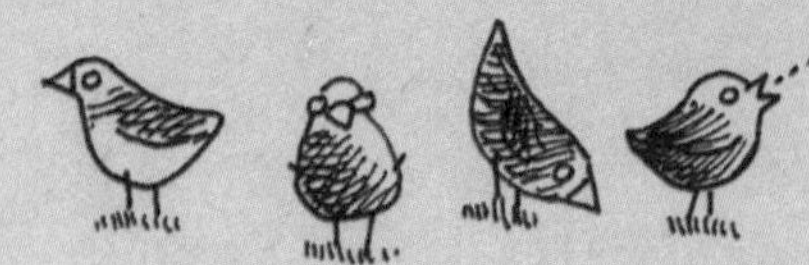

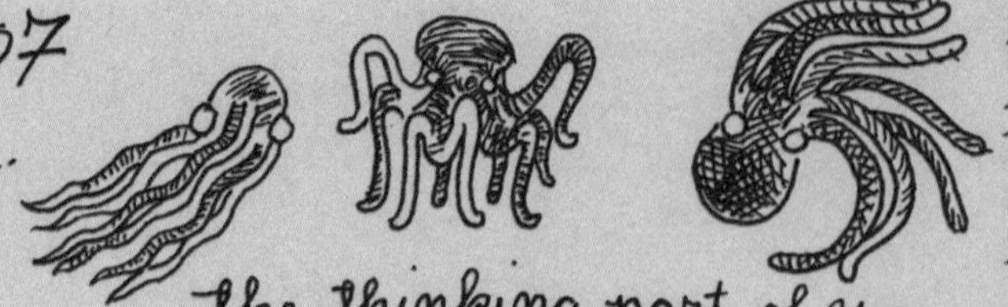

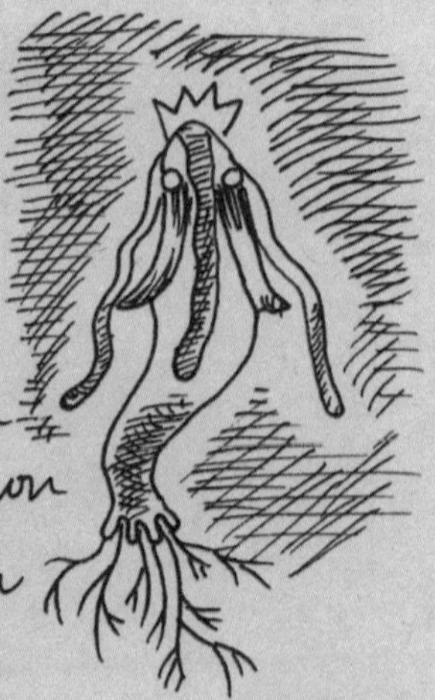

The thinking part of you
is not the doing part of you
or the experiencing part of you

The thinking part of you can
tell you that a decision has
been made but it's not the
part of you which decides things

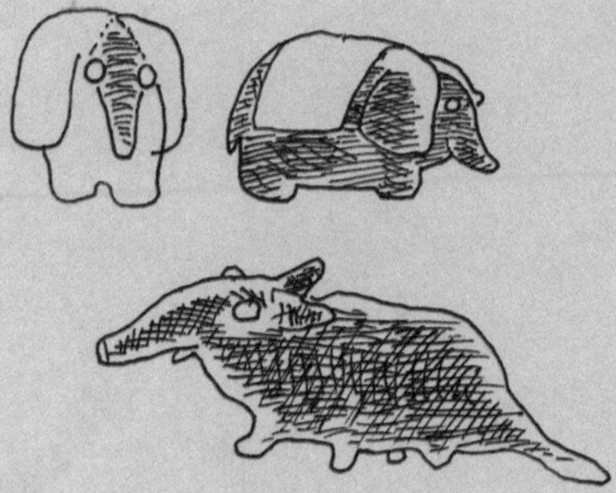

This is why thinking is not
the same as creating though
the thinking part of us seems
completely ~~at~~ unaware of this

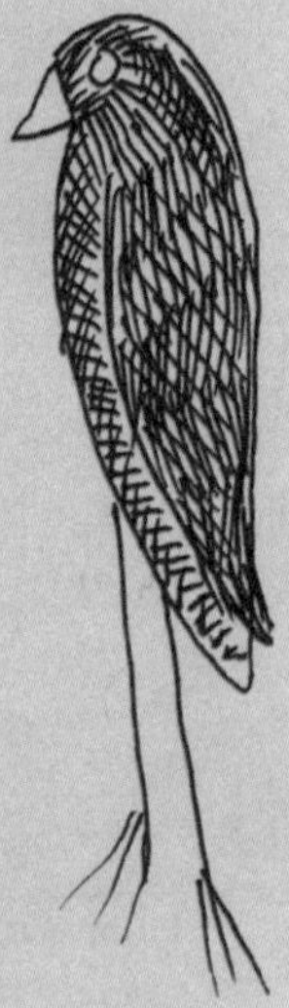

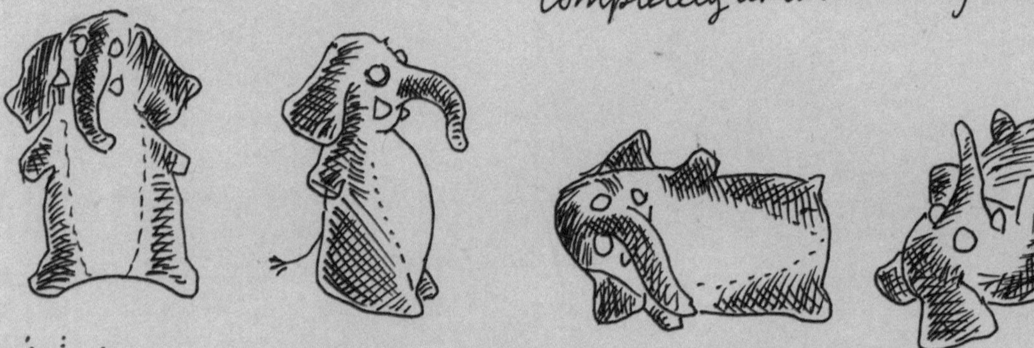

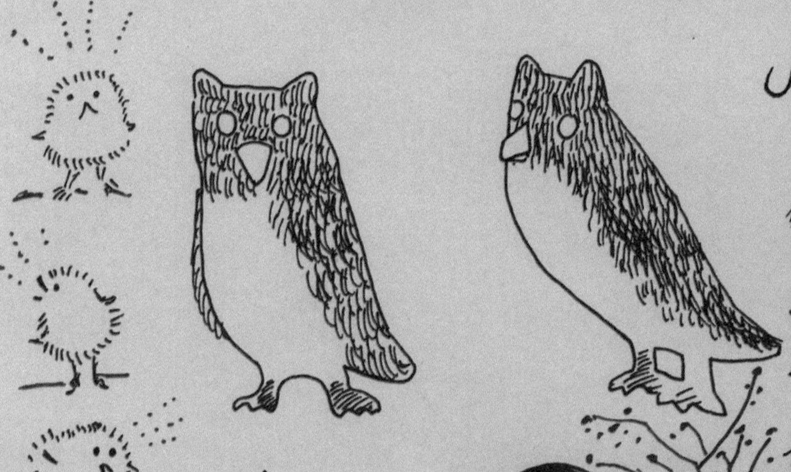

January 3rd 2007

A WEDNESDAY

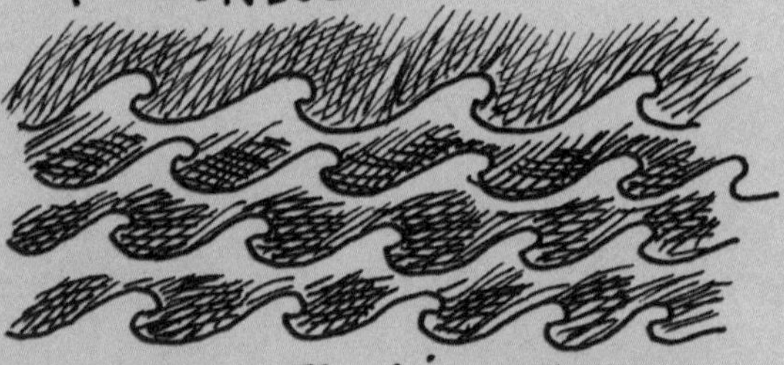

yesterday the Piggots brought
us a truck load of elm, saying,
HAPPY NEW YEAR. It was so kind
of them. I love heating and cooking
with wood. There is something
deep in it. Covalent bonds
released. This morning I looked
at the oaks in the grove. All
trunks and branches were lines.
Veins + arteries.

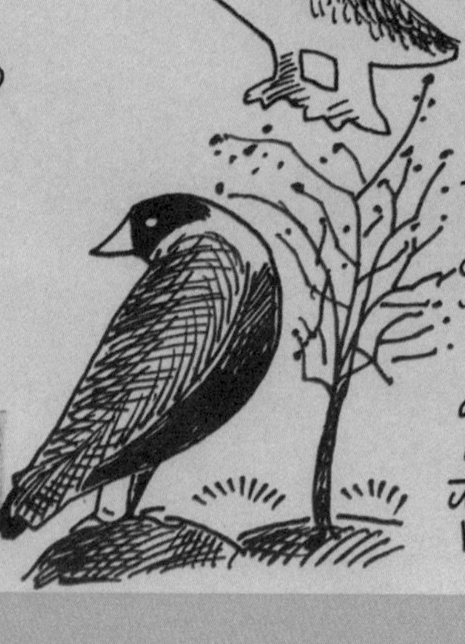

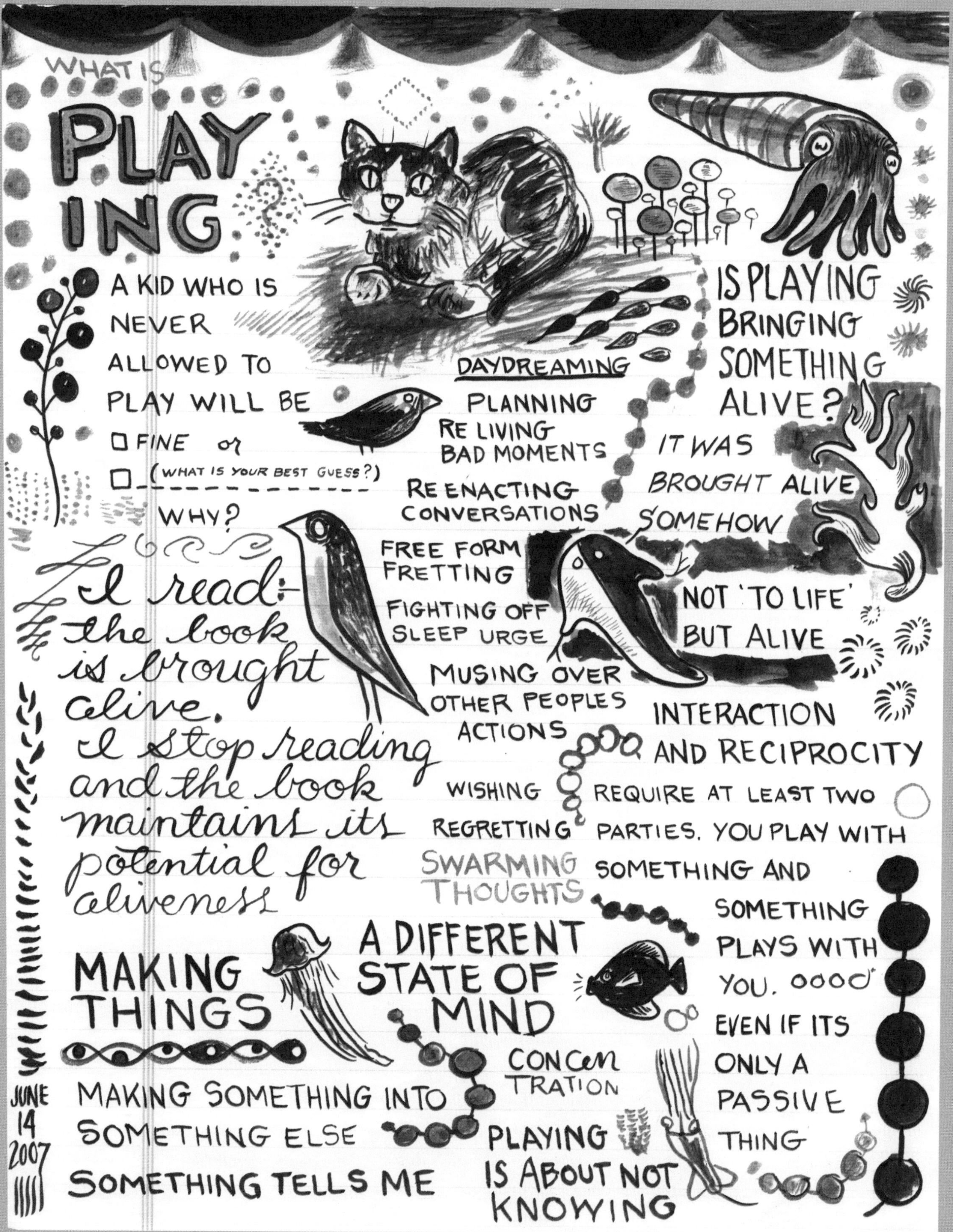
WHAT IS
PLAYING
?
A KID WHO IS NEVER ALLOWED TO PLAY WILL BE
☐ FINE or
☐ _(WHAT IS YOUR BEST GUESS?)
WHY?
DAYDREAMING
PLANNING
RE LIVING BAD MOMENTS
RE ENACTING CONVERSATIONS
FREE FORM FRETTING
FIGHTING OFF SLEEP URGE
MUSING OVER OTHER PEOPLES ACTIONS
WISHING
REGRETTING
SWARMING THOUGHTS
IS PLAYING BRINGING SOMETHING ALIVE?
IT WAS BROUGHT ALIVE SOMEHOW
NOT 'TO LIFE' BUT ALIVE
I read: the book is brought alive. I stop reading and the book maintains its potential for aliveness
INTERACTION AND RECIPROCITY REQUIRE AT LEAST TWO PARTIES. YOU PLAY WITH SOMETHING AND SOMETHING PLAYS WITH YOU. oooo EVEN IF ITS ONLY A PASSIVE THING
MAKING THINGS
A DIFFERENT STATE OF MIND
CONCENTRATION
MAKING SOMETHING INTO SOMETHING ELSE
SOMETHING TELLS ME
PLAYING IS ABOUT NOT KNOWING
JUNE 14 2007

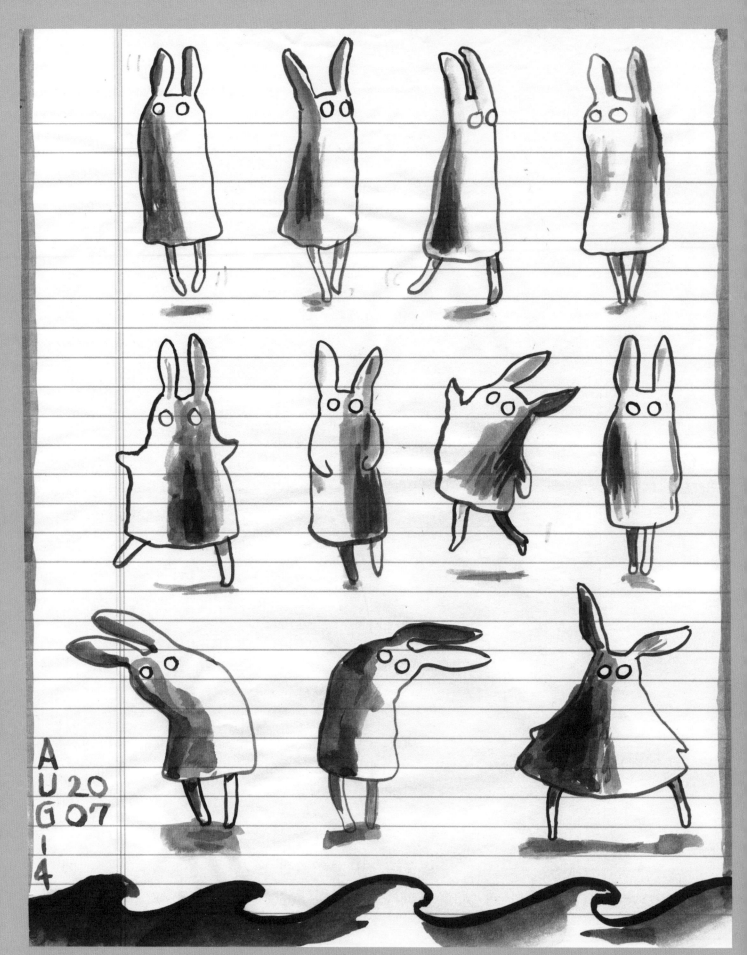

AUG 2007 14

209

I owe a great deal to both Marilyn Frasca and Mark Levensky who taught a class called 'IMAGES' at The Evergreen State College in 1976-77 that much of this book is based on. I also owe a debt to the work of L.A. Cleaver, D.W. Winnicott, Marion Milner, M.P. Follett and Shunryu Suzuki. Thanks also to Everyone at Drawn and Quarterly, especially Chris Oliveros. THANK YOU TO LIZ DARHANSOFF ROS PERROTTA SUSAN GRODE, CHRIS WARE, KELLY HOGAN, FUNKLORD OF USA MATT GROENING AND especially to My husband KEVIN KAWULA WHO helped me watercolor (HE IS VERY GREAT)

Dear Teacher

To

school teacher

Wisconsin Gal

Miss Mitchell

Doris Mitchell

Dear Doris

MANY MANY Thanks

to Donavon and Joanie Mitchell who 'introduced' me to the late Doris Mitchell who began her elementary school teaching career in the mid 1920's. many of the hand written bits and children's school work are from her vast collection of papers she kept all through her life. I am lucky to have access to such treasure while making this book. Thank You to the Mitchells!

THINK CONSTRUCTION. THINK JEFF MITCHELL

and a special thank-you to all of my students

Play always involves anxiety

(T)

ntal alth + ANXIE

NO Feedback + MARILYN'S class
the lesson is to Stop manufacturing Feedbn

KIDS PLAYING (6)

IDEA OF PLAY AS THIS SWEET INNOCENT THING BUT ALWAYS ANXIETY T TROUBLE + NAUGHTY

- NAKED PICNIC BARBIE
- ARMY MEN

ONE CHARACTERISTIC OF PLAY IS BEING TOTALLY ABSORBED — Time gets all warped.

PLAY FOR KIDS IS WHAT CREATIVE CONCENTRATION IS FOR ADULTS.

~~KIDS DRAW~~

KIDS DRAWING (7)

Totally absorbed
sound effects
Bro draw entire army
eat a bowl of cereal + Stare at it
then Blow it up — paper looks like battle field
Thinks he's done.
HIS EXPERIENCE ISN'T THE PAPER ONLY.
he doesn't care about the paper afterwards
Where is the experience?

His ability to bring it all alive in an absorbing way

we tell the ...y of our lives
an obituary
...y no feeling
... list
...ctivated
dried yeast
... not active
(monkeys)

THE BODY

DOING

TRYING WON'T GE(T) YOU THERE, YOU NEED A TOY TO SH(OW) YOU THE WAY.

no expectatin

LOOKING FOR MEANING ~~AS~~ before ~~letting~~ something Acquires meaning

reading poetry that way

№ 237
RECEIPT
To be retained by the Subscriber
Name Doris Mit...
Address Hillsbo...
Date 12/1/5...
In behalf of SAINT (JOS)EPH'S MEMORIAL HO(SPI)TAL, Hillsboro, Wisco(nsin)

accept chaos as a temporary state

NAPOLEON
MONKEYS
BANANAS

BACKWARDS
We're not having the experience in order to make an image ☆

We're making an image in order to have an experience. (T)

Toy plays with us

why are kids drawings so much better to the eye than teen drawings

INTENTION

AFTER CARS talk about working in Series

BOCA RATON RESORT & CLUB
Meeting Jeff Keane —
Seeing an imaginary friend in 3-D
FAMILY CIRCUS

STAY BEHIND THE IMAGE

start with what ...re familiar with
Autobiography — always false in some way
and Fiction — being truer
Bengali alphabet
Air From Heaven — uninteresting and unbearable
Hell — interesting but unbearable
...mpn

TRYING

- remembering
- forgetting
- imagination
- realization
- revelation

(CANT BE FORCED)

DANCING
FALLING IN AND OUT OF THE GROOVE

FLY + TURN INVISIBL(E)
(not sure how — can make a living at that) ok

Gradual belief in a spontaneous ordering force

an internal spontaneous ordering

(composition)

WHAT DOES THE TV See ~~If It~~ when It watches you?